Business, Government and Labor

Essays on Economic Development in Singapore and Southeast Asia

Business, Government and Labor

Essays on Economic Development in Singapore and Southeast Asia

Linda Y C Lim
University of Michigan, USA

World Scientific

NEW JERSEY • LONDON • SINGAPORE • BEIJING • SHANGHAI • HONG KONG • TAIPEI • CHENNAI • TOKYO

Published by

World Scientific Publishing Co. Pte. Ltd.
5 Toh Tuck Link, Singapore 596224
USA office: 27 Warren Street, Suite 401-402, Hackensack, NJ 07601
UK office: 57 Shelton Street, Covent Garden, London WC2H 9HE

British Library Cataloguing-in-Publication Data
A catalogue record for this book is available from the British Library.

BUSINESS, GOVERNMENT AND LABOR
Essays on Economic Development in Singapore and Southeast Asia

ISBN 978-981-3225-25-1

Desk Editor: Sandhya Venkatesh

Typeset by Stallion Press
Email: enquiries@stallionpress.com

PREFACE AND ACKNOWLEDGEMENTS

Economic development, especially of Singapore, has been the passion of my professional career. It began when I was a teenager growing up, first, under "merger with Malaysia", then through Singapore's reluctant independence, when the gravity of our uncertain economic survival was very real. Exposure to 'A' level economics offered the hope of policy solutions, and my infatuation with the discipline continued through my undergraduate studies at Cambridge University, in the department of Marshall, Keynes and Joan Robinson. Economic development was a hot topic, focused not only on the large socialist countries of China and India, but also on Britain's controversial entry into the then European Community and what it might mean for trade with us in the Commonwealth.

Influenced by Malaysian fellow students at Cambridge and Yale, most of them not economists but equally preoccupied with their country's development challenges, I continued to graduate school in the U.S., eventually choosing to do my PhD in economics at the University of Michigan, because of its twin strengths in economic development and Southeast Asian Studies. There, in addition to economics, I took courses in Southeast Asian history, attended Southeast Asia seminars, conferences and performances, studied Bahasa Indonesia (as a proxy for Malay), and prepared for my dissertation research on export-manufacturing multinationals. My fieldwork visiting electronics factories in Malaysia and Singapore in 1975–76 was greatly facilitated and enhanced by friends and colleagues in both countries.

Popular demand on the academic lecture/conference/publication and international development consulting circuits caused me to extend my research beyond trade, investment and industrialization, to labor markets and women workers, and from Singapore and Malaysia to East and Southeast Asia. I also focused more closely for some years on analyzing Southeast Asian Chinese businesses, which accounted for all the local private sector enterprises that I interviewed during and since my dissertation days. Teaching in a business school allowed me to apply my research in a more practitioner-oriented manner, enriched later in my career by independent director board service for publicly-listed U.S. tech companies manufacturing for export in China, with regional operations in Singapore.

I have thus been privileged in my career to see economic development and especially industrialization unfold in different countries, over decades, and from the diverse perspectives of economic globalization, business strategy and management, government public policy, labor and women. The papers included in this volume have been selected not necessarily for their scholarly significance (like peer-review journal publication and citation counts), but rather to reflect this diversity in engagement with enduring questions of economic development that are of contemporary relevance, analyzed within the contextual richness of Asian, and especially Southeast Asian, studies, usually with an eye toward challenging ideological and policy orthodoxies.

I am deeply grateful to the many individuals who have enabled me to pursue this personal and professional passion. First and foremost are my parents, who supported all my endeavors even if they did not necessarily agree with them. My late father, Lim Hee Seng, a progressive father of daughters, funded my studies in Cambridge and Yale, thereby allowing me to pursue an independent career without debt or bondage; my interest in Overseas Chinese business and entrepreneurship was both piqued and informed by exposure to clients of his public accounting practice. My mother Irene kept me constantly updated on matters Singaporean during my long years abroad, including by assiduously reading, selecting and cutting out news articles to send to me.

Chief among the others to whom I am indebted are my co-authors of papers in this volume. Pang Eng Fong, the longest and most frequent of my scholarly collaborators, who became a close family friend, added intellectual excitement, companionship, humor and gastronomic hawker delights to fieldwork and the many articles and books we co-authored, often procuring international consulting contracts that funded our work. My uncle Lee Soo Ann, one of Singapore's leading early economists, inspired me early on to pursue economics and academia, and continues to inspire many with his long-lived devotion to studying and teaching about the Singapore economy, and mentoring Singaporean economists. Gillian Foo, who housed, fed and befriended me during part of my dissertation research in Malaysia, then had me serve on her PhD committee at Michigan, becoming a close family friend in the process, is representative of the many Malaysian friends and colleagues whose comradeship enlivened my intellectual journey and social life.

Above all, my geographer husband L.A. Peter Gosling, deserves the utmost credit for co-founding the Center for Southeast Asian Studies that drew me to Michigan in the first place (and which I subsequently served as Director); for educating me about Southeast Asia through his own deep insights and vast knowledge of the area, its people and cultures, his network of friends, colleagues and former students, and our many visits, particularly to rural and remote areas; for prioritizing and supporting my work over his, and raising our delightful Burmese-named, Thai-speaking, Javanese gamelan-playing, Ramayana-loving, Shakespeare webcomic-artist-entrepreneur daughter, Mya, and generally enriching our lives. Pete, whose involvement in and understanding of Southeast Asia far exceeds my own, is also responsible for my segue into studying Overseas Chinese, a research interest of his on which we co-edited a two-volume conference-based book, *The Chinese in Southeast Asia*, Vol. 1, *Ethnicity and Economic Activity*, Vol. 2, *Identity, Culture and Politics* (Maruzen Asia, 1983).

Finally, the book would not have been possible without the dedication, thoroughness and patience of my editor at World Scientific, Ms. Sandhya Venkatesh, to whom I am indebted for bringing it to fruition. Tilak Abeysinghe and Donald Low invited me to speak at conferences and seminars, while Tilak, Manu Bhaskaran and Tan Kim Song contributed papers (as did Lee Soo Ann and Pang Eng Fong) to the SG50 Special Issue of the *Singapore Economic Review* (Vol. 60, No. 3, 2015), subsequently republished as a book, *Singapore's Economic Development: Retrospection and Reflections*, in World Scientific's SG50 series. Choy Keen Meng recruited me to guest-edit the Special Issue, and also encouraged me to publish this volume of my selected essays, while Donald Low invited me to contribute chapters to his book co-authored with Sudhir Vadaketh, *Hard Choices: Challenging the Singapore Consensus* (NUS Press, 2014). I have learned so much from them all.

Linda Y.C. Lim, PhD
Professor Emerita of Corporate Strategy and International Business

Stephen M. Ross School of Business
University of Michigan

INTRODUCTION

SINGAPORE'S ECONOMIC DEVELOPMENT

Economic development remains a subject of central interest in the world today, not only among countries which are still in the process of developing from low income levels, but also among countries which have successfully developed to middle- and high-income status, many if not most of which are encountering difficulties sustaining continued development.

Singapore's experience is, perhaps uniquely, of interest to countries at different stages. Widely regarded as one of the most successful cases of economic development in the past half-century, its rapid transition to advanced economic status is thought to provide useful lessons to countries "further behind" in the developmental trajectory. At the same time, it now faces many of the same problems that beset other rich countries, such as low GDP and productivity growth, increased inequality, an ageing population ill-equipped for retirement self-sufficiency, and uncertainty about the sources of future growth.

My first essay in this volume, "Singapore's Success: The Myth of the Free Market Economy" (1983) challenged the ideology popular during the Thatcher–Reagan era, that allowing "free market" forces to allocate resources was the best way to ensure economic growth. With its long history of free trade and capital flows, and very rapid growth since independence in 1965, Singapore was often held up as an exemplar of the superiority of the free market model, including by the economics Nobel prize-winner Milton Friedman, who had visited in 1980.[1]

---

[1]Singapore has elicited a great deal of interest and commentary from Nobel prize-winning economists. Paul Krugman's "The Myth of Asia's Miracle" (1994) highlighted other scholars' work emphasizing the factor-accumulation-based, low-productivity nature of Singapore's rapid economic growth, while Joseph Stiglitz, a frequent visitor, cited

In reality, as any Singaporean knows, the state intervened heavily in the economy, beyond just the public provision of infrastructure and social services which characterized most other countries. It also practiced industrial policy, using controls on land, labor and capital to direct resource allocation. This essay added Singapore to the "East Asian developmental state" literature then emerging to explain the equally rapid economic growth and industrialization of Japan, South Korea and Taiwan — all of which, unlike Singapore, employed trade and investment protectionism as part of their development strategies.

But at the time this paper was written, Singapore was also embarking on "privatization" in two ways — turning many previously state-run "natural monopolies" into corporatized, publicly-listed enterprises now called GLCs (government-linked companies), and reducing state responsibility for the provision of many social services that had until then been a hallmark of PAP (People's Action Party) governance.

The second essay here, on "Social Welfare" (1989), details the roles that government health, education, housing and social security policies played in Singapore's economic development, contributing as they did to lower costs, increased efficiency, higher productivity, female labor force participation, and the political and social stability that enabled export manufacturing success particularly during the labor-intensive phase. The early attention to social policy, and its integration with industrial policy, is one of the distinctive features of Singapore's development, simultaneously enhancing economic growth and welfare-oriented distribution.

Yet, as this paper also shows, the 1980s saw social welfare being transformed in ways counter to what standard economic logic would prescribe. In health and education, where abundant externalities exist, state subsidies were reduced, while in housing and management of retirement savings, which elsewhere would be delivered by private markets, state provision and control were expanded to cover the vast majority of the population. I speculated that this could be due to an anti-welfare ideology reminiscent of Thatcher and Reagan on the one hand, and a desire for greater state political control on the other. (At the time, South Korea and Taiwan had just transformed

its social policies as a model the U.S. should follow (2013); both are referenced in my "Singapore's Success: After the Miracle" (2014) essay reprinted in this volume. Earlier, Franco Modigliani on a July 1992 visit to Singapore proclaimed its savings rate "excessive", saying that "wages could be raised", decades before other economists, myself included, raised the same issue (cited in "After the Miracle").

from military-authoritarian to pluralist democratic regimes, while Singapore retains its single- or dominant-party government to this day.)

A second feature of Singapore's development which distinguishes it from other successful East Asian newly-industrialized economies is its extreme dependence on foreign capital and labor, discussed in "Globalizing State, Disappearing Nation: Foreign Participation in Singapore's Economy" (with Lee Soo Ann, 2010). This paper notes that independent Singapore's rapid early growth was achieved through factor accumulation, as in other developing countries. But, distinctively, after barely a decade, high growth was maintained chiefly by adding ever-increasing amounts of foreign capital, technology and unskilled as well as skilled labor to the economy as it progressively restructured in a higher-value direction. This restructuring, though necessitated by the market forces of shifting comparative advantage, was shaped by dirigiste state policy which targeted particular sectors for privileged investment, providing capital incentives and liberalizing the import of labor and skills needed by multinationals producing for global markets.

Our paper cites many other economists in questioning the benefits of such state-directed globalization for the local population, given its correlation with the sharp drop, to historic and comparative lows, in the share of GDP going to employee compensation and aggregate consumption (below 40 percent each), and the high share (50 percent) going to corporate profits, interest and dividends, as the foreign share of domestic production and income increased to 40 percent by the late 2000s. These trends were accompanied by high income inequality, stagnation in median and decline in low-income real wages, while local private enterprise was arguably "crowded out" of both product and factor markets (by the state as well as foreign enterprises). This led us to posit that Singapore's social cohesion and national identity, as well as local economic welfare, might be undermined rather than supported by continuation of the state-directed input-intensive growth model, itself already facing challenges of sustainability in a changing domestic and global economic environment.

In "Singapore's Success: After the Miracle" (2014), I consider these challenges to a now mature, high-income economy at the technological frontier. Since the turn of the 21st century, Singapore's GDP growth had slowed, volatility and inequality increased, productivity turned negative, consumer and asset inflation increased, median real incomes stagnated, and various non-income indicators of "well-being" fell behind those of other developed and East Asian countries, even as the country climbed to near the top of global per capita income and wealth rankings. Like other

Singapore economists, I attributed these shortcomings to excessive GDP growth targets, the multiplicity of new high-tech, high-skill sectors targeted by state subsidies for capital-intensive investment, the vast number of foreign workers (at all skill levels) admitted in a very short space of time, continued privatization and thus increased cost of previously affordable public goods (housing, transportation, utilities, healthcare), and failure of state agencies and GLCs to plan for and provide adequate infrastructure for the suddenly increased population.

Following unprecedented losses for the ruling party in general and presidential elections in 2011, the government announced major new investments in increasing housing and transportation availability, a reduction (but not a reversal) in the rate of increase of foreigners in the workforce, macro-prudential measures to reduce housing price inflation, and increases in social subsidies for the elderly and low-income under a new rhetoric of "inclusive growth". It also unveiled policies to increase skills and productivity, but did not lower growth targets until 2015, and continued to incentivize new sectors, though now with a new rhetoric of "entrepreneurship" and "innovation" still focused on attracting foreign actors.

The lessons of Singapore's experience for both emerging and developed economies are that social and industrial policy are linked, and there are limitations to globalization as a development strategy, particularly in the current era, and to state industrial policy as a country moves up the income and technology ladder. At a capital- and skill-intensive stage of development, privatizing public goods and social services while subsidizing the corporate sector delivers diminishing returns to growth and aggravates rising inequality: what is good for the corporation, particularly the foreign corporation, is not necessarily good for the country.

In "Beyond the 'Global City' Paradigm" (2015), I explore in greater detail market and institutional changes in the global economic environment which have already initiated a period of "de-globalization" that make it difficult if not impossible for Singapore to continue with its state-directed, multinational-led, export-oriented, manufacturing-focused development strategy of the past half-century. New technologies, competitors, consumer behavior, business models and corporate strategies — reinforced recently by populist-nationalist movements and international tax law reforms — now encourage consolidating production in large final markets rather than globally distributed supply—chains in which Singapore could occupy specialized niches.

Singapore's future economic growth will thus require a reorientation toward more market-driven, services-based, domestic and regional market-oriented enterprise led by local private entrepreneurs, in a reversal of past strategy and a return to its pre-independence economic role in Southeast Asia. After decades of heavy investments in infrastructure and education, the country's comparative and competitive advantage in capital- and skill-intensive activities should enable it to succeed in providing complementary goods and services to its faster-growing regional neighbors, even as the ageing domestic population adjusts to lower, but hopefully more stable and equitable, income growth.

LABOR AND WOMEN IN ECONOMIC DEVELOPMENT

The next four papers delve deeper into the role of labor in economic development. "Labor, Productivity and Singapore's Development Model" (with Pang Eng Fong, 2015) discusses how labor market policies have been shaped by and contributed to Singapore's development model — from expanding female labor force participation and raising education levels to controlling labor organization and wage costs and, above all, increasingly heavy dependence on foreign labor and skills to attract foreign investment and enable continued high GDP growth based on factor accumulation. The predictable outcomes of this dependence — low productivity growth, delayed economic restructuring, congestion and social costs — were anticipated by the government as early as the 1970s, but policies to reduce it were repeatedly stayed by short-run exigencies, namely business demands to lower labor costs to maintain export competitiveness especially during increasingly frequent recessions.

"Beyond Gender: The Impact of Age, Ethnicity, Nationality and Economic Growth on Women in the Singapore Economy" (2015) shows how economic restructuring, labor and social policy have impacted women in the labor force, dramatically yet incompletely reducing gender disparities in education, labor force participation, sectoral and occupational distribution, and wage incomes. Remaining disparities, including women being clustered in lower-income occupations and in the lower-income tiers within occupational categories, compared with men of the same age and education, appear to be the result of women's continued disproportionate responsibility for child and elder care which constrains their career choices and advancement, and retirement income adequacy.

Women workers were central to the success of the labor-intensive export manufacturing strategy followed by Singapore and many other developing countries, not only by providing labor, but also by contributing to capital formation through the higher savings which resulted from lower fertility and population dependency ratios. Yet much of the scholarly and popular literature since the 1980s has depicted women factory workers as victims of capitalist exploitation rather than as empowered agents of their own upward mobility and (partial) liberation from gender subordination in traditional society.

"Poverty, Ideology and Women Export Factory Workers in South-East Asia" (with Gillian H.C. Foo, 1989) challenges this stereotype by showing, through survey data and the voices of women workers in Singapore and Malaysia, that they were not poor and factory employment enhanced their living standards while enabling them to fulfil traditional family obligations of "parent repayment", and individual desires for consumer autonomy and personal independence unavailable to their mothers' generation. Women workers also expressed a preference for gender equity in decision-making, though not a strong sense of class consciousness, at least at that time and those places.

"Women's Work in Export Factories: The Politics of a Cause" (1990) further challenges stereotypes of worker exploitation popular in the West, exposing their empirical inaccuracies, methodological flaws, ethnocentric orientation and ideological motivation, particularly the vested political interests which sought to justify protectionist measures against labor-intensive imports from developing countries by devaluing the jobs they create there. This has turned out to be an enduring "cause", revitalized by U.S. campus anti-sweatshop campaigns which I have had occasion to publicly rebut,[2] and most recently and ominously, the elevation of President Donald Trump's virulent anti-trade views on Mexico and China to the brink of destructive policy action.

BUSINESS-GOVERNMENT RELATIONS AND SOUTHEAST ASIAN CHINESE IN ECONOMIC DEVELOPMENT

Singapore's economy has always been intertwined with those of its Southeast Asian neighbors, several of which paralleled, with a lag, its labor-intensive export manufacturing strategy, and also experienced decades of rapid GDP growth. "The Evolution of Southeast Asian Business Systems" (1996) describes the complex dynamic historical, economic, political and cultural underpinnings of the region's "business systems", noting the respective

[2]See e.g., Linda Y.C. Lim, "The Antisweatshop Movement: A Rebuttal", in *Challenge: The Magazine of Economic Affairs*, Vol. 46, No. 4 (July/August 2003), pp. 1–5.

roles of national governments, Western and Japanese multinationals, and ethnic Chinese and indigenous capitalists in the region's developing market economies. These business systems were and are diverse and dynamic, and the paper also outlines how they may be expected to change with economic and political liberalization and maturity.

"Strengths and Weaknesses of Minority Status for Southeast Asian Chinese" (1997, with L.A. Peter Gosling) examines the impact on inter-ethnic relations in Thailand, Indonesia, the Philippines, Malaysia and Singapore of the business dominance and disproportionate economic benefit to "Overseas Chinese" of rapid economic growth and liberalization during a period of political democratization. We conclude and explain why growth eases but does not eliminate longstanding ethnic tensions that may be expected to intensify with the enhanced ethnic pride, cultural assertiveness and pan-Chinese identification that accompany economic success, and the concomitant rise of China as a regional economic power.

The much-reprinted "Whose 'Model' Failed? Implications of the Asian Economic Crisis" (1998) considers whether the late 1990s crisis-induced implosion of Southeast Asia's economies was caused by excessive Western-style "openness" (such as capital market liberalization and political democratization), or by Asian-style statist industrial policy, "crony capitalism" and "culturally embedded networks", a subject much debated in academic and policy circles at the time. I predictably conclude that "*neither* the Western open-markets-and-democracy model *or* the Asian strong-government-and-cultural-values model" satisfactorily explains Asian countries' pre-crisis economic success or their subsequent spectacular (if in most cases short-lived) failure, and further caution against the application of simplistic ideological models to "the messy practical business of public and private sector economic management in developing countries whose political, economic, and business systems are not only diverse and complexly intertwined, but also still evolving." I argue instead for returning to each country's particular history and contemporary circumstances to discern both causes and solutions to the crisis.

That said, "Southeast Asian Chinese Business: Past Success, Recent Crisis and Future Evolution" (2000) seeks to model commonalities in Southeast Asian Chinese business organization and behavior to explain both their success and vulnerability to the crisis. I argue that their success derives from a complex of situational variables: immigrant self-selection, "minority middleman" status, ethnic networks, firstcomer advantage, politics and government relations, multicultural facility, familism and entrepreneurialism. Individual entrepreneurs operate within family firms (particularly diversified conglomerates) and social networks from which they develop and manage relationships with governments, and foreign and indigenous (*pribumi*) partners. This gives them superior access to scarce resources and valuable business opportunities, but also encourages excessive reliance on moral hazard, related-party lending, over-leverage and poor risk management, leading to "bad investments" that collapse in a crisis. Future success will require greater reliance on modern professional management and development of firm-specific competitive advantages, encouraged by greater competition for capital, talent and market share in more liberalized, globalized economies.

"Southeast Asian Chinese Business and Regional Economic Development" (2013) retraces the role of ethnic Chinese in Southeast Asia's economic development, from the colonial era through national independence, the import-substituting industrialization and export-oriented manufacturing phases, and the Asian financial crisis, as a backdrop to analyzing the more recent ASEAN regional economic integration, and China's rise, including its greatly increased trade, investment and tourist linkages with the regional economy. I argue that while Southeast Asian Chinese business probably contributed to their nations' higher economic *growth* than experienced by other post-colonial developing countries, their impact on national economic *development* is more ambiguous. The state- and multinational-centered investment strategies favored by these countries, in part to counter the dominance of ethnic Chinese minority business, may partly explain "the failure of Southeast Asian countries to replicate the vigorous local capitalisms and both large and small-scale, globally competitive private enterprises that emerged in Northeast Asia.. . .despite similar macroeconomic and industrial policies which contributed to rapid output and employment growth based on exporting manufactures to world markets."

Going forward, reduced ethnic discrimination would help to "normalize" entrepreneurship and business development in Southeast Asia. Expanded economic relations with China are likely to preserve the economic advantages of Chinese ethnicity for local Chinese minorities, but could also increase ethnic tensions and political vulnerability depending on how greater "Chinese dominance" in the region is articulated and perceived.

"State Power and Private Profit: The Political Economy of Corruption in Southeast Asia" (2002) reviews the 1990–2002 literature on corruption — a prevalent form of business-government relations–in Indonesia, Philippines, Thailand, Malaysia and Singapore. It finds "no conclusive relationship" between state intervention, liberalization and privatization on the one hand, and rent-seeking and corruption on the other. Particular forms of patronage and clientelism condition the role of the private sector in each country, while political democratization and decentralization appear to have little systematic impact on the prevalence of corruption, which also has not severely dampened economic growth. Neither economic liberalization nor political democratization are sufficient to eliminate corruption.

CONCLUSION: SINGAPORE, GLOBALIZATION AND REGIONALIZATION

Taken together, essays in this volume trace Singapore's economic development from its post-colonial early-industrial transformation from a regional trade-and-services hub to a global manufacturing and logistics hub for multinational corporations, which it remains in the late-industrial era. Singapore was a major beneficiary of the wave of globalization which accompanied the first half-century of its economic transformation as an independent nation state. Facing both severe domestic resource constraints as a now high-cost production location, and external market- and policy-dictated "de-globalization" trends, a reorientation of economic development strategy, from multinational-led manufacturing for world markets to local private enterprise-led services for the Southeast Asian region, is now warranted. As Pang Eng Fong and I noted in 1981, based on an article not included here,[3] "Singapore has a much stronger international competitive advantage in the export of services.....based on its long experience and large human and capital investment in these sectors. Another asset is its location in a rapidly growing regional economy of which it is the service hub."[4]

That region is Southeast Asia, destined by demographics, geography and stage-of-development to outperform the rest of the world in economic growth in the next half-century when Singapore should ease into post-industrial status. Other essays reproduced here outline the ongoing evolution of Southeast Asian business systems, locating them in the particular historic, political, economic and cultural contexts of individual countries, and exploring in greater depth the nature and impact of the dominant local entrepreneurial class, the ethnic Chinese minority. It is in this regional business world that Singapore's economic future lies, and in which our private enterprises should venture, as our predecessors did during the colonial era.

---

[3]Pang, EF and L Lim (1982). Foreign Labour and Economic Development in Singapore. *International Migration Review*, Vol. 16 No. 2, pp. 548–576.

[4]Pang, EF and L Lim (1981). Singapore's Foreign Workers: Are They Worth the Costs?, *Asian Wall Street Journal*, August 4.

CONTENTS

Preface and Acknowledgements v

Introduction ix

Part I: Singapore's Economic Development **1**

1. Singapore's Success: The Myth of the Free Market Economy 3
   Linda Y. C. Lim

2. Social Welfare 17
   Linda Y. C. Lim

3. Globalizing State, Disappearing Nation: The Impact of Foreign Participation in the Singapore Economy 49
   Linda Y. C. Lim and Lee Soo Annj

4. Singapore's Success: After the Miracle 69
   Linda Y. C. Lim

5. Beyond the "Global City" Paradigm 105
   Linda Lim

Part II: Labor and Women in Economic Development **137**

6. Labor, Productivity and Singapore's Development Model 139
   Pang Eng Fong and Linda Y. C. Lim

7. Beyond Gender: The Impact of Age, Ethnicity, Nationality and Economic Growth on Women in the Singapore Economy 177
Linda Y. C. Lim

8. Poverty, Ideology and Women Export Factory Workers in South-East Asia 197
Gillian H. C. Foo and Linda Y. C. Lim

9. Women's Work in Export Factories: The Politics of a Cause 217
Linda Y. C. Lim

Part III: Business-Government Relations and Southeast Asian Chinese in Economic Development 241

10. The Evolution of Southeast Asian Business Systems 243
Linda Y. C. Lim

11. Strengths and Weaknesses of Minority Status for Southeast Asian Chinese at a Time of Economic Growth and Liberalization 267
Linda Y. C. Lim and L. A. Peter Gosling

12. Whose 'Model' Failed? Implications of the Asian Economic Crisis 301
Linda Y. C. Lim

13. Southeast Asian Chinese Business: Past Success, Recent Crisis and Future Evolution 313
Linda Y. C. Lim

14. Southeast Asian Chinese Business and Regional Economic Development 329
Linda Y. C. Lim

15. State Power and Private Profit: The Political Economy of Corruption in Southeast Asia 347
Linda Y. C. Lim and Aaron Stern

Part I

SINGAPORE'S ECONOMIC DEVELOPMENT

Chapter 1

SINGAPORE'S SUCCESS: THE MYTH OF THE FREE MARKET ECONOMY*

LINDA Y. C. LIM†

With the apparent failure in recent years of Keynesian economic policies in advanced capitalist countries and of state-centered development efforts in the Third World, and with the rise of such political leaders as Margaret Thatcher and Ronald Reagan in the West and Edward Seaga of Jamaica in the Third World, it has become increasingly fashionable, even orthodox, to advocate a return to the ideology of the free market as the way to economic growth and prosperity in both developed and developing countries. This 19th-century ideology incorporates such notions as the "Invisible Hand" as the best allocator of resources, and unbridled competition as the means to efficient production. Government intervention in the economy is frowned upon as inefficient, costly, and a threat to personal liberties of the individual and the community — worse still, as "creeping socialism".

Governments of both developed and developing countries which have recently embraced this ideology look for models both to emulate and to point to as justification for their so-called return-to-the-marketplace policies. Singapore is a popular model for this purpose. Margaret Thatcher has cited it as an exemplar of free market economic success. Third World countries like Jamaica and Sri Lanka explicitly look to it for development policies

*This chapter first appeared in *Asian Survey*, Vol. 23, No. 6 (June 1983), pp. 752–764. Reprinted with permission.

†This article is a revised version of a talk presented at the Center for South and Southeast Asian Studies, the University of Michigan, Ann Arbor, February 19, 1982. Much of the material in this paper was collected in collaboration with Dr. Pang Eng Fong for other projects. The analysis, interpretation, and conclusions here presented, including any errors, are the author's.

to emulate.[1] Indeed, Singapore is widely recognized as *the* most successful economy in the world, even in comparison with other members of the so-called Gang of Four, the spectacularly successful, newly industrializing Asian countries of Hong Kong, Taiwan, and South Korea.

My contention in this article is that, contrary to popular belief, this success is *not* due to free market policies which can be emulated by other countries. While Singapore *is* a success story of *capitalist* development, this is not the same as a success story of *free market* development.

THE WORLD'S MOST SUCCESSFUL ECONOMY

Let us first look briefly at the facts making Singapore the world's most successful economy.[2] In the 1960s, GNP growth averaged 10% a year, accelerating to 14.3% a year in the 1970s. Real GDP — domestic output and income discounted for inflation — grew at an annual rate of 8.7% in the 1960s and 9.4% in the 1970s. The GNP growth rate in 1980 was 10.2%, and about the same rate was sustained in 1981. Annual inflation in the Consumer Price Index was 1.2% in the 1960s, 5.6% in the 1970s, and 8.5% in 1980.[3] In other words, Singapore has for twenty years sustained an economic growth rate far above, and an inflation rate below, world averages, and has managed to achieve the often elusive ideal of rapid growth with relative price stability.

During this period, the economy diversified from one based on entrepot trade and British military services to export manufacturing, transport and communications, and financial and business services. The country has become a major node in international manufacturing, trade, communications, banking, and financial networks. The overall balance of payments has been in constant surplus,[4] resulting in the constant appreciation of the

[1]For example, Singapore government officials and private businessmen are directly involved in many Sri Lankan development projects, mainly in joint ventures in real estate, tourist resorts, and the running of the state airline Air Lanka by Singapore Airlines.

Chile is another developing country which has recently shown interest in learning from the experience of Singapore and other successful Asian countries. The Faculty of Economic and Administrative Sciences of the Catholic University of Chile organized a *Conference on Experiences and Lessons of Small Open Economies*, in Santiago, November 11–13, 1981.

[2]For details on the information provided in this section, see Linda Lim and Pang Eng Fong, *Trade, Employment and Industralisation in Singapore*, Working Paper WEP 2-36/ WP 17, World Employment Programme Research, International Labour Office, Geneva, June 1982, Chapters 1 and 2.

[3]Annual inflation in the GDP deflator was 1.2% in the 1960s, 4.9% in the 1970s, and 3.4% in 1980.

[4]Singapore has a persistent deficit in the balance of trade, but this is more than covered by net service inflows and long-term capital inflows.

Singapore dollar[5] and the accumulation of huge foreign exchange reserves which the government is now investing in long-term as well as short-term assets abroad.

What has all this prosperity done for the ordinary people of Singapore? Beginning from a situation of double-digit unemployment in the late 1950s, full employment was reached in the early 1970s, and the unemployment rate is currently 3% of the labor force. The country has had to import labor from other Asian countries to make up the shortfall of domestic labor, which is inadequate to meet demand despite the vastly expanded participation of women in the labor force. In 1980, 11% of the Singapore labor force was foreign — mostly from Malaysia, but also from Indonesia, Thailand, the Philippines, India, Sri Lanka, Bangladesh, etc.[6]

Per capita indigenous GNP (the average income of local residents) tripled between 1970 and 1980, and rose by 5.9% a year in real terms during the 1970s. This increase in average income and purchasing power has been accompanied by a slight *improvement* in the national income distribution, at least through 1976.[7] Per capita income is now more than US $4,000 per year, making Singapore rank 31st of 126 nations in the United Nations, and two to three times higher than per capita income in other newly industrializing countries like Taiwan, South Korea, and Malaysia.[8]

Judged by these conventional economic indicators, Singapore is the world's most successful economy, achieving sustained rapid growth with relative price stability, full employment, a strong balance of payments, rising real incomes, and constant if not declining income inequality. It has also been judged, in at least one major business survey, as the best investment location in the world, based on a system of weighted rankings of various criteria.[9] Most notably, Singapore ranked first among the 45 nations

[5]The Singapore dollar appreciated from 33 U.S. cents in 1970 to 50 U.S. cents in the late 1970s.

[6]See Pang, EF and L Lim (1982). Foreign Labour and Economic Development in Singapore. *International Migration Review*, 16(3), pp. 548–576.

[7]See Pang, EF (1975). Growth, Inequality and Race in Singapore. *International Labour Review*, 111(1), pp. 15–28; V. Bhanoji Rao and M. K. Ramakrishnan, *Economic Growth, Structural Changes, and Income Inequality, Singapore*, 1966–1975, Council for Asian Manpower Studies, Discussion Paper Series No. 77-15, December 1977; Department of Statistics, *Report on the Household Expenditure Survey, 1977/1978* (Singapore: Singapore National Printers, 1979).

[8]The World Bank, *1980 World Bank Atlas.*

[9]By Dr. F. T. Haner, head of Business Environment Risk Information Ltd., an American firm which prepares reports on business environment risks in 45 countries, three times a year, for the heads of 250 multinational companies. Quoted in John Drysdale, "How Singapore became No. 1," *The Straits Times*, Singapore, January 2, 1982.

surveyed in "lack of future political risks" (Japan ranked fourth) and first in "labor force quality"[10] (Taiwan ranked second, South Korea fifth, and Japan seventh). It tied for first place with the U.S., Japan, Switzerland, and West Germany for "future profit opportunities," and ranked fourth, behind the U.S., Switzerland, and West Germany, and ahead of Japan (which ranked eighth) in "free market environment for investors." So it is Singapore, and not Japan, which is Number One.

THE MAGIC OF THE FREE MARKET?

How has this success come about? According to free marketeers like Milton Friedman (who visited Singapore in 1980), it is the result of economic liberalism and the free market. They point to the fact that Singapore is a free port, with only a very few revenue tariffs and protective tariffs which are progressively being removed, and no foreign exchange controls or domestic price controls common in many developing countries. There are also virtually no controls on private enterprise and investment, no anti-monopoly laws, no approval or licensing required of foreign or local private investments, no limitations on profit remittances and capital repatriation, and so on. The financial sector has also been increasingly liberalized. Free trade and free capital flows are thus seen as the basis of Singapore's economic success.

The Long Arm of the State[11]

But in addition to Milton Friedman, the free marketeer, Singapore is also greatly admired by a man often seen as his polar opposite in the spectrum of American mainstream economists — John Kenneth Galbraith, the Keynesian economist and government interventionist who held Singapore up as an ideal in his television series, "The Age of Uncertainty." The state in Singapore is in fact heavily interventionist. It owns, controls, and/or regulates land, labor, and capital resources, and their allocation. It sets or influences many of the prices on which private investors base their business calculations and investment decisions.

[10]This is a composite measure including labor laws, unions, hire/fire/lay off flexibility, relative labor productivity, worker attitude, and technical skills.

[11]For details on the information provided in this section, see Lim and Pang, *Trade, Employment and Industrialisation in Singapore*, Chapter 3; Pang Eng Fong and Linda Lim, "Rapid Growth and Relative Price Stability in a Small Open Economy: The Experience of Singapore," paper presented at the conference cited in note 1 above; Tan Chwee Huat, *State Enterprise System and Economic Development in Singapore*, Ph. D. dissertation in Business Administration, University of Wisconsin, 1974.

Like governments in most developed capitalist countries except the United States, the Singapore government is the exclusive provider of infrastructure and social services. State monopolies provide all utilities, telephone and postal services, port and airport services, industrial estates, and radio and television. Government ministries provide a large part of medical and health services, all sanitation services, and all education for the population from primary to tertiary level. The state Housing and Development Board houses nearly three-quarters of the population in public housing estates. What differentiates these state activities in Singapore from those in other countries is that, with the exception of health, education, and the lowest-income public housing, they all at least break even, and most are profit making. They are not subsidized by tax dollars. This is achieved by a combination of cost efficient operation and by charging users full costs of the services provided.

State enterprises also venture outside the realm of infrastructure and social services. They engage in direct production in competition and partnership with foreign and local private enterprise. The state airlines — Singapore Airlines (SIA) — is probably the world's most successful international carrier. There is a state trading company, a state shipping company, two state joint-venture shipyards, and various other wholly and partly state-owned productive and profit-making companies, including both private joint ventures and publicly quoted companies. The Development Bank of Singapore is a publicly quoted company with a majority government share which operates as a commercial bank and invests in many private enterprises as a kind of government holding company. The government is not hesitant to close down or pull out of its enterprises and investments that are unprofitable — for example, a pulp and paper mill, and very recently, the multinational German camera manufacturer, Rollei, one of the largest industrial employers in the country, which went bankrupt.

The government is the major actor in the *land* market, where it holds about 75% of all land in the country, and is empowered to acquire whatever of the remainder it wishes.[12] Some of the land is used for public housing estates, in which all apartments of three rooms or more make a profit over their construction and administrative costs, with only the smallest flats being subsidized. The government thus competes with the private sector

[12]Owners of land thus acquired are compensated at the 1973 pre-inflation values of their property.

in providing middle-income housing.[13] Some of the land is allocated to the Urban Redevelopment Authority, which engages in urban renewal and property development on a commercial basis and has annual revenues larger than those of the highly profitable Singapore Airlines. Some of the land is resold to private developers at prices far above those at which the government acquired it. Thus there has been criticism from citizens that government activity in the property market has contributed to the excessive inflation in real estate values in recent years.

The government is also the major actor in the *capital* market, given its large direct participation in the financial sector. Its Central Provident Fund and Post Office Savings Bank hold a majority of national savings, while the Development Bank of Singapore is a major commercial bank which holds deposits and grants loans. The Monetary Authority of Singapore acts as a central bank and is responsible for monetary policy, while the new Government of Singapore Investment Corporation will manage foreign reserves and make foreign investments. More than half of domestic income passes through government hands in one way or another — through the 42% share of earned income which goes to the Central Provident Fund in compulsory employer and employee contributions, the 2% payroll tax and 4% Skills Development Fund levy on wages, personal and corporate income taxes, indirect taxes, and the tariffs charged and incomes earned by the various statutory boards and state enterprises.

The government also influences the private allocation of investment funds by various investment incentive schemes administered by the Economic Development Board, which grants tax exemptions, write-offs, other subsidies and allowances, state equity participation, and low-interest loans to desired investments. Penalties are also sometimes used, as in the denial of Multi-Fibre Agreement export quotas to textile and garment manufacturers who have not upgraded their operations in line with government policy.

Above all, the government is the major actor in the *labor* market. It is the largest employer in the economy, accounting for 20% of total employment. It regulates wages through the National Wages Council, which sets annual wage guidelines for the economy as a whole. It regulates labor supply through variable controls on foreign labor, which have been increasingly liberalized in recent years. It invests heavily in manpower training programs to benefit private industry. It has ensured labor peace and discipline through

[13]Government middle-income apartments are cheaper than those in the private sector, but subject to many restrictions, such as income ceilings, limits on the number and relationship of occupants, on rental and resale, etc.

political moves, administrative regulations governing the registration and deregistration of unions, compulsory arbitration procedures to limit strikes, an Employment Act which standardizes terms and conditions of employment (including limits on fringe benefits), and an Industrial Relations Act defining management prerogatives which are not subject to union negotiation and defining the framework and procedures for labor negotiation and conflict resolution.[14] Ninety percent of total union membership (which includes about a quarter of the labor force) is affiliated with the ruling People's Action Party-led National Trades Union Congress (NTUC), which is headed by a government minister and run by government bureaucrats. For over ten years, man-days lost through strikes and other labor actions have been negligible and in the last few years, nonexistent.

THE IMPACT OF STATE INTERVENTION

These state policies and actions have influenced resource allocation by changing relative prices. For example, the showcase sector of Singapore's economic development is the large export manufacturing sector. Tax concessions, efficient infrastructure, wages kept low by government subsidies on low-income housing and other social services, by many years of low National Wages Council wage increases, by easy access to foreign labor, and by docile unions, and the low level of risk and uncertainty afforded by political stability and labor peace — all these have made investment in Singapore very attractive, especially to multinational corporations engaged in labor-intensive manufacturing for export, despite the fact that wage costs *are* higher than in other competing newly industrializing countries in Asia. In other words, state interventions have given Singapore a comparative advantage in export manufacturing which it would not have if free market forces alone prevailed.

But state actions to influence prices and private investment decisions based on those prices, while highly successful in the short run, may have slowed the long-run adjustment of the economy to underlying market forces. In the second half of the 1970s, especially, low wages encouraged excessive use of labor and delayed technological upgrading of the economy. The government recognized this, and in 1979 it instituted a three-year

---

[14]See Pang Eng Fong, "Singapore," in AA Blum (ed.), *International Handbook of Industrial Relations: Contemporary Developments and Research* (Westport, Conn.: Greenwood Press, 1981), pp. 481–497. Existing labor legislation and industrial relations system may be changed in line with the government's "Privatisation" strategy: for example, the system of collective bargaining is now considered by the government to be "anachronistic."

policy of "corrective" large wage increases to "return wages to market levels," discourage labor use, and encourage capital-labor substitution in a labor- scarce economy.[15] The development strategy for the 1980s is to shift the economy away from labor-intensive activities and technologies into more capital- and skill-intensive investments, higher-productivity, higher-wage activities, with manufacturing continuing as the leading sector of the economy. To do this, the government has restructured its investment incentives and labor market policies, and set up a new National Productivity Council to promote and oversee technological and skill upgrading and measures to increase labor productivity.

Once again, the policy of the government is not to let market forces take their course, but rather to intervene to make relative prices (distorted — albeit with beneficial results — by earlier government interventions) attract the type of investment that it wants. Once again, the question may be raised as to whether the government should be creating an artificial comparative advantage for Singapore in high-technology manufacturing and, indeed, whether it can succeed in doing so.[16] The new strategy requires, apart from the foreign capital, technology, and markets that Singapore's labor-intensive export manufacturing sector is already dependent on, increasing dependence on foreign skilled labor and expertise, which are being actively courted and recruited abroad.

State intervention in the Singapore economy has had a positive impact not only on the profitability of private business, but also on the welfare of the working population. Apart from the jobs that have been created in the private and public sectors for workers, the government provides subsidized housing and health, educational, and recreational services, as well as public transportation for the mass of the population, and manages the bulk of savings for retirement through the Central Provident Fund and the Post Office Savings Bank. It also decides annual wage increments (which have usually meant real wage increases) and sets minimum fringe benefits in the public and private sectors.

State responsibility for workers' welfare has won the government the support and dependence of the population, thus guaranteeing the political stability that encourages private investment. In general, state intervention

[15]The wage increase recommended for 1979 and 1980 was 20% in both years, declining to 14% in 1981, after which the policy of large increases was abandoned.

[16]For the arguments behind this statement, and a discussion of alternatives to high-technology manufacturing, see Pang Eng Fong and Linda Lim, "Political Economy of A City-State," *Singapore Business Yearbook* 1981/1982, pp. 7, 9, 13, 15, 19, 21, 25, 27, 29, and 33.

in, and control and even direction of the economy have managed to be pro-business without being anti-labor, at least in the sense of material welfare.

Singapore enjoyed free trade and free capital flows when it was a colonial entrepot, but these were insufficient to bring about high growth and full employment. Since independence, what has made Singapore successful is not the Invisible Hand of the free market, but rather the very Visible Hand, indeed the Long Arm, of the State.

THE WITHERING AWAY OF THE STATE?

Despite the success of its state development policies, the Singapore government itself has also swallowed the free market ideology. It believes that its so-called Second Industrial Revolution — technological upgrading and moving upmarket — requires a dismantling of much of the state apparatus. This does not mean that the state will divest itself of its profit-making functions, like the various state monopolies engaged in infrastructure provision, other state enterprises, and joint ventures. What it intends to do is divest itself of the loss-making functions of government, chiefly the responsibility for providing subsidized housing and health care. This will be shoved onto private employers and workers themselves, with consumers of the part remaining in government hands being charged increased rates to approximate full costs.

This new strategy is called "Privatisation", and involves a shift from what might be called a system of state welfarism to company welfarism, or Singapore's version of the New Federalism — the decentralization of responsibility for social welfare. It is motivated by two factors. First, the government is increasingly unable or unwilling to provide subsidized social services to match the ever-increasing demands and expectations of the population, given rising costs and its own philosophical aversion to subsidies.

Second, it has been noted that dependence on the state has prevented the development of company loyalty and long-service employment, which characterize the Japanese model that the government seeks to emulate and considers essential to employment stability and the development of "good work habits" which lead to high productivity.[17] It is hoped that stronger

[17]In 1981, the government embarked on a campaign of criticizing labor for its "poor work habits," "job hopping," etc., and low productivity. When it was pointed out that potential investors might actually believe the government criticisms and be discouraged from investing in the country, it retracted (e.g., an announcement was made that statistics showed that job hopping was not a problem). Many multinational employers in Singapore have praised the attitudes and productivity of their workers. It should also be noted that

company-worker ties will reduce labor mobility in a tight labor market and permit the emergence of a more direct relationship between labor remuneration, productivity, and company profitability.

The success of Privatisation depends on the extent to which it is accepted by both companies and workers — neither of whom will be happy if they stand to lose anything from the change. Already many companies, including multinationals, have voiced their unwillingness to bear the costs of responsibility for workers' housing, medical care, and pensions, though they are eager to recoup from the government part or all of the 20% of employees' wages they must pay into the Central Provident Fund. Many companies, especially local companies, are too small or insecure to provide such benefits. All companies, especially multinationals and others that are subject to international market forces, will not wish to have their freedom of operation restricted by costly responsibilities for a fixed and, increasingly, aging labor force — particularly in technologically dynamic industries where labor turnover can be a positive factor.[18] In addition, multinationals have no national loyalty to Singapore, and some may wish to retain their freedom to leave the country without costly retrenchment procedures and benefits should their parent corporate interests so dictate.

Workers' reservations about Privatisation are the other side of the coin from employers' concerns. They are reluctant to surrender the security and relative equity of state-provided social benefits. Privatisation means greater insecurity (for example, if the company fails or mismanages workers' pension funds) and greater inequality (those who work for larger, richer companies will get more and better benefits than those who work for smaller, less rich companies). Workers are unlikely to form great attachments to foreign employers who may not be in the country forever[19] and may resent being tied to one company.[20] For many workers, especially the skilled and professional, often the only way up the job ladder is by moving out of one company to

in the business survey mentioned in note 9 above, labor productivity in Singapore was rated first among the countries considered, and much better than in Japan, which had a low ranking. One reason given for this was the lifetime employment system in Japan, which kept labor productivity *lower* than it otherwise might be.

[18]This is one reason why the Japanese, for example, are trying to develop alternatives to their system of lifetime employment.

[19]The nationalism which is arguably one factor in the Japanese worker's loyalty to his company and motivation to work well is not operative in a manufacturing sector as dominated by multinationals as that in Singapore.

[20]Quite likely, the workers who want to and have the opportunity to move out of one company to another are the more ambitious and able ones, while those content to stay are the less able and ambitious who have less opportunity to move.

another, given the relatively small size and shallow internal job ladders of manufacturing firms, including multinational subsidiaries, in Singapore, and the relatively young age of those who occupy the upper rungs of existing job ladders. Internal promotion prospects for those further down the job ladder will be further dimmed if the mobility of their superiors is reduced by the tying of benefits to seniority in one employer.

Overall, tying workers' benefits to individual companies will severely reduce labor mobility — the major means of adjustment to market forces — and make the economy more rigid if companies cannot readily lay off workers and hire new ones and workers cannot readily move to where better opportunities present themselves. The allocation of resources will be more inefficient, and inflationary pressures, now held down partly by the large share of national savings going compulsorily into government coffers, will increase. Labor productivity may well decline rather than improve as intended, since workers resentful about their limited mobility and workers grateful for the assurance of lifetime employment — who are likely to be, respectively, those who are more and less competitive on a "free" labor market — are both unlikely to perform their best.

In addition to the demise of a free labor market, Privatisation in Singapore will likely also mean less, rather than more, laissez-faire. The government may well interfere *more* in companies' internal production and employment decisions — for example through the National Productivity Council whose tasks include concern about technology choice, skill training, etc. The government will also retain, and even increase, its social and political control of the population. Already it tells citizens how many children they can have,[21] what they must study in school and the university[22] (including compulsory religious instruction), what language they must speak at home and in public,[23] and where they can live.[24] To this list will now be added, by means of a combination of incentives and disincentives, where they can work. In addition, the government has recently announced that it will soon

[21]Two children per couple is the official norm, and there are disincentives to discourage more than three children, such as discrimination in the allocation of school places and other public benefits.

[22]For example, a top student may be denied a place in medical school in order to channel him into some other faculty, such as engineering, and scholarships for needy or deserving students are given only for government-approved courses of study.

[23]There has been vigorous campaigning in the past few years to wipe out the indigenous provincial dialects spoken by the majority Chinese population, and to substitute Mandarin. This includes some penalties — e.g., fines for hawkers and taxi drivers who do not speak Mandarin.

[24]This arises out of government allocation and control of public housing units.

pass legislation making it compulsory for children to look after their parents when they are old.[25] This may be viewed as a measure to reduce not only the state's responsibility for caring for the aged in a progressively aging population,[26] but also employers' responsibility for providing benefits to retired workers.

In return for these curbs on personal liberties and choices — curbs on which Singapore's order and efficiency are based, but which would be anathema to citizens of less successful but freer market economies elsewhere — the government promises more costly housing and health care (including that provided by the public sector), and greater insecurity from diminished state welfare responsibilities. The government itself acknowledges that the new policy is not likely to be popular and may have been one of the factors leading to the election to parliament in 1981 of the first opposition member of parliament in eighteen years.[27]

Thus the long arm of the state in Singapore is unlikely to wither away. What it will do is change its role from that of direct provider of social and business amenities to that of director and overseer of a much wider and deeper range of private, social, and business institutions, and behaviors and relationships.

CONCLUSION

In sum, Singapore's spectacular economic success to date is the result more of the Long Arm of state intervention than it is of the Invisible Hand of the free market. Privatisation — the reduction of the state's responsibility for social welfare — will further limit free market adjustments and personal freedoms, and possibly pose a threat to continued economic success while undermining the government's political support on which both political stability and labor peace — the strongest investment attractions of Singapore — are based.

So why is the government doing this? Part of the answer is the same as the answer to why Ronald Reagan and Margaret Thatcher insist on following their economic policies despite opposition from business and labor. First, there is faith; for Ronald Reagan and his supply-side advisors the *belief* that

[25]See Michael Richardson, "Back to Confucius," *Far Eastern Economic Review*, February 26, 1982, p. 26.

[26]By the turn of the century, it is forecast that 300,000 Singaporeans, 10% of the population, will be aged 60 and over. Ibid.

[27]As one of the government's "second echelon leaders," Goh Chok Tong, said after this happened, the electorate in the constituency which elected the opposition party candidate did so because they have "a low threshhold of pain."

tax and welfare cuts will lead to increased investment and work effort; for the Singapore government the *belief* that Privatisation will lead to increased labor productivity. This faith is related to ideology: to Ronald Reagan, a decrease in "Big Government" is a desired end in itself, regardless of its economic and social costs; and to the Singapore government, Privatisation is also a desired goal in itself. "The PAP maintains that excessive government involvement in social welfare undermines individual motivation to work and excel, saps human dignity and drains the public purse."[28] There are also other reasons peculiar to the Singapore situation. One is the confidence — some might say, arrogance — of a government which cannot believe that anything it decides to do will not succeed, since it always has.

Another is the possibility that, quite unconsciously, the state bureaucracy in Singapore is evolving into a separate "class" with motivations and interests independent of, and more than simply intermediary between, those of capital and labor. Government members overwhelmingly do not belong to the private property-owning, domestic entrepreneurial class, and some would say that it does not even serve their interests. Their reward comes not from a share of profits — not even the profits of state enterprise — or from corruption, which is nonexistent (a rarity in both the developed and developing world), and only partly from salary and perquisites (which, though increasing, are still inferior to those in the private sector). Rather it comes from the power of control over the vast assets of the state itself, and indirectly of the private sector as well, and from the reflected glory of the very success the state has created in the economy.

If the past actions of the government are any indicator, this success is likely to continue, notwithstanding the weaknesses of the new strategy noted above. For unlike Ronald Reagan or Margaret Thatcher, the Singapore government is not rigidly doctrinaire in its ideology. Pragmatism has led to the revision of state policies in the past, and no doubt will again, despite government pronouncements to the contrary. There are signs that such revision has already begun — for example, in the announcement by a junior government minister that the state "would continue to provide the basic subsidies in housing, education and health."[29]

Privatisation in Singapore was developed as a means of tackling a central problem of all developed capitalist countries: how to motivate the worker in a situation of affluence and security when his job, housing, recreation,

---

[28] Michael Richardson, "Back to Confucius."

[29] Dr. Wong Kwei Chong, Minister of State for Labour, and Chairman of the National Productivity Board, on February 10, 1982, quoted in ibid.

health care, education, etc. are assured, and he quite naturally may be tempted to put greater emphasis on enjoying the fruits of his labor than on increased work effort. To this problem the free market provides no answer beyond the periodic "discipline" of recessions and the withdrawal of state benefits advocated by its proponents. Singapore's experience shows that for capitalism to survive and prosper with labor's support, the state must intervene.

In the end, the state in Singapore is paternalistic in its attitudes and actions towards both capital and labor. It has been suggested that "Singapore's goal is to create a corporate state similar to Japan in which both government and industry are an extension of the family with all three entities sharing responsibility for individual welfare."[30] But though "all three entities" may share such responsibility, they do not share the power to enforce such sharing when it is not voluntarily forthcoming through free choice or market forces: that is the preserve of the state. While the forms of state intervention in Singapore may change, their essence remains: the manipulation of polity, society, and economy to build and maintain a peculiar, and peculiarly successful, brand of state-dependent capitalism.

---

[30]Ibid.

Chapter 2

SOCIAL WELFARE*

LINDA Y. C. LIM

INTRODUCTION

Social welfare has traditionally been thought of as one of the goals of development, a view which has been reinforced by recent emphases on the importance of providing for the basic needs of the populations of developing countries. Such needs typically include adequate nutrition, health care, clothing, housing, utilities (electricity and water), education, employment and (sometimes) social security (provision for unemployment, disability, and old age). By any absolute or comparative standards, Singapore has excelled in providing for these needs of its population over more than a quarter century of development. Although its per capita income ($7,260 in 1984, according to the World Bank's calculation[1]) is still below that of most developed nations, Singapore has comparable or superior standards of social welfare by most indicators.[2] For example, the infant mortality rate has fallen by three-quarters since 1960, and is now below that of many developed nations, including the United States, Belgium, Austria, Italy, and New Zealand.[3] Life expectancy at birth (seventy years for males, seventy-five years for females) is about comparable with that of developed nations, and per capita caloric supply was 115 per cent of the average daily requirement in 1983, the same as in Japan and the Scandinavian countries.[4] Unlike

*This chapter first appeared in *Management of Success: The Moulding of Modern Singapore*, edited by KS Sandhu and Paul Wheatley, Chapter 8, 1989. This work is reproduced here with the kind permission of the publisher, ISEAS — Yusof Ishak Institute, Singapore. http://www.bookshop.iseas.edu.sg.

[1]World Bank (1986), Table 1, pp. 180–81.

[2]The statistics cited in this paper do not go beyond 1985.

[3]Ibid., table 27, pp. 232–33.

[4]Ibid., table 28, pp. 234–35.

the situation in most developed countries, there has been full employment (defined as an unemployment rate of less than 4.5 per cent of the labour force) in most years since the early 1970s, and real incomes have risen rapidly. In 1985, 77 per cent of employed persons held forced savings for retirement and medical expenses in the government-run Central Provident Fund (CPF), which has helped give Singapore the highest rate of personal savings in the world. Singapore also has probably the best public-housing programme in the world, with 84 per cent of the population (including middle- and upper-income professionals) in 1985 living in government-built and administered housing units, 64 per cent of them owner-occupied. The population is further served by other excellent infrastructure — a modern transportation system, telecommunications, utilities, and even public recreational facilities widely dispersed throughout a highly urbanized island city-state.

It is tempting to regard this high standard of social welfare as simply the outcome of more than two decades of rapid economic growth, industrialization, and urbanization, reflecting the successful achievement of developmental goals. But at least two more interesting questions can be raised about the relationship of social welfare to economic development in the Singapore case. First, there is the possibility, indeed the likelihood, that advances in social welfare may have been instrumental in furthering development, that is, that improved social welfare has been part of the means as well as one of the ends of the developmental process. Second, there is the question, implicitly raised by the severe recession of 1985/86, as to whether the level of social welfare achieved in Singapore has been too high for its stage of development (or level of per capita income): in other words, whether or not excessive investment in social welfare has become a constraint on further economic growth.

Both questions have familiar antecedents in the literature on social welfare and development. The first question derives from the premises of human-capital theory,[5] which views social-welfare improvements — particularly in education, and to a lesser extent in health — as an investment contributing to growth in the future by improving the quality of labour.[6] Education, for example, directly increases job skills and worker trainability, while adequate health and nutrition reduce absenteeism due to sickness and make possible a better work effort and a longer working life. Both increase labour productivity and output. They also result in externalities which benefit society as a whole, thereby justifying government investment

[5]For a comprehensive survey, see Blaug (1976).

[6]See, for example, Schultz (1962), Musgrave (1966), and Mushkin (1982).

since the net public or social benefits from such investment exceed the net private benefits to individual workers or employers.[7]

The second question has been raised in ongoing analyses of the limits of the welfare state, especially in the social-democratic countries of Western Europe but also in social-spending debates in the United States.[8] In this context social welfare is viewed as a consumption good, the cost of providing which might undermine economic growth since it competes with directly productive investment for scarce resources. Some also fear that government provision of social welfare — what is commonly referred to as a "social safety net" — might encourage an unhealthy dependence on the state and sap individual initiative and enterprise, thereby also undermining growth. While this is a risk that developed nations might be able to afford — and indeed guaranteed social welfare may even be viewed as a definitional feature of an advanced society — it is generally considered un-affordable, if not inappropriate, for developing countries, many of which have in recent years abandoned such "welfarist" policies (for example, Sri Lanka, Jamaica, and China).

These two opposing interpretations of social-welfare spending obviously lead to different policy prescriptions. The "investment" interpretation would encourage state spending on social-welfare, while the "consumption" interpretation would discourage such spending and advocate the currently popular privatization of social-welfare services, thereby reducing public expenditure on health, education and welfare services — as is happening in countries such as the United Kingdom and the United States.

Singapore fits rather curiously between these two interpretations. The social-democratic origins of the ruling People's Action Party (PAP) initially led it to favour heavy social-welfare spending, even before the take-off into rapid economic growth, and for both consumption and investment reasons. Pang and Chan, for example, refer to the PAP policy during the early years of government as "redistribution before growth".[9] More recently, the government has reversed itself and, in public pronouncements at any rate, now claims to favour partial privatization,[10] at least of health services, which it views as getting consumers to bear a larger proportion of ever increasing social costs. Singapore is curious in some other respects as well.

[7]For a concise but comprehensive discussion of health and education in development, see Meier (1984), pp. 580–636.

[8]See, for example, OECD (1981).

[9]Pang and Chan (forthcoming).

[10]Note that the term "privatization" is used in Singapore only to describe the government's programme of divestment of state enterprises. Here I use the term in its broader general sense to include a reduced public share of expenditures on social welfare.

One is the extraordinary emphasis on public housing, which is usually viewed much more as a consumption than an investment good, and does not lend itself easily to the human-capital interpretation. Another is the possibility, often raised in public and political discourse in Singapore, that some of the government's social-welfare services may not in fact be subsidized by the state, but may actually be profit-making.

This chapter will examine social welfare in Singapore in the context of these two broad questions (or theoretical approaches). It will evaluate social-welfare developments in four major areas — health, education, housing, and social security — considering policy goals, policies and their effects, and analysing some proposed changes.

HEALTH

The PAP government took office in 1959, and in 1960 health accounted for 13.4 per cent of its main expenditures, or S$20 per person. The proportion peaked at 19.7 per cent in 1964, and then began declining steadily to 7 per cent in 1970, 4 per cent in 1980, and between 3 and 4 per cent in the 1980s.[11] The sharp decline in the late 1960s in large part reflected the increase in defence expenditures following the birth of Singapore as a sovereign nation in 1965, and especially the withdrawal of British military forces in 1968 and the institution of compulsory national military service. Defence has since remained at slightly more than one-quarter of government expenditures.

Despite this disproportionate decline, government health expenditures have grown steadily in real terms, both overall and per capita. In 1985 they amounted to S$195 per person, a quadrupling in real terms since 1960. The number of government hospitals rose from nine in 1960 to fourteen in 1974, before declining to ten in 1985; outpatient dispensaries rose from thirteen in 1959 to twenty-six in 1964. Maternal and child health clinics grew from forty-nine in 1959 to sixty-four in 1965 before declining steadily to twenty-nine by 1980. These numbers reflect rapid changes over time in the country's demography and urban geography.

In 1960 there was one doctor for every 2,573 persons, a ratio which had improved to 1:972 by 1985.[12] The proportion of doctors working for the government remained constant at around 45 per cent. The number of

[11]Except where otherwise noted, figures quoted here are obtained from the two publications of the Department of Statistics, Singapore, noted in the "References".

[12]Most developed countries average between 400 and 500 persons per physician. See World Bank (1986), table 28, pp. 234–35.

dentists remained at around one to 5,000 people through the entire period from 1960 to 1985, while the ratio of people to hospital beds rose from 229 in 1960 to 259 in 1985. The number of beds in government hospitals rose from 6,537 in 1960 to 8,005 in 1975 and has remained roughly stationary since then, as the ratio of government hospital beds to private hospital beds has dropped from 10:1 in 1960 to 4:1 in 1985.

Life expectancy at birth has risen from sixty-three years in 1965 to seventy-one years in 1985, while infant mortality rates have fallen steadily from 34.9 deaths per thousand births in 1960 to only 9.3 in 1985. The primary causes of death for the adult population resemble those in developed countries, with heart disease and cancer ranking first and second, followed by pneumonia. Tuberculosis, an important cause of death in the 1950s and early 1960s, has virtually disappeared. The results of student medical check-ups have also undergone a dramatic change, with dental caries, the major problem in 1960, dwindling in incidence to be replaced by defective vision,[13] followed by obesity, in the 1980s.[14]

Declining fertility in Singapore has attracted a great deal of national and international attention, with the crude birth rate falling from 37.5 per thousand in 1960 to 16.6 per thousand in 1985, when the rate of natural increase was 1.1 per cent. This crude birth rate is almost the same as that of the United States, a little higher than in most other developed countries.

These health and population changes may be positively related to economic growth in the following ways: a healthier, longer-lived work-force is more productive, while smaller families have facilitated the large increase in female labour-force participation (from 17 per cent in 1957 to 45 per cent by 1985) which contributed so importantly to labour supply, especially in high-growth, export manufacturing industries and services. But these changes are not necessarily the result only or even primarily of PAP government health policy.

For one thing, most health indicators — life expectancy, infant mortality, and so forth — had been improving even under the old colonial regime, before the PAP took office. If anything, the improvements before 1960 (since the end of World War II in 1945) were much greater than the improvements after 1960. Singapore was, after all, a relatively modern and well serviced city even in 1960, the administrative seat of the remaining British Empire in

[13]This rose from 487 cases per 10,000 males examined in 1960 to 3,490 in 1985, with the rate being higher for females.

[14]The rate of obesity was 1,144 per 10,000 twelve-year-old males examined in 1985, with the rate being lower for females.

Asia, and richer than any other location in Asia outside Japan. The health improvements which occurred after the achievement of self-government in 1959 continued previous trends without any major discontinuities — except in the practice of modern contraception which began in the 1960s. They were not noticeably more favourable than similar improvements in other countries at a similar stage and pace of development but with different government policies.

For example, infant mortality rates in Hong Kong were identical to those in Singapore in both 1965 and 1985, while in 1985 life expectancy in Hong Kong was actually higher, and the birth rate lower, than in Singapore, despite a somewhat lower per capita income level. The (colonial) government in Hong Kong did not pursue a vigorous family-planning policy as the PAP did in Singapore, yet the percentage of married women of childbearing age using contraception was higher in Hong Kong (80 per cent) than in Singapore (71 per cent)'in the mid-1980s, though it had been lower in 1970: 42 per cent in Hong Kong as against 60 per cent in Singapore[15] (the similarity between Hong Kong and Singapore in fertility behaviour has been frequently noted by demographers[16]). There was one doctor to 1,260 persons in Hong Kong in 1981, compared to one doctor to 1,100 persons in Singapore, and daily per capita caloric consumption in 1983 was higher in Hong Kong (122 per cent of the daily requirement) than in Singapore (115 per cent of requirement).[17]

These similarities between Hong Kong and Singapore in health outcomes despite different government health policies suggest that the rapid economic growth and rising incomes which both cities experienced were probably more responsible than government policy for improving health standards. As people become more affluent, they eat better and enjoy higher living standards, which contribute to better health. In Singapore, moreover, health indicators have continued to improve despite the falling share of government expenditures going to health and the stationary number of government hospital beds over the past dozen years or so. In line with the government's own stated preference (discussed below), the private sector appears to be caring for a higher proportion of medical patients, particularly those requiring hospitalization.

In short, government health policy does not appear to be either a necessary or a sufficient condition for improving health status. Government

---

[15]World Bank (1986), pp. 230–31.
[16]See, for example, Salaff and Wong (1977).
[17]World Bank (1986), table 28, pp. 234–35.

economic policies may have been more effective in this regard by ensuring the rising incomes without which the health status of the population would not have improved. Other government social policies may also have played a role, notably those resulting in improved housing with less crowding and better sanitary facilities.

Whether or not it realized the *relative* unimportance of health policy in improving health status, the Singapore Government has long been unhappy about the inability of the public-health services to pay their own way in the manner of many other government-provided services, despite health's already small and ever shrinking share of government expenditure. In the early 1980s, health care became the first major social-welfare item which the government proposed should be increasingly funded by user fees rather than by government tax revenues. There appear to have been many reasons for this. Philosophically (or ideologically), the government has become increasingly opposed to subsidies. It may be unwilling to bear the likely ever-increasing costs of providing for the health care of a population soon to age rapidly, and has repeatedly pronounced itself horrified by the high cost and reputedly poor service of socialized medicine in Western Europe. It may feel that, with rapidly rising incomes, the people now can afford to, and should, pay for their own health care. This may be justified by the argument that, with improved basic health from rising incomes, the investment component of health expenditures has declined while the consumption component has increased.

At the same time, health and medical services have figured prominently in government plans, first announced in 1979 and re-emphasized during the recession of 1985/86, to restructure the Singapore economy in the direction of higher-value services for export. The emphasis is now on health care and medical services not as a consumption or investment good but rather as a commodity to be sold for profit, even by government hospitals and as "exports" to foreign visitors — a development already initiated by the private sector (which, however, fell on hard times in the 1985/86 recession). Reduced government provision of subsidized medical services was envisioned as a spur to the development of the private market for such services (for instance, by removing any "crowding out" effects), as well as a means of reducing the government's financial responsibility for them.

The government also saw health care as one of the benefits most easily provided for employees by private employers, and this figured prominently in its short-lived effort to get employers to inculcate company loyalty in employees by providing them with enhanced social benefits, in the manner of the traditional labour management system found in large Japanese corporations. Such "company welfarism" was viewed as a means of reducing job-hopping and thereby increasing worker productivity in a tight labour market, as part of the economic restructuring process. The government was concerned to reduce the economic and psychological dependence of the population on the state as provider and guarantor of social welfare, which it felt undermined company loyalty and the private employer-employee relationship considered crucial to high productivity. Company Welfarism through Employer's CPF Contributions (or COWEC scheme) was never widely implemented and became a casualty of the 1985/86 recession and the ensuing reduction in CPF contributions which funded it.

So far there have been no studies of the effects of these shifts in government health policy. A priori, shifting the burden of paying for health and medical services from the public to the private sector, and from society to the individual consumer, almost invariably has regressive distributional consequences, even in more affluent societies. This is because the poor are generally the least able to afford private medical care although the most likely to be sick. Only if the supply of private medical services increases sufficiently to reduce their price without depressing quality — a development always resisted by the medical profession — will the poor benefit from reduced public provision of medical services.

In Singapore, the availability of public care for the really destitute and differential pricing of medical services according to what patients can afford (for example, hospital wards ranked from Class A to Class C) probably mitigate the worst of these regressive effects, despite periodic increases in government healthcare charges. But the CPF Medisave Account (see below) covers an employee's hospitalization expenses in proportion to his income rather than his need (that is, it is not an insurance programme), and is therefore regressive virtually by definition. There has also been a reduction in government services to the poor (as by a disproportionate reduction in the number of low- or non-paying beds in government hospitals, reductions in government subsidy for Class C ward costs,[18] and suchlike) accompanying increased expenditures on technological upgrading at the high end of the scale. Overcrowded out-patient clinics contrast with a proliferation of empty VLP rooms and high-tech medical-research laboratories, and the government charges rates similar to or even higher than (at the National University Hospital, for instance) rates prevailing in the private sector for similar care.

[18]Kalirajan and Wiboonchutikula (1986), p. 136.

Because of its still large share of the health- and medical-services sector (46 per cent of all doctors), the government's rate setting influences that of the private sector and cannot, therefore, be considered competitive or market-determined.[19]

These potentially regressive distributive effects do not, however, necessarily threaten the overall health status of Singaporeans, especially if economic factors dominate government policy in determining health status, as suggested by the comparison between Singapore and Hong Kong. If the health status of Singaporeans does deteriorate with the current shifts in government health policy, this would suggest that government health policy has been more important to Singaporeans' health status than was argued above. If, on the other hand, the health status of Singaporeans remains the same or improves with the new policies, we can conclude that the earlier policies were not that significant — compared with, for example, rising incomes — in bringing about better health.[20]

Whatever the underlying determinants of health status, the PAP has come a long way from its early view of health care as a social welfare or public consumption good, and even from a more economistic consideration of it as an investment good. Today health care is viewed as a commodity to be marketed for profit, and subsidies are consequently disapproved. The move towards a reduced public and concomitantly enlarged private sector, and the fact that the consumer is increasingly expected to pay the full cost of health services (whether rendered by the public or private sector) implies outright rejection of the human capital (or investment) approach, which holds that government subsidies of health care are justified because the social costs and benefits of good health outweigh its private costs and benefits, not least in improving the productivity of the work-force. There is also explicit rejection of any redismbutive motive for subsidization:

> We want to teach people that the government is not a rich uncle. You get what you pay for. We are moving in the direction of making people pay for everything... We want to disabuse people of the notion that in a good society the rich must pay for the poor.[21]

---

[19]To the extent that it is the "better" and more experienced doctors who can survive in the private sector, and who offer better service (for example, shorter queues), it may even be argued that patients in the public sector are overcharged for a lower-quality service at the same rates.

[20]The *ceteris paribus* assumption (for example, no change in income levels) is obviously important here, as is a multivariate analysis.

[21]Senior Minister S. Rajaratnam, quoted in Vasil (1984), p. 168.

EDUCATION

Education is a simpler case than health, as the human-capital perspective has been dominant throughout the PAP's long rule. In 1960, education was the largest single item of government main expenditure, accounting for 23.5 per cent of all expenditures. It remained the largest item until 1969, when it was overtaken by defence and police expenditures,[22] and by the public debt. Education's share of all government expenditures peaked at 32 per cent in 1963 and 1964 (reflecting high initial capital and training expenditures), then steadily declined to less than 9 per cent in 1980, after which it began climbing again to 14 per cent in 1985, the highest ratio since 1970. A drop to 10 per cent was planned for the 1986/87 fiscal year, reflecting in part the effect of declining revenues from tax reductions aimed at stimulating the economy after the 1985/86 recession. In per capita terms, educational spending rose from S$35 in 1960 to S$591 in 1985, a nearly sevenfold increase in real terms over the period. In 1985, government expenditure per student was S$1,619 at the primary level, S$2,515 at the secondary level, and S$9,885 at the tertiary level.

As with health status, indicators of educational attainment in Singapore have improved over time. Population census data show a literacy rate of 72.2 per cent of the population over ten years of age in 1970, rising to 84 per cent in 1980, when more than 90 per cent of the population under thirty-five years of age was literate. Among the literate, 23.7 per cent were literate in two or more official languages in 1970, compared with 60.5 per cent in 1980. The proportion of the labour force with secondary or higher education rose from 16.1 per cent in 1966 to 27.4 per cent in 1980. In 1974, 40.3 per cent of the labour force was still uneducated, or had less than a primary-level education; by 1985 this proportion had fallen to 22.8 per cent. Persons in the labour force whose highest educational qualification was at the primary or post-primary level accounted for 31.4 per cent of the labour force in both years, but those with a secondary education rose from 19.7 per cent in 1974 to 29.3 per cent in 1985, those with a post-secondary education nearly doubled from 6.2 to 11 per cent, and those with a tertiary education more than doubled from 2.4 to 5.2 per cent of the labour force. The proportion of children aged 6–17 years who were enrolled in school rose from 76.7 per cent in 1972 to 92 per cent in 1985. The enrolment in higher education (tertiary institutions) doubled from 6.7 per cent in 1970 to

[22]See the explanation given in the previous section on health.

13.9 per cent in 1985,[23] with the female proportion rising from 25.2 per cent in 1960 to 37.2 per cent in 1985.

These are real achievements, but they are not particularly impressive by international standards, or by the standards of Singapore's achievements in other areas, including other aspects of social welfare. According to World Bank data, Singapore's adult literacy rate of 75 per cent in 1978 was considerably below that of many developing countries with a lower per capita income: for example, the literacy rate was 90 per cent in Hong Kong, 93 per cent in South Korea, 94–95 per cent in Trinidad and Tobago, Argentina and Uruguay, 90 per cent in Costa Rica, 86 per cent in Jamaica, and 84 per cent in Thailand.[24] Developed countries generally reported literacy rates of 99–100 per cent.

More recent data show that, while as early as 1965 all children in the relevant age group were enrolled in primary school in Singapore, the proportion enrolled in secondary school was only 69 per cent in 1983, about the same as in Hong Kong (68 per cent) but much lower than in South Korea (89 per cent), despite the fact that both countries had started from lower bases than Singapore in 1965, when Singapore had 45 per cent of the relevant age groups enrolled in secondary school, Hong Kong 29 per cent, and South Korea 35 per cent.[25] South Korea's achievement is particularly remarkable since it is a much larger and poorer country with a sizeable rural population which is harder to serve with adequate schools. Yet South Korea managed to raise the proportion of 20–24 year-olds who were enrolled in higher education from 6 per cent in 1965 to 24 per cent in 1983, compared with Singapore's increase from 10 to only 12 per cent over the same period (Hong Kong raised its proportion of tertiary-level students from 5 to 12 per cent of the age group during this time). Developed countries generally have between one-quarter and one-half of this age group enrolled in higher education.

Singapore's relative underachievement in education has not gone unnoticed by the government, and may be explained by several factors peculiar to the Singapore situation. First, the relatively low adult-literacy rate is almost entirely confined to older segments of the population, those over forty years of age, who did not have the ease of access to public education enjoyed

[23]These figures are approximate, expressing total enrolment in higher education as a proportion of the population aged 20–24 years, which is accurate for men but not for women, who typically attend university between the ages of eighteen and twenty-two.

[24]Presented in Exhibit IX.6, pp. 603-9 of Meier (1984).

[25]World Bank (1986), table 29, pp. 236–37.

by later generations. Secondly, the government itself acknowledges that the rapid mass expansion of education in the 1960s sacrificed quality for quantity, even in the recruitment and training of schoolteachers, some of whom are still employed within the educational system today.

Thirdly, Singapore is a multiethnic and multilingual society, with even the majority immigrant Chinese population originally speaking a variety of different regional dialects. The government at first focused on national integration and the development of a national identity as a goal of the school system; later it turned to an emphasis on bilingualism — mastery of English and one's own so-called "mother tongue" — as a means of ensuring the preservation of traditional cultures and cultural values. By its own admission, the bottom 20 to 25 per cent of the intelligence hierarchy is probably incapable of fully mastering two languages — for the Chinese majority in Singapore these languages were English and Mandarin, neither of which was commonly spoken among the poorly educated, predominantly dialect-speaking working class. The situation has been complicated by the rapid ascendancy and dominance of English, the non-native language, in the market-place, and the consequent total eclipse of schooling in the native languages, including Mandarin Chinese. English is now the primary language of instruction in all Singapore schools. The language problem is probably responsible for lower achievement levels and higher drop-out rates than one would expect in a homogeneous, monolingual situation.

Fourthly, the government's announced concern about the spectre of graduate unemployment, so common in other developing countries, probably resulted in an under-investment in tertiary education through the 1970s.

Fifthly, the educational system in Singapore has been subject to much experimentation, with many and varied changes being implemented from time to time, and occasionally revoked, according to shifting government priorities. Not all the changes have had academic goals — early streaming on the basis of bilingual ability, testing and special education for gifted children, computerization, and foreign-language instruction are some of those which do have such goals. An earlier emphasis on practical and technical skills as part of the regular academic curriculum has all but been abandoned.

But an important sixth feature of the Singapore educational system is the multiplicity of goals which it has been constantly called upon to meet. Here it would appear that many educational policies have not been primarily academic or even economic in intent. For example, the early neglect, if not discouragement, of Chinese-language education, especially at the tertiary level, had the aim of weakening a Chinese-educated, and often left-leaning, political opposition. The later promotion of Mandarin at the expense of regional Chinese dialects had the goal of unifying a linguistically divided Chinese community, but also served to undermine dialect-based Chinese clan associations (a potential source of political opposition to the predominantly English- and Western-educated PAP leadership) and to equip Singapore Chinese with the language capability required for participation in increased economic exchange with China. The English language was also promoted as the lingua franca of the world business so important to this open city-state, but with the safeguard of simultaneous promotion of bi-lingualism as necessary for the preservation of so-called "cultural ballast" in a rapidly changing society open to world, especially supposedly decadent Western, influences. In addition, compulsory moral and religious education has been instituted for the inculcation of appropriate (namely, conservative, traditional) values in schoolchildren, especially the value of filial piety which it is hoped will ensure that adult children will physically and financially care for their aged and infirm parents, rather than imposing that burden on a very reluctant state.

Besides its usefulness in socializing (or, to the less charitable, propagandizing) the young, the educational system has been a tool for the achievement of other government social goals. For example, family planning goals were promoted by granting priority entry to the schools of their choice to children of parents who had been sterilized. Later, the same priority was granted to the children of women university graduates (known as "graduate mothers" in Singapore) as an incentive to such women to have more children in accordance with the Prime Minister's belief that this would improve the gene pool and intelligence of the population. This policy was quickly withdrawn as being "ineffective"; it was also politically unpopular. Now, in a complete reversal of the earlier anti-natalist policy, priority school entry is to be granted to children from families with three or more children.

Whatever their academic or social merits, it is likely that the multiplicity of goals and frequency of policy changes endured by the educational system are at least partly responsible for Singapore's relative underachievement in education. Within Singapore itself the system has been criticized for being too élitist, by which is meant that it focuses on the superior academic achievements of a small group of students, while selectively weeding out weaker students from a young age. This tends to result in a high wastage rate with many drop-outs at each stage and no flexibility for the inclusion of late bloomers, older re-entrants, and suchlike — a serious limitation in a small nation facing chronic domestic-labour shortages. The system is competitive, rigorous, and rigid — the weeding out process assigns students to particular educational streams with different curricula, which then determine the range of jobs they are equipped to fill on completion of their schooling.[26]

More recently, the education system has been criticized for being excessively examination-oriented, resulting in a high degree of technical competence and conformity which produces excellent state bureaucrats but which may stifle the creativity, originality, individual initiative, and risk-taking required of the successful scientists, designers, and business entrepreneurs that the nation is thought to need in the emerging era of high-tech industry and services. It has been pointed out, for example, that Singapore has a much smaller number and proportion of local entrepreneurs than its Asian NIC competitors — South Korea, Taiwan, and Hong Kong — and than its role model, Japan, and that this may constrain its future economic growth. It is interesting that Japan and South Korea are also increasingly critical of their existing educational systems, and are exploring educational reforms which will encourage individual creativity and thus equip them better to succeed in the inventive and entrepreneurial culture of high-tech industry.

The government has announced that it will considerably increase public expenditure on education as a major means of enhancing productivity in the wake of the 1985/86 economic recession. Two other innovations — development of private-sector educational service exports, and development of "independent schools" — are complex and controversial and will not be discussed here. For the moment, it seems likely that the human-capital approach will remain dominant — at least for practical, if not ideological, reasons — although human-capital appreciation is by no means the only goal of Singapore's educational system, and is in fact arguably undermined by the multiplicity of economic, social, and political as well as academic, goals that the system is expected to serve.

PUBLIC HOUSING[27]

If the education sector in Singapore has been characterized by underachievement, the public-housing sector may be characterized by overachievement. When the newly elected PAP government took office in 1959, 8.8 per cent of the population was living in 20,907 public-housing units constructed by

[26]This contrasts with the much admired (in Singapore) Japanese educational system, which does not "stream" or "track" students according to ability and has a uniform curriculum and yet a very low drop-out rate.

[27]References for this section include Yeh (1975), Wong and Yeh (1985), Low (1985), and Chng (1986).

the colonial government since 1947. In 1960 the Housing and Development Board (HDB) was established, and by 1965 23.2 per cent of the population was being housed in 54,430 units under its management. By 1985, 84 per cent of the population was being housed in 551,767 HDB units.[28] Housing is the largest single item of government development expenditure, accounting for about 40 per cent of the total.[29] Like other major government statutory boards, the HDB has in recent years run current, and sometimes overall (that is, including development expenditure) surpluses.[30]

Public housing in Singapore has clearly been a tremendous achievement, attained without undue strain on the government budget. In most other countries, public housing is viewed simply as a consumption good provided by the government at subsidized cost to low-income families, and this certainly was the dominant original goal of the HDB — to clear Singapore's urban slums and provide decent housing for the people. This had political and economic gains as well, by providing a most visible example of government benefaction, no doubt winning electoral support for the ruling party, and perhaps also by subsidizing the private-sector wage (in the early years when most public housing was still subsidized by the government), thereby stimulating employment creation. The HDB also built and managed multi-storey "flatted factories" for labour-intensive industries located in the housing estates to supply jobs to the neighbourhood population.

But the HDB did not stop at merely providing subsidized rental housing for low-income groups. Instead, it progressively extended its reach into providing un-subsidized, and even profit-making, luxury housing for middle- and upper-income groups. In 1985, excluding land costs, which are insignificant on a per-unit basis because of high density and the HDB's acquisition of land at below-market values, the HDB earned surpluses of $10,600 per unit on five-room Model A flats and $25,200 per unit on Executive Apartments which it built, while subsidizing three-room flats at $700 per unit and four-room flats at $5,400 per unit.[31]

At the same time, the HDB was facilitating the government's political and social goal of creating "a nation of home-owners". The government felt that Singapore's ethnically diverse population of immigrant origin was more likely to develop a commitment to the nation if it had a real stake in it through home ownership (which, incidentally, also returned funds to the

[28]Figures from Yeh (1975), pp. 5 and 9, and Department of Statistics (1986), p. 18.
[29]Asher (1984), pp. 78–107.
[30]Ministry of Trade and Industry (various years).
[31]Low (1985), Table 4.

HDB's coffers[32]). People, including tenants, were encouraged and enabled to buy public-housing units which continued to be maintained and strictly regulated by the HDB (in much the same manner as condominium flats). In 1970, less than a third of public-housing units were owner-occupied, but by 1985 more than three-quarters were, housing 64 per cent of all HDB residents. During the recession in 1985/86, the government announced a programme to help even lowest-income workers own their own homes, something which had been thought impossible a few years earlier.

The term "public housing" is thus something of a misnomer in the Singapore context, since most public-housing residents in fact own equity in the units they inhabit (and may even rent out units they own but do not inhabit), although their ownership rights are restricted as compared with those of owners of fully private property. For example, the HDB imposes limitations on the number and family status of people who can live in the units, has to approve their renovation, rental and resale, forbids the conduct of business in the units, and has the right to evict residents found guilty of morally inappropriate behaviour, not necessarily with compensation for their equity in the unit. This gives the government tremendous potential control and leverage over the vast majority of the population, which may be considered a social cost or externality partly offsetting the social benefit of the housing provision. The goal of one hundred per cent home ownership also has economic costs, since it would practically eliminate the rental market (except for that serving foreigners), thereby increasing mobility and transaction costs since it is more costly to buy and sell homes than to rent.

Like education, public housing in Singapore has been used by the government to fulfil a multiplicity of goals. It is clearly a major element in the spatial planning of the densely populated island, including planned dispersal of population concentrations out of the overcrowded city centre, and the integration of residential and industrial developments. Especially in the early days, compulsory urban resettlement provided the PAP with the opportunity of breaking up established and potential opposition electoral communities by dividing up old ethnic, working-class communities for resettlement in dispersed locations. At the same time, the public-housing estates, and the new towns of which they were a part, were expected to foster ethnic integration and national identity through the homogenization of life-style and experience in the same neighbourhoods, schools, stores, playgrounds,

---

[32]The HDB also receives some portion of the payment when units are sold and resold.

and so forth. With the move to providing more middle- and upper-income units, the HDB first segregated these units in like clusters, but more recently has preferred dispersal — some believe in part to allow for the possibility that members of a like-income group (educated professionals, for instance) might vote in a like manner, resulting in housing patterns biassing voting results.

The allocation of public housing — including time of delivery, choice of neighbourhood, size and location of unit — could be, and has been, used as an incentive or disincentive to promote desired, or discourage undesired, behaviour. For example, to encourage small families in the 1970s, large families were subjected to longer waiting periods for public-housing units; while to encourage "three-generation families" in the 1980s (one of the government's attempts to ensure private shouldering of the old-age burden), such families were given priority allocation of housing units. Family members in different nuclear units are also now encouraged and allowed to locate in the same estate or block of flats, and even in adjacent units with direct access between them. In 1983, reflecting the government's concern with the so-called "lop-sided procreation pattern",[33] low-income, poorly educated couples who had themselves sterilized after no more than two children were offered S$10,000 to be paid into the wife's CPF account, where it could be used to purchase (a considerable portion of the value of) a public-housing unit for the family.

Public housing estates have also become the bases for new forms of social organization and political mobilization. Community centres established to provide common recreational facilities are often also the headquarters of PAP branches which, among other things, run kindergartens for young children and a variety of adult and youth programmes. They are the venues for weekly "Meet-the-People" sessions held by PAP Members of Parliament (MPs). Residents' Committees have become increasingly powerful and involved in political, as well as merely administrative, affairs; their leaders are usually PAP supporters; some consider them to be the neighbourhood "eyes and ears" of the ruling party. To quote the Prime Minister himself:

> Look at our new towns with community centres, parks and stadiums. Think of their channels of communication for the constituents to reach the HDB, PUB, TAS, the government ministries, and the administrators who manage

[33]This term, which for a time was a favourite of many a PAP minister and MP, refers to the fact that the poorest families tend to have the largest number of children. See, for example, Ow (1984).

> them. They have their MPs, RCs, MCs, CCCs, who act like the network of nerves and sensors which monitors signals and feedbacks and sends out messages in return. It is these invisible ties that make for the sense of belonging, a sense of security of life in Singapore.[34]

Before and after the 1984 election, the government (including the Prime Minister himself) threatened public-housing constituencies voting in opposition MPs with the loss of some state-provided services. The then Minister for National Development Teh Cheang Wan considered this "a very practical political decision".[35] While the HDB threat to serve opposition constituencies last has sensibly lapsed, certain political services such as meet-the-people sessions have been withdrawn.[36] More recently, the government has changed the political process by allowing three adjacent electoral constituencies to vote in a team of MPs. The political party with the most votes would win the area and run its Town Council of elected representatives. Promoted as a move to decentralize responsibility for running public-housing estates, this electoral change would also provide the government with new opportunities to dilute opposition votes by combining constituencies with dominant opposition sympathies with neighbouring constituencies which strongly support the PAP.

Clearly, public housing in Singapore (as indeed, elsewhere) is used to fulfil social and political, as well as purely housing, goals. Its economic consequences have also been manifold, although these are not fully known. At a minimum, such a massive public undertaking (with the government owning 75 per cent of all land and housing 84 per cent of the population in 1985) must have distorted local land and property markets and prices and crowded out some private enterprise, particularly in middle- and upper-income housing and commercial and industrial property (also provided by the HDB and other statutory boards such as the Urban Redevelopment Authority and the Jurong Town Corporation). The HDB has certainly not been immune to, and must have contributed to, the property-market collapse of 1985/86, which depressed the values especially of middle- and upper-income HDB units competing with the private sector. Owners of such units have had to pay heavy mortgages pegged to the high buying prices of depreciated units, and

---

[34]Quoted in the *Straits Times*, 20 August 1984; cited in Low (1985), p. 17. PUB stands for the Public Utilities Board, TAS for the Telecommunications Authority of Singapore, MPs for Members of Parliament, MCs for Management Committees, and CCCs for Citizens' Consultative Committees.

[35]*Straits Times*, 22 March 1985.

[36]Low (1985), p. 18.

pay out of forced-saving contributions which had been reduced by a cut in CPF contributions (see below). A large number of middle- and upper-income HDB units remained unsold, as home-buyers tended to favour private-sector units whose prices also fell drastically in an overbuilt condominium market. This could hardly have endeared the government to this segment of the voting population.

Private ownership of government-built housing units gives the government increased political and social control over the large majority of the population that it houses, but it also makes it the focus of many normal discontents — about, for example, the market value and maintenance of one's home, which is seen as a government rather than a private responsibility. Even discontent about the pricing or delivery of transport, utility, and telecommunications services may be focused on the government as sole provider or regulator of such services, and could at some time or other be translated into political opposition. Dependence is always a two-edged sword, and the dependence of the Singapore population on the government — much of it arising from the government's role as property developer and landlord — is extreme for a supposedly market-oriented economy.[37]

This discussion has so far treated public housing as a social-consumption good which also serves government political and social ends. Can it also be considered a form of social investment? A priori, to the extent that public housing, by lowering the price of a major wage-good, has lowered the wage, it may be credited with stimulating faster economic growth and employment creation. It may also have released private-sector resources for other forms of productive investment, thereby increasing productivity and growth. By ensuring a higher standard of living for the working population at a given wage, it may have contributed to better worker productivity and certainly to political and social stability and labour peace, which are necessary underpinnings of private investment and economic growth.

The home-ownership programme, by giving most workers a realistic chance to own their own homes, may have been an important motivator inspiring greater work effort and saving. The one-shot creation ol nuclear-family units may have stimulated demand for a variety of household products such as furniture, cookware, and electronic items (which would be shared in the extended-family household), some of which would be locally made. At

[37]For more on the "dependency mentality" in Singapore, see Wong (1985).

the same time, increased costs of living, and consumer desires (including the desire for home ownership), together with the greater supply of female jobs in light industries located in flatted factories in public-housing estates, increased female labour-force participation and family incomes, making possible higher output growth than would otherwise have occurred. Finally, there is the fiscal stimulus, manifested in both multiplier and linkage effects, of government spending occasioned by a massive public-housing construction programme, a stimulus which could be, and was, used counter-cyclically to smooth out fluctuations in economic growth, thereby encouraging more private investment.

It is likely that Singapore's public-housing programme has had many or all of these positive effects on productivity and economic growth; but it may also have hindered growth through, *inter alia*, the "crowding out" effect, the exact overall impact of which is difficult to gauge. It is probable that the positive effects dominated in the earlier years of the programme when it was relatively small, while negative effects surfaced only later when the public-housing sector had already become very large and was encroaching on what should have been the preserve of the private sector by building middle- and upper-income housing for a profit. The sharp increase in housing values in both the public and private sectors in the late 1970s and early 1980s — and its sequel, the property-market collapse of 1985/86 — also cannot have been unaffected by such a large actor in the market as the government. For example, the release of CPF funds for private housing purchases in 1981 fuelled high demand which pushed up prices and contributed to the subsequent oversupply. This particular action, together with the acceleration of public-housing construction after 1981, may have been motivated by the desire to win back voter support after the loss of a parliamentary seat to an opposition party leader in the 1981 by-election. Ironically, it was these possibly politically motivated actions which led to overbuilding in both the private and public sectors, and thus to the subsequent property slump and decline in home values which — in a nation where more than three-quarters of the population consists of "home owners" whose homes constitute the bulk of their savings — has undoubtedly lost the government some of its political support.

Whatever the growth and productivity effects, however, it is undeniable that Singapore's remarkable public-housing programme has been extremely successful in achieving consumption goals. Indeed housing is the one area where the government has clearly made a (positive) difference to social welfare, with progressive distributional consequences.

SOCIAL SECURITY[38]

Even in the early heyday of its social-democratic commitment, the Singapore Government has never committed significant government funds to social security for the unemployed, disabled, aged, or indigent. Transfer payments to households, for example, accounted for 12.8 per cent of main government expenditure in 1960, then declined steadily to 8.5 per cent in 1965 and to 1.4 per cent in and since 1975. In per capita terms, there was an increase from $19 per head in 1960 to $60 per head in 1985, a 25 per cent real increase. Part of the decline in proportionate expenditure may be attributed simply to the growth and prosperity of the economy, especially since 1965. With high employment, rising wages, and a relatively young population, the number of people needing to be on public welfare declined. The traditions of extended-family responsibility and filial piety have also remained relatively intact. Part of the relative decline is explained by the large increases in new or other categories of expenditure, such as defence and education.

But part of the explanation also lies in the government's oft-noted "philosophical aversion" to subsidies, and especially its horror of the magnitude of public-welfare commitments in Western countries. Public assistance is awarded only on extremely stringent criteria: nearly 90 per cent of its recipients are single elderly persons, most of them immigrants who have spent a lifetime at hard labour, never married, and have no family ties, with the remainder being the mentally or physically handicapped, widows and orphans, and abandoned wives and children. Public assistance payments are also meagre: by one estimate, in 1980 they covered only 50 per cent of the minimum household requirement of a single person, and 34 per cent of the minimum household requirement of a four-person household with children in school.[39] There is no system of unemployment compensation. This reflects the government's philosophy:

> We want to disabuse people of the notion that in a good society the rich must pay for the poor. We want to reduce welfare to the minimum, restricted only to those who are handicapped or old. To the others we offer equal opportunities and it is up to them what they make of [them]. Everybody can be rich if they try hard.[40]

---

[38] A useful reference on this subject is Kalirajan and Wiboonchutikula (1986).

[39] Author's interview with a representative of the Singapore Council of Social Services, 1986.

[40] Senior Minister S. Rajaratnam, quoted in Vasil (1984), p. 168.

Transfer payments do not, of course, account for all government expenditure on what might be called "social security", which also includes such other items as the operation of three homes for the aged and portions of the health and education budgets. For the most part, however, the government mostly leaves the care of those who cannot care for themselves to private charities and voluntary, often religious, agencies. In 1985 the Ministry of Social Welfare was disbanded and incorporated into a new Ministry of Community Development.

Although there is no publicly provided social safety net as such in Singapore the Central Provident Fund (CPF) does provide social security for employees.[41] It was begun in 1955 under the colonial government, but has been vastly expanded and changed under the PAP. In 1985, there were 889,600 CPF contributors, about 77 per cent of the total labour force.[42] The CPF is essentially a pension fund managed by the government, with compulsory contributions paid by employers and employees, and earning a rate of interest determined by the government. Contributors are allowed to withdraw their CPF balances at retirement (still set at fifty-five years, although extensions are increasingly common), subject to the maintenance of a recently imposed "minimum balance" to ensure that those who prematurely dissipate their withdrawn balances do not become destitute and thus burdens on the state. Before retirement, CPF balances may be used only to purchase housing or stock in approved public and private companies, and to pay members' hospital bills (the Medisave Account) and some insurance premiums. A recently introduced "topping up" scheme also allows CPF members to transfer part of their savings or cash to parents over fifty-five years of age as a means of providing support for their old age.

CPF contribution rates have been rising through time, from 10 per cent of the wage, evenly split between employer and employee, in 1955, to 16 per cent, also evenly divided, in 1970, to 38.5 per cent in 1980 (20.5 per cent contributed by the employer, 18 per cent by the employee), and finally 50 per cent, evenly divided, in 1984. In 1986, in response to the 1985/86 recession, caused in part by the high CPF rate and its contribution to declining labour-cost competitiveness and an excessively high

[41]For a comprehensive micro-economic treatment, see Lim Chong Yah *et al.* (1986). A brief macro-economic analysis is provided in Lim, Pang, and Findlay (1987). See also Kalirajan and Wiboonchutikula (1986), and Tsao (1986).

[42]Employers, the self-employed, and unpaid family workers are among the categories of working persons who are not required to contribute to the CPF.

national-savings rate,[43] the employer's rate was reduced to 10 per cent, for a total contribution of 35 per cent of the wage. When the economy subsequently emerged from the recession, the employer's CPF rate was increased by 2 per cent to 12 per cent in 1988, for a total contribution of 36 per cent. The merits and demerits of the CPF have been much debated, especially in the context of macro-economic growth and micro-economic cost structures. The discussion here will focus only on its social-welfare effects.

The situation is complex as, once again, the CPF fulfils a multiplicity of roles and goals. It provides the government with a huge amount of relatively cheap funds with which to invest in domestic-development expenditures and income-earning financial assets, including foreign assets. This may make possible a higher rate of productive social investment, including investments in housing, infrastructure, and economic services which improve consumption standards as well as increase productivity, and are funded in a non-inflationary way. However, the CPF's importance as a source of funds for such social investment has declined over time. By the late 1970s, government surpluses were more than enough to finance public-sector development spending, and CPF funds were increasingly "sterilized" as foreign reserves, thereby ensuring non-inflationary growth in an era of high wage increases.[44]

The CPF also ensures that the individual contributor builds up savings with which housing may be purchased, mostly from the government, thereby serving one of the goals of public housing itself. The Medisave Account, which takes up 6 per cent of the wage, provides for payment of hospital accounts, again mostly to the government, but it is not an insurance scheme and affords protection to the individual only in proportion to his or her actual contribution and income. With the rise in unemployment as a consequence of the 1985/86 recession, the government also briefly considered allowing unemployed citizens to withdraw portions of their CPF balances to meet living expenses during the period of their unemployment, but this has apparently been abandoned following the economic recovery. In short, the CPF is the means by which the government ensures that the working population pays for its own retirement, health care, housing, filial responsibilities, and perhaps also unemployment income, through its own forced savings and without charge to the government budget.

Whether or not the CPF proves to be an efficient method of providing social security can only be assessed after large numbers of working persons

[43]Ministry of Trade and Industry (1986).
[44]See, for example, Low (1985).

eventually retire and withdraw their balances. Much, of course, depends on the financial performance of the assets in which CPF balances are invested before retirement. For example, if the bulk of a contributor's CPF balances are invested in housing and/or stocks which have depreciated, or not increased, in real value at the time of withdrawal, he or she may have to choose between having housing and a disposable income. There is also the government's fear that many retirees will spend their money unwisely (in gambling perhaps), and end up destitute anyway (hence the "minimum balance" scheme). And if an unemployment-income scheme is enacted, the use of CPF balances to cover living expenses during a prolonged period of unemployment could seriously diminish the balance available at retirement. (However, this particular problem could be solved for all but the chronically and older unemployed if withdrawals for support during unemployment were made up through higher rates of contribution during subsequent periods of employment). Despite the existence of the CPF, the government itself seems to feel that the family circle is ultimately the best guarantee of social security for the elderly — hence its constant emphasis on traditional values and filial piety, and the effort and expenditure spent in promoting them, for example, in schools. So far, the family unit has remained strong in this regard: most adult children do care for aged parents who are in need, and the "topping up" scheme is designed to facilitate this.

There remains the question as to whether in the context of providing social security — its major goal — the CPF has also been a social investment; in short, whether it has contributed to or detracted from increased work effort and productivity. A priori, it might be argued that the CPF, simply by raising the savings rate, has added to investment and hence to productivity and growth. However, this result depends on the debatable assumption that publicly managed investment is more productive than private investment, and that housing, which accounts for the largest expenditure of CPF funds, is a productive form of investment. Indeed, it might be counter-argued that the encouragement of home ownership for social and political reasons, and restrictions on the expenditure of forced savings for other purposes, has diverted excessive savings into essentially nonproductive expenditure for consumption (of housing services); and, further, inflated home property values before they crashed in 1985/86, representing a loss of investment and depressing growth. If the CPF reduced the supply and raised the cost of capital to the private sector, and perhaps also reduced individual risk-taking behaviour, thereby discouraging local entrepreneurship, this inhibiting effect on productive investment would have been accentuated. The extremely high incremental capital-output ratio in Singapore does suggest that capital is not being used as productively as it might be.[45] The concentration of such a huge amount of savings in government hands also severely limits Singapore's prospects for developing into a funds-management centre, as is clearly desired.

Interestingly, Singaporeans interviewed in 1984 as to the reasons for their (overwhelming) objections to the government's proposal (later withdrawn) to increase the retirement and CPF-withdrawal age beyond fifty-five, often cited their desires to use their retirement balances for productive purposes — most commonly to begin a business enterprise and to fund children's higher education abroad; that is, for investments in business and human capital, which should result in higher growth and productivity. Some did say they wished to spend part of the money on consumption — most notably travel abroad; but most seemed to feel that they could obtain a higher return on their forced savings than the government had achieved — which may not, of course, be true, bearing in mind that, if the government offered a lower return on CPF funds, it also offered lower risk on the investment of those funds. Recent measures to allow individuals a greater say in investing the discretionary portion of their CPF funds may somewhat mitigate this problem of differential returns on private- and public-sector investments.

It is clear that it is not the CPF scheme itself, but rather its progressively — and eventually excessively — high rates of forced saving contributions, together with the market distortions resulting from restrictions on individuals' use of their CPF funds, which are responsible for any negative effects of this social-security system on growth and productivity. Counteracting positive effects would have to derive from any positive results that the CPF might have on work effort, length of working life, unforced savings and the pattern of investment. It is difficult to come to any definitive conclusion on the basis of this brief discussion.

In general, however, it appears that the CPF social-security scheme represents private investment in consumption (home ownership and/or a financially secure retirement) rather than social investment in production. Most economists in Singapore concur that the CPF over-provides for retirement, and results in overinvestment in housing, distorting resource allocation, investment flows and the intertemporal distribution of consumption — thereby ultimately reducing both economic growth and consumer welfare.[46] But the CPF has functioned at many levels and served many

[45]Lim, Pang, and Findlay (1987).

[46]See references in note 41 above.

goals besides those of social security and economic growth *per se*, particularly the social and political goals associated with the public-housing programme.

CONCLUSION

The preceding discussion of the four major aspects of social welfare in Singapore — health, education, housing, and social security — suggests that the subject is highly complex. In general, high levels of social welfare have been attained, with achievements in education being somewhat less than ideal, and the eventual outcomes in social security being still a little uncertain. Not all these achievements have been due only or mainly to government policy: health and education improvements, in particular, might have occurred without it, although perhaps more slowly, as a natural consequence of increasing prosperity. On the other hand, the extensiveness of the government's housing policy suggests that mass housing could not have been achieved as rapidly or completely without it. Housing remains one of Singapore's greatest social achievements, although perhaps carried too far in the more recent government provision of housing for middle- and upper-income groups. As for social security, its particular form in Singapore is very much a creature of government policy.

Government expenditures on health and housing have been mainly orientated towards social consumption rather than investment goals, while the reverse is true of expenditures on education. As discussed above, health and housing expenditures, as well as government uses of CPF funds provided by employers (including itself) and employees, may also have had implications for investment and productivity — in both positive and negative directions in the cases of housing and the CPF. The net effect on investment has probably been positive, but the hypotheses raised here need to be explored and tested further before definitive conclusions can be reached.

More importantly, the discussion has suggested that government social-welfare policy in Singapore reaches beyond the consumption and investment approaches conventionally employed by economists in several ways. First, as in other — both democratic and socialist — countries, social-welfare provisions have, as the government itself admits, been used as political instruments to ensure social stability and greater political support for, and less effective political opposition to, the governing party. Housing is the prime example of this, as described above. It is noteworthy that a government already embarked on privatizing other state agencies and enterprises has not yet proposed large-scale privatization of its largest enterprise, public housing.[47] Yet this is the one social-welfare provision for which there is the least theoretical economic justification for state provision, and which most crowds out the private sector — especially when it is on the scale found in Singapore. It is also, significantly, the one social-welfare provision which arguably affords governments providing it the greatest degree of social and political control.

Secondly, social-welfare provisions have been used as instruments for the furtherance of various government social policies, including language policy, family-planning policy, and the effort to preserve the traditional family and its values. This again has occurred in other countries, particularly in the context of (largely unsuccessful) pro-natalist policies in both East and West European countries, where governments have, for example, paid citizens to have children and (especially in Eastern Europe) given young married couples priority in the allocation of state housing. In Singapore, with the exception of language policy (which has its own complex political, social, and economic goals), it is not clear what the effectiveness of these policies has been, since one cannot be sure what would have happened in their absence. In particular, fertility behaviour in Singapore has not been significantly different from that in other countries undergoing similar rapid social and economic transformation. Furthermore, while in some cases the use of a single policy instrument to achieve a variety of different ends results in some economies and heightened efficiency (perhaps in housing, for example), in others it may mean the opposite, that is increased inefficiency (as in education).

Thirdly, whereas in most countries government social-welfare provisions are expected to lower private-sector costs, thus providing the wherewithal and stimulus for greater private investment, productivity and growth (the human-capital approach), in Singapore in recent years the opposite has been true. Overall the Singapore Government runs a public-sector surplus, which some have argued mirrors the private-sector deficit of recent years. High CPF contribution rates, for example, while providing the government with huge amounts of relatively cheap captive capital, raised private-sector costs and dampened private demand in non-housing markets, resulting in declining and distorted patterns of private investment, and eventually in the severe 1985/86 recession. Recognizing this,[48] CPF rates have been at least

[47]The government is, however, beginning to contract out some HDB maintenance services, and attempting to include land costs in the prices of HDB flats.
[48]For example, Ministry of Trade and Industry (1986).

temporarily reduced, and the government has embarked on a programme of privatization to reduce its own very large role in the economy.

Fourthly, in recent years the government has begun to shift to individual consumers the cost burden of the social services it provides, while encouraging the private sector to offer more such services, at least in the health sector. The result of this will be to reduce government, and increase private, responsibility for social welfare. While this may a priori have some regressive distributional consequences for consumption, the likely impact on investment and productivity cannot be predicted. More interestingly, any relative — but not necessarily absolute — reduction in government social-welfare provisions will reduce the government's leverage in several policy areas and issues, given the multiplicity of economic, political, and social goals which each social-welfare provision currently serves. It will simultaneously reduce the government's control over the population and the population's dependence on the government, possibly promising greater political and social independence which may not be viewed entirely favourably by the government itself.

In summary, it appears as if the high level of social-welfare consumption in Singapore has been achieved in combination with a high degree of government political, social, and economic control. These are both related, and in the past they have been credited with increasing private and social investment, productivity, and growth. But more recently both have been considered constraints on private investment and growth, as well as on political and social freedoms, which are apparently of greater importance to a now more sophisticated citizenry. While the government's proposed privatization of social services could reduce the level of social welfare consumption, especially if regressive distributional effects weigh heavily in total welfare, the government has not yet indicated its willingness to accept a commensurate reduction of its own political and social control.

It remains to consider the implications of the Singapore experience with social welfare for ideology and developmental theory. In its early days, the PAP subscribed to a social-democratic ideology which strongly emphasized public provision for social-welfare needs, and it did succeed admirably in increasing social consumption both through its economic policies and through public social-welfare provisions. This clearly contributed to development by enhancing human capital, increasing private investment, and ensuring political stability and social peace (including well deserved popular support for the government itself). But the PAP very quickly shifted its ideology to incorporate a strong bias against state subsidies, reflecting a partial rejection of the human-capital approach — notably in the health sector. It continued to maintain impressive social-welfare programmes, but they were increasingly funded directly by consumers themselves. In education, the human-capital approach was employed to justify shifting the costs to consumers: for example, by arguing that university students, already heavily subsidized, should pay more of the costs of their education from which they would eventually derive substantial benefits.

It was when the government began to use social-welfare programmes — mainly housing and the CPF — to achieve other goals, and especially to earn a surplus for the government itself, that positive impacts on social productivity and private investment began to be displaced by negative impacts. This problem ballooned in the 1980s, finally contributing in part to the 1985/86 recession and economic crisis. As part of its response to this recession, the government has undenaken to reduce its role in the economy, including aspects of social-welfare provision. On the theoretical level, this reflects a partial rejection (or, in some cases, revision) of the human-capital approach to development. On the ideological level, it represents a somewhat extreme embrace of the now popular conservative, free-market economic doctrine which extols privatization and the down-sizing of government — "extreme" because even the most ardent political exponents of such a doctrine (Margaret Thatcher and Ronald Reagan, for example) did not go so far as to contemplate the privatization of social-welfare services. Indeed, both Thatcher and Reagan maintained huge budget deficits and heavy social-welfare expenditures such as unemployment payments in Britain and medical and social-security payments in the United States.

But the PAP has never been rigidly doctrinaire or ideological in its approach to government, instead displaying a pragmatic bent which has been one of its enduring strengths. Although social-welfare policy in Singapore has variously achieved consumption, investment, political, and social goals, this has probably only rarely been the outcome of a conscious grand design. More likely the PAP has merely seized on the opportunities for exercising social and political influence presented by social-welfare programmes such as housing and the CPF, rather than constructing these programmes specifically to fit a dominant desire for control. The multiplicity of goals which have been hung on many social programmes, and their progressive encroachment on the private sector, all reflect attempts to use existing institutions, established for different purposes, as the means for effecting new policies. They often bear the hallmark of bureaucratic, rather than political, decision-making.

Curiously, while economic logic and history both suggest that the government should divest itself of its role in housing and social security (for example, selling off unsubsidized public-housing estates and converting the CPF into one or many private corporations like the massive group-pension funds in developed countries), it is to these two programmes that it is clinging, presumably because they represent both economic gains and political and social controls which are considered too important to relinquish. Instead the government is proposing partial privatization of the smaller health and education services, the two aspects of social welfare which are most characterized by externalities and which human-capital theory suggests are most deserving of social subsidy. This inverted interpretation of the ideology of privatization is peculiar to Singapore. It remains to be seen if this inversion is justified by pragmatism, in which case social investment and productivity will be enhanced, or if it represents the dominance of political goals over economic rationality, in which case social investment and productivity will suffer.

REFERENCES

Asher, MG (1984). The Financial System in Singapore. In *Singapore: Twenty-Five Years of Development*, Seng, YP and Yah, LC (eds.), pp. 78–107. Singapore: Nan Yang Xing Zhou Lianhe Zaobao.

Blaug, M (1976). Human Capital Theory: A Slightly Jaundiced Survey. *Journal of Economic literature* 14, 827–55.

Chng, MK (1986). The Political Economy of Public Housing in Singapore. Paper presented at the Workshop on the Political Economy of Development in ASEAN, 4–5 April 1986, Institute of Southeast Asian Studies.

Department of Statistics (1983). *Economic and Social Statistics, Singapore 1960–82.* Singapore.

______. *Yearbook of Statistics, Singapore 1985/86.* Singapore, 1986.

Kalirajan, K and P Wiboonchutikula. The Social Security System in Singapore. *ASEAN Economic Bulletin* (Special Issue on "Social Security Systems in ASEAN") 3, no. 1 (1986): 129–39.

Lim Chong Yah *et al.* Report of the Central Provident Fund Study Group. *Singapore Economic Review* (Special Issue) 31, no. 1 (1986).

Lim, L, Pang EF, and R Findlay. The Political Economy of Poverty, Equity and Growth: Singapore 1959–1987. Paper prepared for the World Bank Workshop on the Political Economy of Poverty, Equity and Growth, 25 April to 4 May 1987, in Fez, Morocco.

Low, L (1985). The Financing Process in the Public Sector in Singapore. *Bulletin for International Fiscal Documentation* 39, 148–65.

Meier, GM, ed. *Leading Issues in Economic Development.* 4th ed. New York: Oxford University Press, 1984.

Ministry of Trade and Industry. *Economic Survey of Singapore.* Singapore, various years.

———. *The Singapore Economy: New Directions.* Report of the Economic Committee. Singapore, 1986.

Musgrave, RA. "Notes on Educational Investment in Developing Nations". In *Financing of Education for Economic Growth.* OECD Study Group in the Economics of Education. Paris: Organization for Economic Co-operation and Development, 1966.

Mushkin, SJ. "Health as an Investment". *Journal of Political Economy* (Supplement), 1982, pp. 129–57.

Organization for Economic Co-operation and Development. *The Welfare State in Crisis.* Paris, 1981.

Ow, CH. "Singapore: Past, Present and Future". In *Singapore: Twenty-Five Years of Development*, edited by You Poh Seng and Lim Chong Yah, pp. 366–88. Singapore: Nan Yang Xing Zhou Lianhe Zaobao, 1984.

Pang EF and Chan HC. "The Political Economy of Development in Singapore: 1959–1986". Paper presented at the Workshop on the Political Economy of Development in ASEAN, 4–5 April 1986, Institute of Southeast Asian Studies.

Salaff, JW and AK Wong. "Chinese Women at Work: Work Commitment and Fertility in the Asian Setting". In *The Fertility of Working Women: An International Synthesis of Research*, edited by Stanley Kupinsky, pp. 81–145. New York: Praeger, 1977.

Schultz, TW. "Investment in Human Capital in Poor Countries". In *Foreign Trade and Human Capital*, edited by P.D. Zook. Dallas: Southern Methodist University Press, 1962.

Tsao, Y. "Comment" (on a paper by Kalirajan and Wiboonchutikula). *ASEAN Economic Bulletin* 3 (1986): 140–44.

Vasil, RK. *Governing Singapore.* Singapore: Eastern Universities Press, 1984.

Wong, AK. "Social Transformation in Singapore". Paper presented at the Conference on Singapore and the United States into the 1990s, in November 1975, at the Fletcher School of Law and Diplomacy, Tufts University.

Wong, AK and SHK Yeh, eds. *Housing a Nation: 25 Years of Public Housing in Singapore.* Singapore: Maruzen Asia, for the Housing and Development Board, 1985.

World Bank. *World Development Report 1986.* Washington, D.C., 1986.

Yeh, SHK, ed. *Public Housing in Singapore.* Singapore: Singapore University Press, for the Housing and Development Board, 1975.

Chapter 3

GLOBALIZING STATE, DISAPPEARING NATION: THE IMPACT OF FOREIGN PARTICIPATION IN THE SINGAPORE ECONOMY*

LINDA Y.C. LIM and LEE SOO ANNJ

FROM HUB TO NATION

Singapore has been a global city, and a hub for international trade, investment and migrant labour, since its modern-day "founding" as a free port by the British colonial officer Stamford Raffles in 1819. During the colonial period, free trade and capital flows, a common currency with neighbouring British territories on the Malay peninsula and north Borneo, and the free inflow of migrant labour from China, India, and present-day Indonesia, turned Singapore into a trading, transport-and-communications, financial and managerial services hub for Southeast Asia as the region became a major exporter to world markets of tin, rubber, rice, timber, petroleum, and other commodities.

As a regional hub for global markets, Singapore's economy was heavily dependent on political as well as economic developments in the region and world at large. Thus the Great Depression of the 1930s, World War II and the Japanese Occupation of the 1940s, post-war decolonization, associated regional conflicts, and the establishment of communist governments in China, North Korea and North Vietnam in the 1940s and 1950s, all served to disrupt Singapore's hub relations with its neighbours and the world. Flows of people in and out of the island diminished, all but ceasing in the 1950s, while its neighbours' new national import-substituting trade barriers and currency

*This paper by Linda YC Lim and Lee Soo Ann first appeared in *Management of Success: Singapore Revisited*, edited by Terence Chong, Chapter 9, 2010. This work is reproduced here with the kind permission of the publisher, ISEAS — Yusof Ishak Institute, Singapore. http://bookshop.iseas.edu.sg.

regimes reduced their links with Singapore as their external intermediary with world markets.

By 1959, when Singapore achieved internal self-government from the British, and voted in the People's Action Party (PAP), the island's regional hub-based economy was faltering. Slow GDP growth and high (double-digit) unemployment were accompanied by labour unrest and political turmoil, which naturally discouraged new investment. The PAP's initial proposal to stimulate growth was political and economic integration with present-day Malaysia, with the combined nation then following a strategy of import-substituting industrialization for a "Malaysian common market" for which Singapore would still serve as the "New York", or commercial and financial hub.

The two territories did indeed unite in 1963, but separated just two years later, in 1965. Anticipating continued decline in its regional hub function, as well as the eventual withdrawal of British military services (then accounting for nearly a third of the GDP of the newly independent nation), the PAP government embraced a new strategy of labour-intensive export manufacturing for world markets. By then such manufacturing was delivering strong growth and employment creation in Hong Kong, Taiwan and South Korea. Singapore already enjoyed the free trade and capital flows required by such a strategy, and had substantial domestic surplus labour, but lacked indigenous manufacturing capability. For this it turned to multinational corporations, particularly in the electronics industry, which was beginning to outsource labour-intensive assembly from developed home countries such as the U.S. and Japan, to labour-abundant developing countries.

This export manufacturing strategy would integrate production facilities in Singapore into the evolving offshore supply chains of foreign multinationals producing for their home and global markets. It was thus clearly a strategy of globalization rather than localization (as import-substituting industrialization within Malaysia would have been) or regionalization (continuation of a regional hub function in traded services). But its subsequent success also derived from a set of national development policies on which the PAP government had already embarked since 1959, which had a local nation-building as well as global economy stimulating goal and function.

These national development policies included: expansion of the Central Provident Fund (CPF) to mobilize domestic savings which were then invested in long-term government bonds to fund government development expenditures; compulsory state acquisition of private land for investments in physical infrastructure such as housing, roads, utilities, industrial estates, the port and airport; formation of the Housing and Development Board (HDB) to build high-rise public housing units for the rapidly growing domestic population; building of industrial estates to accommodate — first import-substituting then export-oriented — factories; and investments in public education and health care.

Together with generous tax breaks and subsidies for foreign investors, restrictive labour and industrial relations legislation enacted in 1968, and annual wage increase guidelines recommended by a tripartite National Wages Council (NWC), these policies greatly increased the attractiveness of Singapore as an investment location for foreign companies. They provided investors with cheap land, labour and efficient infrastructure, increased the productivity of the working population, and reduced risk by ensuring political stability and labour peace. In line with the PAP's social-democratic ideology of the time, all these public goods were provided by state agencies and enterprises.[1] The government's control of the economy increased as land went from 80 per cent privately owned to 80 per cent publicly owned in less than ten years, labour rights were reduced, foreign capital was dependent on the government for investment incentives and inputs, and local capital was increasingly crowded out by both the state and multinationals in factor and product markets. At the same time, political, legal, and media controls were enacted which weakened and eventually eviscerated any political opposition.[2]

Singapore's post-independence globalization of the 1960s and 1970s was thus heavily directed by an authoritarian state, imposing some costs on the local citizenry in terms of property rights, political liberties, and human rights.[3] But globalization and the "developmental state" also "delivered the (economic) goods" to a mostly grateful electorate in terms of employment generation, increased incomes and improved social welfare.[4] Real GDP doubled between 1960 and 1969, and its annual growth accelerated to double-digit rates between 1966 and 1973.[5] This was based not only on

---

[1]Lim, LYC (1983). Singapore's Success: The Myth of the Free Market Economy. *Asian Survey* 23(6), 752–64.

[2]See Tan Tarn How's "Singapore's Print Media Policy: A National Success?" in this volume for a discussion on political control over local media.

[3]See Thio Li-ann's "'More Matter, with Less Art': Human Rights and Human Development in Singapore" in this volume for a discussion on human rights in Singapore.

[4]Lim, LYC (1989). Social Welfare in Singapore. In *Management of Success: The Moulding of Modern Singapore*, Sandu, KS and Wheatley, P (eds.). Singapore: Institute of Southeast Asian Studies.

[5]Lee Soo Ann, "Patterns of Economic Structure in Singapore", in *Singapore: Twenty Five Years of Development*, edited by You Poh Seng and Lim Chong Yah (Singapore: Nanyang Xing Chou Lianhe Zaobao, 1984).

favourable regional and world market conditions (including a Vietnam War-induced boom in the export of commodities and traded services), but also on the domestic mobilization of capital, labour and land, and the establishment of institutions to facilitate this, beginning with self-government in 1959.

In the process, Singapore was transformed from a regional hub to a national economy whose integration into world markets and the global production networks of multinational corporations was deliberately shaped by an increasingly powerful and nationally oriented state. The state's own political legitimacy hinged not only on the economic performance it enabled, but also on a nationalist rhetoric of the vulnerability of a resource-poor "small island nation" cast adrift in the potentially hostile waters of a then turbulent region. The transformation from hub to nation also provided opportunities for the development of new state agencies and enterprises which steadily grew their share of the economy and of employment, gradually morphing from statutory boards headed by civil servants into publicly listed government-linked corporations (GLCs) headed by well paid CEOs. Thus the abandoned British naval base facility and the semi-skilled labour it employed became government-owned shipbuilders Sembawang and Keppel, now both major conglomerates that no longer build ships; various defence-related industries that grew up to develop the national military forces later became another conglomerate Singapore Technologies; government land and urban development agencies spun off real estate developer Capital Land; utilities provider Singapore Telecoms, the former Development Bank of Singapore (now DBS), and the iconic Singapore Airlines, among others, became profit-oriented regional and global players in their respective industries.

At the aggregate level, these national development policies led to striking shifts in the domestic macroeconomy: private consumption fell from 89.4 per cent of GDP (at market prices) in 1960 to 68.5 per cent in 1969, while government's share of GDP rose, and that of investment more than doubled, rising from 11.3 per cent in 1960 to 28.6 per cent in 1969.[6] Despite the large increase in exports, the economy ran a persistent balance of payments current account deficit, with domestic demand exceeding GDP until 1985. This gap was more than covered by large inflows of foreign capital, with the result that the foreign share of the country's GDP increased from 9 per cent of GDP in 1966 to 20 per cent of GDP in 1973 and 28 per cent by 1980.[7]

---

[6]Ibid.
[7]Ibid.

The foreign share comprises "the share of resident foreigners and foreign resident companies in GDP",[8] which presumably includes temporary foreign workers. When the booming economy led to full employment and rising wage costs in 1973, foreign workers were imported to increase the supply of labour and, together with conservative NWC recommendations, maintain competitiveness in the still labour-intensive export manufacturing sector.[9] This continued through the global recession of 1974–75, which affected Singapore, and the subsequent recovery. By 1979, however, the government decided that low wages had discouraged capital deepening and investments in increased productivity. It launched a so-called "second industrial revolution" by raising salaries and wages (including through CPF contributions and NWC recommendations) between 1980 and 1982, to force industrial upgrading and capital-labour substitution in the export manufacturing sector. The salaries of government employees were also raised, even though they did not face international competition.

This "high-wage" policy is believed to have contributed to the severity of the 1985–86 global recession's impact on Singapore, following which compulsory CPF contributions by employers and employees were reduced in an effort to regain lost competitiveness versus other Asian export economies. This was successful in attracting more foreign investment, and GDP growth recovered from 1987 until the Asian financial crisis of 1997–98. However, income inequality also increased (discussed below), as did the foreign share of the economy.

FROM NATION TO HUB

At the aggregate level, the economy in 1985 turned from a net importer to a net exporter of capital. High domestic savings (including CPF "forced savings") in both the private and public sectors, combined with large surpluses (net exports) in the services account of the balance of payments, and large net inflows of foreign capital, created huge external surpluses and probably the world's largest foreign exchange reserves, as a share of GDP and in per capita terms, for a non-oil-exporter. The ratio of official foreign reserves to GDP was 102 per cent in 2004, and to indigenous GDP was

[8] *Yearbook of Statistics Singapore* (annual) subtracts "foreign share" from GDP to give "indigenous GDP". Adding net factor receipts from the rest of the world, gives indigenous GNP, which in Singapore is much less than GNP at market prices. Indigenous GNP is also less than GDP, which includes production in Singapore contributed by foreigners.

[9] Pang, EF and Lim, LYC (1982). Foreign Labour and Economic Development in Singapore. *International Migration Review* 16(3), 548–76.

165 per cent in 2006, with the reserves valued at historical cost rather than their market value which would be two to three times larger, increasing the reserve ratio to as much as five times indigenous GDP.[10] Foreign asset accumulation occurred not only through the investment of official reserves by the Government of Singapore Investment Corporation (GIC) responsible for investing persistent large budget surpluses, but also through the foreign direct and portfolio investments of government-linked companies (including the holding company Temasek Holdings, which manages the surpluses of GLCs) and large local corporations. From the late 1980s, the government encouraged outward investment by Singapore firms in, and relocation by foreign multinationals manufacturing in Singapore to, neighbouring countries such as Indonesia, Malaysia and China, including in Singapore Government-owned industrial estates in Batam (Indonesia), Vietnam and Suzhou (China).[11]

Singapore's fellow export-oriented Newly Industrialized Economies (NIEs), or "Asian tigers" South Korea, Taiwan and Hong Kong, also experienced rising production costs in the late 1980s, the result of tight domestic labour markets and more aggressive labour movements following political democratization in Korea and Taiwan, and strong appreciation of the won and New Taiwan dollar. In response, these other "tigers" also began exporting capital and relocating manufacturing to Southeast Asia and China, but as part of a cross-border vertical disintegration of the supply-chains of domestic companies, following shifting comparative advantage and trade policy liberalization. In the process Hong Kong and Taiwan companies in particular became regionally integrated into evolving "Greater China" production networks that also took in parts of South east Asia as well. But they remained linked to sources of capital, technology, and managerial skills and to sourcing, marketing and design functions in their home territories.

In contrast, export producers who relocated out of Singapore, also to China and Southeast Asia, were mainly foreign multinationals, whose relocation was part of a process of globalization, which in many cases

---

[10]Lee Soo Ann, "From Nation to Hub: The Economy and Christian Life in Singapore Today", unpublished manuscript.

[11]Pereira, A. (2005). Singapore's Regionalization Strategy. *Journal of the Asia Pacific Economy* 10(3), 380–96; Phelps, NA (2007). Gaining from Globalization? State Extraterritoriality and Domestic Economic Impacts: The Case of Singapore. *Economic Geography* 83(4), 371–93; Yeung, HWC (2000). State Intervention and Neoliberalism in the Globalizing World Economy: Lessons from Singapore's Regionalization Programme. *Pacific Review* 13, 133–62.

disengaged them from the Singapore economy, except as a residual services intermediary, where required, between different parts of their now regionally distributed value chains. Responding to this, the Singapore Government embarked on a strategic plan to develop "clusters" of high-value activities that would attract multinational investment in new sectors, most notably the "life sciences" or biomedical sciences and pharmaceuticals, financial services, health and medical services, and education, for foreign markets.[12] These and other capital-intensive investments helped push the foreign ownership share of the economy up to 40 per cent of GDP by 2000, the level at which it remains today. As a consequence, the increasing stream of profit repatriation abroad, far exceeding inward investment income flows, portends a likely negative balance of services account in the future.[13]

Together with the increase in outward investment flows, continued large inward foreign investments contributed to the national economy reverting to its earlier historical role as a regional hub by importing and re-exporting capital, as well as goods and services, particularly financial, commercial, transport and communications services, and now also health and education to regional neighbours. But in the late 1990s, the Asian financial crisis put a severe if temporary crimp in demand from regional markets. So, entering the twenty-first century, these hub activities were expanded and extended to serve the world increasingly, and not just the region, particularly in financial services and the life sciences. The 2001–03 U.S. tech recession, which hit Singapore hard, reduced the government's enthusiasm for activity in the long-established electronics-computers-telecommunications cluster. The subsequent massive economic booms in China and India, which trickled down into Southeast Asia, appeared to validate the regional-services-export part of this post-industrial development strategy, which culminated in the government's locally controversial 2006 decision to welcome international gaming casinos to Singapore, as part of what is euphemistically called an "integrated resort" for foreign (mainly Asian and especially Chinese) tourists.

Singapore's development is distinguished from that of the Northeast Asian NIEs in other ways besides its dependence on foreign multinationals rather than on local private enterprises. These include: continued state

---

[12]Economic Planning Committee, Ministry of Trade and Industry, *Strategic Economic Plan* (Singapore: Ministry of Trade and Industry, 1991).

[13]Teh Kok Peng, "The Singapore Economy 2030", in *Singapore Futures: Scenarios for the Next Generation*. Paper presented at the Institute of Policy Studies (IPS). Singapore Perspectives 2008 Conference, January.

dominance of the economy, including through corporatized GLCs; continued one-party dominance and lack of government "turnover" in the political sphere; and heavy reliance on foreign labour and skills ("foreign talent").[14] In the first two decades of Singapore's post-independence economic development, foreign labour was mainly imported to fill cyclical shortages of low-skilled labour required in labour-intensive export sectors such as manufacturing and shipbuilding, and in occupations requiring physical labour, such as domestic service and construction, which became unattractive to increasingly well educated Singaporeans. But since recovery from the 1985–86 recession, inflows of foreign labour have been expanded, though they are still subject to various regulatory controls, such as a foreign worker wage levy. Foreign labour imports were also liberalized to include workers from "non-traditional" sources besides the "traditional" source, Malaysia, and they began coming from the Philippines, Thailand, Indonesia, Myanmar, Bangladesh, India, Sri Lanka, China and beyond.

While there are official numbers on the number of foreign workers in the labour force, there is no breakdown of foreign-born and Singapore-born citizens. The importance of foreigners in the labour force is much greater than it seems. (Permanent residence has been made easier for skilled and even semi-skilled foreigners to obtain, and this is readily converted into Singapore citizenship after a few years.) But various indirect calculations suggest that foreigners constituted about 40 per cent of the labour force in 2006, up from 26 per cent in 1986,[15] and a quarter or more of the nearly 5 million resident population of Singapore.[16] With numbers such as a six million or eight million population being bandied about by government officials, and the ageing and low birth rates of locally born Singaporeans despite a quarter-century of pro-natalist population policies giving tax and other benefits to those having more children, it is clear that the government's intention is for the share, as well as the number, of foreign-born residents and citizens to continue rising (though this has been set back by mass layoffs in the wake of

[14]Linda Y.C. Lim, "The State and Private Capital in Singapore's Economic Development", in *Political Economy, Studies in the Surplus Approach* 3, No. 2 (1987), pp. 201–22; Lim, LYC, Pang Eng Fong, and R Findlay, "Singapore", in *Five Small Open Economies*, edited by Ronald Findlay and Stanley Wellisz (New York: Oxford University Press for the World Bank, 1993).

[15]Lee, "From Nation to Hub".

[16]For example, the difference between the number in the labour force and the number of CPF contributors (which includes only higher-level foreign workers eligible for permanent residence and citizenship) amounts to about one-quarter of the labour force *(Yearbook of Statistics Singapore*, various years).

the global financial crisis and severe recession of 2008–09). This will make the Singapore population resemble more closely that of its colonial past, when it was populated mostly by immigrants and transient workers, serving as a denationalized regional hub for inflows and outflows of labour as well as of capital, goods and services.

GLOBALIZATION'S LOCAL IMPACT

Whether a regional or global hub, or a national economy, any normative evaluation of Singapore's state-led development strategy needs to consider its impact on "indigenous" Singaporeans, and on Singapore as a nation, and not just on the rate of growth of a GDP 40 per cent owned by foreigners, or employment creation for a labour force of whom 40 per cent are foreigners. As earlier literature on the economic growth of Singapore and the other Asian NIEs pointed out, rapid growth can readily be achieved by simple factor accumulation, or increasing inputs of capital, labour, skills, and technology to produce greater output, without yielding higher productivity or involving increased efficiency in the use of scarce resources.[17] Adding large amounts of foreign capital and foreign labour to an economy can certainly grow that economy, and the returns it delivers to the foreign capital and labour, but the benefit to local citizens may be more ambiguous.

In the early decades of Singapore's post-independence economic development, foreign investment which brought capital, technology and foreign market access to an economy with surplus labour not only contributed to GDP, employment and income growth, but also reduced income inequality, by increasing the demand for lesser-skilled, lower-wage labour.[18] While the mass import of low-skilled foreign labour beginning in the mid-1970s might be expected to depress the wages of low-skilled local labour, this effect was probably outweighed by the rising skill levels of local labour as state investments in public education started to yield results. The "high-wage

[17]Krugman, P (1994). The Myth of Asia's Miracle. *Foreign Affairs*, 73(6), 62–78; Young, A. Tale of Two Cities: Factor Accumulation and Technical Change in Hong Kong and Singapore. In *NBER Macroeconomics Annual 1992*, O. J. Blanchard and S. Fischer (Cambridge and London: MIT Press, 1992), pp. 13–54; Alwyn Young, "The Tyranny of Numbers: Confronting the Statistical Realities of the East Asian Growth Experience", *Quarterly Journal of Economics*, 110, No. 3 (August 1995), 641–80.

[18]Wood, A (1999). Openness and Wage Inequality in Developing Countries: The Latin American Challenge to East Asian Conventional Wisdom. *World Bank Economic Review*, 11(1), 33–57; Fields, G (1994). Changing Labor Market Conditions and Economic Development in Hong Kong, the Republic of Korea, Singapore, and Taiwan, China. *World Bank Economic Review*, 8(3), 395–414.

policy" implemented by the government as part of its push for a "second industrial revolution" in the 1980s also raised wages and labour productivity through capital-labour substitution, and the exit of very labour-intensive activities. However, the shift to more capital- and skill-intensive activities, dictated by market forces as well as state strategy, probably increased income inequality by raising the returns to capital and skills relative to the returns to low-skilled labour. The 41 per cent share of Singapore's GDP going to employee compensation (wages and salaries) in 2007 is one of the lowest such shares in the world, as is the similarly low share of aggregate consumption in GDP,[19] while the more than 50 per cent share of GDP going to corporate profits, interest and dividends is one of the world's highest. At the same time, the foreign share of domestic production and income also increased, to around 40 per cent.

A Department of Statistics study in 2002 revealed that between 1990 and 2000, there was "a widening disparity in the overall household income distribution in Singapore ... in line with the trends observed in countries such as Hong Kong, Taiwan, Korea and U.S."[20] Recent studies show that globalization has been accompanied by increased income inequality throughout Asian and other countries including developing ones.[21] The reasons given for this that apply to Singapore include: increases in capital inflows and the complementarity of capital with skilled labour, skill-biased technological change, and "upgrading of the average product quality in export plants, which in turn generates demand for a better qualified

---

[19]Ermisch and Huff claim that forced saving extracted through compulsory CPF contributions and high statutory board charges for providing utilities and other public services are responsible for Singapore's high saving and low consumption rates. But Abeysinghe and Choy (2004) point out that private consumption as a share of disposable income, and not just of GDP, has also trended downward and is low, which they attribute to high residential property prices requiring rising loans and withdrawals from CPF to fund house (and car) purchases. In large part because of high asset prices, consumption and living standards are much lower than per capita income levels suggest, resulting in greater economic volatility with changes in GDP growth, since consumption is typically the most stable component of GDP. See Ermisch, JF and Huff, WG (1999). Hypergrowth in an East Asian NIC: Public Policy and Capital Accumulation in Singapore. *World Development*, 27, 21–38; Tilak Abeysinghe and Choy, KM (2004). The Aggregate Consumption Puzzle in Singapore. *Journal of Asian Economics* 15, 563–78.

[20]"Income Distribution and Inequality Measures in Singapore" (Singapore: Department of Statistics, 2002).

[21]Goldberg, PK and Pavcnik, N (2007). Distributional Effects of Globalization in Developing Countries. *Journal of Economic Literature*. XLV, 39–82; Asian Development Bank, *Key Indicators 2007: Inequality in Asia* (Manila: Asian Development Bank, 2007).

workforce".[22] All these contribute to the widening of the skill premium or wage differential between highly skilled and low-skilled workers. Increased returns tend to be particularly high for tertiary degree recipients employed in managerial, professional, and technical jobs, whose ranks expand rapidly with the transition to a "knowledge-based economy". While these inequality-increasing developments can happen in a closed national economy, they are likely to be exacerbated by globalization, particularly cross-border flows of capital and technology, and the "global war for talent", which can bid up the wages of the highly skilled in developing countries, almost to developed country levels.[23]

In a market economy, external demand would increase domestic inequality if trade disproportionately increases demand for capital- and skill-intensive products and services, and thus the returns to scarce but highly valuable capital and skills. A shift in the comparative advantage of national economies, from activities and sectors which intensively use relatively immobile low-skilled labour, towards those which intensively use relatively mobile capital and high-skilled labour, would have this effect. In Asia over the past two decades, trade and investment liberalization, and market-oriented domestic economic reforms, especially but not only in China and India, greatly increased these countries' competitiveness in labour-intensive export industries, based on their relative abundance of low-wage labour. The now more capital- and skill-abundant Asian NIEs, including Singapore, had to turn to capital-deepening and increased skill-intensity to compete, which in turn increased income inequality within their domestic economies.

In Singapore's case, this widening in income disparities is enhanced and complicated by the strong role of the state in shaping the country's integration into regional and global economies. The adjustment to shifting comparative advantage in the other "Asian tigers" was undertaken mainly by their national private enterprises engaging in capital-labour substitution at home, and the relocation of more labour-intensive activities abroad, in a largely market-determined process and increasingly democratized polities where, for example, labour movements gained strength (particularly in South Korea) and succeeded in pushing up wages.

In Singapore, however, the still authoritarian state led and directed this process in a number of ways. The "second industrial revolution" and

[22]Goldberg and Pavcnik, "Distributional Effects of Globalization", p. 67.
[23]It should be noted, however, that these increases in inequality "are not a story of the 'rich getting richer and the poor getting poorer'. Rather, it is the rich getting richer faster than the poor." (Asian Development Bank, 2007), p. 6.

subsequent development policies, including regionalization and the move into the life sciences and high-value services, accelerated the shift out of labour-intensive activities employing lower-skilled workers, and into capital- and skill-intensive activities favouring owners of capital and the highly skilled, who received state subsidies for their investments in the form of tax breaks, R&D and training grants, together with higher education. CPF and NWC recommendations, and continued ruling party control of the union movement, together with large increases in foreign labour imports, probably limited wage increases at the lower-skill end of the domestic labour force, in contrast to developments in the other Asian NIEs. At the same time, competing with many more locations than previously to attract mobile capital and "talent" required the enhancement of a business environment, infrastructure, and regulatory framework conducive to foreigners, including relaxed residency and citizenship requirements for those with capital and skills.[24] In the wake of the 2001–03 tech recession and the SARS incident, both of which hit the Singapore economy hard, the government

> In its bid to adapt Singapore's economy to international competition ... has tried hard to reduce business costs. This has meant slashing labor prices, which has helped push wages down. According to official figures, over the past five years Singapore's wealthiest 10 per cent have seen their income rise by 2.3 per cent annually (and that doesn't include nonwagc earnings such as capital gains or dividends). At the same time, the poorest 10 per cent have suffered a staggering 4.3 per cent drop in their salaries each year. The government has also allowed employers to cut their contributions to Singapore's Central Provident Fund, which pays for pensions, public housing, medical expenses and education ... Together, these factors have led to lower- than-expected private consumption, which has risen by just 3 per cent in the past two years.[25]

In January 2007, senior government economist Yeoh Lam Keong warned that "median real-wage stagnation and low-income decline", despite very strong GDP growth, if left unchecked, could lead to "the formation of an underclass (and) the makings of social instability".[26] Given this coincidence of widening income disparities, an increased foreign share of the economy and of the labour force, and the state's leading role in restructuring the

[24]Following the government's own reasoning, some scholars have argued that participating successfully in globalization requires increased rather than diminished state action (Shin 2005), and that meeting Singapore's GDP growth targets requires increased dependence on foreign labour (Hui and Hashmi 2007).
[25]"Singapore Swing", *Newsweek International*, 29 January 2007.
[26]Ibid.

economy and mediating globalization, including especially its encouragement and employment in GLCs, for example, of highly paid "foreign talent", it is no surprise that there is a sense among some of the Singapore citizenry that they are no longer lords of their own nation, that the nation itself is being increasingly "taken over" by foreigners, and that their own government governs more for the benefit of foreign capital and talent than it does for local labour, capital and talent. At the same time, globalization has also meant that many Singaporeans with globally marketable skills now work abroad as expatriates for extended periods of time with foreign companies, or emigrate permanently, causing a "loss" of locally produced and subsidized talent who might otherwise be relied upon to provide economic, political, and social leadership for the nation. Concerned about this, the government in 2006 created an Overseas Singaporeans Unit in the Prime Minister's Office to maintain links with Singapore's own "foreign talent", estimated at about 200,000, living abroad. Whether they stay or leave, the government has also voiced concern that a growing cultural and social as well as income gap, is emerging between a highly educated and globalized elite dubbed "cosmopolitans", and so-called "heartlanders" who are less geographically and economically mobile.[27] Or as an opposition politician vividly stated during the 2006 General Election campaign,

> Singapore is like a 6 star hotel. In this hotel, the elite are either managers or guests. The managers want to retain the hotel's 6 star status and attract foreign guests who will pay the expensive room rates. You don't need three guesses to guess who the managers are. The elite locals on the other hand enjoy the good facilities and can afford the expensive room rates. However they are guests with no ownership and have no desire to contribute to the running of the hotel apart from paying high room rates. Both the foreigners and local elites use our country as a good place to make money but when it becomes uncomfortable they move out. The rest of us are the worker bees: chamber maids, waiters etc. We work hard for our children and dream they will become either managers or the guests of the hotel. This hotel although a good one is home to no one. There is no soul of a nation in a hotel.[28]

This disengagement of nation and economy may be considered inevitable given the transformation from national to global hub economy outlined above, and in a nation whose national identity is predicated primarily on economic progress which can be ephemeral or attainable elsewhere. The

[27]These terms were first introduced in the 11 August 1991 National Day Rally Speech of then Prime Minister Goh Chok Tong. See discussion in Tan (2007).

[28]Eric Tan, unsuccessful Workers' Party candidate for Parliament.

inevitability of this disengagement may be questioned since it is the product of state policy more than of private enterprise and market forces, and has not happened in South Korea and Taiwan, for example, where local private enterprises such as Samsung, Hyundai, Acer and Quanta have become successful global multinationals, in part with assistance from their national governments. Inevitable or not, the nature of the Singapore economy's recent articulation into the global economy poses challenges for the state which has shaped this articulation, and arguably maintains itself in power, paying its top members the world's highest public servant salaries, precisely by making itself indispensable to the global capital and talent which it has welcomed to the economy.[29] The consequence, intended or unintended, is the "crowding out" of domestic enterprise and labour, perhaps even of the indigenous electorate, and the undermining of national identity which contributes to social stability and can help the economy "hold on" to its scarce citizen talent. There is potential political risk in the perception or actuality of a widening gap in income and economic opportunity between the locally born who are lower skilled and lower paid, and both foreign- and local-born "talent" who are increasingly compensated at "global" rates of pay, including in the state and government-linked sector. In other words, economic progress and national unity, which in an earlier era were mutually reinforcing, may now run counter to each other.

> We may even end up with a situation where Singaporean 'heartlanders', emotionally committed to their birthplace and relatively immobile in the global job market, are ruled by potentially footloose 'foreign talent', while members of the Singapore-born elite, raised to be 'global', depart for foreign shores.[30]

Several recent developments in Singapore's economy illustrate the role of the state in shaping a new domestic political economy predicated on a particular form of state-mediated globalization which arguably empowers and enriches wealthy foreigners, and the state itself, more than it does average local citizens. For example, in the capital- and skill-intensive field of the life sciences, foreign talent is imported (sometimes at above world-market rates of compensation), and capital subsidies provided to foreign firms, to produce medical breakthroughs for (mostly rich) global consumers. This might make Singapore a profitable place for parts of the life sciences'

---

[29]Wei, SJ "Corruption in Economic Development: beneficial grease, minor annoyance, or major obstacle?" Working Paper No. 2048 (World Bank, Washington D.C., 1999).
[30]Lim, LYC "Singapore: Place or Nation?" *Straits Times*, 19 June 2006, adapted from a talk given at the Institute of Southeast Asian Studies, 8 June 2006.

global value chain to locate. But it is not clear where Singapore the nation benefits, since the jobs, profits and products are produced overwhelmingly by and for foreigners. Employment creation for ordinary Singaporeans in this highly risky and capital-intensive sector has proved disappointing, and the economic, political and scientific problems of global pharmaceutical companies, to whose locomotive the Singapore state has hitched its life sciences carriage, are well known.[31] As the 2008–09 recession has shown, output and employment volatility in this sector is as great as that in export-oriented electronics manufacturing.

Another example is the government's decision to develop an "integrated resort" in Singapore around gambling casinos established by international gaming companies. Responding to local objections, including from within its own ranks, based on "moral values" as well as economic concerns, the government argued that casinos would not undermine Singapore society because Singaporeans would not be involved in the business as consumers but only as workers — though casino employees may be expected to be disproportionately foreign. The near collapse in 2008–09 of this global industry, and of the larger of the two international gaming companies investing in the Singapore project,[32] again highlight the volatility occasioned by yet more state-induced dependence on foreign corporations and markets.

Singapore has also been expanding its financial services industry to focus on private banking for high net-worth individuals from around the world. There is a visible physical aspect to the economy's makeover into a global services centre for very wealthy foreigners. Real estate developments led by GLCs such as Capital Land and foreign as well as local mega private property developers are using "en bloc" sales to clear desirable downtown areas of public housing and older middle-class residential properties, replacing them with expensive high-end properties affordable only to a small local elite and very wealthy foreigners, such as is seen in places like Macau, Dubai and Monaco, which have much smaller local populations. To make room for rich foreigners, the Singaporean "middle class" living in both public and private housing units is being "pushed to the margins" of the already heavily populated island. The government's policy role in transforming extremely scarce land from a national patrimony to global real estate, replacing

[31]See, for example, "Pharma companies try different routes on rocky road to renewal", *Financial Times*, 13 March 2009, p. 20.

[32]"Will gambling continue to grow? All bets are off", *Wall Street Journal*, 2 January 2009; "Sands project causes worry", *Wall Street Journal*, 14 November 2008; "Singapore concern for casino project", *Wall Street Journal*, 9 November, 2008.

traditional neighbourhoods, familiar buildings, cemeteries and other social landmarks, including the elimination of much of the island's green space, may contribute to a sense of dislocation and loss of identity.[33] On the issue of urban planning,

> Nature Society president Geh Min has noted that viewing Singapore as a city results in its physical environment being managed by urban planners and our land resources treated as real estate defined by their globally determined commercial market value. Open spaces are seen as having value only as manicured parks, improving the urban quality of life ... Considering Singapore as a nation, however, would result in its physical territory, including the biodiversity found in wild areas, being valued as a national treasure and birthright. Wild lands might then be preserved in their natural state for their emotive and affective appeal for nationals.[34]

The shrinkage of global capital flows following the 2008–09 global financial crisis, and the anticipated tightened national and multilateral regulation of such flows as remain,[35] also highlight the fragility, riskiness and volatility of a growth strategy reliant on servicing foreign financial flows.

Singapore's sovereign wealth funds such as the GIC and Temasek Holdings, with richly compensated "foreign talent" disproportionately represented in their managerial ranks, have also made world headlines with the billions of dollars they have spent to acquire sizeable shares of some of the world's largest financial services corporations, such as Union Bank of Switzerland, Citigroup and Merrill Lynch, as they stumbled from their own errors that led to the U.S. subprime mortgage crisis and its global financial market spillovers. These assets add to already substantial portfolios held by state funds in Singapore's neighbouring Asian developing countries. The high (and partly forced) savings of Singapore's citizens and its numerous government entities addicted to earning massive surpluses have been converted into global capital itself, bringing the economy full circle from its early days as a recipient of inward foreign direct investment from rich developed countries to a provider of outward portfolio investment to these same countries. Unfortunately, the collapse in the financial crisis of the Western banks in which Singapore's sovereign wealth funds invested has caused a major decline in the value of their portfolios, leaving the

[33]De Koninck, R, J Drolet and M Girard (2008). *Singapore: An Atlas of Perpetual Territorial Transformation*. Singapore: NUS Press.

[34]Lim, "Singapore: Place or Nation?"; see also Geh Min's "The Greening of the Global City" in this volume for a discussion on conservation and urban planning in Singapore.

[35]See, for example, "Harbours of Resentment", *Financial Times*, 1 December 2008.

Singapore Government as the second largest investor and rescuer, after the U.S. Government, of Citigroup.[36]

CONCLUSION

The PAP government has been more adept than any other at devising and implementing national policies that selectively attracted international capital and technology, and foreign labour and skills, to create competitiveness in particular niches of the global market economy chosen by the state. This nationally oriented globalization strategy worked spectacularly well for four decades in increasing productivity, employment, and incomes for Singaporeans as well as foreigners.

The twenty-first century presents the Singapore economy with new challenges. These include its inevitably high cost structure (reflecting increasing local shortages of land and labour, but not of capital), the restructuring of global value chains in industries in which it had specialized (such as electronics and computers), and the emergence of new competitors for capital, technology, skills and global markets, particularly China and India. In response, rather than leaving the risks of restructuring the national economy to local and global market forces and the private sector, and loosening the bonds of state control with economic maturity, as other developmental states such as Taiwan and Korea and economies-in-transition such as China and India have done, the PAP government has chosen a strategy of "more of the same".

This includes bureaucratic targeting of favoured sectors for receipt of (now much more costly) state subsidies and tax breaks directed at attracting capital investment and technology from foreign companies and institutions serving international markets. But unlike the earlier era of labour- and then skill- and capital-intensive multinational export manufacturing, the newly favoured sectors (such as "life sciences", gambling casinos and high value-added services such as finance, medicine, and education) create disproportionately more jobs for foreigners than for locals, at all skill levels, and can only be sustained by massive immigration. They are also much more capital-intensive and risky, and subject to stronger global and regional competition, than was the case in the past. Because of these simultaneous "big bets" in a small place, the reliance on external factors of production

[36] "Two years of Temasek growth wiped out in months", *Business Times*, 11 February 2009; "Singapore government fund's loss pegged at $33 billion", *Wall Street Journal*, 18 February 2009; "GIC raises Citigroup stake to 11.1 per cent", *Straits Times*, 28 February, 2009.

and the costs of failure are much higher, arguably requiring even greater state control to maintain social stability.

Besides the greater economic risks involved in "more of the same" state policies applied to non-manufacturing sectors in an era of extremely rapid global and technological transformation, Singapore's continued policy of importing foreign capital, foreign labour, and foreign technology, and privileging foreign/global companies, to serve foreign markets, poses obvious local political, social, and cultural challenges for the nation and the state. Whereas the past four decades have seen the state successfully mould a colonial place into a postcolonial nation, the economic policies of the past four years raise the likelihood of the local nation dissolving into a global place, through the agency of the state.

These policies, together with changes in the global economic environment and the globalization processes of multinational companies, have resulted in much more ambiguous impacts on the local population. GDP growth, hinged to globalization in specific ways dictated by the state, has in the past decade suffered multiple setbacks that reflect continued if not increased vulnerability to the vicissitudes of volatile regional and global economies, most notably in the 2008–09 crisis which may see GDP plunge by as much as 10 per cent in one year.[37] The growth which has occurred has seen low shares in GDP for labour incomes (relative to capital returns), and consumption (relative to investment and government expenditure), increased income inequality, and a decline in the relative incomes of local Singaporeans relative to foreigners. The specific forms and requirements of GDP growth have also contributed to the undermining of national identity and social cohesion which previously held together the people of this "hub economy" and sustained their support for their government.

Why the government chose these state-dependent "enhanced hub" policies, rather than considering potential alternative market-determined, locally-oriented and private enterprise-led models of post-industrial development is a matter of some speculation. Lee suggests that the nation's founders, one of whom, Lee Kuan Yew, is still active in the government, never envisaged Singapore as an independent nation, but as a hub, and have retained a deep sense of insecurity about "going it alone".[38] Besides being an argument for path dependence which is not uncommon in bureaucratic

[37] "MM does not rule out GDP shrinking 10% ", *Straits Times*, 5 March 2009, p. 1.

[38] Lee, "From Nation to Hub". As recently as a few years ago, Lee Kuan Yew mentioned in a surprising public speech that Singapore might one day have to rejoin Malaysia, a statement that was equally unpopular in both countries.

policy-making, especially given past success, this approach also suggests that being important to foreign capital, governments, and "talent" might provide some assurance of security against potentially hostile neighbours. It has also earlier been suggested that "the self-interested bureaucracy (is) likely to resist privatization (and) the ruling party is increasingly motivated primarily by the wish to keep itself in power".[39] Besides addiction to political control for its own sake, reasons for this might include lack of trust in an increasingly disadvantaged and disempowered indigenous electorate, and an understandable eagerness to hold on to the extraordinarily high salaries and perquisites given to leaders of the ever-expanding state economic apparatus, including a remarkable 60 per cent increase in salaries for government ministers already earning seven-figure U.S dollar salaries, that generated considerable local disaffection.[40] (This did not abate when ministers' and senior civil servants' salaries were subsequently reduced by 20 per cent at the onset of the 2008–09 recession.) The fact that government officials are rewarded economically, through salaries and bonuses, as well as politically, through promotion in the ruling party hierarchy, for delivering GDP growth,[41] may also lead to "growth fetishism" (or "people for growth" rather than "growth for people") and thus to preference for the easiest route to growth, which is through the addition of inputs of foreign capital, labour, and skills.

Singapore's continued rapid GDP growth in the post-industrial era has thus been bought at the price of expanding and entrenching the economic as well as political dominance of a one-party state that maintains its power in part by brokering the increased and even privileged participation of foreign capital, talent and labour in the "local" economy. Foreigners beholden to the state for its beneficence and their own presence are unlikely to challenge its authority, in the way that an independent, globally competitive and non-state-dependent domestic entrepreneurial class — still weak and largely absent in Singapore — might.

---

[39]Lim, "The State and Private Capital", p. 222.

[40]Singapore blogs exploded with outrage at the news, while Lee Kuan Yew "painted a horrifying picture of a Singapore governed by ministers who earn no more than ministers anywhere else ... ". "Your apartment will be worth a fraction of what it is", he said, "your jobs will be in peril, your security will be at risk and our women will become maids in other people's countries. "See Seth Mydans, "Singapore announces 60 percent pay raise for ministers", *International Herald Tribune*, 9 April 2007.

[41]Note though that government officials and politicians are never penalized for growth slowdowns and recessions, which are always attributed to external market factors beyond their control.

In addition to this "inward globalization" of the Singapore economy, its growing "outward globalization", dominated by large state investments abroad, can also provide both external and internal security for the state's denizens, expanding its scope and power through extraterritoriality.[42] But "outward globalization" also has its risks, most recently seen in the antagonism towards Singapore over its sovereign wealth funds' acquisitions of strategic telecommunications assets in Thailand and Indonesia. There are also the risks of capital loss and nationalist political backlash in foreign countries where Singapore state funds have purchased large stakes in private sector corporate "crown jewels". State-led outward globalization may thus be politically destabilizing and security-undermining rather than the intended opposite. Add to this the uncertain long-term market success, certain high capital costs and risks, and some early failures (in life sciences and higher education)[43] in "winning" sectors "picked" by an unchallenged, authoritative state, and it is not at all clear that Singapore's transition from nation to global hub will be an easy or unmitigated success.

[42]Phelps, "Gaining from Globalization?" pp. 371–93.

[43]Fuyuno, I (2006). Singapore Pulls Plug on US Collaboration. *Nature* (3 August, P. 493); Montlake, S (2007). Singapore's Failing Bid for Brainpower. *Far Eastern Economic Review*, 170(8), 46–48.

Chapter 4

SINGAPORE'S SUCCESS: AFTER THE MIRACLE*

LINDA Y.C. LIM[1]

Singapore has long been widely recognized as possibly the most successful case of development among emerging economies in the 20th century. This has resulted in a large literature — both academic and popular — on the country's economic development, quite out of proportion to its small size and unique circumstances.[2] This chapter will not repeat or synthesize this literature, since it is well known. Instead I shall, first, provide a brief retrospective summary of the country's economic policy and performance in the 20th century since independence in 1965, considering the extent to which these are replicable (or not) in other countries; and second, discuss the many developmental challenges the now-rich country faces in the 21st century, reflecting on whether they cast doubt on the wisdom and sustainability of some of its past and current policies, and the prospective implications for

*This chapter first appeared in *Handbook of Emerging Economies*, Robert E.Looney (Ed.), pp. 203–226. Reprinted with permission from Routledge, London.

[1]Thanks are due to Tilak Abeysinghe, Manu Bhaskaran, Richard Doner, Gunter Dufey, Donald Low, Irene Ng, Pang Eng Fong, Kanwaljit Soin and others for their very helpful comments on earlier versions of this paper. Any remaining errors of fact or interpretation are mine alone.

[2]My own early contributions to this literature include: Pang Eng Fong and Linda Lim, 'Rapid Growth and Relative Price Stability in a Small Open Economy: The Experience of Singapore', in Vittorio Corbo, Anne O. Kreuger and Fernando Ossa (eds), *Export-Oriented Development Strategies: The Success of Five Newly Industrializing Countries*, Westview Press, Boulder, CO, 1985, 79–110; Linda Lim, Pang Eng Fong and Ronald Findlay, 'Singapore', in Ronald Findlay and Stanley Wellisz (eds), *Five Small Open Economies*, Oxford University Press for the World Bank, New York, 1993, 93–137.

other developed as well as emerging economies that may seek to emulate Singapore as a 'model'.[3]

Given this focus, the chapter draws heavily on current public policy debates in Singapore and recent research by Singapore-based economists and other social scientists. A collective conclusion is that industrial policy, population policy, immigration policy, housing, health, social security, monetary and fiscal policy are all heavily interconnected and interdependent in a 'complex system', such that operating one policy lever has consequences (including unintended and undesirable consequences) for other policy arenas and the system as a whole. This reality limits both the replicability of the Singapore model in other economies, whether emerging or developed, and the policy options for Singapore as it struggles to emerge from its current development dilemmas.

THE 'MIRACLE' ECONOMY: FROM INDEPENDENCE TO MATURITY IN THE 20TH CENTURY

Singapore's transformation from colonial port-city to newly industrialized economy in the 20th century shared much with the experience of the other 'Asian Tigers' of the Republic of Korea (South Korea), Taiwan and Hong Kong, as noted in the voluminous scholarly literature of the time, the World Bank's 1993 study of *The East Asian Miracle*,[4] and continued policy reflections since, focused on lessons for other emerging economies.[5]

From a market perspective, these economies in the 1960s and 1970s developed through free trade by specializing in the export of labour-intensive manufactures based on comparative advantage (relative resource endowments). From a 'developmental state' perspective, they relied heavily on state-interventionist policies which used industrial policy of selective protection and subsidies to direct capital investment to particular sectors, and provided public investment in infrastructure and education to increase productivity. Industrialization was further facilitated by conducive macroeconomic policy (including fixed and undervalued exchange rates, and

[3]The Singapore 'model' has been praised and singled out for emulation (often for different reasons) by a wide range of noted economists, including Michael Porter, Robert Reich, Paul Romer, Joseph Stiglitz, Lester Thurow and many media columnists; some of these will be considered later in this chapter.

[4]World Bank, *The East Asian Miracle: Economic Growth and Public Policy*, Oxford University Press, 1993.

[5]See, for example, Dani Rodrik, 'Normalizing Industrial Policy', Commission on Growth and Development, Working Paper No. 3, The World Bank, 2008.

high domestic savings[6]) and authoritarian political regimes which ensured labour peace and 'affordability', and efficient, centralized policymaking with effective implementation.

Singapore resembled Hong Kong, but differed from South Korea and Taiwan, in continuing with the free trade and capital flows of the British colonial era, including openness to foreign direct investment (FDI, whereas both trade and FDI were only selectively 'free' in South Korea and Taiwan). It resembled South Korea and Taiwan, but differed from Hong Kong, in practising industrial policy.[7] Significantly, it also differed from all three other 'Tigers' in relying much more heavily on multinationals than local enterprises, and on imports of foreign labour and talent, in addition to tight state control of land and the domestic labour market.[8]

Political democratization in Taiwan in 1987 and South Korea in 1988 accelerated the shift in resource-based comparative advantage that both economies experienced, as now-permitted labour activism raised wages, currencies were allowed to float upward (but remained 'managed'), the influence of state industrial policy and enterprises moderated (but did not disappear), and local private enterprises rapidly expanded and globalized their operations. There were no similar political changes in Hong Kong and Singapore, but China's opening around 1980 facilitated the relocation of Hong Kong's labour-intensive manufacturing there, to be replaced by finance and other services.

In Singapore, manufacturing competitiveness was maintained through the 1980s and 1990s by state industrial policy that encouraged the substitution of capital for labour, and technological upgrading, even as foreign labour imports preserved some labour-intensive parts of the manufacturing value chain. Exchange rate management also helped, with Singapore running

---

[6]For a summary explanation of high East Asian savings, see, for example, Linda Y.C. Lim, 'Rebalancing in East Asia', in Stijn Claessens, Simon Evenett and Bernard Hoekman (eds), *Rebalancing the Global Economy, A Primer for Policymaking*, Center for Economic Policy-Making, London, 2010, 32–35.

[7]See, for example, Robert E. Wade, *Governing the Market: Economic Theory and the Role of Government in East Asian Industrialization*, Princeton University Press, 1990; Jung-en Woo, *Race to the Swift: State and Finance in Korean Industrialization*, Columbia University Press, 1991; Linda Y.C. Lim, 'Foreign Investment, the State and Industrial Policy in Singapore', in Howard Stein (ed.), *Asian Industrialization and Africa: Case Studies and Policy Alternatives to Structural Adjustment*, St Martin's Press, London and New York, 1995, 205–38.

[8]Lim, LYC (1983). Singapore's Success: The Myth of the Free Market Economy. *Asian Survey* 26, 756–64, summarises the role of the state in Singapore's early economic development.

globally unprecedented current account surpluses of around 25% of gross domestic product (GDP) every year for over 30 years in a row. This has maintained manufacturing at over 20% of GDP[9] — again unprecedented among high-income countries — largely by attracting huge amounts of FDI into particular targeted sectors ranging from petrochemicals in the 1960s to pharmaceuticals in the 2000s, with electronics in between. It has also maintained and even expanded the economic role of the state, with a proliferation of government-linked companies or GLCs (resulting from the partial privatization of state agencies and enterprises) and two of the world's leading sovereign wealth funds, GIC (Government of Singapore Investment Corporation) and Temasek.[10]

This state-driven development model succeeded in delivering high rates of GDP growth over nearly four decades, such that Singapore now ranks as one of the world's richest countries by per capita income.[11] It also ranks high globally in many private-sector comparative indices, such as for 'competitiveness',[12] 'economic freedom',[13] 'business environment',[14] 'science and mathematics education',[15] among others. However, the model is of limited relevance to other countries today, given recent changes in the dynamics of the world economy (and political economy), and peculiarities of the Singapore case itself.

When Singapore and the other Asian Tigers embarked on their export manufacturing development strategy, they were individually and collectively small players in a world market where there were few other open-economy

---

[9]Manufacturing was over 25% of GDP until the downturn following the 2008–09 global financial crisis.

[10]GIC's funds come from government surpluses, which include foreign exchange reserves accumulated from balance of payments surpluses, and other government cash surpluses. Temasek developed from a holding company for entities such as DBS (Development Bank of Singapore), Singapore Airlines and other GLCs, often referred to as TLCs (Temasek-linked companies).

[11]In 2010 Singapore had a per capita income of US$40,070 in nominal terms, and $55,790 in purchasing power terms, which ranked seventh in the world, according to the World Bank's *World Development Indicators* 2012, table 1.1, www.worldbank.org.

[12]Singapore perennially ranks second (to Switzerland) in the annual *Global Competitiveness Report* rankings of the World Economic Forum, most recently in 2012–13, www.weforum.org.

[13]Singapore perennially ranks second (to Hong Kong) in the Heritage Foundation's annual *Index of Economic Freedom*, most recently in 2013, www.heritage.org.

[14]Singapore ranked first in the World Bank and International Financial Corporation's *Doing Business 2013* report, www.doingbusiness.org.

[15]Singapore typically ranks among the top 10 countries in the OECD's Program for International Student Assessment, including in 2012, www.oecd.org/pisa.

competitors with the same market comparative advantage (relative labour intensity) and policies to develop sector-specific competitive advantage (investment incentives, industrial targeting, export promotion). Today, there are many more large emerging economies with similar market advantages (most notably the People's Republic of China), while the evolution of World Trade Organization (WTO) trade rules has limited international tolerance for 'export subsidies', 'trade-related investment measures', 'currency manipulation' and other 'beggar-my-neighbour' policies. Singapore gets away with continuing many of these policies because it is both relatively small, and very open in trade and capital flows; because its policies benefit multinationals, their home countries are unlikely to protest 'unfair competition'.

From the 1960s to the 1980s, Singapore and the other Asian Tigers also found ready access for their exports in the robustly growing and open USA, other developed Western and Japanese markets, at a time when those countries' companies were rapidly internationalizing their production networks amid global trade liberalization. Today, most rich countries face stagnant or slow-growing economies burdened with ageing populations and unsustainable fiscal burdens, making them less tolerant of imports from countries perceived as not observing 'a level playing field'. Following the global financial crisis of 2008–09, tightening financial regulations and reduced tolerance for 'tax havens' may also reduce the scope of offshore financial services and industrial investment incentives that countries like Singapore can offer international capital.[16] With political liberalization accompanying market economic reforms around the world since the 1990s, many emerging economies today also have limited tolerance for the type of state-heavy policies that propelled authoritarian Singapore's economic development.

BEHIND THE 'MIRACLE' IN THE 20TH CENTURY

Singapore's economic development benefited from many favourable 'initial conditions', including an excellent geographical position and deep-water port

[16]In the short term, regulatory tightening benefited Singapore's financial centre as tax-avoiding global capital fled there from Switzerland and other Western countries. The bulk of Singapore's private wealth management services are accounted for by Asian investors, so its 'strict bank-secrecy laws and a poor record on exchanging information' (*The Economist* 'Special Report on Offshore Finance', 16 February 2013, 14) may continue without detriment to this sector. A potentially more serious concern is the international effort to require that taxes on MNCs be assessed in the geographical location where particular activities occur, such that transfer pricing to shift income (e.g. attributable to intellectual property) to low-tax jurisdictions like Singapore is limited.

at the crossroads of intra-Asian and international maritime trade, good infrastructure and commercial institutions developed by the British colonial authorities, free trade and capital flows which facilitated its role as a regional entrepôt within South-East Asia, and an entrepreneurial, largely immigrant population engaged in trading networks with their neighbouring countries of origin.[17] Despite this, GDP growth was slow and unemployment high at independence in the mid-1960s, when the city of 1.5 million was already middle-income (with the second highest income in Asia after Japan). The beginnings of offshore sourcing in labour-intensive manufacturing by Western and Japanese corporations, and the experiences of Puerto Rico, Mexican border *maquiladoras*, and South Korean and Taiwanese export-processing zones, provided a model for industrialization and employment creation that was also adopted in the 1970s by some of Singapore's South-East Asian neighbours, especially Malaysia and the Philippines in the electronics industry.

As in these other economies, government policies and institutions in Singapore played an important role in attracting FDI in labour-intensive export manufacturing. The role in investment promotion of Singapore's lead development agency, the Economic Development Board (EDB), is well-known,[18] but perhaps less attention has been paid to the complementary roles of other government agencies and policies in facilitating rapid industrialization. The efficiency-enhancing role of infrastructure agencies — the Port of Singapore Authority, Changi Airport, Jurong Town Corporation (industrial estates), Public Utilities Board, Urban Redevelopment Authority, etc. — is obvious, but social policy has also played a less obvious role in increasing productivity and creating the conditions for successful growth.

Most notably, Singapore's Housing Development Board (HDB) has housed some 85% of the population since the 1980s, building and maintaining 'public' housing units which most residents own. The provision of affordable housing helped keep wages low, while the integration of industrial premises into residential housing estates provided an easily accessible supply of factory

[17]Singapore also had unfavourable initial conditions, such as lack of natural resources and domestic market, labour unrest and the withdrawal of British military services accounting for a third of GDP, which conditioned its choice of development strategy. See, for example, Richard F. Doner, Bryan Ritchie and Dan Slater, 'Systemic Vulnerability and the Origins of Developmental States: Northeast and Southeast Asia in Comparative Perspective', *International Organization* 59, 2005: 327–61.

[18]www.edb.gov.sg.

labour.[19] Investments in public health and education increased labour productivity and skills, while a vigorous family planning campaign encouraged low fertility and greatly increased female labour force participation. Social security was provided through a Central Provident Fund (CPF) or 'forced savings' scheme under which employers and employees contributed mandated proportions (ranging from 20% to 50%) of employees' salaries to individual accounts managed by the CPF. Though meant to be savings for retirement, employees could and did use these funds to purchase housing — and later, also for medical and (limited) educational expenses, and equity investments in certain 'blue chip' GLCs.[20]

Such institutional innovations enabled the Singapore government to provide high-quality public and social goods and services without running public-sector deficits. It frequently articulated its abhorrence of 'subsidies' and a 'welfare state' even while extending the long arm of the state, directly and indirectly, into more and more sectors of the economy.[21] Most public-sector agencies earned surpluses through user charges, and the government budget itself was almost always in surplus, with revenues exceeding expenditures nearly every year. 'Singapore Inc.' became a frequently invoked moniker in the international business press, even before the privatizations of the 1990s and 2000s turned monopolistic state agencies into publicly listed corporations (e.g. Singapore Airlines, Neptune Orient Lines, Singapore Telecoms, Singapore Mass Rapid Transit, etc.), dominating the market capitalization of the Singapore Stock Exchange. State agencies and GLCs (in which the government holds controlling minority shares) essentially prosper by providing goods and services at profit-making prices to the private sector.[22]

---

[19] HDB was particularly successful in rebuilding communities dislocated by extensive urban redevelopment. Its public housing estates included community centres, residents' committees, child-care and recreational facilities, all of which helped to form new communities and promote peaceful social relations in a multi-racial and multi-religious society (though an alternative interpretation was that these social goods and the 'grassroots' organizations that managed them were designed to consolidate the ruling party's popularity and power).

[20] Linda Y.C. Lim, 'Social Welfare in Singapore', in Kemial Singh Sandhu and Paul Wheatley (eds), *Singapore: The Management of Success*, Oxford University Press, 1989, 171–97, describes the rationales (including ideological rationales) for Singapore's housing, education, health and social security policies from the 1960s to the 1980s.

[21] One example is the National Trades Union Congress (NTUC), nominally an autonomous labour movement co-operative, but controlled by the ruling party for decades, headed by PAP cabinet ministers or members of parliament and widely seen as an extension of the government. NTUC runs many enterprises including the island's largest supermarket chain, insurance, taxis and resorts.

[22] See, for example, Linda Low, *The Political Economy of a City-State: Government-Made Singapore*, Oxford University Press, 1998.

The government also influences wages and salaries in a number of ways. First, it controls the supply of labour through visa and immigration policies. Second, it influences the demand for labour through its investment promotion activities. Third, it is a major employer through the public sector and GLCs (influencing both demand and the supply price of labour). Fourth, it is the dominant participant in the tripartite (government, unions, employers) National Wages Council which comes up with annual wage increase guidelines for the private sector. Fifth, it controls the labour movement[23] and exerts considerable influence on the private business sector.[24]

The state's early ability to organize itself efficiently enabled it to 'get the basics right' with lightning speed and limited political backlash as it embarked on an 'extreme makeover' of the city. Being able quickly to deliver good infrastructure, low inflation, fiscal balance, political stability,[25] policy predictability and low corruption enabled it to outcompete cheaper neighbours to become the preferred regional headquarters of multinationals. This, then, developed agglomeration and other first-comer advantages that became part of its competitive advantage in later years.

The fact that Singapore has been politically a 'one-party state' for three generations has much to do with the social and institutional underpinnings of its economic success in the 20th century. Unchallenged political authority enabled the ruling People's Action Party (PAP) to undertake many developmental policies that in more pluralistic democracies might have encountered opposition, including from vested interests, and threatened a loss of power. Potentially contentious policies included labour controls, compulsory land acquisition and allocation, and the 'crowding out' of the local private sector in both product and factor markets by multinationals and the state sector (which has not happened in the other Asian Tiger economies). The country

[23]See footnote 21. Strikes are also illegal throughout the economy; in 2012, the 'first strike in 25 years' resulted in striking bus drivers from the People's Republic of China being arrested, prosecuted, jailed and deported; one subsequently complained of 'lack of freedom' and workers' rights in Singapore, and the unfriendliness of Singaporeans, and claimed that some Bangladeshi workers were paid so little that they went without food, sg.news.yahoo.com/former-smrt-bus-driver-why-we-went-on-strike-part-ii-083616951.html. However, earlier, control of the labour movement facilitated adjustments such as redundancies, as argued in Yuen Chi Ching and Lim Ghee Soon, 'Globalization, Labour Market Deregulation and Trade Unions in Singapore', in Chris Rowley and John Benson (eds), *Globalization and Labour in the Asia-Pacific*, Frank Cass, London, 2000, 154–73.

[24]For example, membership of the Singapore Business Federation is compulsory for all businesses in Singapore, and it is often headed by former civil servants (including currently).

[25]This was achieved in part through vigorous suppression of a left-wing labour movement and political opposition.

also ranks far below its per capita income rank in comparative rankings which include variables such as 'political freedom', 'human development' and 'well-being'.[26]

AFTER THE 'MIRACLE': DEVELOPMENTAL CHALLENGES OF THE 21ST CENTURY

Singapore's development model of the 20th century might not be replicable in other emerging economies because they do not face the same favourable initial conditions that Singapore and other Asian Tigers enjoyed then, and/or they do not possess the political will or institutional capacity necessary to enact and implement the comprehensive social as well as economic policies that Singapore could undertake in the 20th century. Another reason why countries might not follow the Singapore model is that 21st-century internal and international developments have revealed the model's own shortcomings in continuing to deliver positive results for its population.

The most critical shortcoming of Singapore's growth model is its sustainability — or lack thereof. Almost from the beginning, studies have shown that GDP growth in most periods was achieved mainly through increasing the quantum of inputs — of capital, labour, even land[27] — rather than their productivity.[28] This strategy may have been efficient in developing a middle-income economy with underutilized resources (e.g. the

[26]For example, Canada's Fraser Institute ranks Singapore as 'partly free' (4 out of 7, where 1 is most free) in terms of political and civil liberties, www.fraserinstitute.org; the United Nations Human Development Index ranks it far lower in HDI than in per capita income (though granting a major jump since 2011 based on political liberalization), www.hdr.undp.org. Charles I. Jones and Peter J. Klenow, 'Beyond GDP? Welfare Across Countries and Time', National Bureau of Economic Research (NBER) Working Paper No. 16352, September 2010, find that Singapore has the greatest (negative) gap between per capita GDP and well-being of any of the 134 countries studied, with a welfare score of less than half that of Hong Kong despite a slightly higher per capita GDP.

[27]Singapore has thus far reclaimed about 20% of its land from the sea, a process that is slowing due to the technical difficulties of reclaiming land from deeper waters, and the difficulty of obtaining reclamation materials (sand, rocks, earth) from neighbouring countries, most of which have now banned the export of such materials.

[28]See, for example, Lee, TY (1985). Growth without Productivity: Singapore Manufacturing in the 1970s. *Journal of Development Economics*, 19, 25–38; Alwyn Young, A Tale of Two Cities: Factor Accumulation and Technical Change in Hong Kong and Singapore, in O.J. Blanchard and S. Fischer (eds), *NBER Macroeconomics Annual 1992*, MIT Press, 1992, 13–54; Young, A (1995). The Tyranny of Numbers: Confronting the Statistical Realities of the East Asian Growth Experience. *Quarterly Journal of Economics*, 110, 641–80; Paul Krugman, The Myth of Asia's Miracle, *Foreign Affairs 73/6*, 1994: 62–79; Koji Nomura and Tomomichi Amano, Labor Productivity and Quality Change in Singapore: Achievements in 1974–2011 and Prospects for the Next Two Decades, KEO Discussion Paper No. 129, September 2012, Keio Economic Observatory, Keio University.

high unemployment of the 1960s), and the ability to 'borrow' internationally (e.g. by participating in multinational networks) to 'catch up' to the global technological frontier. It becomes much more difficult in a high-income (and thus high-cost) economy with fully employed resources now at the global technological frontier, but lacking the domestic market size, production scale and indigenous entrepreneurs to innovate for global markets.

The logic of international economics is that resource-based comparative advantage shifts, sometimes rapidly, such that activities that are competitive in one location at one period of time eventually become uncompetitive as domestic and international factor markets change. Given its small size and extreme openness to and dependence on world markets (with exports, including re-exports, accounting for over 200% of GDP), Singapore would be particularly vulnerable to shifts in comparative advantage. Indeed, barely half a dozen years after the launch of its labour-intensive export manufacturing strategy in the late 1960s, the country reached full employment and began importing foreign labour (initially from Malaysia) as a means of delaying the loss of comparative advantage in labour-intensive manufacturing. A few years later (1979–82), the government switched course, launching what it called a 'second industrial revolution' with a 'high-wage policy' aimed at increasing labour productivity and upgrading technology through capital-labour substitution. Ever since, variable labour importation has been an important policy tool in creating competitiveness and in counter-cyclical management (with 'tightening' taking place in times of weak GDP growth and slack labour market demand, to limit domestic unemployment, and 'easing' taking place when demand was strong, to reduce inflationary pressures). This has arguably delayed the 'economic restructuring' to higher productivity levels that the government itself has called for more than once a decade since the 1970s.[29]

[29]See, for example, Pang Eng Fong and Linda Lim, 'Singapore's Foreign Workers: Are They Worth the Costs?' *Asian Wall Street Journal*, 4 August 1981; Pang, EF and Lim, LYC (1982). Foreign Labour and Economic Development in Singapore. *International Migration Review*, 16, 548–76; Pang Eng Fong and Linda Lim, 'Wage Policy in Singapore', in *Government Wage Policy Formulation in Less-Developed Countries: Seven Country Studies*, International Labour Office, Geneva, 1989, 75–101. For a more recent study, see Hui, WT and Hasmi, AR (2007). Foreign Labour and Economic Growth: Policy Options for Singapore, *Singapore Economic Review* 52, 53–72. For a gender perspective, see Linda Y.C. Lim, 'Beyond Gender: The Impact of Age, Ethnicity, Nationality and Economic Growth on Women in the Singapore Economy', unpublished manuscript presented at the 25th anniversary of the Association for Women in Action and Research (AWARE) at the National University of Singapore, 5 March 2011, revised 13 July 2011.

In seeking to manage and facilitate inevitable shifts in comparative advantage, the modus operandi of Singapore state development agencies, led by the EDB, has been to pick particular 'new' sectors they think are promising, then attract foreign companies in these sectors to Singapore by showering them with investment incentives (tax breaks, R&d and training subsidies, employment subsidies, cheap land, special buildings). Since these are capital- and skill-intensive industries, offering capital subsidies and the freedom to hire specialized employees from around the world are effective inducements. Singapore has also worked on constantly improving its competitive advantages of location, infrastructure, logistics, legal, regulatory and tax regimes, and the general business environment — all of which contribute to its popularity as a global financial centre and regional headquarters for multinationals. However, these efforts have not been entirely successful,[30] given the high capital cost and risks of picking new industries at the uncertain technological frontier, Singapore's chronic lack of the scale required to develop robust, long-lived clusters, and the rising local costs inevitably associated with the simultaneous development of many different sectors competing for scarce land, labour and talent resources, and with the privatization (and hence profit-seeking higher prices) of some previously publicly provided goods and services.

The turn of the 21st century saw Singapore's economy suffer in quick succession from several external shocks: the late 1990s Asian Financial Crisis which hurt financial services, the early 2000s crash of the dotcom bubble which hurt high-tech and IT, and the SARS near-epidemic which temporarily devastated tourism and hospitality. An Economic Review Committee in 2003[31] affirmed the continued importance of manufacturing, particularly

---

[30]The Singapore government claims that it is quick to stop supporting sectors that fail to perform, for example, scaling back on support for life sciences (biomedical) research when this cluster was (predictably) slow to deliver on commercial results, and when some of the 'international research stars' recruited from abroad to lead the effort left the country. However such a trial-and-error method of choosing sectors to subsidize has a high opportunity cost. In my field research in Singapore in 2012 and 2013 I came across partially or completely empty new buildings in dedicated technology research parks, and what other tenants told me were 'white elephant' operations soon to leave the premises that were occupied. Both local and foreign technology start-ups I visited, as well as larger multinationals with hundreds of employees, said that as many as 85% of their employees were foreigners, including recent Asian scholarship graduates from Singapore universities, who could obtain permanent residence (PR) status 'in one month', before foreign labour visa rules were tightened beginning in 2011.

[31]www.mti.gov.sg/ResearchRoom/Documents/app.mti.gov.sg/data/pages/507/doc/1%20 ERC_Main_Committee.

the 'four key clusters' of electronics, chemicals, biomedical sciences and engineering, as well as the development of educational, medical, financial and tourist services, and 'creative industries', for a growing Asian middle class. Following the global financial crisis of 2008-09, an Economic Strategies Committee in 2010[32] expanded these activities to include 'green urban solutions' and developing Singapore as a global 'hub' and 'node' for financial and business services, R&d, consumer research, 'commercialization and innovation', and 'complex manufacturing and manufacturing-related services', on top of established industries like trading, logistics and ICT, though the most visible addition to the economy was the opening of two major casinos (called 'integrated resorts').

Despite (or perhaps because of) this proliferation of diversified new sectors, GDP growth declined, volatility increased (particularly in the highly capital-intensive and 'lumpy' pharmaceuticals sector), and productivity growth slowed as GDP growth was achieved largely by input-intensive means (increasing capital and labour). While the government was mainly concerned with maintaining GDP growth, economists (and even some ruling party 'backbencher' MPs) were already questioning the quality of growth and distribution of its benefits, noting: 1. increased volatility (and its negative impact on domestic investment, employment and growth);[33] 2. the very low ratio of wages and of domestic consumption (about 35% each) in GDP and concomitantly high savings (45%) occurring disproportionately in the highly profitable multinational and state corporate sectors;[34] 3. stagnation in median incomes and decline in incomes of the bottom decile; 4. worsening income inequality with one of the highest Gini coefficients among rich countries (0.478 before and 0.459 after government taxes and

---

[32] www.mti.gov.sg/ResearchRoom/Documents/app.mti.gov.sg/data/pages/885/doc/ESC %20Full%20Report.pdf.

[33] Choy Keen Meng, 'Singapore's Changing Economic Model', in Terence Cheong (ed.), *Management of Success: Singapore Revisited*, Institute of Southeast Asian Studies, Singapore, 2010, 123–38. See also various essays in Choy Keen Meng, *Studies on the Singapore Economy*, World Scientific Publishing, Singapore, 2012.

[34] Abeysinghe, T and Meng, CK (2004). The Aggregate Consumption Puzzle in Singapore. *Journal of Asian Economics*, 15, 563–78; Linda Y.C. Lim and Lee Soo Ann, 'Globalizing State, Disappearing Nation: The Impact of Foreign Participation in the Singapore Economy', in Terence Chong (ed.), *Management of Success: Singapore Revisited*, Institute for Southeast Asian Studies, Singapore, 2010, 139–58; Hoon Hian Teck (Singapore Management University, Economics), 'The Future of Wages in Singapore', *The Straits Times*, 5 February 2013.

transfers)[35] and declining social mobility;[36] 5. persistent consumer price and asset inflation, particularly of land and housing;[37] 6. Singapore's relatively poor performance in newly popular measurements of 'well-being' that include non-income metrics such as working hours, consumption, inequality and life expectancy;[38] and 7. environmentalists added concerns over high energy consumption, the loss of green and wild spaces, and the intensifying negative externalities of congestion, pollution and loss of cultural heritage sites in what was already the most densely populated country in the world (7,253 people per sq. km in 2010).[39]

---

[35]Department of Statistics, Singapore, cited in Goh Chin Lian, 'Gap Widens but Workfare Helps', *The Straits Times*, 21 February 2013; and Fiona Chan, 'Reducing Inequality', *The Straits Times*, 9 March 2013; this represented a worsening since 2000 (0.430) and 2010 (0.452), during which time the ratio of the average income of the top quintile of employed households to that of the bottom quintile also increased, from 10.1 to 12.9. For discussions of the causes of high and rising inequality, see Donald Low, 'The Four Myths of Inequality in Singapore', 26 April 2011, sites.google.com/site/reflection singapore/Downhome/Topic1/thefourmythsofinequalityinsingapore; Manu Bhaskaran, Ho Seng Chee, Donald Low, Tan Kim Song, Sudhir Vadaketh and Yeoh Lam Keong, 'Inequality and the Need for a New Social Compact', in Kang Soon Hock and Leong Chan-Hoong (eds), *Singapore Perspectives 2012 Singapore Inclusive: Bridging Divides,* World Scientific Publishing, Singapore, 2013, 125–78, and other chapters in this volume from the Institute of Policy Studies, Lee Kuan Yew School of Public Policy, National University of Singapore; Hui, WT (2013). Economic Growth and Inequality in Singapore: The Case for a Minimum Wage. *International Labour Review* 152, 107–23; Linda Y.C. Lim, 'Beyond Gender'. For an early analysis, see Pang, EF (1975). Growth, Inequality and Race in Singapore. *International Labour Review*, 25, 508–23.

[36]Ng, IYH (2013). The Political Economy of Intergenerational Income Mobility in Singapore. *International Journal of Social Welfare*, 22, 207–18; Irene Y.H. Ng, 'Education and Intergenerational Mobility in Singapore', *Educational Review* (forthcoming, posted online April 2013).

[37]Abeysinghe, T and J Gu (2011). Lifetime Income and Housing Affordability in Singapore. *Urban Studies*, 48, 1875–91.

[38]Jones and Klenow, 'Beyond GDP?' 'In 2010 full-time resident male workers worked 50.7 hours a week ... sales and service workers worked 52.5 hours (54.2 hours for those aged 50–59) and plant and machine operators 52.1 hours (54.7 hours for those aged 50–59)', Singapore labour force data cited in Linda Y.C. Lim, 'Beyond Gender'.

[39]For one of many examples, see Geh Min, 'Singapore: Home or Hotel?' *The Straits Times*, 4 March 2013, and an earlier commentary by Linda Lim and Geh Min, 'When Less is More', *The Straits Times*, 30 June 2008. See also www.bukitbrown.org, www.bukitbrown.com and other sites on the government's plan to demolish part of Singapore's oldest cemetery, a green area, to make way for roads, mass rapid transit, and new housing for an expanded population, similar to the planned demolition of an historic downtown school complex for condominium development, www.facebook.com/saveoldschool.

Several factors appear to have contributed to the real or perceived decline in Singaporeans' well-being, even as the country climbed the charts of the richest nations in the world, ranking first in the proportion of households with over US$1 million in assets under management (15.5%).[40] First, pushing growth in many different new high-tech, high-skill sectors divided Singapore's already limited talent pool, preventing the development of critical mass in any given industry, while requiring heavy dependence on specialized foreign talent, given the desire to 'develop new capabilities in emerging technologies such as micro-electromechanical systems, nanotechnology and photonics'.[41] Second, the vast expansion in numbers of foreign workers admitted in a very short space of time[42] led to inevitable national clustering in workplaces and residences, alleged discriminatory hiring practices, a perceived 'glass ceiling' for Singaporean professionals, and extreme congestion in transportation and housing scarcity as the government's physical planning fell behind the numbers it admitted. Third, a massive influx of low-skilled foreign workers (in construction, domestic service, cleaning and other services), and of white-collar clerical and retail workers, depressed wage growth among low- to middle-income Singaporeans, while a similar influx of highly skilled 'global talent' attracted with above-world-market salaries, and ultra-wealthy tax haven-seeking capital owners/investors[43] contributed

[40]Boston Consulting Group, 2010, reported in *Bloomberg News*, 4 April 2012 with this caveat: 'Singapore is ending a program that allowed wealthy foreigners to "fast track" their permanent residency if they kept at least S$10 million in assets in the country for five years. The moves are aimed at slowing the rapid surge in property prices, which have been driven in part by wealthy investors and which have rankled Singaporeans.'

[41]Economic Review Committee, 2003. For example, the expansion of financial services diverted local university students from engineering to business and finance, resulting in university engineering departments recruiting students from China and other countries, who then fulfilled their scholarship bonds by working for the required number of years in Singapore's semiconductor, petrochemical and other industries. Many of these subsequently left Singapore for China or other countries (such as the USA, Canada and Australia).

[42]About two thirds of jobs created in Singapore between 2006 and 2011 went to foreigners, or well over 100,000 per year; together with their dependents, it is likely that the foreign population grew by nearly 1 million (or 25% of Singapore's total population) in just six years. The increase slowed to 32,200 in 2012 (excluding construction and domestic service workers), Amelia Tan, 'Inflow of Foreign Workers Slows Down', *The Straits Times*, 16 March 2013. In 2010, the foreign-born accounted for 45% of the population and 38% of the total labour force.

[43]The government and media have been particularly proud that Brazilian Facebook co-founder Eduardo Saverin and American investor Jim Rogers both left the USA to take up residence (instantly granted) in Singapore.

to visibly widening income and wealth disparities in the already densely packed island city-state.[44]

Fourth, at the same time, the ruling party stuck to its longstanding aversion to social (but not corporate) subsidies, raising a consumption tax while maintaining low income tax rates, and privatising what were previously public goods like health care, housing, transportation and utilities. With only a few large, now profit-seeking, players in what might be considered 'natural monopoly' sectors, the predictable result was rising user charges and oligopolistic rents.[45] The impact on social welfare was particularly noticeable in health care.[46] In housing, a change around 2000 in the goal of public housing policy from 'affordability' to 'asset enhancement' penalized new buyers, resulting in large and long mortgage burdens for young couples whose starting professional salaries have increased only fractionally relative to the cost of public as well as private housing over the past decade. 'The government itself has acknowledged that the emerging homelessness problem is due in part to some who gambled on asset appreciation and lost.'[47] Not surprisingly, Singaporeans complain that they are 'paying more and more for less and less' (including residential housing space in HDB flats), while living costs (pushed up in part by foreign demand) escalate much

[44]A slew of recent articles in the international press have highlighted Singapore's attractiveness to ultra-wealthy global elites. See, for example, Shibani Mahtani, 'Singapore Takes a Gamble on Glitz', *Wall Street Journal*, 3 October 2012, and 'Singapore: Wealth over the Edge', *WSJ Money*, Spring 2013. A recent report ranks Singapore third (behind London and New York) among cities 'important to high net-worth individuals', predicting that it will outrank New York in 10 years with property continuing 'to feature strongly in the investment portfolios of the rich', Cheryl Ong, 'Singapore "Set to be No. 2 Wealth Centre in the World"', *The Straits Times*, 12 March 2013.

[45]At one time minimum rentals were set for hawker stalls in food centres, benefiting landlords at the expense of small entrepreneurs and relatively low-income consumers. However, telecoms charges did fall with privatization and increased competition.

[46]Singapore lacks a comprehensive health insurance programme, such that a high proportion of citizens' medical costs are borne out of pocket. Public health services have been squeezed by the deliberate expansion of the high-earning private medical sector, an 'exportable service' catering disproportionately to wealthy foreigners, and overwhelmed by the sudden large increase in population, such that waiting times as well as service quality are perceived to have declined, even before population ageing has increased demand.

[47]Irene Y.H. Ng, 'Can we Fix Inequality?' 23 September 2010, www.salt.org.sg. It is not known how many of the growing numbers of homeless and poor are the victims of 'problem gambling' following the opening of the casinos, which have delivered high profits to their foreign owners (Las Vegas Sands of the USA and Genting of Malaysia) and large tax revenues to the government, including from the entrance fee imposed on Singaporeans (but not on foreigners) in an effort to discourage their visits.

more rapidly than average wages (held down by foreign supply, and the related low productivity gains), resulting in a sense of 'downward mobility'[48] in what residents are constantly reminded is one of the world's richest countries.

That the situation had become politically and socially, if not economically and environmentally, unsustainable, was revealed by two elections in 2011. In the May general election, the PAP which had ruled since the 1960s with only one or two token opposition parliamentarians, saw its share of the popular vote drop to 60% (the lowest since independence), while its share of parliamentary seats dropped from 98% to 93%.[49] In the four-way contest for the elected presidency in August, the government's candidate won with 35% of the vote, or a 0.3% margin. These unprecedented results were seen by the ruling party as a loss of popularity; the prime minister apologized to the population, the cabinet was reshuffled with some of the most unpopular ministers replaced, and many new policies were hurriedly announced, particularly to increase the availability of public housing and transportation. Also politically significant was the decision to reduce cabinet ministers' salaries — then and still today the highest in the world.[50] Since then, two by-elections were also won by the main opposition Workers' Party, most recently in January 2013 with a 55% majority against the PAP candidate.

Right after this last by-election loss, the government released a White Paper on Population Policy,[51] which met with overwhelming public opposition, including some from ruling party backbenchers (reflecting the

[48]Tan Ern Ser (National University of Singapore, Sociology), quoted in Joyce Hooi, 'Singapore's Emigration Conundrum', *Business Times*, 6 October 2012.

[49]Decades of gerrymandering explain the large discrepancy between the popular vote and parliamentary representation. Besides some genuine appreciation for the government's achievements, tight media control, pre-election distributions (popularly known as 'goodies'), a limited nine-day election campaign, and lingering fears from the past persecution of opposition politicians, explain what in other countries would be considered a respectable popular vote share for the government.

[50]No. 1-ranked Singapore Prime Minister Lee Hsien Loong's annual salary of US$2.85 million in 2011 was five times that of No. 2-ranked Donald Tsang of Hong Kong, seven times that of No. 5 President Barack Obama of the USA, and 40 times that of average per capita GDP in Singapore (as calculated by *The Economist*, 5 July 2010). As part of the post-2011 salary revision, political leaders' and senior civil servants' annual bonuses are now linked to unemployment and median and bottom quintile wage increases, as well as to GDP growth which previously was the sole metric.

[51]*A Sustainable Population for a Dynamic Singapore*, www.population.sg.

views of their electoral constituents).[52] It laid out plans for what Singapore might be in 2030, with a 6.9 million population (vs. 5.3 million currently), of whom 45% would be immigrants or temporary foreign workers (with 15,000 to 25,000 new permanent residents a year, down from 79,000 in 2008[53] and on top of a current stock of 500,000 permanent residents), required because native Singaporeans' abnormally low total fertility rate of 1.2 children per woman and rapidly ageing population would make it otherwise impossible to achieve 3%–5% GDP growth (high for a developed economy). The government later acknowledged that a lower GDP growth rate was likely, given the maturity of the economy, that it would focus on increasing productivity and reducing (but not eliminating) reliance on foreign labour, and that the 6.9 million figure was not a target, but a 'planning parameter' for infrastructure purposes, and even 'a worst-case scenario'. It also enacted yet more pro-natalist policies to encourage Singaporeans to have more children, including shorter waits for HDB housing for young couples, and cash bonuses for each baby, though such policies have been around for 30 years without having much impact (though one could argue that without them, the birth rate might be even lower).[54]

Many of Singapore's problems today are shared by other high-income developed economies, especially by their dense urban areas. These include low birth rates, rising income and wealth inequality, reduced social mobility, traffic congestion, expensive housing and reliance on an immigrant labour force. The difference in Singapore is mainly one of degree — its birth rates are lower, income and wealth inequality greater, housing more expensive,[55] and reliance on foreign labour most extreme. Because its economy is also

[52]See, for example, Donald Low, Yeoh Lam Keong, Tan Kim Song and Manu Bhaskaran, 'Economic Myths in the Great Population Debate', www.ipscommons.sg; Linda Lim, 'How Land and People Fit in Singapore's Economy', 21 February 2013, www.sg.news.yahoo.com; and numerous traditional media articles and blog posts from January to March 2013. On 17 February 2013, a protest rally against the White Paper attracted 4,000 people at Hong Lim Green; the gathering was the 'largest in 40 years', given strict limitations on freedom of assembly.

[53]For comparison, note that the much larger USA grants only 65,000 H1-B visas a year for highly skilled foreigners, though this number has been as high as 180,000 in the past and is expected to be raised in the near future.

[54]For more on this subject, see Youyenn Teo, *Neoliberal Morality in Singapore: How Family Policies make State and Society*, Routledge, London, 2011, and the White Paper on Population Policy (footnote 51).

[55]See, for example, www.economist.com/houseprices for international comparisons by various metrics.

more state driven (e.g. with the government housing 85% of the population, admitting the large numbers of foreign workers and actively pursuing industrial policy), public policy must explain some of the differential, though the ultimate constraint may simply be the country's extreme land shortage.

The government's growth and investment promotion policies, and their requirement for large inputs of foreign labour and talent, probably have the greatest impact on the economy, since they distort the allocation of resources by influencing relative prices. In terms of sectoral targeting, the White Paper mentioned the government's intention to grow the following 'new industries': biomedical, digital media, petrochemicals, advanced electronics, green energy, in addition to existing sectors of logistics, fashion, food, marine and environmental engineering. Not mentioned were the already large established sectors of trade, finance and tourism/hospitality, other sectors identified (above) by the Economic Review Committee (2003) and Economic Strategies Committee (2010), or the new sectors of 'space industries' and 'Big Data' analytics and storage, announced after the release of the White Paper (2013). All these sectors require investment incentives or corporate subsidies (because they would not be market competitive otherwise); all would compete with each other for scarce local resources including land and skills, pushing those costs up; all would require heavy recruitment of foreigners (with the resultant negative externalities of congestion, asset inflation and social unease); while simultaneous development of multiple sectors would undermine the likelihood that each would be able to reach the critical size and scale required for global market competitiveness. Since these sectors are selected for being capital- and skill-intensive, their returns would accrue disproportionately to high-income owners of capital and skills (mostly foreigners), thus worsening income inequality. Large inflows of capital would either cause currency appreciation that would reduce the competitiveness of more labour-intensive export sectors (such as tourism) or aggravate (already rising) domestic inflation (if the currency were not allowed to appreciate). Some sectors would add to Singapore's already high energy consumption and consume scarce land, with negative consequences for environmental sustainability and 'spatial justice'.

The impact of these industrial and labour policies on birth rates probably works through the housing market. Young dual-income couples needing both to work longer and save more to purchase housing[56] delays the age of marriage, while the need to service housing loans, the high costs of child care,

[56]Tilak Abeysinghe (National University of Singapore, Economics), research reported in 'Move Beyond Economics to Boost Fertility', *The Straits Times*, 25 January 2013.

limited living space (especially for those who take in renters to help pay for their mortgages), and expensive and inconvenient transportation, discourage childbearing. This is true also in other cities around the world. To the extent that children are an 'inferior good' (for whom demand falls as income rises) in a materialist consumerist society and among the highly educated, this trend should continue in Singapore as the proportion of university-educated Singaporeans rises from the current 27% to the targeted 40% of the age cohort, and population density increases. Some scholars also argue that corporate career pressures, long working hours and a highly stressful school system are responsible for young Singaporeans' low marriage and fertility rates.[57] High housing prices, the use of CPF retirement savings to pay for them, and the erosion of CPF savings given the low interest rate they earn relative to inflation, also causes many Singaporeans to fear that they will be unable to support themselves in retirement, with a recent survey revealing that 56% of 2,000 respondents would like to emigrate.[58] Complicating the situation, several GLCs are now dominant players in private property development of high-end commercial and residential properties, with their REITs (Real Estate Investment Trusts) profiting handsomely from soaring prices and rentals.[59]

In their criticisms of the White Paper and its vision of Singapore in 2030, Singaporeans have generally called for slower GDP growth with better distribution, including a higher share of the proceeds of growth for Singaporeans (vs. foreign workers and employers) and the low-income; a recent poll by the government's 'feedback unit' found that nearly nine in ten

---

[57]See, for example, reports on The Population Conundrum Roundtable on Singapore's Demographic Challenges, Institute of Policy Studies, Singapore, 3 May 2012, www.spp.nus.edu.sg, especially remarks by Pauline Straughan (National University of Singapore, Sociology).

[58]Mindshare survey reported in Joyce Hooi, 'Singapore's Emigration Conundrum', *Business Times*, 6 October 2012. Some 65% of respondents did not believe that they would be able to retire comfortably in Singapore, 73% thought that public housing prices are 'getting out of hand', 75% agreed that 'I should not be spending my entire working life paying off my housing loan', 72% said they 'could not afford to get sick due to high medical costs', and 69% said that 'there are too many foreign workers taking up job opportunities in our society today'. According to the World Bank, there are 300,000 Singaporeans living and working abroad (about 9% of the total native population, although government figures put the number at 200,000 or 6%, a third of whom left in the last 10 years), with Malaysia the top destination, followed by Australia, the UK and USA (all with lower per capita incomes than Singapore).

[59]GLCs in the property development and REIT business include Capital Land, Mapletree, Keppel (core business: shipbuilding and marine services), and Singapore Press Holdings (core business: media).

Singaporeans support measures to tighten the inflow of foreign workers.[60] The government itself proposes higher productivity growth as a means to assuring higher incomes, but it appears to assume continued dependence on low-skilled foreign workers and labour-intensive methods in sectors such as construction, food and beverages, and domestic service, even though this itself discourages investments in productivity improvements, technological and institutional innovations,[61] and sociological transformations that are commonplace in other rich countries, and discourages Singaporeans from entering these occupations because they remain low-wage, low-status and populated by low-skilled foreigners. Instead the government's approach, as revealed in its 2013 Budget, for example, is a two-pronged one: lifting more Singaporeans into what are called PMET (Professional Management Executive and Technical) jobs that pay higher wages (rather than allowing wages for non-PMET jobs to rise), and providing more social subsidies to low-income households (rather than enabling them to earn higher wages through the market), in direct contradiction of its longstanding opposition to income transfers because they make people 'lazy'. In short, its plan appears to be to continue with resource allocation distortions and then to compensate those who lose by such distortions (such as the wage repressing effects of low-wage foreign labour imports) through fiscal handouts (known locally as 'giveaways').[62]

Apart from local objections, and the questionable wisdom of 'growing new sectors' which mainly provide jobs for foreigners and can only survive by hiring them, there is concern that foreign workers may not be available in the medium to long term. As the gap between employment and living standards in Singapore and migrant source countries like China, India, Malaysia and the Philippines narrows, and as the multinationals that employ these workers increasingly move to their home locations because they have larger labour and talent pools, as well as lower costs and larger, more rapidly growing markets, it may become harder for Singapore to attract such workers, while those who do come may not stay permanently since they have family in their home countries and eventually better economic opportunities there for

[60] Tessa Wong, '"Most Support Curbs" on Foreigner Inflow', *The Straits Times*, 19 March 2013.

[61] 'Has the Ideas Machine Broken Down?' *The Economist*, 12 January 2013, reviews work by Paul Romer and others that suggests that the availability of abundant cheap labour not only discourages investment in productivity but also reduces innovation and increases income inequality.

[62] The recent appearance of credit and training programmes for small-scale entrepreneurs like hawkers is a potentially hopeful sign of a different philosophy emerging.

themselves and their children. It is possible, even likely, that 'new industries' heavily subsidized by the Singapore state may eventually move to the larger origin countries of their migrant employees. Thus the strategy of attracting investment by providing capital subsidies and ease of hiring foreign labour and talent is probably not sustainable. Already multinationals say that inflation, rising costs and expensive property prices, as well as shortages of staff, are making Singapore a less attractive location for investment.[63] Local businesses, which tend to be more labour intensive, are also challenged by rising costs and labour shortages;[64] the government has instituted a variety of assistance schemes to help them upgrade, and will cover wage increases for most of their workers over the next three years.[65] Like multinationals, some will have to relocate as businesses have always done with shifting comparative advantage.[66]

These 21st-century developments suggest that the past success of Singapore's economic model is not sustainable. Even the government argues in support of its policies that the country has 'no choice' but to import large numbers of foreigners, and does not have a strategy for what it can and should do after 2030, since then there will be even more rapidly diminishing returns to the policy of adding yet more capital and labour to the already overcrowded island.[67] Singapore's accumulation of excess foreign reserves and its early establishment of sovereign wealth funds to manage government surpluses and invest them abroad was originally designed to provide the country with a financial cushion against external shocks and domestic downturns. It appears now that foreign reserves will be further increased 'to strengthen our social safety nets, and to cope with volatility

---

[63]Survey by *The Economist* Corporate Network, reported by Yasmine Yahya in 'S'pore Losing Shine Among MNCs: Poll', *Business Times*, 8 January 2013. In February, eight international chambers of commerce signed a letter to the government expressing their concerns with the tightening of employment visas for foreigners.

[64]Aaron Low, 'Bosses Fear Further Curbs on Foreign Manpower', *The Straits Times*, 31 January 2013.

[65]Note that local SMEs, like MNCs, have long received a variety of government subsidies, mostly for upgrading and retraining; however, because they are less capital-intensive than MNCs and less likely to be in the targeted high-tech and 'new industries' which receive the bulk of 'incentives', they receive fewer subsidies each.

[66]Besides productivity growth, moderating property prices, rents and inflation from a slower-growing population, and slower appreciation of the Singapore dollar with lower inward FDI, could partly compensate for rising labour costs. Linda Lim, 'Can Slower Growth Lead to a Stronger Nation?' *The Straits Times*, 22 February 2013.

[67]In addition to replacing 20-storey buildings with 50-storey ones, the government is also promoting joint development of the Iskandar project in the neighbouring Malaysian state of Johor, and exploring more ways for Singaporeans to live and work underground.

and uncertainty',[68] since the government continues to be averse to raising revenues through taxes (which range from 12% to 17% of GDP, compared with the 34% Organisation for Economic Co-operation and Development (OECD) average).[69]

LESSONS FOR EMERGING ECONOMIES

Many lessons have been, and continue to be, drawn from Singapore's economic development experience for other emerging economies; they range from the general[70] to the specific.[71] There is certainly much to admire and emulate from public policy in Singapore. Two recent books by former Singaporean civil servants engaged in policymaking are particularly recommended. *Dynamics of the Singapore Success Story: Insights by Ngiam Tong Dow* outlines the political and institutional, educational and social, financial and banking 'pillars' of Singapore's building of a knowledge-based economy, and also considers the implications of its experience for China.[72] The chapters in *Behavioural Economics and Policy Design: Examples from Singapore* show how behavioural economics informs policies such as traffic management, environmental management, electricity retail, discretionary transfers, health and retirement policy, and provide useful lessons for developed countries as well.[73]

---

[68]Prime Minister Lee Hsien Loong at the first Singapore Summit, quoted in Teh Shi Ning, 'S'pore to Build up its Foreign Reserves Shield', *Business Times*, 22 September 2012.

[69]Chia Ngee Choon (National University of Singapore, Economics), 'How Progressive is the New Tax Structure?' *The Straits Times*, 28 February 2013, also notes that overall social spending is 'just above a third of the OECD average'; the 2013 Budget raises various levies on luxury car and investment housing purchases, mainly to reduce traffic congestion and housing price inflation, but they also have a progressive distributional impact.

[70]For example, Mac Margolis, 'The Next Singapore: Honduras Ponders an Extreme Economic Makeover', *Newsweek*, 8 October 2012, reports on an effort to create a 'semi-autonomous, free-market charter city' like Hong Kong or Singapore 'to tap investment, migrant workers and innovation from around the world', an idea inspired by Paul Romer (New York University, Economics), www.chartercities.org.

[71]Ravi Velloor, 'S'pore Held up as Model in Reducing Trade Barriers', *The Straits Times*, 24 January 2012, notes the World Bank's and Bain & Co.'s praise for Singapore's 'strategic initiatives to cut trade barriers', which facilitate the globalization of multinational supply chains.

[72]Zhang Zhibin (ed.), *Dynamics of the Singapore Success Story: Insights by Ngiam Tong Doiv*, Singapore: Cengage Asia Learning, 2011. Note that in the past several years, Mr Ngiam, once Singapore's top civil servant in charge of economic development, has been publicly critical of the government's more recent 21st century policies, including the emphases on property and finance as sources of employment and income.

[73]Donald Low (ed.), *Behavioural Economics and Policy Design: Examples from Singapore*, Singapore: World Scientific Publishing, 2012, for the Civil Service College.

In terms of the broader themes of this volume, another book, by a long-time International Monetary Fund economist on South-East Asia, *Singapore's Success: Engineering Economic Growth*, perhaps best captures international development agencies' enthusiasm for Singapore's development as a model for developing countries.[74] It concludes with these words:

> Key themes emerged from Singapore's success story. These include: the role of saving in allowing the buildup of first-rate infrastructure; the growth potential of increased labor force participation and immigration; the central importance of economic development among national goals; sharing opportunities for growth widely to make people more productive through better health and education; the macroeconomic resilience and employment- creating potential provided by flexible wage policy; competent civil service and integrity of governance; fiscal discipline and setting aside surpluses during boom years; win-win relations with MNCs [multinational corporations] and labor; maintaining racial harmony; learning from others pragmatically; the rule of law; and well-designed policies ...
>
> Singapore followed an integrated approach to development. Outcomes, policies, institutions, social and cultural values, and the political dynamics of implementation all reinforced each other. The government pursued this comprehensive strategy across a range of areas such as fiscal, monetary policy, education, health, transportation, housing, finance, wage policy, legal system and law enforcement, labor markets, and political stability and legitimacy ...[75]

From this expert practitioner perspective, then, Singapore's economic development was a success because it was comprehensive and integrated across all dimensions of public policy, and social and cultural institutions. This alone can be a daunting and difficult path for other emerging economies to follow, which is presumably the reason for Paul Romer's suggestion of establishing a separate city-state.[76] Ghesquiere and other foreign admirers of the Singapore model skirt around the one institution which has arguably been essential to the 'growth-enhancing institutions' and 'political economy of implementation' that enabled its economic success — and that is the

[74]Henri Ghesquiere, *Singapore's Success: Engineering Economic Growth*, Singapore: Thomson Learning, 2007. Dr Ghesquiere served on the staff of the IMF in 1978–2005, and was director of the IMF's Singapore Regional Training Institute in 2004–05.
[75]Ibid., 167–68.
[76]However, see also Jonathan Watts, 'Plans for Honduras Start-up City Hit by Transparency Concerns: Blow to Plan's Credibility as NYU Professor Paul Romer Says he has been Unable to Act as its Guarantor and Watchdog', *The Guardian*, 7 September 2012.

political institution of the one-party authoritarian state. A very different view is projected by some other Western writers focused on the country's non-economic institutions, where they find governance a problem due to its concentration in a small interrelated elite.[77] It is beyond this author's expertise and this chapter's scope to consider governance issues, except to note that in other emerging economies such a concentration of political and economic power is typically considered antithetical to, rather than supportive of, successful economic development.[78]

More interesting, in my view, is how and why the Singapore model — so admirable in so many respects and for so long — has stumbled in the 21st century, in terms of maintaining high living standards, economic opportunity and social satisfaction for its citizen population, requiring a return to the input-intensive growth that is typically associated with less-developed economies that have fewer strategic choices. After four decades of rapid GDP and income growth, Singapore's economy today is even more dependent on increasing inputs of foreign labour and talent, foreign capital and technology, and even increasing land area by artificial means, at the cost of increased inequality, reduced social mobility, rising inflation, greater risk and volatility, and declining quality of public and social goods and services (all of which the government, to its credit, acknowledges). It has failed to develop a model of sustainable growth despite achieving a highly educated population (human capital) and accumulating huge amounts of financial capital through the world's highest savings rate and foreign exchange reserves (which indicate that wages and consumption continue to fall behind top-line GDP growth, or that Singaporeans are much less well-off than their nominal or even real GDP per capita suggests).

[77]See, for example, Ross Worthington, *Governance in Singapore*, London/New York: Routledge-Curzon, 2003; Michael D. Barr and Zlatko Skrbis, *Constructing Singapore: Elitism, Ethnicity and the Nation-Building Project*, Copenhagen, Denmark: Nordic Institute of Asian Studies (NIAS Press) Democracy in Asia No. 11, 2008. One of the well-known facts about governance that these authors note is that Singapore has had only three prime ministers since 1959, with the third, current Prime Minister Lee Hsien Loong, being the son of the founding Prime Minister Lee Kuan Yew, while his wife Ho Ching is the long-time head of the sovereign wealth fund Temasek.

[78]As Ghesquiere also notes, 'Good institutions can take a variety of forms. Each country must fashion the specifics of its policies and institutions tailored to its own local geographical and historical conditions' (Ghesquiere, *Singapore's Success*, 168). Singapore's model differs from those of South Korea and Taiwan, but all had the political will and determination to impose their chosen models on their populations in the early stages of industrial development.

Seen in this light, the ruling party's declining political popularity is unsurprising.[79]

Theories about domestic causes of these public policy shortcomings relate mainly to failures of governance arising from the single-party system and its concentration/overlap of political and economic power, leading to lack of diversity of thought and competition of ideas ('groupthink'), the persistence of cognitive ideological biases long after they have ceased to be valid, and the self-interest of an academically selected elite of lifetime civil servants heavily networked with state and quasi-state agencies and GLC senior management, all of them highly compensated for their responsibilities over the allocation of public resources.[80] However, for the purposes of this volume, it is more useful to consider if any general lessons may be derived from the Singapore experience for economies that are still 'emerging'.

A first possible lesson is the limitations of globalization as a development strategy. There is no question that Singapore and other emerging economies would not have succeeded as they did in industrializing, raising incomes and moving towards post-industrial status, without participating in globalization, particularly liberalizing trade and foreign direct investment, and

---

[79]With rising affluence, education, and the spread of the internet and social media, especially among youth and post-Arab Spring, it is tempting to suggest that this unpopularity is due to a desire for greater political freedoms. However, the public discourse and popular rhetoric including online is heavily weighted toward so-called 'bread-and-butter' issues of stagnating incomes and worsening distribution, housing and health care costs, etc. for which government policy allowing the massive influx of foreigners is held partly to blame. Singaporeans did not seem to mind high salaries for political leaders and senior public officials, when their own economic situation was good, and the public sector appeared to be perfonning well; their ire was raised only when several repeated failures in public services (escape of a terrorist suspect from jail, mass transit overcrowding and breakdowns, frequent severe flooding, high cost and reduced availability of housing and health care, etc.) called into question the competence of highly compensated civil servants whom 'we pay well to do the job'. As many of the commentators cited here note, the past 'social compact' in which Singaporeans supposedly accepted curbs on their political freedoms in exchange for economic and social advancement has broken down because of the state's failure to deliver the latter, even as political freedoms have gradually improved.

[80]For thoughtful reflections on post-2011 governance challenges in Singapore, see the following essays by former civil servant Donald Low: 'What Went Wrong for the PAP in 2011?' www.facebook. com/notes/donald-lows-fc/what-went-wrong-for-the-pap-in-2011/209993849034597; 'Sustaining Good Governance in an Era of Rapid and Disruptive Change', speech at the IPS Singapore Perspective Conference, February 2013; 'Reframing the National Conversation', IPS Commons, www.ipscommons.sg/index.php/categories/politics/86-reframing-the-national-conversation; 'Governing in the New Normal', *The Straits Times*, 10 September 2011. Singapore justifiably ranks as the least corrupt country in Asia, No. 5 globally in 2012, www.transparency.org, though recent years have seen a rise in high-profile cases of corruption related to government procurement contracts.

exporting to global markets. However, the 21st century has also revealed some of the downsides of globalization especially for small open economies like Singapore. These include: extreme volatility arising from external GDP shocks; vulnerability to destabilizing global capital flows resulting from other countries' monetary and currency policies; and the unreliability of multinational investors as long-term members of a national private sector, since their own corporate fortunes and strategies change with globalization and the accompanying shifts in comparative and competitive advantage, such that 'piggy-backing' on specific multinationals is no longer an assured path to growth given heightened technological dynamism, business cycle volatility and general uncertainty in the world economy.[81]

Singapore's attempt to deal with export volatility through industrial diversification has had limited success, while its accumulation of foreign reserves managed by sovereign wealth funds has been variously criticized for: 1. maintaining currency undervaluation; 2. depriving the economy of funds that might be better used for domestic consumption, investment and a more robust social safety net; 3. resulting in financial losses from bad investments overseas; and 4. undermining the sovereignty of other nations.[82] Singapore's extreme openness to capital inflows puts upward pressure on its currency (undermining export competitiveness), contributes to domestic inflation (including politically sensitive house price inflation)[83] and income and wealth inequality, and has exposed it to criticisms at home and abroad of being a tax haven and money-laundering centre.[84]

The heavy and prolonged reliance on multinationals is what most differentiates Singapore from other successful Asian emerging economies — Taiwan, South Korea, Hong Kong, even Malaysia, Thailand and China — all

[81]See, for example 'Here, There and Everywhere', *The Economist* Special Report on Outsourcing and Offshoring, 19 January 2013.

[82]For example, during the financial crisis Singapore's sovereign wealth funds incurred large losses from their investments in Western financial institutions such as Citigroup, Merrill Lynch and UBS; their telecommunications investments in Indonesia, Thailand and Australia caused political controversy and also resulted in losses.

[83]Emerging economies suffering from the same problems have in recent years imposed a variety of capital controls that are increasingly sanctioned by the IMF; see, for example, Dani Rodrik, 'Global Capital Rules', www.project-syndicate.org, 7 April 2013. This is not possible for Singapore, given the reliance of its financial services sector on open capital flows, but in 2012 the Monetary Authority of Singapore added macroprudential measures to what had previously been only exchange-rate management in its monetary policy.

[84]For example, in 2013 Singapore was found to be the centre of a global soccer-fixing syndicate, presumably facilitated by the ease of money transfers.

of which have developed large local private enterprises with the capacity for competitive survival at home and successful globalization abroad as national comparative and competitive advantages have shifted. Singapore, in contrast, has remained heavily dependent on foreign multinationals, not simply by being open to FDI, but actually attracting specific state-chosen investments with extensive subsidies of capital expenditures and of labour (through liberal labour importation policies, training and education).[85] The subsidies required to attract and retain such foreign investment tend to increase with capital and skill intensity and technological specificity, yet are no assurance that the companies will remain, since from a corporate perspective subsidies are only one variable in location and investment decisions.[86] Providing subsidies to any company or industry also diverts scarce resources (land, labour, talent, capital) from other companies and industries. While multinationals do provide supply-chain opportunities for local companies, they also 'crowd out' or compete with them for scarce resources, given limited land and full employment. This is one reason why many local Singapore companies are 'much bigger abroad than at home', given larger markets and more resources in neighbouring countries, and competition at home from MNCs and GLCs. Concerns have also been expressed that the heavy dependence on foreigners may distort economic development and hamper the continued evolution of participatory democracy.[87]

---

[85] At the extreme, the Singapore EDB has paid for the salaries of engineers and other skilled employees of multinationals such as Microsoft and Hewlett-Packard; such jobs tend to disappear when subsidies are withdrawn, since by definition they do not make market sense for the employing multinationals. There have also been media reports of young Singaporeans graduating with previously encouraged 'life sciences' degrees being unable to find suitable employment (e.g. the celebrated case of a Stanford PhD 'new citizen' from China found driving a taxi).

[86] During my 2013 research visit to Singapore, more than half of the taxi drivers I engaged were in the business (which, unusually, is limited to Singapore citizens only), after being laid off (after 8–20 years as production managers, logistics and procurement officers, warehouse supervisors, sales and marketing managers, even an engineer) from MNCs, mostly in electronics (e.g. disk drives), but also in consumer goods; many blamed age discrimination for the loss of their previous jobs.

[87] 'Foreigners beholden to the state for its beneficence and their own presence are unlikely to challenge its authority, in the way that an independent, globally competitive and non-state-dependent domestic entrepreneurial class — still weak and largely absent in Singapore — might', Linda Y.C. Lim and Lee Soo Ann, 'Globalizing State, Disappearing Nation', 155. Some Singaporeans (particularly active online) go further in subscribing to the 'conspiracy theory' that the goal of the government's immigration policy is to 'dilute' native Singaporean votes with those of 'new citizens' who are much more likely to support the ruling PAP.

A second possible lesson for emerging economies is the limitations of state industrial policy as a country moves up the technology and income ladder, and it becomes more costly, risky and difficult to pick sectors in which to 'strategically invest' (or subsidize). Some sectors may not survive when subsidies are withdrawn, and the resources, e.g. labour and skills, they leave behind might be too specific (geared to fill niches in MNCs' global value chains) to be transferable to other sectors. There are also other risks associated with industrial policy, such as vested business interests (lobbying for subsidies), bureaucratic entrenchment (of state agents responsible for industrial policy), and the 'crowding out' of private business by state agencies and GLCs as well as MNCs. The main problem is that after decades of resource allocation distortions, downsizing the state and 'unwinding' to market forces is difficult, and there may be few local entrepreneurs available to drive the growth of a market economy.[88] However, public policy in a market economy is supposed to focus on the well-being of (domestic) consumers, not (foreign) producers. A national economy should begin with its domestic resource base, paying attention to both comparative advantage and strategic differentiation in the sectors it chooses to develop. In a developed economy, this resource allocation decision should be made by private enterprise actors risking their own money in response to (local and global) market forces, not by state actors. The transition from a state-driven to a market-driven economy which comes with development is a difficult one, at which Singapore has not yet shown itself successful. Fortunately, the government's new focus on 'inclusive growth' shows that it recognizes that it is important that growth benefit everyone; unfortunately (in my view), it seems to want to achieve this by continuing with its problematic growth model to date (subsidize foreign skills and capital) and then compensating locals who do not benefit, out of the public purse.

A third possible lesson, somewhat counter to the previous one, is that privatization is not always the answer, certainly where public goods and social services are concerned. Since the 1990s, the Singapore state has progressively privatized what used to be social goods, even as it continued with and even ratcheted up its subsidies of the multinational (and local) corporate sector. The housing, transportation, health and education sectors have been liberalized or corporatized to allow prices to be set by international market forces, including foreign demand, prioritizing returns to foreign as well as local shareholders, with social goods being 'commoditized' as export

[88] Linda Lim, 'Why Local Entrepreneurs are Vital', *The Straits Times*, 12 May 2009, makes the case for local entrepreneurs as agents of economic growth going forward.

products. This has contributed to rising costs of living for Singaporeans, whose wages did not rise in tandem, in part because of increased labour market competition from foreign workers, culminating in the problems already identified.

LESSONS FOR AND FROM DEVELOPED COUNTRIES

Singapore has become something of an icon for many 'policy wonks' in developed countries. In the West, conservative politicians and economists like it for its low taxes, lack of welfare spending, big budget surpluses,[89] free trade and capital flows, corporate subsidies, labour controls, pro-business policies and pro-market rhetoric; liberals like it for its activist state and industrial policies, what they think are social subsidies, good education and anti-market fundamentalism; everyone likes the absence of corruption and regrets the lack of political freedoms. What, besides an impressively successful state public relations apparatus, explains the dissonance between the foreign plaudits and the local dissatisfactions highlighted in this chapter?

A recent *New York Times* blog post by Nobel prizewinning economist and Columbia University Professor Joseph Stiglitz,[90] widely reprinted in Singapore and elsewhere, illustrates some of the reasons. First, foreign commentators are often inadequately if not wrongly informed about Singapore. For example, Professor Stiglitz asserts that a quarter of the Singapore labour force was unemployed at independence in 1963 — it was half that (at 12%); he praises Singapore for having a progressive tax system when it is less progressive than that in the USA and Western Europe, with a top corporate tax rate of 17% and top personal income tax rate of 20%; his claim that the government's intervention in wage bargaining between workers and firms 'tilts the balance towards groups with less economic power' is unsubstantiated, certainly given the stagnation and decline of median and especially low-decile wages since 2000; he totally disregards the hundreds of thousands of low-wage foreign workers with no bargaining rights; his claim that the education system ensures that it is 'not just the children of the rich'

[89]Conservatives do not seem to realize that public-sector surpluses are derived from private-sector deficits, since they mean that the state collects more in revenues from the population than it delivers in expenditures.

[90]Joseph E. Stiglitz, 'Singapore's Lessons for an Unequal America', *The New York Times*, 18 March 2013, opinionator.blogs.nytimes.com/2013/03/18/ singapores-lessons-for-an-unequal-america/. Professor Stiglitz has been a frequent visitor to Singapore over many years.

who have a chance at upward mobility is contradicted by the government's own efforts to counter demonstrated low social mobility, which it considers troubling.

Second, information about Singapore is selectively and uncritically presented, primarily to serve the foreign commentator's own policy agenda in his home country. Thus Professor Stiglitz lauds the fact that 90% of Singaporeans own their own homes, paid for by their CPF savings, which he praises for inculcating 'individual responsibility' for personal welfare. He does not note that the conflation of savings for retirement and home payments has become a serious social issue given housing price inflation and population ageing, with 47% of Singaporeans over the age of 60 having insufficient CPF savings to support themselves in retirement; he fails to note that this 'individualized' solution to social welfare needs disadvantages those — particularly women — who are unable to have continuous, lifelong, full employment, and being tied to earnings, translates wage differentials into unequal access to health care (also provided out of CPF forced savings) and retirement income. He also disregards the disadvantages that lower-income parents and children suffer in the education system, which has given rise to large private investments in expensive out-of-school tuition and enrichment classes that they are less able to afford.[91]

Third, there is a tendency by Western commentators especially to judge Singapore by different (and lower) standards than they uphold for themselves and other Western societies. For example, Stiglitz says of Singapore that:

> It's true that Singapore, a highly centralized state, has been ruled for decades by Mr. Lee's People's Action Party. Critics say it has authoritarian aspects: limitations on civil liberties; harsh criminal penalties; insufficient multiparty competition; and a judiciary that is not fully independent. But it's also true that Singapore is routinely rated one of the world's least corrupt and most transparent governments, and that its leaders have taken steps toward expanding democratic participation.

while he says of the Nordic countries that:

> I believe the economic achievements of the Nordic countries are in large measure a result of the strongly democratic nature of these societies. There is a positive nexus not just between growth and equality, but between these two and democracy.[92]

[91]These arguments were cogently made by Teo You Yenn (Nanyang Technological University, Sociology), 'How Stiglitz Weakens Change in S'pore', www.todayonline.com/print/98231, one of many critical comments on the Stiglitz article.
[92]Stiglitz, 'Singapore's Lessons for an Unequal America'.

Professor Stiglitz is not alone among liberals in his infatuation with Singapore. *Washington Post* and NPR (National Public Radio) commentator Matt Miller is a self-described 'gushing fan of Singapore's public policy achievements', recently praising its high ministerial salaries, low expenditure on health care (just 4% of GDP), home ownership policies, transport facilities, 'fiscal stewardship' based on a 'culture of self-reliance' and 'no redistributions', and 'low-tax, business-friendly environment'.[93] For former Democratic Governor of the state of Michigan Jennifer Granholm, it is Singapore's practice of industrial policy to attract foreign investment that is attractive, recounting that a panel of multinational CEOs she interviewed all agreed that Singapore 'has the best formula for attracting their investment'.[94]

This, then, is the reason for the dissonance. As US liberals have long argued, what is good for the corporation — minimal regulation, offshore tax havens, outsourcing — is not necessarily good for the country. Singapore ranks high on indices that measure the business environment for multinational investors — low taxes, no corruption, lots of state subsidies, freedom to take capital in and out and hire people from anywhere in the world.[95] However, this is not the same as the well-being of native Singaporeans, as measured by income, inequality, working hours, access to affordable housing, health care, social security, education and social mobility — without even considering negative externalities like congestion, environmental degradation, loss of cultural heritage and even 'nationhood'.

Interestingly, many Singaporean social scientists find themselves attracted to the 'Scandinavian model' of small, open economies with modest growth, low income inequality, strong social safety nets and high measurements of well-being, even 'happiness'. However, in a speech to economists and parliamentarians in June 2012, Prime Minister Lee Hsien Loong said this would not work because 'higher taxes would likely be unpopular among Singaporeans and make the economy less competitive'. Some of his audience (including ruling party MPs) argued that a 'middle ground' is possible, since Singapore can increase public spending over the current 17% of GDP

---

[93]Matt Miller, 'What Singapore can Teach Us', *Washington Post*, 2 May 2012.

[94]Cited in Sharon Chen, 'Can the Singapore Model Solve US Unemployment Crisis?' www.asiancorrespondent.com, 21 October 2011.

[95]For example, as noted by Hoon Hian Teck, 'The Future of Wages in Singapore': 'The ready access to the supply of foreign workers kept labour costs low while the increase in value-added per worker boosted the profitability of manufacturing firms. This boost to profits very likely benefited both multinational corporations (MNCs) as well as small and medium-sized enterprises (SMEs).'

(perhaps to the over 20% ratio that prevailed up to the late 1990s), and that tax rates alone are not the only source of Singapore's competitiveness.[96]

CONCLUSION

In this chapter I have reviewed one of the most successful cases of economic development in modern times: one that, unusually, has been held up as a model for both emerging and developed economies, and has won plaudits from all sides of the political spectrum. I argue, in line with other development researchers and practitioners, that Singapore's economic success in the 20th century was the product not just of 'the right' policies, but also of favourable initial conditions (domestically and internationally), and 'the right' institutions, for the times. I further argue, as some others have, that Singapore's policies and institutions worked to deliver the results they did because they were *integrated* across economic, social and political arenas. Thus the relevance for other countries is limited, since few, if any, can (or want to) marshal and implement such a complex, interrelated set of public policies under the aegis of a strong centralized state whose political power has been unchanged for over half a century.

I deviate from the international development establishment consensus, but concur with local Singaporean scholars and analysts, in noting that the results of Singapore's public policy complex have been less positive for average Singaporeans than they have been for international business and for global and local elites, in the 21st century; that this view is widely shared in Singapore and is reflected in recent electoral results and a much more open public discourse.[97] I further argue that the past Singapore growth model is unsustainable, because of changes in the international environment, and domestic resource and social constraints.[98] In particular I note the limits

[96]Robin Chan and Aaron Low, 'Find Middle Ground: Economists, MPs', *The Straits Times*, 11 June 2012. See also Donald Low, 'Squaring the Circle the Scandinavian Way', www.facebook.com/notes/donald-lows-fc/squaring-the-circle-the-scandinavian-way/389281347772512.

[97]Contrary to Professor Stiglitz's attributing Singapore's recent political liberalization to its 'leaders' having 'taken steps to expand political participation', this is more the result of the spread of the internet and social media, and the emergence of a 'new generation', as acknowledged by Prime Minister Lee Hsien Loong in a recent *Washington Post* interview, reported by Andrea Ong, 'Govt Will Need to be More Open, Says PM', *The Straits Times*, 17 March 2013. There has been a notable increase in well-educated young professionals participating in the political opposition, motivated in large part by the perception of declining living standards and economic opportunities for themselves and their fellow citizens in 21st-century Singapore.

[98]For details, see Lim, LYC (2009). Singapore's Economic Growth Model: Too Much or Too Little? *Ethos*, 6, 32–38.

of globalization, state industrial policy and privatization of social services as contributors to growth and welfare, especially for a high-income country; and like other Singaporeans, I question the efficiency and equity of growth based on continuous large imports of foreign capital and labour induced by ever-expanding corporate subsidies.

The Singapore government is nothing if not responsive to the developmental and political challenges it faces, and is finally embarking on policies (long recommended by local economists) to limit foreign labour dependence, increase productivity and increase social subsidies for Singaporeans, even if it means slower GDP growth and 'painful restructuring'. It has accepted that manufacturing's share of the economy will continue to decline. The low productivity of the services sector (measured by value-added per employee and as compared with other high-income countries) offers many opportunities for increased efficiency, growth and higher incomes,[99] as does the continued growth and rising incomes of Singapore's 600 million South-East Asian neighbours, for whom it will continue to serve as a regional financial, commercial, trade, transport, information and recreational 'hub'.

The public policy dilemma the government now faces arises from the very interdependence of economic and social policies and institutions which led to the country's past success; it turns out that they cannot be easily disentangled and restructured. Take, for example, housing policy which once contributed to economic growth but is now a drag on it due to asset inflation. Turning housing from an affordable social good into a financial asset interacts negatively with demographics — both on fertility rates of the young, and on consumption of retirees who have 'nowhere else to go'. Allowing the free inflow of foreign capital and labour also contributes to housing price inflation,[100] reducing cost competitiveness while undermining social stability, all of which discourage investment, growth, entrepreneurship and innovation.[101] CPF 'locks up' individuals' forced savings, channelling them disproportionately into housing (and state assets), leaving inadequate

[99]See, for example, Choy Keen Meng, 'Rethinking Singapore's Growth Model', *Today*, 7 November 2009.

[100]For example, residential property (and REITs) are major investment asset classes for foreigners attracted to Singapore as a 'safe haven' for international and offshore capital (private banking and wealth management are promoted as part of the financial services sector), while permanent residents compete with citizens for scarce public housing, and foreign workers crowd and push up rents in both the public and private housing sectors.

[101]An example of resulting resource misallocation was the discovery that government-subsidized industrial space was being illegally converted into dormitories to be rented out to foreign workers (also with 'nowhere else to go') for a much higher return than manufacturing could yield.

amounts for health care and retirement subsistence, and inhibiting the development of a healthy domestic (as opposed to global) financial services sector that could channel savings into local value-creating enterprises. HDB and GLCs in the property development business employ large numbers of low-wage foreign construction workers and earn their profits (and senior management bonuses) off the increased costs of households and businesses, creating potential conflicts of interest. This results in Singaporeans, as they get richer and older, saving more and more — now, nearly half their income — for basic subsistence (housing, health care), which limits the growth of the domestic consumer sector and the entrepreneurship it could generate. The government is now taking steps to reduce housing speculation and inflation (by increasing supply, increasing transaction and mortgage costs for those with more than one private property, and limiting the increased demand from more foreign workers), but this risks diminishing the asset values (and retirement savings) of property-owning households, as well as the profits and equity values of property GLCs in which citizen savings and offshore capital are invested. Encouraging and rewarding state agencies (and their management) for earning surpluses (a source of pride for 'Singapore Inc.') also transfers income from households and the private sector to the state, which then invests the surpluses offshore in sometimes risky private investments in foreign countries rather than in public or social goods at home. Meanwhile a well-compensated state and quasi-state bureaucracy and GLC management have little incentive to restructure themselves out of their high-earning jobs to relinquish scarce resources and market space for private-sector investment.

From a governance perspective, the expansion of the state and the proliferation of individual ministries and agencies and their activities has resulted in duplication, competition and a weakening of the central co-ordination function of the state.[102] The recent launch of the Population White Paper from the National Population and Talent Division in the Prime Minister's Office revealed a lack of co-ordination and consultation among different government departments, most notably exemplified by the controversial (and

[102]For example, nearly every ministry has its own research and training units which both conduct in-house activities and outsource them to private-sector (often foreign) consultancies, professional service providers and commercial market research firms (e.g. McKinsey, KPMG, Gallup, Nielsen, etc.). Anecdotally it appears that Singapore government agencies and GLCs may account for as much as one third of the business in the professional services private sector; their custom (like their capital) is also a reason for other companies to set up in Singapore, e.g. US start-ups with which I have had contact, in the medical technology, IT and telecoms sectors.

hastily withdrawn) identification of nurses (a short-supplied profession into which the Ministry of Health has long been trying to attract more students and workers) as 'low skilled'. Multinational employers have also mentioned their frustration with conflicting messages they get from different ministries: for example, the Ministry of Trade and Industry's EDB promises them they can hire skilled foreigners freely, while the Ministry of Manpower rejects their applications for employment visas.[103] Equally important, a now larger but less centralized state is less able to impose its own, perhaps more divided, political will on an increasingly politically restive and active citizenry.

Perhaps then the main quandary in Singapore's current economic policy conundrum is what to do about the role of the developmental state *after* the miracle of growth has been achieved. As other rich countries have found upon maturity, it is extremely difficult to 'stay on top', especially without a vibrant indigenous entrepreneurial class. How should and can the state reduce and reshape its role at a stage and era when innovation, and not imitation or superior execution, is the source of sustainable competitiveness? How does it deal with the limits to changing comparative and competitive advantage through state action (e.g. immigration policy, capital flows, technology and infrastructure development, and tax and regulatory regimes)? How does the state balance its political obligation for the social welfare of its citizenry with its economic goal to be 'No. 1' in servicing international capital? How does it manage the challenges that both bureaucratic division and democratic pluralism pose to economic growth? What is the proper nature of a state, or a nation, in a globalized era which some argue is increasingly defined by competing state — or even national private — capitalisms? It may be that Singapore's development conundrum is a general one after all, not just for economies that are still 'emerging', but also for all high-income, open economies. However, there is a special poignancy to the Singapore case, given the apparent belief of its long-time political leaders that here subordination of the hitherto carefully nurtured nation is necessary for economic survival. The resulting tension is perhaps best summed up by this recent foreign comment on a local heritage-conservation controversy:

> This is what Singapore's government has always done: look around corners on behalf of its people and plan ahead, confident enough in the infallibility of its policymaking and in the inevitability of its re-election to ignore pressure

[103]Meanwhile, the Ministry of Home Affairs grants permanent residence (permission to immigrate and settle permanently, not just to work temporarily) on other criteria, including education and race, given the government's longstanding belief that the racial proportions of the population existing at independence should be preserved.

groups and to scorn pandering to populism. Even its critics contend it has been successful. But times have changed. Social media have turned silent, isolated dissent into more concerted, vocal protest. The political opposition — with less than 10% of the seats in parliament — seems a long way from power. But with 40% of the popular vote in 2011, it can no longer be dismissed as irrelevant. For its part, the government makes much these days of its willingness to 'listen'.

In this context, the struggle over Bukit Brown takes on a wider meaning. The improbable coalition of birdwatchers, conservationists and heritage buffs trying to stop the road are testing the government's promises of a new responsiveness, or, put another way, the strength of its conviction that it still knows best. The argument over the fate of the graveyard may look like a tussle over Singapore's past. But it is really about its future.[104]

[104]Banyan, 'Grave Concerns', *The Economist*, 6 April 2013. See also Linda Lim, 'Singapore: Place or Nation?' *The Straits Times*, 16 June 2006; Linda Lim, 'Can Money Ease Loss of Memories?' *The Straits Times*, 21 June 2007; Geh Min, 'Singapore: Home or Hotel?' (2013).

Chapter 5

BEYOND THE "GLOBAL CITY" PARADIGM*

LINDA LIM

THE ECONOMY AT INDEPENDENCE

At independence in 1965, Singapore's economy remained heavily dependent on its colonial-era role as a regional entrepot, or import-export hub, linking South-east Asia to world markets through the provision of port, transport, commercial and financial services as well as British military services, which constituted nearly a third of the gross domestic product (GDP). Though Singapore's per capita income was already Asia's second highest, after Japan, unemployment was 12% of the labour force.

A decade earlier, a World Bank mission to Malaya (including Singapore) had recommended that the two British colonial territories embark on import-substituting industrialisation for what became known after the merger in 1963 as a "Malaysian Common Market" (International Bank for Reconstruction and Development, 1995).[1] Political separation in 1965, and the circumstances under which it occurred, made this an unlikely, or at least difficult, prospect. At the same time, there was occasional social unrest at home and political turbulence abroad, including Indonesia's *Konfrontasi* against Malaysia, the war in Vietnam and the Cultural Revolution in China.

*This chapter first appeared in *Singapore Perspectives 2015 : Choices*, Su-Fern Hoe and Carol Soon (Eds.), 2015, pp. 51–89. Reprinted with permission from World Scientific Publishing and Institute of Policy Studies, Singapore.

[1]International Bank for Reconstruction and Development. (1955). *The Economic Development of Malaya*. Baltimore, Maryland: Johns Hopkins Press.

THE POST-INDEPENDENCE DEVELOPMENT STRATEGY

Fortunately for Singapore, another promising development strategy had already emerged elsewhere in the developing world — that of labour-intensive manufacturing for export to world markets. Puerto Rico's "Operation Bootstrap" began as early as 1948, soon to be followed by the export of garments manufactured by Chinese industrialists who fled to Hong Kong after the communist takeover of China in 1949. In 1965, Mexico established its Border Industrialization Program, or *Maquiladora*, and in 1966 the Kaohsiung Export Processing Zone (EPZ) was inaugurated in Taiwan, followed by the Masan zone in South Korea in 1970 and multiple EPZs in Malaysia and the Philippines in the 1970s.

This development strategy fit with the theory of comparative advantage, which argues that countries should specialise in the production and export of items that intensively use their relatively abundant factors of production. High unemployment suggested that Singapore too might be competitive in relatively labour-intensive industries. But the strategy was driven not just by comparative advantage, or supply-side factors. Technological and public policy changes in developed countries also contributed to favourable demand-side conditions for labour-intensive manufactured exports from developing countries.

Most notable in trade policy was the institution of Items 806.30 (in 1956) and 807.00 (in 1963) of the US Tariff Schedules, which exempted US-origin value-added from import duty (U.S. Tariff Commission, 1970).[2] In the contrary case of textiles and garments, low-wage developing countries were so successful in displacing production in developed countries that the General Agreement on Tariffs and Trade (GATT, precursor of the World Trade Organization) imposed Multifibre Arrangement (MFA) quotas limiting exports from individual countries from 1974 to 2004. Fortunately, as a relatively early exporter, Singapore, like Hong Kong, retained textile quotas much larger than those awarded to lower-wage later entrants like Bangladesh, giving it a measure of protection that preserved competitiveness in this labour- intensive sector longer than market forces would allow. From 1975, Singapore also benefited from the GATT/WTO's Generalised System of Preferences (GSP) for developing countries until, together with the other Asian newly industrialised countries (NICs) of Hong Kong, Taiwan and

---

[2]U.S. Tariff Commission. (1970, September). *Economic Factors Affecting the Use of Items 807.00 and 806. 30 of the Tariff Schedules of the United States.* Tariff Commission Publication 339, Washington, DC.

South Korea, it was "graduated" (ruled ineligible by income level) by the US, (1989), European Union (1997) and Japan (2000) (Ow-Taylor and Ow, 1991).[3]

Technological developments in the semiconductor and consumer electronics industries also enabled and encouraged subdivision and offshore sourcing of labour-intensive parts and components of the electronics value-chain by multinationals like Fairchild Semiconductor, Texas Instruments and Hitachi, a subject I examined in 1975–76 through field research in Singapore and Malaysia for my PhD dissertation (Lim, 1978).[4] The other industry that Singapore bet big and successfully on was the then-also-labour-intensive shipbuilding and repair, transforming the abandoned British naval base facilities into commercial shipyards run by new government-linked companies (GLCs) like Keppel and Sembawang.

Resource-based comparative advantage was not the sole reason why these labour-intensive export industries developed. Also key to Singapore's success here was the parallel development of complementary competitive advantages through strategic industrial and social policy that built on the country's already established economic assets of good geographical location, deep-water harbour, free trade and capital flows, and commercial and physical infrastructure.

Industrial policy measures undertaken by new state institutions (primarily the Economic Development Board, or EDB, founded in 1961) consisted mainly of a streamlined bureaucracy (then called a "one-stop shop" for investors), the provision of infrastructure such as subsidised industrial estates (e.g., Jurong Town Corporation, or JTC) and industrial financing (Development Bank of Singapore, or DBS), and various tax incentives, including one to explicitly encourage manufacturing for export, that were

[3]Taylor, OCH and CH Ow (1991). Graduation from U.S. GSP: The Case of Singapore. *Journal of Asian Economics*, 2(2), 285–299.

[4]Lim, LYC (1978). Multinationals and Manufacturing for Export in Less-Developed Countries: The Case of the Electronics Industry in Malaysia and Singapore (PhD dissertation in Economics), University of Michigan, Ann Arbor. See also Leontiades, J (1971). International Sourcing in the Less Developed Countries. *Columbia Journal of World Business*, 6(6), 19–26. Moxon. R. W. (July 1974). Offshore Production in Less Developed Countries: A Case Study of Multinationality in the Electronics Industry. Bulletin. Nos. 98–99, New York University Graduate School of Business Administration, Institute of Finance and Reynis, L. A. (1976). The Proliferation of U.S. Firm Third World Sourcing in the Mid-to-Late 1960s: An Historical and Empirical Study of the Factors Which Occasioned the Location of Production for the U.S. Market Abroad (PhD dissertation in Economics). University of Michigan, Ann Arbor.

introduced in 1967.[5] Taiwan and Korea had similar policies but Singapore's were distinctive in two ways.

First, they focused largely on promoting inward foreign direct investment whereas policies in the other NICs privileged domestic private enterprises, which soon came to dominate their export manufacturing sectors. Second, Singapore integrated social policies into industrial development to a much greater extent than in other locations. Its signature social policy — "public" housing (Housing Development Board or HDB flats) that residents paid for through their own "forced savings" (in the Central Provident Fund, or CPF) — co-located labour-intensive factories, including the then iconic "flatted factories", with HDB residential high-rises. This facilitated employers' access to workers, especially young females who made up the vast majority of workers in textiles and electronics factories and typically worked around the clock (requiring rotating shifts). It also helped maintain low labour costs by reducing workers' costs of housing (due to a combination of scale economics and state subsidies) and transportation. At the same time, large state investments in healthcare and education raised labour productivity, and in education also provided vocational and technical training for specific manufacturing industries (Lim, 1989).[6]

Political stability and labour peace were necessary to encourage investment because they ensured that export manufacturing for distant global markets, especially in short product life cycle industries like fashion garments and electronics, would not be disrupted by political upheaval or labour unrest. Notably, among the other NICs, Taiwan and Korea were under military rule with strict labour controls until democratisation in the late 1980s while Hong Kong was a British colony, all throughout the period of labour-intensive export manufacturing. Unlike these NICs, Singapore was nominally a parliamentary democracy, albeit one that had seen the left-wing political opposition eviscerated in the early 1960s, resulting in a one- or dominant-party government by the People's Action Party

---

[5]Singapore's industrial policies during the first two decades of independence have been extensively discussed in many studies, including Pang, EF and L Lim (1986). *Trade, Employment and Industrialisation in Singapore.* Geneva: International Labour Office and Chia, SY (1989). The Character and Progress of Industrialization. In K. S. Sandhu and P. Wheatley (Eds.), *Management of Success: The Moulding of Modern Singapore* (pp. 250–279). Singapore: Institute of Southeast Asian Studies.

[6]Lim, LYC (1989). Social Welfare. In K. S. Sandhu and P. Wheatley (Eds.), *Management of Success: The Moulding of Modern Singapore* (pp. 171–197). Singapore: Institute of Southeast Asian Studies.

(PAP) that helped ensure political stability (Chan, 1989).[7] On the labour front, the PAP's control of the labour movement (National Trades Union Congress, or NTUC) and legislation restricting labour organisation and action (particularly the 1968 Employment Act) ensured that there were virtually no incidents of significant labour unrest over the next decades (Raj, 1989).[8]

Thus both market forces (comparative advantage) and domestic government policies (creating competitive advantage) made Singapore's new export manufacturing industries competitive in a fortunately favourable global market context. At the same time, the focus on foreign investment linked its economy closely to the developed home markets of multinational employers. Between 1965 and 1973, just before Singapore suffered its first globally-induced recession as an independent nation, manufacturing value-added grew by 23.2% per year at current factor cost and 18.1% at 1968 constant prices while its share of GDP rose from 15% to 23% and the share of manufacturing output exported rose from 27% to 54%, and to 63% by 1985 (Chia, 1989, pp. 253–256).[9] By then, less than a decade after independence, the combination of very rapid labour-intensive growth and Singapore's small labour force meant that "surplus labour" had been absorbed, full employment had been reached and labour shortages appeared, indicating a shift in comparative advantage.

Yet the initial policy response was to seek to maintain GDP growth and preserve the eroding competitiveness of labour-intensive activities by holding down wages through the institution of a tripartite National Wages Council (NWC) in 1972 and importing low-wage foreign labour. It was not until 1979 that a "second industrial revolution" was launched, with the goal of moving into higher-value industries, increasing productivity and wages, and reducing reliance on low-skilled and foreign labour. It was recognised that:

> *The economic success of the 1970s was, in retrospect, achieved not so much because of improvements in labour productivity but as a result of the influx of foreign labour and the increased numbers of women joining the labour force...*

---

[7]Chan, HC (1989). The PAP and the Structuring of the Political System. In K. S. Sandhu and P. Wheatley (Eds.), *Management of Success: The Moulding of Modern Singapore* (pp. 70–89). Singapore: Institute of Southeast Asian Studies.
[8]Vasil, R (1989). Trade Unions. In K.S. Sandhu and P. Wheatley (Eds.), *Management of Success: The Moulding of Modern Singapore* (pp. 144–197). Singapore: Institute of Southeast Asian Studies.
[9]Chia (1989), op. cit.

> *...the availability of cheap low-skilled workers allowed many employers to continue with inefficient operations, thus threatening to defeat the national plan to move up the technological ladder.*
>
> *In line with the wage-correction policy introduced in 1979 to help employers automate their operations, the government decided to phase out all foreign workers and have a wholly Singaporean work-force by 1991... A foreign worker levy ... was introduced in 1982... in order to deter employers from becoming overly dependent on them.*[10] (Pang *et al.*, 1989, p. 134)

THE "SECOND INDUSTRIAL REVOLUTION" AND AFTER

One of the downsides of being a "global city" hitched to the wagon of multinationals based in distant foreign markets is vulnerability to economic shocks in those markets. The externally driven recession that Singapore suffered in 1974–75 was partly responsible for the delay of policymakers to adjust to the loss of comparative advantage in labour-intensive manufacturing. Another severe recession in 1984–85 led to hesitation in following through the "Second Industrial Revolution", as its high-wage policy was blamed for the severity, though it was not the cause, of the recession.

> *In the 1970s, a low-wage policy encouraged labour-intensive activities, thus negating attempts to achieve high productivity. In the 1980s, wage increases were to be tied to productivity, but instead the high increases recommended across the board did not reflect inter-industry differences in productivity growth. In most cases, wage increases exceeded productivity and pushed labour costs beyond internationally competitive levels.*[11] (Pang *et al.*, 1989, as cited in Pang and Lim, 1989, p. 136)

---

[10] Pang, EF, CH Tan, and SM Cheng (1989). The Management of People. In K. S. Sandhu and P. Wheatley (Eds.), *Management of Success: The Moulding of Modern Singapore* (pp. 128–143). Singapore: Institute of Southeast Asian Studies. See also Pang, EF and L Lim (1982). Foreign Labour and Economic Development in Singapore. *International Migration Review*, 16(4), 548–576.

[11] See also Pang, EF and L Lim (1989). Wage Policy in Singapore. In *Government Wage Policy Formulation in less-Developed Countries: Seven Country Studies* (pp. 75–101). Geneva: International Labour Office. Other relevant studies include Rodan, G. (1985). *Singapore's Second Industrial Revolution: State Intervention and Foreign Investment.* ASEAN-Australia Joint Research Project, Rodan, G. (1987). The Rise and Fall of Singapore's 'Second Industrial Revolution'. In R. Robison, K. Hewison and Richard Higgot (Eds.), *Southeast Asia in the 1980s: the Politics of Economic Crisis* (pp. 149–176). Sydney, Australia: Allen and Unwin and Leggett, C (1994). Labour and Singapore's Second Industrial Revolution. In S. Jackson (Ed.). *Contemporary Development in Asian Industrial Relations* (pp. 77–97). Sydney, Australia: University of New South Wales Studies in Human Resource Management and Industrial Relations in Asia.

Dependence on foreign manufacturing investment for which there was growing international competition arguably also reduced the degrees of freedom that Singapore's policymakers had in adjusting to declining competitiveness. In retrospect, they appear to have responded in two ways: first, by seeking to change the factor endowments that underlie comparative advantage, specifically by relaxing immigration rules for highly educated or skilled professionals (Pang *et al.*, 1989, p. 134)[12]; second, by continuing to add location-specific competitive advantages that would particularly appeal to capital- and skill-intensive industries, primarily infrastructure and investment incentives targeted to specific industrial "clusters". These policies reflect the view of Professor Michael Porter (1990)[13] who states that a nation can escape the limitations of its factor endowments like land, natural resources, labour and the size of the local population by creating "new advanced factor endowments", such as skilled labour, a strong technology and knowledge base, government support and culture.

The policies were successful in maintaining and even growing manufacturing's share of GDP, which went from 22% in 1985 to 26% in 1990, where it remained through 2005 (Choy, 2010, p. 129).[14] This was in striking contrast to the sharp (roughly 50%) share drop in all other developed economies, except Korea, and the virtual disappearance of manufacturing in Hong Kong (Perry, 2012)[15], as predicted by the Fisher-Clark hypothesis that demand for, and employment in, services rises with income over time. The share of high-value-added (capital-intensive) sectors also increased, as reflected in the decline in manufacturing's share of employment from 26% in 1990 to 17% in 2005, and the "steady migration of industrial production over the last twenty years into technologically advanced and skill-intensive clusters, in particular electronics, petrochemicals, specialty chemicals and pharmaceuticals" (Choy, 2010, p. 131).[16]

However, this policy-induced move up the manufacturing value-added ladder was accompanied by a more concentrated industrial structure, heavily

---

[12]Pang and Lim *et al.* (1989), op. cit., p. 134.

[13]Porter, ME (1990). *The Competitive Advantage of Nations.* New York, NY: The Free Press.

[14]Choy, KM (2010). Singapore's Changing Economic Model. In T. Chong (Ed.), *Management of Success: Singapore Revisited* (pp. 124–138). Singapore: Institute of Southeast Asian Studies.

[15]Perry, MJ (2012, March 22). Manufacturing's Declining Share of GDP is a Global Phenomenon, and It's Something to Celebrate. US Chamber of Commerce Foundation. Retrieved from http://www.uschamberfoundation.org/blog/post/manufacturing-s-declining-share-gdp-global-phenomenon-and-it-s-something-celebrate/34261.

[16]Choy, op. cit.

reliant on an electronics and, more recently, pharmaceutical cluster, both of which transmitted their highly volatile business cycles to Singapore's own GDP growth (Choy, 2010, p. 131).[17] In addition, studies have shown that in all stages of Singapore's industrial development — from the labour-intensive 1970s to the capital- and skill-intensive 2000s — productivity growth has been weak to non-existent.[18] This most likely reflects the input-intensive nature of Singapore's growth, which has been achieved by adding mostly foreign capital, skills and labour to production rather than by increasing the productivity of domestic factors of production. As an example, a recent international innovation index ranked Singapore No. 1 in "Overall Innovation Input" each year from 2011 to 2014, but only No. 17 in "Overall Innovation Output" in 2011, declining to No. 25 in 2014, and No. 94 in "Innovation Efficiency" in 2011, declining to No. 110 in 2014 (INSEAD) 2015).[19] Other studies have attributed Singapore's high inequality, stagnant median wages, low wage-to-income and low consumption-to-GDP ratios and comparatively weak performance on "well-being" indices to this input-intensive growth model (Lim, 2014).[20] Professor Tan Kong Yam's contribution to this volume explicitly links social discontent to the fact that "the bottom 30% and some of the aspiring members of the middle class" have lost out from globalisation

---

[17]Ibid.

[18]See, for example, Lee, TY (1985). Growth without Productivity: Singapore Manufacturing in the 1970s. *Journal of Development Economics*, 19, pp. 25–38; Young, A (1992). A Tale of Two Cities: Factor Accumulation and Technical Change in Hong Kong and Singapore. In Blanchard, OJ and S Fischer (Eds.), *NBER Macroeconomics Annual 1992.* MIT Press; Young, A (1995). The Tyranny of Numbers: Confronting the Statistical Realities of the East Asian Growth Experience. *Quarterly Journal of Economics, 110,* 641–80; Krugman, P (1994). The Myth of Asia's Miracle. *Foreign Affairs* 73/6, 62–79; Chuang, PM (2009, March 23). S'pore scores low in labour productivity. *The Business Time*, citing a comparative study of 17 developed economies by the U.S. Department of Labor; and Nomura, K and T Amano (2012). Labor Productivity and Quality Change in Singapore: Achievements in 1974–2011 and Prospects for the Next Two Decades, KEO Discussion Paper No. 129, Keio Economic Observatory, Keio University. The most detailed and excellent analysis of Singapore's productivity policies and performance since independence can be found in a three-part case from the Lee Kuan Yew School of Public Policy, *Singapore's Productivity Challenge,* Parts I, II and III, prepared by Hawyee Auyong under the supervision of Donald Low, Case Study Unit. Singapore: Lee Kuan Yew School of Public Policy. Auyong's analysis shows that economic planners expressed concerns about excessive dependence on foreign capital and labour, the limits of the export manufacturing model and their depressing impact on productivity growth from very soon after independence, and continuing to the present day.

[19]INSEAD (2015), *INSEAD Global Innovation Index.* Retrieved from: https://www.globalinnovationindex.org/content.aspx?page=past-reports.

[20]Lim, LYC (2014). Singapore's Success: After the Miracle. In R. E. Looney (Ed.), *Handbook of Emerging Economies* (pp. 202–226). London: Routledge.

while the government, local and global elites, and owners of capital have benefited.[21]

SINGAPORE'S ECONOMIC MODEL AT 50: A LOOK BACK

Becoming a "global city", and specifically a "node" in the evolving global supply chains of multinationals, was the best and probably only path to economic development that Singapore could have followed fifty years ago. It succeeded because external global forces, including multilateral trade liberalisation and the information and communications technology revolution, and internal domestic policies and outcomes were conducive. Comparative and competitive advantage together created the international competitiveness that enabled Singapore to develop a successful export manufacturing sector within a few years of independence. But comparative and competitive advantages are dynamic, and Singapore's small size and high growth meant that shifts in international competitiveness happened very rapidly, with comparative advantage in labour-intensive activities yielding quickly to skill- and capital-intensity.

Singapore's policymakers recognised all of the limitations and weaknesses of its economic model as they emerged. The Ministry of Trade and Industry reviewed the model and recommended new policies in 1986 (after the 1984–85 recession), 1991 (after a 1990 downturn), 1998 (after the 1997–98 Asian financial crisis), 2003 (after the tech bubble burst, the September 2011 terrorist attacks in New York and the SARS crisis) and 2010 (after the 2008 global financial crisis) (MTI 1986; 1991; 1998; 2003; 2010).[22] All the reports emphasised the need to increase productivity [23] and move into higher value-added activities, though the actual sectors prioritised changed over time (to eventually include a cumulatively broad slate of industries and services). All assumed a continued global role for Singapore in multinational networks, and a leading role for government in the "restructuring" or "transformation" of the economy. Until the 2010 committee report, all featured a continued

---

[21]Please see the chapter by Professor Tan Kong Yam in *Singapore Perspectives 2015 Choices.*

[22]Ministry of Trade and Industry, Singapore (MTI). (1986). *The Singapore Economy: New Directions*, Report of the Economic Committee; MTI. (1991). *Strategic Economic Plan: Toward a Developed Nation;* MTI. (1998) *Committee on Singapore's Competitiveness Report*; MTI. (2003) *Economic Review Committee*; MTI. (2010). *Economic Strategies Committee.*

[23]For details, see Auyong (2014) op. cit.

major role for manufacturing, referred to in 2003, as in 1986, as one of "the twin engines of manufacturing and services". And despite the earlier (1979) stated intention to reduce dependence on foreign labour, all reports emphasised the need for continued, if reduced, imports of foreign labour and, especially, foreign talent. To varying degrees, they also mentioned the need to develop domestic private entrepreneurship, recognised as a deficiency of the Singapore model compared with those of Hong Kong, Taiwan and South Korea.

Interestingly, relatively early on, as well as recently, Singaporean economists, myself included, voiced scepticism about high-tech manufacturing as a durable and desirable development strategy for Singapore in the long term, as these representative remarks show:

> *The question may be raised as to whether the government should be creating an artificial comparative advantage for Singapore in high-technology manufacturing, and indeed, whether it can succeed in doing so. The new strategy requires, apart from the foreign capital, technology and markets that Singapore's labor-intensive export manufacturing sector is already dependent on, increasing dependence on foreign skilled labor and expertised.*[24] (Lim, June 1983, p. 758)[25]

> *It is not apparent that Singapore has a comparative advantage in high-tech industry, at least in the short term. The prerequisites for success in high-tech industries are an abundance of scientific skills, large expenditure on R&D, and the availability of venture capital and dynamic entrepreneurship... Although much has been spent on technical, scientific, and engineering education and training in the past decade so that the talent pool is growing, it lacks experience and critical mass, and is expensive in comparison with that available in the other NICs, and even in some advanced countries.... Singapore does not have a ready availability of venture capital, in spite of its very high savings rate and its well-developed financial markets.* (Chia, 1989, p. 274)[26]

> *In manufacturing, though, the planners are banking heavily on the biomedical industry... to spearhead industrial upgrading. Unfortunately... biomedical output tends to be as volatile as electronics exports, being constantly subject to unpredictable demand fluctuations and changes in product mixes. Furthermore, the government is taking a calculated gamble in picking this industry as a putative winner. It is well known that the*

[24]This paper refers to alternative development strategies discussed in Pang, EF and L Lim (1982). Political economy of a city-state. In *Singapore Business Yearbook*, 7–33. Research Collection Lee Kong Chian School of Business.
[25]Lim, LYC (June 1983). Singapore's Success: The Myth of the Free Market Economy. *Asian Survey*, 26(6), 752–764.
[26]Chia (1989). op. cit.

> *huge R&D investments in biotechnology have long gestation periods before basic research can be applied to the commercial production of new drugs and medical technologies, not to mention stiff competition in this area from other countries such as Korea, which arguably has a comparative advantage over Singapore.* (Choy, 2010, p. 136)[27]

Reservations were also voiced about the continued dependence on both foreign and state enterprises

> *Secondly, the dominance of foreign enterprises and the public sector have to some extent crowded out domestic private enterprise. Foreign-owned enterprises and state-owned enterprises compete with domestic private enterprises in both the product and factor markets....*
>
> *The crowding-out effect is likely to be more serious in the labour market, as foreign investors and the public sector compete for scarce skills, and cream off the best talents by offering attractive salaries and career perks, thus inducing an upward pressure on salaries. The ready availability of remunerative jobs in government and MNCs, continuing full employment, and rising wages tend to discourage entrepreneurial risk-taking among the younger generation.*
>
> *The crowding-out effect also operates with regard to access to capital. The high contribution rates for employees set by the Central Provident Fund (CPF) have reduced personal disposable incomes and voluntary savings, and thus contributed to a scarcity of personal and household venture and risk capital....*
>
> *Thirdly, the rising cost of doing business also penalizes domestic entrepreneurs in SMEs. Large-scale urban redevelopment, for instance, has led to serious dislocations of many small businesses... as relocated businesses often face higher rentals in their new premises. Rising labour and utility costs, compliance with... business regulations, have also impinged harder on the SMEs.*
>
> *Fourthly, the tax system is biased against local entrepreneurs in manufacturing activities. The high tax rate on corporate profits and the absence of taxes on capital gains and windfall incomes have distorted entrepreneurial returns, thereby diverting entrepreneurial energies away from industrial production, which is characterized by long gestation periods, towards speculative activities in real estate and the stock market. And while the government offers wide-ranging tax incentives to promote industrial investments, local SMFs tend to benefit less than foreign MNCs because of the selection criteria.*
>
> *Finally, social attitudes have bred risk aversion rather than the entrepreneurial spirit. This is the result of a paternalistic government, a strong regulatory environment, an emphasis on social conformity, an*

[27]Choy (2010). op. cit.

> *educational system emphasizing scholarship rather than creativity and innovativeness, and a growing intolerance of failure.* (Chia, 1989, pp. 265–266[28])

and about the dependence on foreign workers:

> *The question we must answer sooner or later is this, 'When do we stop growing?'... at what point do we stop importing foreign workers and cease to encourage foreign entrepreneurs and capital in Singapore? Because of our limited land area, industrial expansion, together with the concomitant population expansion, will produce overcrowding to increasingly uncomfortable limits.* (Goh Keng Swee, as cited in Teh, 2014)[29]

> *[Given official projections of annual economic and productivity growth rates]... the population of foreign workers, temporary and permanent, will rise in Singapore in the 1980s. The benefits of such workers to the local economy are well known, but the potential social and economic costs they pose have yet to be closely examined. These include the costs of providing housing, public transportation, social services and recreational facilities.*
>
> *...These costs will spill over to the local population, who will have to compete with the foreigners for scarce and increasingly costly housing, and for services such as transportation, recreation and public health facilities. Costs will escalate rapidly and Singaporeans may have to subsidize the increased services to accommodate the foreigners. Their dissatisfaction with the declining quality of life may lead to hostility against foreigners.*
>
> *...These social problems will intensify as the composition of the foreign labor force becomes increasingly weighted toward workers from countries other than Malaysia.... As the nontraditional sources of labor increase, so will ethnic, cultural and linguistic differences, which may limit productivity as well as intensify problems of social cohesion and integration.*
>
> *...The short-term flexibility foreign workers offer must be weighed against the need for a restructuring of the economy.* (Pang & Lim, 1981)[30]

> *To avoid an overdependence on imported labour, however, the government ought to review its policy on the intake of low-skilled foreign workers. By augmenting the size of the labour force, these migrant workers have held down economy-wide wage increase. But the same workers depress earnings at the lower end of the nominal wage scale because of their low productivity, thus impacting on income distribution adversely. Worse, relying on them indefinitely implies that Singapore's economic progress would still be achieved primarily by increases in labour inputs rather than productivity improvements. Since there are upper limits to immigration and the population size, sustainable growth in the long run can only come from*

[28]Chia (1989). op. cit.

[29]Teh, KP (2014). Globalisation and Singapore's Discontent, talk given at the Asia Pacific Real Estate Association (APREA) Chairman/CEO Series, September 5.

[30]Pang, EF and L Lim (1981). Singapore's Foreign Workers: Are They Worth the Costs? *Asian Wall Street Journal, August 4.*

the latter. Hence, a slower pace of economic growth might not be a bad thing if it is achieved through productivity gains and is accompanied by less macroeconomic volatility. (Choy, 2010, p. 135)[31]

These consistent analyses reflect traditional economics, which is the "science" of the allocation of scarce resources among competing alternative uses. As I have explained elsewhere:

Comparative and competitive advantage both allow for government policy to influence a location's competitiveness in particular sectors, through selective investments that shape resource endowments, and tax incentives and subsidies to target resource allocation toward particular sectors.

However, these policies can be imitated with relative ease, leading to "beggar-my-neighbour" outcomes and excess capacity....

As a national economy moves up the technology ladder, the capital and opportunity cost of further state-directed shifts in comparative or competitive advantage escalates, given diminishing returns. Further, competition created by government policy rather than market forces introduces a large element of political risk into business decisions, encourages inefficiency in the allocation of resources, and reduces world welfare.

...These time-tested economic maxims boil down to one prognosis for Singapore's economic model — you can't have everything, even without size and resource constraints. Trying to achieve comparative advantages in too many sectors at once will only push up resource costs, aggravate negative externalities such as inflation and environmental degradation, and result in reduced competitiveness overall. Competitive advantage based on economies of scale, first-comer and agglomeration or cluster advantages derived from government policy rather than geographical advantages, are probably unsustainable. (Lim, 2009)

Singapore itself likely suffered recently from a "beggar-my-neighbour" event when Broadcom, a large US fabless semiconductor firm, announced that it was moving some of its operations out of Singapore to Ireland, leading to speculation that this could be due to the expiry of tax incentives.

Tax incentives reduced Broadcom's Singapore taxes by US$423 million (S$528 million) last year, and by US$399 million in 2012 — significant sums given that its net earnings were US$424 million last year and US$719 million in 2012...

[The company's annual report] said tax incentives such as those it enjoyed in Singapore "often require us to meet specified employment and investment criteria" in the relevant jurisdictions.

---

[31] Choy (2010). op. cit.

> *It added: "In a period of tight manufacturing capacity, our ability to meet Singapore content requirements in our products may be more limited, which may have adverse tax consequences".*
>
> *Broadcom's decision to use its Irish trading company for some foreign operations was expected to "result in a similar foreign tax provision as our current Singapore tax incentive", it said.* (Chia, 2014)[32]

SINGAPORE'S ECONOMIC PROSPECTS: THE NEXT 50 YEARS

Singapore's "global city" economic model, successful in terms of delivering rising incomes and living standards for its citizens through high GDP growth in the first decades of independence, has recently come up against domestic resource and social constraints:

> *Singapore's continued policy of importing foreign capital, foreign labour, and foreign technobgy, and privileging foreign/global companies, to serve foreign markets, poses obvious local political, social, and cultural challenges for the nation and the state....*
>
> *These policies, together with changes in the global economic environment and the globalization processes of multinational companies, have resulted in much more ambiguous impacts on the local population. GDP growth, hinged to globalization in specific ways dictated by the state, has in the past decade suffered multiple setbacks that reflect continued if not increased vulnerability to the vicissitudes of volatile regional and global economies.... The growth which has occurred has seen low shares in GDP for labour incomes (relative to capital returns), and consumption (relative to investments and government expenditures), increased income inequality, and a decline in the relative incomes of local Singaporeans relative to foreigners. The specific forms and requirements of GDP growth have also contributed to the undermining of national identity and social cohesion which previously held together the people of this "hub economy" and sustained their support for their government.* (Lim & Lee, 2010, pp. 153–4)[33]

A great deal of policy and public interest has been devoted to these issues since the general election of 2011, in which opposition political parties made unprecedented gains in popular votes and parliamentary seats (Low

[32]Chia, YM (2014). Clarity needed on whether chip dip a cause for worry. *The Straits Times.* Retrieved from http://www.straitstimes.com/st/print/2792236.

[33]Lim, LYC and SA Lee (2010). Globalizing State, Disappearing Nation: The Impact of Foreign Participation in the Singapore Economy. In T. Chong (Ed.), *Management of Success: Singapore Revisited* (pp. 139–158). Singapore: Institute of Southeast Asian Studies.

and Vadaketh, 2014).[34] This suggests that the industrial and social policies so critical to past success have been found wanting in the current stage of development.

The PAP government has responded by working to improve housing affordability, reduce inflation and transport congestion, expand healthcare and social safety net provisions for the elderly and the lowest-income. It is also slowing (but not stopping) the inflow of foreign workers, subsidising wage increases, putting in place (relatively minor) affirmative action provisions for Singaporeans in the job market and trying (yet again) to increase productivity, so far without success.[35] As noted on the Ministry of Manpower's website (MOM, n.d.)[36]:

> *Over the past decade, Singapore's economy grew by an average of 5% per annum. Singapore's productivity growth over the same period averaged about 1% per annum, a rate on par with that of other developed countries. The broad majority of Singaporeans also enjoyed real wage growth and a rise in living standards.*
>
> *Nonetheless, productivity gains have declined in recent years due to heavier reliance on labour inputs to generate economic growth, especially inputs of foreign manpower.*
>
> *Productivity is the only sustainable way to increase our value-add and grow our incomes and it must be the key driver of our economic growth. The Government will focus on helping businesses and workers improve their productivity and continue to provide support through many programmes and schemes.*

Significantly, the government has also announced a lowering of the target rate of GDP growth to 2% to 3% per year, similar to that in other developed countries, rather than the 3% to 5% (with 2% to 3% annual productivity growth) recommended by the Economic Strategies Committee in 2010 (Lee, 2015).[37] Clearly, it now accepts the limitations on growth imposed by domestic resource — and political — constraints, and maturity

[34]Low, D and S Vadaketh (2014). *Hard Choices: Challenging the Singapore Choices.* Singapore: NUS Press.

[35]Productivity dropped dramatically in 2014. Sec http://www.tradingeconomics.com/singapore/productivity.

[36]Ministry of Manpower (MOM), (n.d.). Skills, Training and Development. Ministry of Manpower. http://www.mom.gov.sg/employment-practices/skills-training-and-development.

[37]Lee, U-W (2014, January 17). PM Lee redefines 'economy faring well'. *The Business Times.* Retrieved from http://www.businesstimes.com.sg/government-economy/pm-lee-redefines-economy-faring-well.

as a developed economy, which also undermine the continued viability of the "global city" model itself.[38] As I noted in a 2009 interview:

> *Certainly, to generate growth, just by adding more input, you can get more output. But what is the opportunity cost? How much did we pay to attract such investment and what else might have been done with the money, tax revenue foregone and other local resources? Because we are a small economy, big, lumpy, capital-intensive investments that we do not control also increase our risk and our vulnerability to downturns, rather than protect us from them.*
>
> *Ultimately, economic growth... should seek to increase the "income, welfare, stability and security of all Singaporeans". It should be "growth for people", not "people for growth".*
>
> *In the long run, a lower rate of growth which delivers a higher ratio of benefits to Singaporeans may be more desirable than a higher rate of growth which is more unstable and inequitable.* (Long, 2009a, p. 10)[39]

The global economic environment, so favourable in the first few decades after independence, is also very different today, presenting both challenges and opportunities for the future.

First, there will be a slowdown, if not a reversal, in the pace of globalisation in the next fifty years; world trade growth has fallen to, or below, world GDP growth, which it dramatically outpaced in previous decades (*The Economist*, 2014, December 13).[40] The reasons for what some

[38]See *The Economist.* (2014, March 7). The world's most expensive city: Sing on a shoestring. Retrieved from http://www.economist.com/blogs/banyan/2014/03/orld-s-most-expensive-city and Milman, O. (2015, January 5). The price of life in Singapore, city of rules: 'It's a Faustian deal'. *The Guardian.* Retrieved from http://www.theguardian.com/cities/2015/jan/05/the-price-of-life-in-singapore-city-of-rules-its-a-faustian-deal. While Singapore has been promoting urban density as a positive attribute of its "liveability" as a city, this does not mesh with studies that show a strong preference of rising middle classes in Asia, particularly China and India, major source countries for immigrants to Singapore, for more physical space, as reflected in growing suburban sprawl. See *The Economist.* (2014, December 6). A planet of suburbs: Places apart. All dense cities also have very low fertility rates, which I and others have commented on in the Singapore context. Ever-increasing density, including through large-scale immigration, could thus compound Singapore's extreme demographic dilemma; see Lim, LYC (2014), How land and people fit together in Singapore's economy, in Low and Vadaketh, op. cit., pp. 31–47.

[39]Long, S (2009a, March 11). Why it can't be more of the same. *The Straits Times.*

[40]*The Economist.* (2014, December 13). International Trade — A troubling trajectory. Retrieved from http://www.economist.eom/news/finance-and-economics/21636089-fears-are-growing-trades-share-worlds-gdp-has-peaked-far.

have called "deglobalisation" include, on the supply side:

- Acceleration in shifts of comparative advantage, with automation in situ taking over from offshoring to more labour-intensive locations as manufacturing wages rise, whether in the US, where "reshoring" is picking up (*The Economist*, 2013, January 19)[41] or China, where electronics contract manufacturer Foxconn is planning to replace its one million workers with robots (*The Economist,* 2011, August 6)[42];
- Revolutionary technologies like 3-D printing enabling mass customisation and small-batch production at or close to where the final consumer resides (*The Economist*, 2013, September 7)[43];
- Continued shrinkage of the already fractional share of manufacturing in the value-chain of physical products like the Apple iPhone, most of whose value is embedded in services like design, marketing, software, retail and return to capital (of the roughly US$500 iPhone retail price in 2011, less than US$10 went to manufacturing in China) (Schuman, 2011)[44];
- Producing where you sell to save on transport and inventory costs and turnaround time, and to reduce currency exposure and risk;
- Lower marginal benefits from further trade and investment liberalisation when most countries have already liberalised, with further liberalisation and standardisation more likely to occur on a regional than global level;
- Environmental and social policy pressures to reduce carbon footprints and thus streamline and shrink currently far-flung global supply chains;
- Narrowing of competitive advantage differences between geographies based on relative productivity levels, infrastructure and government incentives increasingly constrained by international agreements and protocols to "level the playing field", as economic development proceeds around the world.

---

[41] *The Economist.* (2013, January 19). Reshoring Manufacturing: Coming home. Retrieved from http://www.economist.com/news/special-report/21569570-growing-number-americ an-companies-are-moving-their-manufacturing-back-united.

[42] *The Economist.* (2011, August 6). Foxconn: Robots don't complain. Retrieved from http://www.economist.com/node/21525432.

[43] *The Economist.* (2013, September 7). 3-D printing scales up. Retrieved from http://www.economist.com/news/technology-quarterly/21584447-digital-manufacturing -there-lot-hype-around-3d-printing-it-fast.

[44] Schuman, M (2011, May 16). Adding up the iPhone. *Time.* Retrieved from http://content.time.com/time/magazine/article/0,9171,2069042,00.html.

On the demand side, we see:

- A slowdown in global macroeconomic growth as the rich world ages and stagnates and booming emerging markets become more mature;
- Manufacturing's shrinking and services' expanding share of value-added in global value-chains as world incomes rise, populations age and the heavily services-oriented "app economy" takes hold;
- Social innovations like the spread of the "sharing economy" (Lever, 2015),[45] the "on-demand economy" (*The Economist*, 2015, January 3),[46] conservation culture, buy-local norms and a values shift from material to experiential "goods" (like social media communications);
- A much lower rate of employment creation by large companies: for example, Facebook has annual revenues of US$12 billion and a market capitalisation exceeding US$200 billion but serves 1.5 billion customers with only 8,500 employees worldwide, most of whom are in its home country.

All these add up to slower growth in output, a lower ratio of goods to services in output, a lower ratio of manufacturing to services value-added in goods, a greater localisation of goods and services production, and a much lower employment to output ratio, occurring at much lower levels of per capita income than in the present-day developed world. This is the post-industrial society on a global scale.

For Singapore, these global trends indicate a need for transformation beyond the "global city" paradigm of the past fifty years. Today, there are also many more "global cities" competing for this role — Hong Kong, Shanghai, Sydney, Seoul — and more will emerge in the next fifty years. The gap in every dimension (physical infrastructure, income levels, social amenities, shopping, cultural activities) between the first-tier global cities of Shanghai and New York has dramatically narrowed while Shanghai's share of world GDP has increased as New York's has shrunk.[47] The same will eventually be true of the gap between Bangkok and Manila with that of Singapore.

[45]Lever, R (2015, February 3). 'Sharing economy' shapes markets as complaints rise. Agence France-Presse.

[46]*The Economist.* (2015, January 3). The Future of Work: There's an app for that. Retrieved from http://www.economist.com/news/briefing/21637355-freelance-workers-available-moments-notice-will-reshape-nature-companies-and.

[47]In 2000, China's share of world GDP was 3.6% while the U.S. share was 31%. By 2012, China's share had increased to 11% while the U.S. share had fallen to 22%. During this period, China's per capita income rose from 2.6% to 12.2% of the U.S's per capita income. See World Development Indicators at www.data.worldbank.org.

Domestically, Singapore's comparative advantage long ago shifted decisively away from labour- to capital- and skills-intensity, despite decades of this market adjustment being slowed by compensating policy-created competitive advantages such as a liberal foreign-labour-and-talent policy. Such policy advantages will be increasingly difficult to sustain given heightened competition and spreading global norms like the reduced acceptability of tax-avoidance incentives for multinationals, a major feature of Singapore's attractiveness to foreign investors, many of whom would not locate here without them.[48]

> *However, is the real risk to Singapore that the age of the hub in MNC business models is coming under pressure and potentially to an end? A number of Beps proposals could make having a hub in somewhere like Singapore less palatable, if it means higher taxes on a global basis. For example, MNCs could end up paying more in taxes when paying dividends from profitable subsidiaries with a hub in Singapore than if they had just paid to the headquarters directly. In that case, would this negate the operational benefits of having the hub in Singapore?*
>
> *In a more extreme scenario, MNCs could choose to just invest into territories directly rather than through a hub location such as Singapore. This could be bad news for Singapore.*[49] (Pickford, 2015)[50]

Changing US financial regulations such as those removing expatriate tax benefits, enforcing taxation of offshore bank accounts (under the Foreign Account Taxation Compliance Act, or FATCA) and imposing more restrictive credit rating standards on sovereign wealth funds like Temasek

[48]I have heard this from many multinational subsidiaries in Singapore that I interviewed for my research. For the declining global acceptability of "tax arbitrage", see e.g., "EU to accuse Apple of taking illegal tax aid from Ireland", *The Guardian*, September 28, 2014; "More than 50 Countries Sign Tax Deal", *Wall Street Journal*, October 29, 2014; "UK Targets Tech Firms with 'Google Tax'", *Wall Street Journal*, December 3, 2014; "New Leak Shows Scope of Luxembourg Corporate-Tax Deals", *Wall Street fournal*, December 10, 2014; "EU to Widen Sweetheart Tax Deal Probe", *Wall Street Journal*, December 17, 2014.

[49]Beps stands for the Base Erosion and Profit Shifting project that is being carried out by the Organisation for Economic Co-operation and Development (OECD). The current move towards corporate tax reform in the U.S., if effected, would also reduce the need for MNCs to shelter overseas income in offshore tax havens like Hong Kong, Singapore, Luxembourg, Ireland, Bermuda and the Cayman Islands.

[50]Pickford, B (2015, January 27). Responsible taxation — the impact on Singapore's hub status. *The Business Times.* Retrieved from http://www.businesstimes.com.sg/opinion/responsible-taxation-the-impact-on-singapores-hub-status.

and GIC also impact Singapore's financial services sector ("Singapore isn't Greece, Singapore tells S&P in 29 pages", 2015).[51]

LOOKING TO SERVICES AND THE REGION

While Singapore's chosen development strategy of becoming a "global city" was the right one for its time and circumstances fifty years ago, the challenges of remaining internationally competitive in this role emerged rather quickly. It was only sixteen years after independence that Pang Eng Fong and I (1981)[52] wrote:

> *Ultimately, Singapore will have to face up to a fundamental strain in its domestic economy: the competition for labor between the services and the manufacturing sectors.*
>
> *...Because of its labor-intensive base, and the rigidities imposed by fixed capital investments, restructuring in the manufacturing sector must be slow, and its success in the competitive international arena is by no means assured. The projected demands for high-skilled and experienced technical personnel are great and can't be met from the domestic labour pool. It's possible that they can't even be met internationally, given the shortages in skilled labour in most competing countries, including the advanced industrial nations.*
>
> *...Singapore has a much stronger international competitive advantage in the export of services — banking, finance, commercial services, transportation, telecommunications — based on its long experience and large human and capital investment in these sectors. Another asset is its location in a rapidly growing regional economy of which it is the service hub. The service sector is intrinsically labor-intensive, and will become more skill-intensive as it upgrades into high-value services.*
>
> *At the same time, even in export manufacturing industries, Singapore's competitiveness is shifting toward service-oriented activities such as regional warehousing, purchasing, servicing and research and development. Both commercial and industrial services have a demand for skilled professionals that can't be supplied adequately from domestic sources. And, as the Singapore population grows more affluent, it will consume more labor-intensive social and personal services than goods, further increasing the domestic demand for labor.*
>
> *One solution to the long-range problem of labor shortage is to concentrate Singapore's limited domestic resources in the one area in which it has the greatest competitive advantage — the supply of services, including*

[51] *The Straits Times.* (2015, February 6). Singapore isn't Greece, Temasek tells S&P in 29 pages.

[52] Pang, EF and L Lim (1981, August 4). op. cit.

> *industrial-based services. This would mean the phasing out of production-oriented manufacturing, in which Singapore's potential advantage on a global basis is problematic.*
>
> *Unskilled labor would be released for the nontraded services sector, and skilled labor would be available for professional jobs in the highly competitive traded services sector. Reliance on both unskilled and skilled foreign labor would be reduced, and Singapore's historic complementary role to countries in the region would be enhanced.*

A few years later, the Report of the Economic Committee (1986) made similar recommendations:

> *[Singapore should] move beyond our being a production base, to being an international total business centre. We cannot depend only on companies coming to Singapore solely to make or assemble products designed elsewhere. We need to attract companies to Singapore to establish operational headquarters, which are responsible for subsidiaries throughout the region. In Singapore such headquarters should do product development work, manage their treasury activities, and provide administrative, technical and management services to their subsidiaries ...*
>
> *Services account for an increasing share of our GDP, and our service exports have been growing as quickly as world trade in services. Scope for growth is still huge. We need to promote not just Singapore-based activities like tourism or banking, but also offshore-based activities, like construction firms building hotels in China, and salvage firms operating in the Middle East... we have expertise in hotel management, air and sea port management, town and city planning. These skills should be systematically marketed...*
>
> *Our greatest potential for growth lies in this area: banking and finance, transport and communications, and international services. It has been growing rapidly.... The government must promote services actively, the same way it successfully promoted manufacturing.... Suitable incentives, including taxation of income from international services at a lower rate, will speed the shift toward a service economy.* (As cited in Lee, 1989, p. 293).[53]

However, the committee did not recommend any reduction in the promotion of manufacturing:

> *As manufacturing is to be treated equally with services, there appears to be a continuity of the old pattern of concentrating on the overall growth rate as the target of economic policy and of emphasizing the visibility of*

[53]Lee, SA (1989). Expansion of the Services Sector. In *Management of Success: The Moulding of Modern Singapore*, Sandhu, KS and P Wheatley (Eds.), 280–299. Singapore: Institute of Southeast Asian Studies.

> *manufacturing, despite the possibilities and the strength of the services sector.* (Lee, 1989, p. 297)[54]

Furthermore, the Economic Review Committee (2003) continued to emphasise manufacturing as one of the "twin engines" of GDP growth. Services continued to expand, growing from 60% of the GDP in 1985 and 1990 to 63% in 2005; its share of employment rose from 67% in 1990 to 77% in 2005 (Choy, 2010, p. 129)[55], enabled by the liberal foreign labour and talent policy as competition continued with the heavily-subsidised manufacturing sector for scarce resources. As the theory of *comparative* advantage tells us, a comparative advantage in one sector means a comparative disadvantage in another, and even large economies like the US and China cannot be equally competitive in every sector.

Choy (2010)[56] argues thus for a change in Singapore's economic model[57] away from manufacturing to services:

> *the service sector is less risky. Due to its very nature, service industries are less dependent on foreign capital and tend to be influenced to a smaller extent by business cycles. As Singapore establishes itself as a reputable exporter of final services such as financial wealth management, the media business, marketing and design services, tertiary education, and medical treatment — moving away from the current reliance on activities that are cyclically tied to manufacturing production such as intermediate trading, transportation, and banking services — the economy's vulnerability to external shocks will be reduced accordingly. The construction of two world-class integrated resorts to attract high-spending visitors to Singapore can be construed as a step in this direction, though it must be acknowledged that international tourist traffic will remain sensitive to global economic conditions and geopolitical events.*
>
> *More to the point, the development of a heterogeneous and diversified service sector offers the prospect that monetary policy will be a potent tool for mitigating economic fluctuations, as a result of the greater sensitivity of tradable services to exchange rate movements. Since exportable services have much higher domestic value-added and lower import content compared with manufactured goods, theory predicts and empirical evidence confirms that a currency depreciation stimulates the foreign demand for services much more than it does commodity exports.*

---

[54]Ibid.

[55]Choy (2010). op. cit.

[56]Ibid.

[57]The definitive quantitative longitudinal study of the Singapore economy and its institutions is in Abeysinghe, T and KM Choy (2002).

For all this to come to pass, however, government bureaucrats need to intensify greatly their efforts to promote the service sector in general, and expand regional markets for tradable services in particular. Servicing the needs of the burgeoning middle classes in China and India could easily add a percentage point or two to Singapore's potential growth rate. One should also not neglect to mention the untapped potential of domestically-oriented service industries catering to a richer and ever-growing local population. Economic planners in Singapore must, therefore, shed their long-held bias in favour of manufacturing, stemming perhaps from the perception that service jobs are less glamorous and that the average level and growth rate of productivity in the service sector are lower compared with the goods industries. However, service industries have the virtue of being relatively labour-intensive, thus generating more employment and helping to keep both structural and cyclical unemployment at bay. The same cannot be said for high-technology manufacturing. For example, the biomedical sciences cluster currently accounts for only a small proportion of the workforce, its forward linkages with the health care industry notwithstanding. Moreover, if Singapore is going to be compared to the leading cities of the world such as New York and London, having a vibrant and progressive service sector will be essential for success....

...the manufacturing-based export growth engine which Singapore and other Asian economies have relied on so heavily for economic success has run out of steam and left them without domestic demand stabilizers. Therefore, it is time for the government to change Singapore's economic model to meet the new economic circumstances and challenges. (pp. 136–137)[58]

The next question one might ask is services for whom? The Strategic Economic Plan (1991) recommended the launch of what was called a "second wing" for the Singapore economy, encouraging local enterprises to venture out and invest in booming neighbouring countries, with the assistance of government fiscal incentives, tax concessions, equity financing and infrastructure provision to support overseas ventures.

By 1997, S\$75.8 billion in cumulative outward direct investments had been committed by local firms, though the lion's share was, not surprisingly, attributed to government-linked companies (GLCs).

Sadly, though, the Asian financial crisis erupted in July 1997 with the devaluation of the Thai baht and brought to a dramatic end the golden era of strong regional and domestic economic growth that had lasted for nearly a decade. (Choy, 2010, p. 126)[59]

[58]Choy (2010). op. cit.
[59]Ibid.

Despite this slowdown, both large and small Singapore companies have continued to invest abroad, with Asia their top source of overseas revenue, and ASEAN particularly important for SMEs.[60] Recently, Dr Teh Kok Peng (2014)[61] has called for "creating a second Singapore outside Singapore" (as cited in Teh, 2014):[62]

> *while the particular globalization strategy that Singapore embarked on soon after independence was the right one ... we may have overstayed in applying this strategy as the dominant one. As a result, our shortage of land, labour and other capabilities is becoming more obvious and severe. I believe it is time to have a second strategic pillar, which I would describe in short as "creating a second Singapore outside Singapore." ... the economic space of Singapore and Singapore companies should be much bigger than the geographical space of Singapore....*
>
> *Singapore's land and labour constraints are immutable. Since independence in 1965, our planners have done a remarkable job in land reclamation and urban planning such that we have been able to increase our population and the intensity of our land use without the residents feeling unduly overcrowded or congested until recent years.... Nevertheless, in the long term, there is clearly a limit as to how much more we can do in land use intensification, given how much we have already done.*
>
> *With regard to labour, Singapore had actually run up against domestic labour constrains early on, and had begun importing foreign workers, mainly Malaysians, by the early 1970s.... Since then, our dependence rate of foreign workers as a proportion to our total work force has risen sharply, to possibly the highest in the world, with the exception of the Gulf States.... It is this surge in our resident population... that has given rise to... discontent.*
>
> *...It may well be that Singapore can support a population of 6.9 million without being congested or over-crowded, with clever planning and after the current massive construction of MRTs, highways, hospitals, schools, HDBs etc. all reach completion. But it may also be the case that one man's buzz is another man's claustrophobia.*
>
> *The question also arises as to the marginal benefit of such further large capital investments in a limited space and ... with the limited supply of labour. In economic theory, when one factor of production — land — is largely fixed, and another factor — labour — can only grow slowly, adding more and more capital leads to diminishing returns. About twenty years*

[60]See "Asia remains biggest source of overseas revenue for Singapore companies", *The Straits Times*, January 29, 2015, citing the Singapore International 100 ranking by the DP Group.

[61]Teh, op. cit.

[62]Dr Teh, an economist, was President of the Government of Singapore Investment Corporation (GIC) Special Investments division from 1999–2011, and is currently a non-executive director of several large Singapore companies.

ago, Paul Krugman argued that Singapore's growth... was largely driven by inputs of labour and capital rather than productivity. If this is true, are we in the process of doing more of the same, even if the declared intent is to develop a more innovation-based, productivity-driven economy? (pp. 100–101)

Dr Teh goes on to note that more mature developed economies are all large importers *and* exporters of foreign direct investment, which yields higher returns than the portfolio investments in which Singapore currently concentrates its massive foreign reserves (resulting from high savings and large cumulative budget and current account surpluses, managed mainly by MAS and GIC). Given this large stock of accumulated capital and other capabilities, and a per capita income that is one of the world's highest, a "second Singapore" is clearly feasible as well as desirable. Income from foreign investments would also help counter the long-term balance-of-payments outflow of investment income from the huge stock of inward foreign direct investment in Singapore itself. In Dr Teh's opinion, "it seems to me that we are at a stage of development where the greater risk by far is not venturing out".[63]

Such outward direct investment has the following benefits: easing the pressure on Singapore's own land and labour market, as foreign labour is employed in their home countries instead; enabling SMEs to achieve scale more easily and deploy their developed technologies and capabilities more profitably in lower-cost locations; avoiding potential exclusion from promising markets, and acquiring new knowledge and capabilities abroad that could be transferred to enhance parent firms' competitive advantages; and higher returns on investments enabling the payment of higher taxes to help fund the domestic transfer payments put into place to serve growing social needs.

Fortunately, in addition to the physical, financial and human capital built up over the past fifty years, Singapore benefits from an excellent geographical location in the centre of South-east Asia. This is the next large emerging regional market to which global multinationals are already turning their investment attention, as are Singapore and national companies in our neighbouring countries.[64] The tapering off (*note:* not total disappearance)

---

[63]Comment made at IPS Singapore Perspectives 2015.

[64]See, for example, "Indonesia sees surge in foreign investment", *Wall Street Journal*, January 20, 2012; "Foxconn moves into Indonesia, worrying labor groups", *Christian Science Monitor*, September 5, 2012; "Indonesia to Big Chains: Share the wealth", *Wall Street Journal*, May 12, 2013; "Facebookers in Indonesia Rise to 69 million", *Wall Street Journal*, June 27, 2014; "Japan Inc. goes deeper into Southeast Asia", *Wall Street Journal*, September 28, 2014; "Japanese Investment in Southeast Asia: Outward bound", *Economist*, November 1, 2014.

of the 20th-century development model of manufacturing for export through multinational networks to rapidly-ageing, slowly-growing, distant rich markets will be replaced by domestic consumption-led growth in faster-growing nearby middle-income markets like China (as it "rebalances" its economy away from the current investment-driven export-led manufacturing model towards increased domestic consumption of services)[65] and the more youthful India and Indonesia. Singapore's well-developed industrial services referred to above can also integrate with developing manufacturing capabilities in neighbouring countries, for both regional and global markets.

Singapore can build on our natural differentiating advantages versus other "global cities" by playing a role in regional value-chains catering to the hundreds of millions who are already entering the middle class all around us. Based on comparative (capital, skills) and competitive advantage (infrastructure, first-comer advantage, location, culture), our edge is likely to be in value-added services — finance, education, health-and-wellness, recreation — that we already provide to the world's and region's wealthy, and which market research studies already show strong demand growth for in these markets.[66] What we need to do is cater more explicitly to the much larger numbers just slightly further down the regional income distribution, who are likely to consume similar services and at similar price-points to the bottom 80% of our local citizens by income level, who can provide and benefit from such services themselves as skill capabilities and scale economies develop.

Put simply, we will move from manufacturing physical goods for customers richer than we are to providing services to customers poorer than we are. The good news is that services for our regional neighbourhood are more location-specific and scalable, and less capital- and energy-intensive, than manufacturing for distant markets, less reliant on rare specific technical skills unlikely to be found in adequate scale among our small population and more open to small entrepreneurs with different levels of formal education, providing a channel for employment creation, upward mobility and reduced inequality (through SME ownership and the capital returns from operating

[65]This is the same economic model that Singapore should also rebalance away from. See Lim, LYC (2010). Rebalancing in East Asia. In *Rebalancing the Global Economy: A Primer for Policymaking*, Claessens, S, S Evenett and B Hockman (Eds.), 32–35. London: Centre for Economic Policy-Making.

[66]Some examples include McKinsey (March 2012), "Meet the Chinese Consumer of 2020"; Accenture (February 2013), "Meet the New Chinese Consumer"; Boston Consulting Group (March 2013), "Indonesia's Rising Middle Class and Affluent Consumers".

in regional markets). As I have written elsewhere:

> *In both high-tech manufacturing and financial services, Singapore lacks not just market scale and supply-chain depth and diversity, but also a sizeable globally-competitive labour and talent pool. So far it has succeeded by importing the narrowly specific skill sets that these sectors require — like electronics engineers from China and financial and IT experts from India — but this has already bumped up against... constraints. In the next 50 years it will also become more difficult to attract top talent from other Asian countries as their economies develop, giving their talented citizens better career opportunities and lifestyles at home.*
>
> *Fortunately, Singapore's scale also confers certain advantages, in that it only needs to excel (on the supply side) in relatively few, smaller but higher-value, product niches in order to compete globally and provide sufficient employment opportunities for its resident population, with the help (on the demand side) of expanded domestic consumption by the local population, and demand from increasingly affluent regional neighbours. Looking forward 50 years, two major intrinsic assets that the country possesses are its geographical location in the centre of what will be the world's largest fast-growing middle-income regional market (the currently 600-plus million in Southeast Asia, together with the 1.5 billion-plus in South Asia), and its own population's cultural affinity with the populations in that market, which will be particularly important in various professional, personal and social services.*
>
> *In financial services, for example, the principle of portfolio diversification alone will dictate that some segment of the burgeoning mass middle classes of Southeast Asia will place some portion of their savings in or with Singapore-based financial institutions and finance professionals, just as high-net-worth individuals from the region and the world already do. In tourism, there is already a large and vibrant regional market, which will only grow as more families are able to afford short holidays in neighbouring countries. Health and educational services are already well-developed and have further room to grow, especially for average-income customers.* (Lim, 2015, p. 101)[67]

Note that Indonesia is already the largest source of international visitors to Singapore, followed (at some distance) by China, while elder services (that Singapore's rapidly-expanding ranks of elderly could also benefit from at home) are already beginning to take off in China (Burkitt, 2015).[68] From a trade policy perspective, for all its likely disappointments, the ASEAN

---

[67] Lim, LYC (2015). Singapore in the International Economy. In *Singapore 2065: Leading Insights on the Economy and Environment from 50 Singapore Icons and Beyond*, Quah, E (Ed.), 98–102. Singapore: World Scientific.

[68] Burkitt, L (2015, January 20). China's aging boomers are lucrative market. *Wall Street Journal.*

Economic Community, which is due to be launched by the end of 2015 (ASEAN Secretariat, 2014),[69] will enhance the prospects for regional services integration, given its vision of a "single market" for services, regulatory standardisation, infrastructural connectivity (e.g. in telecommunications, to facilitate e-commerce) and promotion of SMEs and SME collaboration.

What of the role of state industrial and social policy, which I argued above was critical to the success of the post-independence "global city" economic model? This transition from being one of many global cities to becoming a one-of-a-kind regional city requires shifts in Singaporean mindsets, educational choices, labour market behaviours and government policies that directly or indirectly influence and incentivise them.

> *Focusing on employment and income creation for the average native Singaporean as opposed to income maximisation for footloose foreign corporations... requires a shift in economic policy and individual thinking from, among others, the global to regional, manufacturing to services, capital to labour and skills, high-end to middle, foreign to local, state to market, large to small, profits to wages, corporate to entrepreneurial, and so on.* (Lim, 2015, p. 101)

Given the strong underlying market advantages, I do not see a role for state industrial policy to micro-manage this shift. Rather, I would propose a downsizing, if not dismantling, of the whole bureaucratic infrastructure that has for decades strived — with some, if incomplete and declining, success — to "manage" Singapore's international competitiveness as a "global city", particularly in manufacturing. Not only is such state management of competitiveness no longer effective or even possible in the changed global environment that is already with us today, but it also distorts resource allocation at home and abroad, discouraging entrepreneurial investments. A reduction in the role of state intervention in the forces of dynamic comparative and competitive advantage would, among other things, release scarce resources of capital and local talent to find their way into the most market-advantageous economic activities which I, and others, have argued are likely to be in services for the domestic and regional market, a process which is already taking place. As noted in my 2009 interview:

> *The way forward for Singapore... is to allow the market to 'diversify on its own', with resource allocation done by market forces and entrepreneurs, instead of the state and bureaucrats.*

---

[69]ASEAN Secretariat (May 2014). *Thinking Globally, Prospering Regionally — ASEAN Economic Community 2015.* Jakarta: ASEAN.

> *Do we devote our carefully husbanded national savings, accumulated over generations, to letting the state make big bets on a few major, capital-intensive, risky and expensive projects?*
>
> *Or do we privatize the economy, releasing capital and talent to local entrepreneurs to create value in smaller but nimbler enterprises? At least, if they fail, it will take only small parts, rather than big chunks, of the economy down with them.*
>
> *It's much better to send out 100 motorboats, rather than one huge aircraft carrier, into the unknown. I would bet on at least some of the motorboats making it, instead of the aircraft carrier, a sitting duck, which could get blown up.* (Long, 2009b, p. 10)[70]

I have been visiting Myanmar for thirty years. About eight years ago, I interviewed some Singaporean businesses there and found to my surprise and delight that there were already about 350 of them, mostly SMEs in services like trading, schools, hair salons, small hotels, shops and restaurants. This was well before Myanmar starred opening out to foreign investment in 2011, after which Singapore GLCs, banks and government agencies like International Enterprise Singapore (IE) and SingBridge, as well as MNCs from many countries, moved in in a big way. Our SMEs had ventured into a very difficult business environment ahead of most of the "big boys", and they were doing well.

Since the 1991 "second wing" initiative, many of our GLCs have also ventured into the region. Mr Chow Yew Yuen, CEO of Keppel Offshore and Marine, shared his company's experience:

> *As offshore and marine, we operate in 15 countries and we have 20 yards worldwide. Most of our operations we manage with a few Singaporeans. We find that Singaporeans are actually, because of our background, able to operate in those countries quite well if you compare with people of maybe more homogeneous societies like the Japanese or the Koreans... In our case, we are moving a lot of our less skill intensive types of operation overseas. For example, we have moved to the Philippines, Indonesia and some of the other regional places. But to protect the mothership, we are consciously making decisions on where we keep our R&D development, our project management development and our supply chain management (in Singapore).*[71]

[70]Long, S (2009b, March 11). New growth model beyond Jack-of-all-hubs needed. *The Straits Times.*

[71]Comment made at the post-panel discussion at IPS Singapore Perspectives 2015 on 26 January 2015.

Individual Singaporean entrepreneurs have also ventured into our Southeast Asian neighbours.

One example is Kwok Kian Tow, a Singaporean economist-by-training whose company runs granite quarries and processing facilities in Singapore, Malaysia and China, branching out into construction materials in Vietnam and Myanmar, and into property development in Malaysia and China. His company also manufactures die-cast aluminium parts in Malaysia. To quote Kwok:

> *The British East India Company sent ordinary Englishmen to the 'Far East' and many became leading businessmen thousands of miles away from home. Each of us who went away from Singapore shores to do business in Southeast Asian countries and beyond had an EIC "eureka moment" — that these lands held opportunities equal to or better than home. As for the drive and the flow to do business in unfamiliar settings, most of us had no EIC to give us a start, a leg up. Each had his own story.*[72]

Some younger Singaporeans are also doing the same thing, and for the same reason, namely, they see the Singapore market as "saturated".

And Sharifah Yuhaniz, a Singaporean MBA entrepreneur in Malaysia, says:

> *In my business, the opportunities are in South East Asia. With lower oil prices, many downstream projects like in situ small-scale power generation projects are becoming viable and are taking off. Especially in an archipelago of small land masses like South East Asia, producing power near demand makes a lot more sense than dealing with expensive transmission.*[73]

Social policy could also have a role to play in enabling or encouraging more Singaporeans to become entrepreneurs, develop service enterprises and venture into Southeast Asia. For example, if Singaporeans did not have to devote so much of their savings to CPF and housing, they would have more disposable income and time to spend on consuming domestic services,[74] creating jobs at home and accumulating start-up capital and developing

[72]Kwok Kian Tow, personal communication with author in February 2015.

[73]Sharifah Yuhaniz, personal communication with author on 23 February 2015.

[74]Abeysinghe, T and KM Choy (2004). The aggregate consumption puzzle in Singapore. *Journal of Asian Economics*, 15, pp. 563–578; Abeysinghe, T and J Gu (2011). Lifetime income and housing affordability in Singapore. *Urban Studies*, 48, pp. 1875–1901; Lim, LYC and J Cheng, "Why Singapore is not Iceland", *The Business Times*, Singapore, January 24, 2014; "'Meaningful correction still unachieved': Tharman", *The Business Times*, October 29, 2014; "Not kicking the habit", *Economist*, February 7, 2015, all refer to the high level of household debt in Singapore. In contrast, in the U.S., entrepreneurs often resort to home mortgages for start-up capital.

capabilities that could be invested both at home and abroad. They might even be able to marry at a younger age, have more children and be able to support themselves in their post-retirement years ("Top concerns for Singaporeans", 2015).[75] A universal social safety net for poverty and pension relief might reduce the risk aversion that discourages entrepreneurial activity. And educational options could be increased at all age levels to provide experiences (e.g. active learning projects in neighbouring countries) and skills (e.g. studying South-east Asian languages, non-university accounting, finance and marketing courses) that would encourage and enable entrepreneurship.[76] Given vested (and competing) interests, including entrenched bureaucratic interests, and the multiple other needs that social policy must fulfil, bold policy changes are unlikely here.

CONCLUSION

The "global city" model served Singapore's economic development well in the early decades of independence when it comported well with the country's mostly market-based comparative and competitive advantages. As these changed, strategic government industrial and social policy interventions managed to preserve international competitiveness, mostly by importing foreign capital, talent, labour and technology to serve global markets. However, this was at the cost of ever-increasing subsidies for foreign investors ("corporate welfare"), distortions and rigidities in the allocation of resources, disappointing productivity growth, increased volatility, inequality and negative externalities, and the "crowding out" of local entrepreneurs and non-favoured sectors, calling into question the model's continued economic, social and political sustainability.

Looking forward to the next fifty years, dramatic and rapid changes in the global economy further undermine the viability of the "global city" model. However, a fortunate geography, and valuable national assets accumulated over the past half-century, provides Singapore with a new opportunity to prosper as a regional city serving the growing service consumption needs of the increasingly wealthy middle classes of South-east and South Asia, and connecting them with the wider world as necessary. This transition

[75]Channel NewsAsia (2015, February 16). Top concerns for Singaporeans: Retirement adequacy, healthcare and cost of living. *Channel News Asia*, Retrieved from http://www.channelnewsasia.com/news/singapore/top-concerns-for/1663084.html.

[76]For a more extended discussion of what Singapore and Singaporeans can do to prepare for the employment challenges of the present and future, see Lim, LYC (2014). What's wrong with Singaporeans? In Low and Vadaketh, op. cit. pp. 79–96.

requires an entrepreneurial spirit that will enable us to create our own jobs rather than slot ourselves into the declining number of jobs that will emanate from large foreign companies. In addition, a mindset shift in geographical orientation is required:

> *For the last 40 years, Singapore has viewed itself as 'an outpost of Western empire, catering to those scared of the jungle and needing an intermediary'...*
>
> *...Instead of trying to be a 'secondary global node', Singapore should focus on being a 'primary regional one' and leverage its 'unique location-specific advantages'.* (Long, 2009a, p. 10)[77]

From the 1910s to the 1930s, my great-grandfather Kung Tian Siong, the first of now six generations of my family to study in Anglo-Chinese School (and, beginning with my great-grandmother, Methodist Girls' School), frequently travelled to and readily conducted business in cities as diverse as Batavia (now Jakarta), Surabaya, Pontianak and Shanghai on the one hand, and Los Angeles, Chicago, New York, London and Frankfurt on the other, while his younger brother Kung Tian Cheng lived and worked for some years in Bangalore and Mysore as well as Penang, Shanghai and Beijing. Their widowed mother was an illiterate seamstress who spoke only dialect, yet both men became fluent and literate in English, Malay, Mandarin and several Chinese dialects, and were clearly comfortable in many different cultural milieus.[78] There have always been Singaporeans like them, and there should be many more in our next fifty years, as we increase the regional, while retaining the global, content and context of our city, and of our nation's economy. Conserving our multicultural national identity will then go hand in hand with economic progress and social well-being.

REFERENCES

Lim, LYC (2009). Singapore's Economic Growth Model: Too Much or Too Little?" *Ethos*, 6, 32–38.

Pang, EE and L Lim (1989). High Tech and Labour in the Asian NICs. *Labour and Society*, 14, 43–57.

[77] Long (2009a). op. cit.

[78] For more details on their lives and careers, see Lim, LYC (2014). *Four Chinese Families in British Colonial Malaya: Confucius, Christianity and Revolution* (3rd Ed.). Retrieved from www.blurb.com. Also available at the National, NUS and ISEAS libraries in Singapore.

Part II

LABOR AND WOMEN IN ECONOMIC DEVELOPMENT

Chapter 6

LABOR, PRODUCTIVITY AND SINGAPORE'S DEVELOPMENT MODEL*

PANG ENG FONG and LINDA Y. C. LIM†

This paper discusses how Singapore's labor market policies since independence have been molded by the state-driven, foreign investment-led, export-oriented, manufacturing-focused development model the country has followed over the past fifty years. The literature we review shows that high GDP growth has been achieved through factor accumulation rather than productivity increase, a strategy of extensive growth that has now run into diminishing returns as well as political, social and resource constraints. Prolonged heavy dependence on imports of foreign labor and skills to attract foreign investment has contributed to low, declining and even negative productivity growth, with low real GDP growth in recent years. In response, the government is pursuing renewed economic restructuring, limiting foreign labor inflows, targeting investments more selectively, and promoting productivity and innovation, so far with uncertain results. This paper suggests that Singapore should let market forces propel the economy toward services, domestic consumption and regional trade, led by domestic private enterprise. But the retreat from established state industrial and social policies will be difficult.

1. INTRODUCTION: SINGAPORE'S DEVELOPMENT MODEL

Singapore's extraordinary journey from relative poverty to impressive prosperity began with its unplanned independence in August 1965.[1] Along the

*This chapter was first published in *Singapore Economic Review*, Vol. 60, No. 3, 2015, 1550033-1–1550033-30. Reprinted with permission from World Scientific Publishing Singapore.

†Corresponding author.

[1]Lee Kuan Yew, Singapore's Prime Minister from 1959 to 1990 said in an interview in Newsweek (18 September 1989) "we did not want an independent Singapore — it went against our logic on how to build a stable long-term future as a multiracial community. We considered Singapore not viable. But we were forced to make it viable".

way from Third World to First, Singapore evolved a distinctive development model based on a large role for multinationals and an extensive involvement of the state in reshaping the economy and society.[2] Local enterprises in Singapore played only a supporting role, not the catalytic one that they did in South Korea, Taiwan and Hong Kong.

The dominant role of the state[3] in Singapore's economy and society began after self-government in 1959, when the government led by the People's Action Party (PAP) under Lee Kuan Yew moved swiftly to tackle the serious problems of a stagnating entrepot economy, high unemployment, and urgent housing and educational challenges arising from a rapidly growing population. It embarked on a mass public housing program, introduced family planning, and made plans for industrialization that involved an expanding role for the state. By independence in 1965, the government had become not only a regulator and planner, but also a significant player in the economy, having taken equity stakes in many companies, in large part because the private sector was unable or unwilling to risk its own capital, and it was believed that state enterprises were necessary to create wealth and jobs. Despite these efforts, development achievements in the first half of the 1960s were modest because of political uncertainties and labor unrest. But the period did lay the institutional groundwork for the evolution of a uniquely activist state.

Separation from Malaysia in 1965 meant that the import-substituting industrialization strategy previously envisaged for the larger combined domestic market was no longer feasible, and the newly-born city-state had to turn to export manufacturing instead. But there were few domestic companies that could be nurtured into national industrial champions capable of competing in international markets, given their concentration in the commercial services of a colonial port-city. So, government policy-makers turned to attracting foreign capital, even though much of the developing world then had serious reservations about its long-term positive contribution to industrialization.

---

[2]The central role of the government in the economy is not due to a large public sector or high level of government spending to GDP. The public sector — civil service and statutory boards — employed 138,000 persons or 6.2% of the resident workforce of 2.2 million in 2013. In 2012, the government spending to GDP ratio was 17%, one of the lowest among developed economies.

[3]The word "state" encompasses more than "government". It includes all the administrative, legal, bureaucratic and coercive systems that influence relations between a people and those in authority. The state is not a unitary institution and conflicts between parts of the state and different groups of people are inevitable.

Separation did not just cause a change in development strategy. The traumatic event produced in the political leadership a profound sense of psychological insecurity and an acute awareness of Singapore's vulnerable position in Southeast Asia — enduring anxieties that arguably continue to shape the city-state's domestic and foreign policies. On top of the daunting challenge of economic survival, Singapore's political leaders had to build a nation out of an ethnically diverse population descended mostly from immigrants. The struggle for political and economic survival was one and the same thing, leading to policies to promote social stability and industrial peace which were critical both to attracting foreign capital and to nation building.[4]

In addition to the normal government controls over the macro-economy through monetary, fiscal and exchange rate policies (the colonial-era regimes of free trade and capital flows remaining largely intact), the Singapore state progressively extended its controls over domestic capital (e.g., Central Provident Fund "forced savings", persistent budget surpluses, huge foreign exchange reserves, and world-scale sovereign wealth funds), land and property (e.g., housing over 80% of the population through the Housing Development Board, and developing commercial and residential private properties through state-linked entities), and the labor market (the focus of the rest of this paper). Government entities including statutory boards and state enterprises (later transformed into government-linked companies (GLCs) through partial divestment or privatization) provide, and profit from providing, infrastructure, finance, and services.[5]

The role of foreign capital or multinationals is itself heavily mediated by state industrial policy, particularly investment promotion led by the Economic Development Board (EDB), which has impacted labor market policy and outcomes, and resource allocation more generally. The basic policy of tax incentives, subsidized infrastructure and labor policies to attract foreign investors has remained unchanged for five decades, with Choy (2012) noting that "Singapore held no attraction then, and now, as

[4]Alternate historical explanations are possible for Singapore's unique and persistent dependence on both state and foreign capital. In the colonial and early post-colonial era, most local private enterprise was in the hands of the "Chinese-educated", many of whom supported anti-colonial and then left-wing opposition politics, whereas the more "moderate" PAP was led by "English-educated" professionals. State and foreign enterprises provided an alternative to reliance on potentially contentious domestic private capital, while foreign capital additionally bolstered national security by giving foreign powers a vested interest in Singapore's political survival (Lim, 1987).

[5]See e.g., Lim (1983), Lim *et al.* (1993) and Huff (1999).

a final market; for FDI to keep flowing in, the state has to continually entice investors with tax concessions."[6] At independence, lacking both a domestic market and indigenous industrial expertise, Singapore had "no choice" but to provide state incentives to attract foreign investment for its capital, technology, international market access and the resulting employment creation and income growth. Foreign direct investment (FDI) inflow and the export earnings it generated also covered and then reversed the city-state's longstanding trade deficit. However, there was "no feedback from these beneficial outcomes to investment itself" (Choy, 2012, p. 5), requiring the constant "chasing after" new foreign investments as Singapore's comparative advantage, external demand and international competition changed. Specifically, since the late 1970s incentives have been constantly redesigned to encourage industrial restructuring, technological upgrading, higher value-added and "knowledge-intensive" activities which market forces would presumably otherwise not direct to Singapore.

Besides industrial policy, policy in social sectors like housing, healthcare, education and pensions served both to entrench the state and serve the needs of foreign capital (Lim, 1989; Lim and Lee, 2010). Being a city-state (Pang and Lim, 1982b) was an advantage, with concentrated population in a small physical area facilitating both industrial and social policy, from external defense and domestic political control to housing and "social engineering". The government intervened in the social system to promote values and attitudes favorable to nation-building, self-reliance and hard work, over the years imposing a multiplicity of controls and regulations which have profoundly shaped Singapore society.[7] While promoting social order and facilitating economic progress, these social interventions have also arguably bred an aversion to risk-taking, discouraging domestic private entrepreneurship. Citizens came to be increasingly dependent on the government, seeing it as not only the provider of basic needs, but also the generator of wealth and opportunities. Periodically since the 1980s, the state itself has noted the limits of a development model based on two key actors — the state and foreign firms, drawing attention to the need for the local private sector to play a bigger role.

---

[6] Choy (2012), p. 5.

[7] Singapore's Prime Minister Lee Kuan Yew said in the Straits Times (20 April, 1987) that "I am often accused of interfering in the private lives of citizens. Yes, if I did not, had I not done that, we wouldn't be here today. And I say without the slightest remorse, that we wouldn't be here, we would not have made economic progress, if we had not intervened on very personal matters — who your neighbour is, how you live, the noise you make, how you spit, or what language you use. We decide what is right. Never mind what the people think."

2. LABOR MARKET POLICIES

At independence, labor was Singapore's only "natural resource", but the labor market had long been characterized by frequent labor unrest which also undermined political stability. Beginning in the early 1960s, the PAP government introduced various legislative and administrative measures to curb rival unionism and promote industrial peace (Vasil, 1989). After independence, to ensure the success of the export-oriented development strategy which hinged on low wages and labor discipline, the government increased its role in the labor market. In 1968, it passed two labor laws to contain labor costs and improve the investment climate. The Employment Act of 1968 standardized terms and conditions of employment and set limits on negotiable fringe benefits. The Industrial Relations (Amendment) Act excluded from collective bargaining issues such as worker recruitment, retrenchment and dismissal, and dictated new procedures for labor negotiation and conflict resolution.

These laws succeeded in depoliticizing the labor movement, established de facto government control over unions, and gave employers considerable bargaining power over workers. They contributed greatly to the huge expansion of jobs in labor-intensive factories, especially for young women, which initiated major social and demographic changes. In less than a decade, export manufacturing by multinationals had reduced the backlog of unemployment. Since then, with the exception of several short recessions in 1973–1974, 1985–1986, 1997–1998, and 2008–2009, Singapore has enjoyed full employment, as low as 2% of the resident labor force.

In 1972, the government made two major interventions in the labor market. First, it relaxed immigration rules to allow labor-short employers to bring in foreign workers.[8] Second, it formed a tripartite National Wages Council (NWC) as an advisory body with representatives from government, employer groups and labor. The NWC was given three objectives — formulate annual wage guidelines, recommend wage structure adjustments, and advise on incentive systems. In practice, it directed its attention to the first objective. In 1972–1978, the guidelines succeeded in moderating wage pressures, keeping Singapore a competitive location for labor-intensive manufacturing. But they also had unintended effects: across-the-board

[8]The transition from a labor-surplus to a labor-importing economy took less than ten years for Singapore. For other rapidly industrializing economies like South Korea and Taiwan, the turning point took longer as they had an agricultural sector (Pang, 1975).

guidelines meant that actual wage increases did not fully reflect wide sectoral variations in labor demand (Pang and Quek, 1980). The burden of adjustment to changing economic conditions fell on the supply side of the labor market, impairing its efficiency (Pang, 1988). Wage suppression to keep wages in Singapore "internationally competitive" also attracted firms in search of low wages, resulting in more demand for cheap labor (Toh and Low, 1990, p. 264).

The government then became concerned that "orderly" wage increases were leading to a "low-wage equilibrium trap". So, in 1979–1981 it pursued a "wage correction" policy which resulted in high wage increases and slower employment growth, with a greater impact on the mostly local small and medium enterprises (SMEs) than on multinational companies. In the early 1980s, the council dropped its practice of issuing annual wage guidelines and instead became a forum for tripartite discussions on the economy and the labor market.

The policy to import foreign workers has had more profound consequences. In the 1970s, the inflow of unskilled foreign workers represented a small proportion of the labor force — 3.4% in 1970 rising to 7.4% in 1980. They were drawn mostly from Malaysia, the city-state's traditional hinterland, and employed in the manufacturing sector. But as labor shortages became widespread, employers were allowed to bring in workers from non-traditional sources and into the non-manufacturing sector. Unskilled foreign workers, less protected by labor laws, provided a useful flexible buffer in economic downturns, and were not subject to the annual leave for military training required of male citizen workers.

Regulations on the importation of skilled and unskilled foreign workers have over the years become increasingly complex, with adjustable levies that vary by industry, dependency ratio ceilings and minimum qualifying salaries for mid-level and high-level pass holders. Until 2004 when employers were allowed to bring in mid-level skilled workers under the S-Pass scheme, there were only two broad categories of foreign workers — highly skilled workers were issued employment passes while unskilled workers were given work permits. The introduction of the S-Pass scheme recognized that manpower shortages had become widespread and were no longer confined to highly-skilled or unskilled groups. It was also a response to representations by labor-short local as well as foreign employers.

The government initially viewed the resort to foreign workers as a temporary solution to manpower shortages. By the late 1970s, it was clear that the growing dependence on unskilled foreign workers could not continue indefinitely without imposing high social and economic costs on

Singapore.[9] In 1981, the government announced a policy to phase out unskilled foreign workers by 1991 (Pang and Lim, 1982a). However, the policy allowing the liberal import of skilled people remained unchanged. In fact, the government encouraged (and still encourages) employment pass holders who can be assimilated easily into Singapore to take up permanent residence.

In 1982, the government tightened conditions on the import of unskilled workers from non-traditional sources (that is, other than Malaysia). A year later, in response to employer complaints, it relaxed the deadline for phasing out unskilled workers from non-traditional sources. In 1984, employers were allowed to bring in unskilled workers from four new sources, namely, South Korea, Taiwan, Hong Kong and Macao. The long-term goal of phasing out unskilled foreign workers was set aside in the interest of short-term flexibility even as a variety of incentive measures were introduced to restructure the economy and reduce its need for unskilled labor.

In 1985, Singapore experienced its worst-ever post-independence recession. Its response was to cut costs, particularly employer CPF contributions, and to ease employer access to foreign workers. As the economy recovered in 1986, the upward trend in dependence on foreign workers resumed. The government still recognized the need to reduce reliance on foreign workers in the longer term, but was being "pragmatic" in responding to the short-term labor needs of employers. Thus foreign labor inflows ebbed and flowed with economic conditions, but the net result was a steady rise in the relative and absolute size of the foreign workforce in Singapore.

From the mid-1980s until the introduction of the S-Pass in 2004, the employment pattern of foreign workers differed significantly from that of local workers. Non-citizen, non-resident workers were over-represented at both the top and bottom ends of the skill hierarchy (Pang and Lim, 1982a). With the opening since 2004 of the mid-skilled job market to foreign workers (whose number jumped four-fold from 44,500 in December 2007 to 164,000 in June 2014)[10] the employment pattern of foreign and citizen workers has become more similar. While access to a huge regional pool of unskilled foreign workers has most likely depressed wages of citizen workers at the lower end

[9]As early as 1972, Goh Keng Swee, Singapore's Deputy Prime Minister had spoken of the risk of a rising dependence on foreign workers to sustain economic growth. See Au Yong (2014), Part 1.

[10]As Table 1 shows, in proportionate terms, this jump was much greater than those for work permits (which increased from 757,100 in 2007 to 980,800 in 2014) and employment passes (99,200 to 164,700).

of the labor market, the opening of the mid-level market to foreigners has enlarged the possibilities for employers to substitute foreigners for citizen workers with similar skills. In theory, employed citizen workers with mid-level skills should not be affected if demand is rising faster than supply. In practice, however, cost-conscious employers seeking greater workforce flexibility find it advantageous to replace older, higher-wage mid-skilled locals with younger replacements from abroad.[11]

The government has long voiced concern about the negative effects of rising dependence on foreign labor. Tony Tan, then Finance Minister, said in his 1985 Budget Speech that "the solution to our labor shortage cannot be an indefinite and ever-growing dependence on foreign workers. The experience of countries, which have indiscriminately allowed large numbers of foreign workers to settle permanently, shows that this gives rise to social and political problems of such a magnitude as to threaten the cohesiveness and stability of their societies." But his speech had little impact on policy. From the mid-1980s to early 2000s, public unease about the rising inflow of foreign workers grew, yet the government did not restrict it, fearing that this would harm the economy. In a 2011 speech at the 50th anniversary of the HDB, Singapore's founding Prime Minister Lee Kuan Yew noted that "we've grown in the last five years by just importing labor. Now, the people feel uncomfortable, there are too many foreigners."[12]

It was only after the PAP suffered its greatest electoral setback in May 2011, when it lost the Aljunied Group Representation Constituency to the Workers' Party, that the government tightened the inflow of foreign workers (excluding domestic workers), slowing the growth rate from 8.8% in 2011 (already down from the 20.7% increase in 2008) to 1% in 2014 (Table 2). Prime Minister Lee Hsien Loong in a speech at the opening of National Productivity Month on 7 October 2014 said "we are controlling foreign worker inflows so that we put pressure on companies to upgrade their workers rather than simply hiring extra bodies. But we still give companies enough access to foreign workers to complement your Singaporean workforce, because if we allow in too few foreign workers, or freeze their numbers, some

[11]There are also complaints from Singaporeans that foreign employers and hiring managers tend to favor fellow nationals, a practice known among sociologists in U.S. academia as "homosocial reproduction".

[12]For some examples of studies of foreign labor policy in Singapore, see Wong (1997), Huang and Yeoh (2003) and Chia (2011).

Table 1. Foreign Workforce Numbers, Singapore, 2007–2014[1]

Pass Type	2007('000s)	2008('000s)	2009('000s)	2010('000s)	2011('000s)	2012('000s)	2013('000s)	2014('000s)
Employment Pass (EP)	99.2	113.4	114.3	143.3	175.4	173,800	175.1	176.6
S Pass	44.5	74.3	82.8	98.7	113.9	142,400	160.9	164.7
Work Permit (Total)	757.1	870.0	851.2	865.2	901.0	942,800	974.4	980.8
— Work Permit (Foreign Domestic Worker)	183.2	191.4	196.0	201.4	206.3	209,600	214.5	218.3
— Work Permit (Construction)	180.0	229.9	245.7	248.0	264.4	293,300	318.9	321,200
Other Work Passes[2]	—	—	5.2	6.0	7.6	9,300	11.3	14.7
Total Foreign Workforce	900.8	1,057.7	1,053.5	1,113.2	1,197.9	1,268.3	1,321.6	1,336.7
Total Foreign Workforce (excluding Foreign Domestic Workers)	717.6	866.3	857.4	911.8	991.6	1,058.7	1,107.1	1,118.4
Total Foreign Workforce (excluding Foreign Domestic Workers & Construction)	527.1	616.8	588.3	638.9	699.1	731.3	748.1	753.7

Source: http://www.mom.gov.sg/statistics-publications/others/statistics/Pages/ForeignWorkforceNumbers. aspx.
Note: [1]Data may not add up to the total due to rounding.
[2]Other Work Passes' includes Letter of Consent (LOC) holders and Training Work Permit (TWP) previously included in published Work Permit (WP) figures. Training Employment Pass (TEP) was included in "Other Work Passes" from Mar 2014 onwards.

Table 2. Annual Percentage Change in Foreign Workforce, Singapore, 2008–2014[1]

Pass Type	2008	2009	2010	2011	2012	2013	2014
Employment Pass (EP)	14.3%	0.8%	25.4%	22.4%	−0.9%	0.8%	0.9%
S Pass	66.9%	11.4%	19.2%	15.4%	25.0%	12.9%	2.4%
Work Permit (Total)	14.9%	−2.2%	1.6%	4.1%	4.6%	3.4%	0.7%
— Work Permit (Foreign Domestic Worker)	4.5%	2.4%	2.8%	2.4%	1.6%	2.3%	1.8%
— Work Permit (Construction)	27.7%	6.9%	0.9%	6.6%	10.9%	8.7%	0.7%
Other Work Passes[2]	—	—	15.4%	26.7%	22.4%	21.5%	30.1%
Total Foreign Workforce	17.4%	−0.4%	5.7%	7.6%	5.9%	4.2%	1.1%
Total Foreign Workforce (excluding Foreign Domestic Workers)	20.7%	−1.0%	6.3%	8.8%	6.8%	4.6%	1.0%
Total Foreign Workforce (excluding Foreign Domestic Workers & Construction)	17.0%	−4.6%	8.6%	9.4%	4.6%	2.3%	0.8%

Source: http://www.mom.gov.sg/statistics-publications/others/statistics/Pages/ForeignWorkforceNumbers.aspx.
Note: [1]Figures have been calculated based upon figures obtained in Decembers of each year.
[2]Other Work Passes' includes Letter of Consent (LOC) holders and Training Work Permit (TWP) previously included in published Work Permit (WP) figures. Training Employment Pass (TEP) was included in "Other Work Passes" from Mar 2014 onwards.

businesses will not survive, especially SMEs, and many Singaporean jobs will also disappear".[13] Even though the foreign worker inflow has slowed, their absolute number is still rising. Public unhappiness with foreign workers, particularly those competing with Singaporeans for mid-level jobs, has not dissipated, despite new policies like the fair consideration framework (FCF) which came into force in August 2014 to prevent discriminatory hiring practices against Singaporeans (Cabuyao, 2015).

[13]In a 2012 May Day Rally Speech, PM Lee recognized that employers and workers see the influx of foreigners differently. "The employers... feel that they cannot find enough workers in Singapore, especially workers who will stay on the job. Hence, better to bring in some foreign workers, seize the opportunities, rather than let the business go somewhere else. At least you keep the jobs, the business in Singapore and you keep some jobs in Singapore. The workers often see it differently, that the foreign workers add to competition against them. If there are too many, it may reduce wages and it may even take away some of the jobs which Singaporeans can do. Better we have fewer foreign workers and let our wages rise."

3. LABOR MARKET OUTCOMES

Singapore's labor market policies contributed to the early attainment of full employment, which has been mostly sustained since. In the early days of independence, domestic labor supply increased largely due to a jump in female labor force participation (FLFP), responding first to new employment opportunities in female-labor-intensive export manufacturing industries, and then to demographic and societal changes, including reduced fertility and increased female education. FLFP rose from 28.2% in 1970 to 43.8% in 1980, then continued a steady climb to 58.6% in 2014, when male LFP was 75.9%, and women accounted for 44.4% of all employed residents. Both participation rates and incomes of women workers remain below those of men, though the gaps have narrowed significantly, and participation continues to decline with marriage, child-bearing and age.[14]

Labor market policies also enabled a long period of high GDP growth based on factor accumulation heavily dependent on imported inputs of both capital and labor. But periodically holding wages below market levels (through the "downward flexibility" afforded by variable CPF contributions), and continually increasing the supply of foreign labor (through liberal immigration policy) discouraged economic restructuring even as a plethora of successive investment incentives and education and skill upgrading measures sought to achieve it. Table 3 shows that real wages of resident workers began stagnating, increasing by 1.5% a year from 2003–2013 (including employer CPF contributions) and by just 1.1% from 2003–2010 and 0.7% from 2010–2013 (excluding employer CPF contributions).[15] Income inequality increased over the same time period: in 2014 Singapore's Gini coefficient before government taxes and transfers was 0.462, one of the highest among developed countries.[16]

---

[14]Department of Statistics and Ministry of Manpower. Yap and Gee (2015) in this volume note that FLFP in Singapore does not increase after children are older, as it does in most other high-income countries.

[15]Real wages are computed for resident workers which include permanent residents who are on average better educated and paid than citizen workers. Data on wage changes for citizens and permanent residents are not publicly available and so it is not possible to analyze the impact of over half a million permanent residents on citizen wages. There are also no publicly available and separate figures on wage changes for unskilled non-resident workers. These data gaps render difficult any attempt to evaluate the effects of the rapid growth of the non-resident population on citizen wages (Basu, 2015).

[16]In 1966, at a much lower level of per capita income, the Gini coefficient was 0.457 (Pang, 1975). It fell by 1973 to 0.415, thanks to rapid employment growth and rising wages for workers at the lower end of the income distribution. Asher *et al.* (2015) in this volume argue that the Singapore Gini understates inequality because it is limited to labor income

Table 3. Annual Percentage Change in Labour Productivity and Real Wages, Singapore, 2003–2013

	Labor Productivity	Real Total Wages (Incl Employer CPF Contributions)	Real Total Wages (Excl Employer CPF Contributions)	Real Basic Wages
2003	5.7	0.3	1.0	0.7
2004	7.7	−0.1	1.9	1.0
2005	3.0	3.8	3.8	2.6
2006	2.1	3.5	3.5	2.6
2007	0.4	4.5	3.8	2.2
2008	−7.2	−1.7	−2.4	−2.2
2009	−3.3	−1	−1.0	0.7
2010	11.6	2.9	2.7	1.1
2011	2.2	0.9	0.1	−0.8
2012	−1.4	−0.4	−0.8	−0.1
2013	−0.2	2.9	2.9	2.7
2003–2010	2.5	1.5	1.7	1.1
2010–2013	3.1	1.6	1.2	0.7

Source: Survey on annual wage changes, MOM; and data from Department of Statistics (DOS).

Still, as the decades passed, education and skill levels, and wages, increased with high growth. In 1980, 83.1% of residents had not completed secondary education, while only 2.7% had a university education; in 2013, 31.2% had less than a full secondary education with 27.3% having a university education (Table 4). These ratios will rise as the existing "stock" of less-educated older workers retires and leaves the labor force. Correspondingly, professional and technical, and administrative and managerial, occupations rose from 13.6% of the labor force in 1980 to 53.1% in 2014 (Table 5). Despite a near-equalization by gender in educational attainment, women are still under-represented in higher-income occupational categories and higher-income levels within occupational categories, while they are over-represented in both mid- and lower-skill occupations.[17]

The sectoral composition of output and employment also changed — first, from regional services to global manufacturing for export from the mid-1960s to the mid-1980s, then back to services, especially high-value global financial and business services, since then. Notably, and contrary to the experience of all other developed economies (except South Korea) and

which accounts for only 40% of national income, excluding capital income, which accounts for 52% and accrues disproportionately to the top decile of the population.

[17]See Lim (2015a) for a more detailed analysis of women in the labor force in Singapore, including discussion of how they may be impacted by the foreign labor policy.

Table 4. Highest Qualification Attained of Residents Aged 25 Years & Over[1] (%)

Education Attainment	1980	1990	2000	2010	2013
Below Secondary	83.1	63.3	45.3	34.5	31.2
Secondary	9.5	23.6	24.0	19.0	18.8
Post-Secondary (Non-Tertiary)	4.7[2]	4.7	8.9	9.5	8.7
Diploma & Professional Qualification		3.6	9.8	13.3	14.0
University	2.7	4.7	12.1	23.7	27.3
Total	100.0	100.0	100.0	100.0	100.0

Source: http://www.singstat.gov.sg/statistics/browse-by-theme/population-and-population-structure.

Notes: [1]Data pertain to residents who are not attending educational institutions as full-time students. The data include those who are upgrading their qualifications through part-time courses while working.

[2]Data refer to post-secondary (non-tertiary) and diploma & professional qualification.

high-income major cities, manufacturing's share of GDP remained high at around one-quarter, though its share of employment predictably declined as state industrial policies targeted specific high-tech and capital-intensive "clusters" such as electronics, chemicals and pharmaceuticals. Unfortunately, these heavily foreign-dependent sectors also contribute to increased volatility and inequality (Choy, 2010), now considered major problems for the economy and society. Industrial restructuring toward male-intensive heavy industry reduced the proportion of women in manufacturing, while the expansion of services increased their representation there.

The proportion of foreign non-resident workers in the Singapore workforce had doubled from 3.2% in 1970 to 7.4% in 1980. Between 1980 and 1990, it doubled again to 16.1% and nearly doubled again to 28.1% in 2000 (Yeoh and Lin, 2012). Between 2004 and 2014, the number of non-resident workers more than doubled from 603,000 to 1.3 million (Table 6), and in 2014, 38.1% or more than a third of the labor force of 3.5 million in Singapore were non-residents.[18]

Very few countries have seen such a surge in foreign workers in recent years or have GDP growth that is driven largely by an influx of foreign labor. In the 1980s when GDP growth averaged 7.8% a year, employment growth was only 2.4% a year. In the decade 2000–2010, GDP grew at an average of 5.2% a year while employment expanded by 3.9% a year (Hui and Toh, 2014). Hui and Toh (2014) found that "employment as the driver of growth has increased its share from 31% in the 1970s to 75% in 2000s".

[18]Table 3 of Yap and Gee (2015) in this volume.

Table 5. Percentage Distribution of Labor Force by Occupation (in Thousands)

	1970		1980		1990		2000		2010		2014	
Year Occupation	No. ('000s)	%	No. ('000s)	%	No. ('000s)	%	No. ('000s)	%	No. ('000s)	%	No. ('000s)	%
Professional & Technical	56.1	8.6	95.1	8.8	240.6	15.6	433.6	29.2	706.9	37.2	1160.341	53.1
Administrative & Managerial	15.5	2.4	52.2	4.8	132.1	8.6	211.8	14.3	250.0	13.2		
Clerical	82.9	12.7	167.5	15.6	201.9	13.1	213.6	14.4	241.8	12.7	541.9296	24.8
Services & Sales	191.3	29.4	244.2	22.7	333.2	21.7	366.0	24.7	252.6	13.3		
Agricultural & Related Workers	26.9	4.1	21.0	1.9	8.9	0.6	1.2	0.1	1.0	0.1	482.9292	22.1
Production & Related Workers	254.9	39.2	435.0	40.4	558.8	36.4	285.5	19.3	254.0	13.4		
Cleaners, Laborers & Related Workers	—	—	—	—	—	—	101.1	6.8	130.3	6.9		
Not Classifiable	23.1	3.6	62.2	5.8	61.4	4.0	52.8	3.6	61.3	3.2		
Total	650.9	100	1,077.1	100	1,537.0	100	1,482.6	100	1,898.0	100	2185.2	100

Source of 1970–2010 data: Saw (2012). In *The Population of Singapore* (3rd ed., p. 291). Singapore: Institute of Southeast Asian Studies.
Source of 2014 data: http://stats.mom.gov.sg/Pages/Labor-Force-Summary-Table.aspx.

Table 6. Resident and Non-Resident Workers in Singapore, 2002–2013

Mid-Year	Total('000s)	Residents('000s)	Residents % of Total	Resident Growth Rate %	Foreigners	Foreigners % of Total	Foreigner Growth Rate %
2002	2,223.2	1,573.7	70.8	−0.6	649.5	29.2	−5.2
2003	2,208.1	1,605.4	72.7	2.0	602.7	27.3	−7.2
2004	2,238.1	1,632.1	72.9	1.7	606.0	27.1	0.6
2006	2,505.8	1,796.7	71.7	10.1	709.1	28.3	17.0
2007	2,670.8	1,842.1	69.0	2.5	828.7	31.0	16.9
2007[a]	2,631.9	1,803.2	68.5	−2.1	828.7	31.5	0.0
2008	2,858.1	1,852.0	64.8	2.7	1,006.1	35.2	21.4
2009	2,905.9	1,869.4	64.3	0.9	1,036.5	35.7	3.0
2010	3,047.2	1,962.9	64.4	5.0	1,084.3	35.6	4.6
2011	3,149.7	1,998.9	63.5	1.8	1,150.8	36.5	6.1
2012	3,274.7	2,040.6	62.3	2.1	1,234.1	37.7	7.2
2013	3,352.9	2,056.1	61.3	0.8	1,296.8	38.7	5.1

Source: Comprehensive labor force survey, Ministry of Manpower, Singapore (2014)
Notes: [1]Data for 1995, 2000 and 2005 are not available as the Comprehensive Labor Force Survey was not conducted in these years due to the conduct of the Census and General Household Survey by Department of Statistics, Ministry of Trade and Industry.
[2]To facilitate comparison with data for 2008 onwards, the 2007 data have been adjusted based on Singapore Department of Statistics' revised population estimates (released in February 2008) which exclude Singapore residents who have been away from Singapore for a continuous period of 12 months or longer. Adjusted data for 2007 are denoted by the symbol a.

From 2010 (which was a truly exceptional year of recovery from the global financial crisis with GDP rebounding by more than 14%) to 2014, annual GDP growth averaged about 3%, already at the low end of the 3%–5% range the Economic Strategies Committee (Ministry of Trade and Industry, 2010) suggested was possible. This was again driven largely by the import of more foreign workers and not by labor productivity growth. The government's own labor productivity growth target set in 2000 of 2% to 3% a year has not been achieved; from 2012–2014, productivity in fact stagnated. The large number of well- funded schemes that the government and its agencies have launched to encourage employers to innovate and substitute capital for labor, and workers to undergo additional training, appear to have had (so far) little effect. Supply-side policies to increase the labor force participation of women and of the elderly have had some success, contributing to a new high resident labor force participation rate of 67% in 2014.[19] But so far there have not been policies to attract back Singaporeans who have emigrated or are working abroad, who are likely to be more highly-skilled.[20]

4. GROWTH WITH LOW PRODUCTIVITY

The story of Singapore's unimpressive productivity record is not a recent phenomenon. As early as the late 1970s, Pang (1977) calculated that Singapore's manufacturing sector had productivity gains (measured as output per worker) of only about 1% a year. Tsao (1982, 1985) found that total factor productivity had stagnated in the 1970s in Singapore manufacturing. She advanced three explanations for this dismal record: the high reliance on foreign capital in manufacturing; the low level of industrial competence; and the use of unskilled foreign labor. A growth accounting study by Young (1992, 1994) suggested that Singapore's economic growth was largely driven by factor accumulation and that the huge influx of capital had not been efficiently used, with Singapore a "victim of its own targeting policies". Krugman (1994) characterized Singapore's rapid economic growth (averaging over 8% between 1966 and 1990) as "an economic twin of the growth of Stalin's Soviet Union growth achieved purely through mobilization of resources", the outcome of perspiration, not inspiration. These conclusions strengthened the government's resolve to intensify the restructuring drive begun in the late 1970s.

---

[19] Tay (2015), citing Ministry of Manpower.

[20] See Footnote 45.

The restructuring effort succeeded in attracting sizeable foreign direct investments in knowledge-intensive, high value-added industry clusters including microelectronics, information technology, logistics, aerospace, marine, clean technology, biomedical, chemicals and precision engineering. Also successfully targeted to broaden the high-value services sector were global finance, wealth management, media, new media, integrated resorts, medical services, logistics, and regional and global multinational headquarters, in addition to the city-state's traditional role as a hub for trade, tourism and transportation. Tax breaks and other incentives were also provided to foreign firms to move more R&D activities to Singapore, in the hope that they would transfer technology to local firms.

These efforts have transformed Singapore's industrial landscape, but they have made little difference to total factor productivity (TFP) growth.[21] According to Vu (2011), annual TFP growth fell from 2% in the 1980s to 1.4% in the 1990s, while from 2000–2008, TFP grew by only 0.5% a year. Using more finely disaggregated data, Nomura and Amano (2012) show that "TFP growth has been poor or even negative" from 1974–2011, while average labor productivity growth of 3.37% per year in the 1980s, 3.33% in the 1990s and 3.54% from 2000–2005 plunged to 0.54% in 2005–2010.[22] A Ministry of Trade and Industry study (2014) says that labor productivity grew by an average of 2.5% a year from 2009–2014 (only 0.3% if the exceptional recovery year of 2010 is excluded); in 2014 it fell by 0.8%.

Singapore's poor productivity performance is not for lack of policy focus or productivity-boosting schemes. Since the 1970s, the government has emphasized higher productivity as the primary engine for raising real wages and so the material standard of living. In developing strategies to increase productivity, it has adopted the approach of giving employers incentives to upgrade their operations through computerization, automation and mechanization and also to invest in manpower development (Au Yong, 2014). One scheme which the government instituted in 2011 and expanded in 2014 is the productivity and innovation credit (PIC), which gives companies tax deductions or cash grants when they invest in machinery and equipment to boost their capabilities. This and other schemes have been criticized for not evaluating their own effectiveness (e.g., how recipient firms have

[21]TFP growth measures the efficiency with which an economy uses factor inputs. It reflects technical change — the only long-run source of economic growth.

[22]Nomura and Amano (2012), Table 4, which also shows that TFP growth averaged −0.3% annually from 1974–2010, but 0.53% from 2000–2010. Png (2015) reports that multifactor productivity (MFP) fell by 2.3% in 2012 and 0.7% in 2013, suggesting that "productivity growth seems to have fallen to the point that the level of productivity is dropping."

performed), and for subsidizing poor management.[23] The government has also expanded continuing education and training support systems to improve the skills of workers already in the labor market as well as new job entrants from the polytechnics and universities.[24]

One explanation for low productivity growth is that the various government schemes introduced in recent years will take time to bear fruit, even though many similar schemes over the past three decades did not. In the highly labor-intensive restaurant sector, for example, Lim (2015) notes that "Restructuring will be difficult for many, after years of liberal foreign worker policies" due to "entrenched practices".... and "The productivity drive is only just gaining momentum among early adopters."

It can be argued too that the 2% to 3% annual productivity growth target established by the Economic Strategies Committee (Ministry of Trade and Industry, 2010) is too ambitious, given that Singapore is now a developed economy and almost all other economies at a similar per capita income level have a trend TFP rate of 1% to 2%. But as noted above, Singapore experienced low productivity growth even in earlier decades at much lower income levels. Nomura and Amano (2012) estimate that TFP contributed negatively to GDP growth from 1974–1980, and in the 1980s and 1990s; from 1974–2011, capital inputs contributed 63.6% and labor inputs 40.7% to GDP growth; capital deepening explained 83% of the average labor productivity growth from 1970–2010.

These data simply reiterate the long-known "extensive growth" model of development that the Singapore state has followed since independence to maintain a GDP growth rate much higher and for much longer than other economies have managed after maturing into high-income status. Growth in any economy is derived from factor accumulation (adding capital, labor, land to create "extensive growth" or more output from more inputs) and/or increases in total factor productivity (the more efficient use of

[23]Png (2015) cites a KPMG survey that found that 30% of survey respondents used the PIC to defray operational expenses rather than to boost productivity. The Singapore Budget 2015 released on 23 February 2015 announced that the PIC Bonus will expire in 2015, but other PIC measures will be extended. Other major productivity-enhancing schemes include the Innovation & Capability Voucher (ICV), the Increase SME Productivity with Infocomm Adoption & Transformation (iSPRINT) and Inclusive Growth Programme (IGP). For a list of productivity-related measures introduced in recent years, see Au Yong (2014), Part 3.

[24]For example, the SkillsFuture programme will give every Singaporean aged 25 and above an initial $500 of SkillsFuture Credit which will be topped up at regular intervals and can be used to pay for approved skill-upgrading courses. See Ministry of Finance (2015).

existing resources, enhanced by technological progress, to create "intensive growth" producing more output per unit of input). Singapore's early post-independence GDP growth was driven by inputs of labor (then primarily domestic and relatively abundant) and capital (readily available, mostly from foreign sources). This continued in the next four decades, with labor quality (human capital and skills) contributing an impressive 1% of the 6.78% annual GDP growth computed by Nomura and Amano (2012), who attribute the slowdown in labor quality improvement after 2005 to the sharp rise in low-skilled foreign workers. A Monetary Authority of Singapore (2010) study which found that labor productivity growth fell from 3.4% per year in the 1990s to 1.1% from 2000–2009 attributed this to "a sharp slowdown in... capital deepening as the economy utilized relatively more labor inputs for production" (p. 72), noting that "there is a large increase in physical labor input in recent years, aided by an inflow of foreign workers" (p. 77).

Crucially, despite economic policy-makers' early recognition that a switch toward intensive growth — or increasing productivity — was necessary, the basic model of state- driven multinational-led export manufacturing did not change, but rather was extended through ever more factor accumulation. Industrial upgrading, for example, required more and more capital investment per unit of output, and of labor, with its attendant need for ever-more-generous tax incentives and other state subsidies. When, as economics predicts, rapid growth at full employment caused the prices of complementary inputs (land and labor) to rise, the policy response was to prevent market adjustments from taking place, by continuing to subsidize scarce land (e.g., in state-provided industrial estates) and allowing greater access to foreign labor which depressed the price of competing local labor. In the many instances where the government back-tracked from its own policy intentions to reduce dependence on foreign labor, increase productivity and encourage high wages, the reason given was the repeated short-run need of foreign investors (and local SMEs which were part of their Singapore supply-chain) for "cost competitiveness" in the face of external demand shocks (global recessions), and increasing international supply-side competition (given the tendency of multinationals to relocate production as comparative advantage shifts), to which the traded goods sector (export-oriented manufacturing) is highly vulnerable.

With each successive policy back-tracking and return to the extensive growth model, diminishing returns worsened and opportunity costs rose — again as economics predicts, making it ever more obvious that "meagre factor productivity growth is the Achilles' heel of the Singapore economy" and there is a pressing need to "reduce the Singapore economy's dependence on capital and labor inputs and strive for slower but more sustainable economic growth through productivity gains instead... As the scope for factor accumulation is exhausted, the long-standing model of extensive growth has run into diminishing returns and needs to be replaced by a new paradigm that achieves intensive growth through making better use of existing resources and technological progress."[25]

This result conforms with research by Paul Romer and others suggesting that "the availability of abundant cheap labor not only discourages investment in productivity but also reduces innovation and increases income inequality." (Economist, 2013) The recent large-scale employment of foreign workers in the UK (roughly a third of the increase in employment since 2010) resulted in higher GDP growth than in its European neighbors, but with much lower productivity (20% below French levels) and wages (a third lower), though company profits have soared. "When people are cheap, firms would rather hire than invest in machines or technology. So productivity is held down." (Economist, 2015).

In Singapore in the end it was political and social constraints, rather than economic inefficiency and unsustainability of the extensive growth model, which led to the most recent and concerted attempt to pursue intensive growth. The sharp increase in the foreign worker population from 2006 was associated with rising housing, healthcare and transportation costs and congestion, and increased "social unease" among Singaporeans at a time when median and lower-end wages were stagnating, and income inequality increasing. This contributed to opposition party electoral and parliamentary gains in the 2011 general election (and subsequent by-elections). Various surveys since then have shown that a very high proportion of Singaporeans ("nearly 9 in 10") believe that the number of foreign workers should be reduced (Wong, 2013), and this proportion has remained high despite the government's policy response to tighten (but not reduce) inflows.[26]

[25]Choy (2012), p. 5. See also Choy (2010).

[26]For example, brokerage and investment group CLSA's latest survey of life in Singapore showed that "83% of respondents (believe) there are too many foreigners in Singapore. This view is largely affected by the sight of too much congestion (35%), job losses (20%) and higher costs of living (19%). Only 9% of respondents believe foreigners should be allowed to work in white-collar jobs. Moreover, there is a surprisingly high correlation between positive views of the transport sector and positive opinions of foreigners." The same survey found that 41% of respondents, and 52% of those under the age of 30, said their primary financial concern was the rising costs of living (Singapore Business, 2015).

In February 2012, Deputy Prime Minister and Finance Minister Tharman Shanmugaratnam said, "We have to reduce our dependence on foreign labor, and do much more to build an economy driven by higher skills, innovation and productivity."[27] The absolute number of foreign workers is still being allowed to increase, albeit at a slower rate. This change has imposed hardship on employers, particularly local SMEs which are still struggling to also cope with high commercial rents due to soaring property market values since 2009 (so far only slightly dampened by macro-prudential "cooling measures"). The 8.7% fall in the revenue of the top 1000 SMEs in 2014 was blamed on difficulties hiring labor and higher wage costs.[28] At the same time, unemployment fell to 1.9% in December 2014, with job vacancies rising to their highest levels in six years, 57.2% of them being in low-skilled jobs such as cleaners, waiters, shop assistants and security guards. Employers themselves cite low pay, unattractive work hours and the physically strenuous nature of work for their difficulty finding locals to fill such jobs, which at a range of $1000–1741 per month do not pay enough to cover the high cost of living in Singapore.[29] In 2012, rejecting calls to establish a minimum wage, the government instead introduced a progressive wage model to help employers upgrade and raise the wages of lowly-paid workers like security guards and cleaners: this approach has so far had little impact, and it is not clear that productivity in such jobs results from labor skills rather than complementary equipment (capital) and efficient management and operations processes (human capital).[30]

The Ministry of Trade and Industry study (2014) found that domestically-oriented sectors lagged behind export-oriented sectors in productivity gains, and said that the shift of workers to less productive but employment-intensive sectors like food and beverages and construction accounts for the disappointing labor productivity performance of the economy.

---

[27]Quoted in Mahtani and Raghuvanshi (2012).

[28]Lim (2015a) citing the 2014 SME Development Survey by DP Information Group.

[29]Ministry of Manpower (2015a,b); Cabuyao (2015).

[30]In economic terms, the Progressive Wage Model seeks to lift wages by raising the demand curve for labor, but the wage may still be depressed if the supply curve of labor is not reduced. A minimum wage would simply impose a wage that might be above (employment-reducing) or below (ineffective) the market-clearing wage determined by the demand and supply curves of labor for particular occupations. In the Singapore case, in low-skill occupations the supply curve (heavily influenced by foreign labor imports) is more likely to dominate the demand curve in setting the wage.

But these sectors[31] are not as labor-intensive in other high-income economies as they are in Singapore, suggesting that it is the distortion of relative factors prices which is responsible for their excess demand for low-skilled, low-wage labor. Employers who can "increase output more readily and cheaply by recruiting foreign workers, particularly from lower-income countries, than by investing in capital-labor substitution and upgrading the skills of the domestic labor force" may be expected to do so since "this is an entirely rational decision for profit-maximizing private enterprises" (Lim, 2014a, p. 32). Wage subsidies paid to employers, like the 2012–2015 Wage Credit Scheme (since extended to 2017), may reduce the effectiveness of incentives provided by automation subsidies like the productivity innovation credit to invest in capital-labor substitution and more efficient management and operations processes. Employers may also assume, based on the record of the past four decades, that the government may yield to business pressures to delay, reduce or reverse the tightening of foreign labor inflows: the 2015 Budget already defers increases in foreign worker levies for S-Pass and work permit holders, except for those in manufacturing and construction (the latter the one sector where the net inflow of foreign workers has not slowed).[32]

Besides employers, Singapore consumers, both local and foreign, may have "got used to" what may be called a First World lifestyle facilitated by Third World wages and labor conditions in the household, retail and food sectors, developing consumption habits and tastes very different from those prevailing in other high-income societies where businesses and consumers have adjusted to the relative scarcity of low-skilled service workers. For their part, Singapore workers may also shun "low-skilled" jobs not only because wages are too low (the most important, and economically rational, response), but also because of their association with low-wage temporary foreign workers willing and able to tolerate poor working and living conditions that would be unacceptable to locals in other rich countries, and the low social status accorded to such occupations — ironically perhaps partly because of decades of a public policy rhetoric promoting "skills upgrading" to "higher value" jobs associated with higher levels of formal education. Thus,

[31]Note that given Singapore's extremely open economy, many "domestic" services are in fact provided for foreign customers, including companies, workers and the large quantum of temporary foreign residents and visitors. "Services" in Singapore also include high value-added export-oriented sectors like finance, information and communications technology, healthcare and education.

[32]For details on the 2015 Budget measures, see Ministry of Finance (2015).

attitudinal changes on the part of consumers and workers may be required in addition to higher wages from employers.[33]

Productivity growth is necessary for real incomes to rise, in any economy. Nomura and Amano (2012) show that Singapore's labor quality growth (in the past, chiefly from rising educational attainment) has declined with the sharp rise in low-skilled foreign workers. Given the ageing population (which limits further improvement in labor quality), they conclude that the prospects for future productivity growth are "bleak", and consequently that Singapore's potential annual GDP growth from 2010–2030 will be around 2%, rising to 3% if TFP growth can be increased.[34] This rate is below the Economic Strategies Committee's (Ministry of Trade and Industry, 2010) projection of 3%–5% GDP growth, which is very high for a developed economy. In January 2015, Prime Minister Lee Hsien Loong announced that 2% to 3% growth is more likely. With slower growth, greater volatility, stagnant lower-quartile wages and increased income and wealth inequality, the government has recently acceded to social pressures to provide more targeted income support and transfers to the low-income and elderly.[35]

5. SINGAPORE'S DEVELOPMENT MODEL RECONSIDERED

Singapore's economic strategy at independence entrenched its state-driven, foreign-led, export-oriented development model, with a heavy emphasis on manufacturing, well beyond its transition from a developing to a mature high-income economy. High GDP growth has been maintained for over four

[33]For consumers, some such changes include getting used to self-service and clearing up after oneself in eating places, keeping public toilets clean and refraining from littering — habits that in the past were inculcated by vigorous promotional campaigns and fines. For society as a whole it requires letting go of the stigma attached to "manual labor" and "blue-collar" work — which higher wages would help encourage. Singapore has a remarkable 70,000 (mostly foreign) cleaners, whereas Taipei has 5000, "many of them graduates" (Chang, 2015).

[34]Note that Nomura and Amano's "Business-as-usual" scenario assumes a total fertility rate of 1.24 and annual immigration of 30,000, following a 2011 Institute of Policy Studies scenario. For higher growth in labor quality and average labor productivity, "the low-skilled non-resident workers are required to decrease".

[35]For example, the 2015 Budget contains new targeted measures to help individuals and households, including more financial support for lifelong learning, an income supplement for lower-income Singaporeans and higher CPF contributions for older workers. These follow on earlier wage supplements for low-wage workers, and healthcare subsidies for the elderly. To cover the costs of the 2015 budget deficit (a rare event in Singapore's fiscal history outside of deep recessions) the top rate of income tax is being raised from 20% to 22%, and more resources will be drawn from the (extremely large) foreign reserves.

decades largely through the addition of ever-increasing amounts of capital, labor and skills, much of it foreign, to an initially very small territory and population. This model of extensive growth has been extremely successful in quickly achieving full employment and raising per capita income to one of the world's highest. These results have been achieved with one of the world's highest savings rates and lowest consumption and wage shares of GDP (about 40% each), even compared with other export-led Asian economies (Lim, 2010). Singapore differs in several key respects: much more interventionist state industrial and social policy; much more dependence on foreign capital, labor and talent; and the corresponding relative weakness of domestic private enterprise — which given the small local market and limited resources, has probably been "crowded out" by the large state-linked and multinational sectors in both product and factor markets.

There are several ways in which this development model may have impacted Singapore's labor market and productivity record. Policies to attract and retain internationally mobile foreign manufacturing investments which would otherwise consolidate production in fewer, larger market locations would include liberal visa rules enabling them to bring to Singapore skills and talent from other parts of their global operations. This speeds up set up time, and maximizes MNC employers' human resource allocation flexibility in increasingly dynamic and uncertain global market and technological environments. The more technologically sophisticated their Singapore operations, the less likely MNCs will be to find locals qualified for very specific narrow-skilled niche positions, which also have a long (and thus expensive) training period. Home- and third-country nationals among MNCs' global employee base are unlikely to be interested in staying permanently in Singapore, but will move wherever their personal or corporate career trajectories take them. The dominance of foreigners in the highly-skilled and managerial ranks of MNC subsidiaries may discourage qualified Singaporeans from working for them due to perceptions of a "glass ceiling", leading to even more dependence on "foreign talent". The fact that "big-ticket foreign investments" have been falling "since Singapore tightened its manpower policies and lost its attraction for companies that depend on cheap foreign labor" (Chia, 2015) confirms that many foreign investments were attracted to Singapore because of the ease of employing foreign labor, rather than any intrinsic locational advantages. That the EDB expects "a sharp reduction in the number of skilled jobs created, lower fixed asset investment, and a decline in business expenditure... in line with the Government's restructuring exercise to raise productivity and reduce reliance on foreign workers" (Teng, 2015) also indicates that foreign investors attracted by capital subsidies had been creating skilled jobs mainly for foreigners.

Foreign manufacturers may also be attracted by a local supply chain (including of services) of SMEs which may be more labor-intensive and thus dependent on the import of low- and medium-skill foreign labor, most of whom would not be candidates for permanent residence due to Singapore's own citizenship rules favoring more highly-educated immigrants. SMEs appear to be the most reliant on the low costs of foreign labor for their competitiveness, and its ready availability may discourage them from undertaking the difficult task of restructuring to increase productivity. As Hoon (2013) noted, "The ready access to the supply of foreign workers kept labor costs low while the increase in value-add per worker boosted the profitability of manufacturing firms. This boost to profits very likely benefited both multinational corporations as well as small and medium-sized enterprises." The high (over 50%) capital share of national income, which is very lightly taxed[36] in addition to being heavily subsidized, also suggests that the business sector is highly profitable even though its productivity may be low.

At all skill levels, foreigners from now fast-growing Asian developing countries like China and India may eventually find more preferred employment in their countries of origin, after gaining education and/or relevant work experience in Singapore. Whatever its cause, high labor turnover reduces worker experience and productivity, while increasing employer costs through the need for frequent recruitment and training. The vulnerability to external demand shocks of export-oriented industry in general, and of Singapore's targeted high-tech clusters of electronics, pharmaceuticals and chemicals, in particular, have greatly increased the economy's volatility since the late 1990s (Choy, 2010: Tan, 2015).[37] Volatility itself reduces productivity — from increased labor turnover and the associated loss of skills from worker redundancies or underemployment ("labor hoarding") in downturns, and by discouraging both workers and employers from investing in skills training. The flexibility afforded by the ease of "turning on and off

[36] Asher *et al.* (2015), in this volume.

[37] Choy notes "While the blame for all this (volatility) cannot be laid on the industrial upgrading measures per se... it is undeniable that the government's pursuit of high growth through restructuring had inadvertently exposed the Singapore economy to new vulnerabilities in the international economy. Ironically too, the SEP (Strategic Economic Plan) had already identified in 1991 the competitive and volatile electronics industry to be a source of vulnerability; as it turned out, the planners' worse fears were confirmed." (Choy, 2010, p. 133).

the tap" of foreign worker supply during the labor-intensive era becomes a liability in capital- and skill-intensive sectors when foreign labor mobility in cyclical downturns leads to the shedding of skilled labor which never returns.

In this development model, it is state industrial policy which has pushed capital investment for growth, and targeted particular sectors for ever more generous and capital- and skill-based investment incentives, without which Singapore would not be a competitive location for such investments. At the same time, complementary sectors such as construction (residential, commercial and industrial, some of it undertaken by GLCs), retail, personal services and food-and-beverages were allowed to import low-wage low-skilled foreign labor, thus adding to the subsidies already enjoyed by high-tech industrial (and high-value services) enterprises employing a large number of foreigners with highly specialized skills.

Social policy — and the need for it — have been distorted by this development model. On the one hand, macroeconomic stabilization policies have been constrained. "The instruments most often deployed in recessions were direct cuts in employers' CPF contributions and reductions in government-controlled fees, charges and rentals. However, econometric research suggests that such measures entail painful adjustments for workers and are inefficacious since export demand is not too responsive to them." (Choy, 2010, p. 134). On the other hand, "low-skilled foreign workers... depress earnings at the lower end of the nominal wage scale because of their low productivity, thus impacting on income distribution adversely. Worse, relying on them indefinitely implies that Singapore's economic progress would still be achieved primarily by increases in labor inputs rather than productivity improvements... a slower pace of economic growth might not be a bad thing if it is achieved through productivity gains and is accompanied by less macroeconomic volatility." (Choy, 2010, p. 135).

Lim (2014) argues that "Higher wages would encourage firms to improve productivity and attract more Singaporeans into particular jobs, giving both employers and employees incentive to invest in upgraded skills (since there will be a higher income payoff). Businesses that cannot afford the higher wages would exit, releasing manpower for the businesses that remain. A reduction in demand would alleviate any labor shortage. Fewer foreign workers would also ease pressures on the housing market and on commercial rents, so businesses may benefit from more moderate rent hikes even as they pay out higher wages. Reduced foreign capital inflows to purchase property, and other investments, would mitigate asset inflation and appreciation of the Singapore dollar, thus helping to maintain cost competitiveness. Higher wages with higher productivity and moderating rents do not necessarily mean higher costs. But if they do, these are costs Singapore's consumers will have to pay. As consumers are also workers, their real incomes may increase with higher salaries, lower rents, and mortgage payments. If those enjoying higher wages are Singaporeans (rather than foreigners, who typically have higher savings rates and remittance outflows), the multiplier impact of their local spending will be greater." (Lim, 2014, p. 35)

Unwinding Singapore's decades of dependence on foreign labor will affect various groups differently. Some Singaporeans (e.g., business or household employers of low wage labor, property owners — including of HDB flats — and rentiers, shareholders of property companies or REITs, including GLCs) will "lose" even as others (lower-wage workers, first-time home-buyers and renters, more innovative and competitive businesses) gain. The long-established integration of industrial and social policy, while effective in "creating competitiveness" and maintaining the profitability of business (especially for MNCs and GLCs), has created policy inter-connections which are difficult to disentangle one from another. Thus, CPF employer contributions provided for wage flexibility, and CPF savings enabled a very high degree of home-ownership, including of publicly-provided HDB flats. But today nearly half of Singaporeans lack sufficient savings at retirement, the high share of income spent on housing reduces consumption in other sectors and limits the stabilizing effect of domestic demand (Abeysinghe and Choy, 2004; Abeysinghe and Gu, 2011), and the bottom quartile of wage-earners finds it increasingly hard to make ends meet,[38] even as some GLCs make record profits (including from property) and Singapore's world-leading sovereign wealth funds Temasek and the Government of Singapore Investment Corporation (GIC) accumulate valuable assets around the world.

This time the government appears more likely to follow through on slowing (though not stopping) the influx of foreign labor and finally staying the course on productivity growth. It is accepting a more realistic and sustainable lower GDP growth target, and is being more selective in attracting foreign investments (Chia, 2015; Teng, 2015). However Budget 2015 is delaying increases in foreign worker levies, and continuing with state-directed productivity schemes and the practice of state industrial targeting — this time the "new growth clusters" of "advanced manufacturing, applied health sciences, smart and sustainable urban solutions, logistics and aerospace, Asian and global financial services", rather than relying on market forces

[38]Low and Vadaketh (2014) discuss the social policy challenges and alternatives facing Singapore today.

to reallocate resources.[39] At the same time, the government is increasing its provisions for social security and income support through budget transfers and social subsidies, rather than through higher market wages.

6. CONCLUSION: LOOKING AHEAD

Singapore's state-driven, foreign-led, export-oriented development model since independence has delivered high GDP growth for over four decades primarily through factor accumulation — chiefly foreign manufacturing investment, high domestic savings, and vast inputs of foreign skilled and unskilled labor. This high-growth achievement, and a very high share for profits in GDP, has occurred at the expense of productivity growth, and more recently, of citizens' social welfare.[40] Singapore economists have long called for a change in this model, recommending a refocus away from subsidized manufacturing for a global market toward market-based services for the Asian and Southeast Asian region, in line with Singapore's unique competitive advantage as a city-state in a fast-growing geography.

We argued in Pang and Lim (1981) that "Singapore has a much stronger international competitive advantage in the export of services — banking, finance, commercial services, transportation and telecommunications — based on its long experience and large human and capital investment in these sectors. Another asset is its location in a rapidly growing regional economy of which it is the service hub. The service sector is intrinsically labor- intensive, and will become more skill-intensive as it upgrades into high-value services... even in export manufacturing industries, Singapore's competitiveness is shifting toward service-oriented activities such as regional warehousing, purchasing, servicing and research and development. Both commercial and industrial services have a demand for skilled professionals that can't be supplied adequately from domestic sources. And, as the

---

[39]Note that increased government expenditure on inputs does not necessarily result in increased output: for example, INSEAD's Global Innovation Index, ranks Singapore No. 1 in Overall Innovation Input each year from 2011 to 2014, but it is only No. 17 in Overall Innovation Output in 2011, declining to No. 25 in 2014, and No. 94 in Innovation Efficiency in 2011, declining to No. 110 in 2014. www.globalinnovationindex.org.

[40]The welfare of low-skilled foreign labor in Singapore has also been a matter of international as well as domestic concern, highlighted by spectacular events like the 2012 illegal strike by bus drivers from China, and the 2013 "Little India" riots, as well as longstanding incidents of abuse of foreign domestic workers from the Philippines, Indonesia and elsewhere. It is beyond the scope of this paper to consider this aspect of the foreign labor situation, on which see, for example, Noorashikin Abdul Rahman (2010) and Low (2015a,b).

Singapore population grows more affluent, it will consume more labor-intensive social and personal services than goods, further increasing the domestic demand for labor. One solution to the long-range problems of labor shortage is to concentrate Singapore's limited domestic resources in the one area in which it has the greatest competitive advantage — the supply of services, including industrial-based services. This would mean the phasing out of production-oriented manufacturing in which Singapore's potential advantage on a global basis is problematic. Unskilled labor would be released for the non-traded services sector, and skilled labor would be available for professional jobs in the highly competitive traded services sector. Reliance on both unskilled and skilled foreign labor would be reduced, and Singapore's historic complementary role to countries in the region would be enhanced." (Pang and Lim, 1981) The Report of the Economic Committee (Ministry of Trade and Industry, 1986) made similar recommendations, saying that Singapore should "move beyond our being a production base, to being an international total business centre... Services account for an increasing share of our GDP, and our service exports have been growing quickly... Scope for growth is still huge."

Choy (2010) points out that services did indeed grow from 60% of output and 67% of employment in 1990 to 63% of output and 77% of employment by 2005, as is typical of all high-income countries. He also notes that the "service economy is less risky... service industries are less dependent on foreign capital and tend to be influenced to a smaller extent by business cycles... a heterogeneous and diversified service sector offers the prospect that monetary policy will be a potent tool for mitigating economic fluctuations, as a result of the greater sensitivity of tradable services to exchange rate movements. Since exportable services have much higher domestic value-added and lower import content compared with manufactured goods... Servicing the needs of the burgeoning middle classes in China and India could easily add a percentage point or two to Singapore's potential growth rate. One should also not neglect to mention the untapped potential of domestically-oriented service industries catering to a richer and ever-growing local population... service industries have the virtue of being relatively more labor-intensive, thus generating more employment and helping to keep both structural and cyclical unemployment at bay." (Choy, 2010, pp. 136–137).

Lim (2015b) argues that the prospects for continued high-tech manufacturing for export in Singapore are poor, given "post-industrial" trends in global market demand and supply, technological change and multinational corporate strategies which "add up to slower growth in output, a lower ratio of goods to services in output, a lower ratio of manufacturing to services value-added in goods, a greater localization of goods and services production, and a much lower employment to output ratio" as well as "spreading global norms like the reduced acceptability of tax-avoidance incentives for multinationals, a major feature of Singapore's attractiveness to foreign investors." But she adds that "The good news is that services for our regional neighborhood are more location-specific and scalable, and less capital- and energy-intensive, than manufacturing for distant markets, less reliant on rare specific technical skills unlikely to be found in adequate scale among our small population, and more open to small entrepreneurs with different levels of formal education, providing a channel for employment creation, upward mobility and reduced inequality (through SME ownership and the capital returns from operating in regional markets)."

Budget 2015 (Ministry of Finance, 2015), like numerous previous budgets and government competitiveness and strategic reports, notes that "Services have also emerged as a major engine of enterprise and jobs", praises the international activities of "our homegrown enterprises" and offers many incentives to develop the capabilities of SMEs and encourage them to go abroad.[41] Singapore has not developed a large cadre of strong local enterprises (outside of the finance, property and GLC sectors) that can venture and compete outside the home country, as South Korea, Hong Kong, Taiwan and even Malaysia and China have. One reason for this could be the lack of incentive in an economy dominated by the state and MNCs for both capital and local talent to undertake the risks of private entrepreneurship. While Singapore's state economic planners have long recognized the limitations of their development model, and from time to time have made determined efforts to transform the economy in other directions, this had mostly been with the addition of new sectors, programs and incentives. To date there has not been any serious attempt to reduce or just stabilize manufacturing or foreign investment, or to re-size the state sector, without which the chronic problem of excess demand for both skilled and unskilled labor, including managers/entrepreneurs and bureaucrats/professionals, cannot be resolved.

Among other Asian countries, even South Korea — which like Singapore has a high ratio of manufacturing to GDP, but with a much larger domestic

[41] Note that following the 1991 Strategic Economic Plan, an official campaign was launched to grow a "second wing" for the economy by encouraging local enterprises to invest in neighboring countries. Several GLCs did do so, with some success, but progress so far has been insufficient to "create a second Singapore outside Singapore" as Teh (2014) points out other developed countries have done through outward investments by their own homegrown multinationals.

market, more abundant labor and skills, and strong domestic enterprises which have been successfully globalizing — now "hopes to reduce its heavy dependence on exports for economic growth. Economists see the process as essential for South Korea's long-term prospects... policy-makers in Seoul fret that Korean exports could lose steam in increasingly volatile overseas markets... The government has called for deregulation in six "promising" services industries: health care, tourism, education, finance, logistics and software development." (Jun, 2015).

China, a much larger and lower-income Asian economy that followed a similar state-dominated, high-savings, high-growth, investment-heavy, export-led development model with large foreign participation, has been seeking for some years now to "rebalance" toward "an economy driven by consumers and entrepreneurial vigor... and job creation by... innovative small businesses", at a lower growth rate. In unveiling the country's 2015 annual budget, Prime Minister Le Keqiang said "The government should be bold in imposing reform on itself so as to leave ample space for the market." (Magnier, 2015) "The growth in investment in factories, infrastructure and other fixed assets is still running 25% higher than growth in consumption. That means wealth is being transferred from households to the government, rather than the other way around, many economists said, leaving less in consumer pockets. Standing in the way are state enterprises... as well as an extensive bureaucracy that benefits from the government's large sway. Premier Li cited "systemic, institutional and structural problems," calling them "tigers in the road" holding up development."... Key to spurring consumption is directing more money toward pensions, health insurance, unemployment benefits and other social transfers, encouraging citizens to consume more and feel more secure." (Magnier, 2015).

Singapore faces similar challenges. Speculating on why the government has so far clung to its state-dependent, foreign-oriented development model "rather than considering potential alternative market-determined, locally-oriented and private enterprise-led models of post-industrial development," Lim and Lee (2010) suggest that, harking back to the country's reluctant birth, "being important to foreign capital, governments, and "talent" might provide some assurance of security against potential hostile neighbors." Other reasons they suggest include: bureaucratic inertia, self-interest, and incentives tied to delivering top-line GDP growth leading to "growth fetishism" and thus "preference for the easiest route to growth, which is through the addition of inputs of foreign capital, labor and skills. Singapore's continued rapid GDP growth in the post-industrial era has thus been bought at the price of expanding and entrenching the economic as well as political dominance of a one-party state that maintains its power in part by brokering the increased and even privileged participation of foreign capital, talent, and labor in the "local" economy. Foreigners beholden to the state for its beneficence and their own presence are unlikely to challenge its authority, in the way that an independent, globally competitive and non-state-dependent domestic entrepreneurial class — still weak and largely absent in Singapore — might." (Lim and Lee, 2010, pp. 154–155).

But Singapore will continue to rely on foreign labor and especially foreign talent and skills, since it "can certainly do with more managers and professionals in view of its ambition to be a dynamic and cosmopolitan city supplying premium services to the region and the world." (Choy, 2010, p. 135). The number and proportions should be reduced, focusing on skilled immigrants who are likely to settle permanently in the city-state and assimilate into its society, not on short-term low-skilled workers as has been the case so far. At the same time, efforts should continue to maximize the labor force participation of female and elderly workers, including by removing existing gender and age discriminations, and by improved housing, transport, other social amenities, and family-friendly infrastructure and employment practices. Above all, the country should continue to invest in expanding and diversifying the education, skills, opportunities and incomes of all its citizens, not merely to increase productivity and economic growth, but so that all may benefit from living in one of the world's richest nations. It should cease its rigid adherence to persistently large public sector surpluses (which amount to transfers from households to the state) and ideological aversion to properly-structured social insurance,[42] which would lift low domestic consumption, reduce extreme inequality, facilitate macroeconomic stabilization, promote the development of the services sector, and even encourage entrepreneurship by reducing risk aversion.[43]

The city-states of the past were regional in their economic orientation (Pang and Lim, 1982b), and a regional focus in line with that of old city-states and our own economic history,[44] has a chance of enabling Singapore to grow sustainably, if slowly, in the longer run. The very success of the "global city" model in earlier decades is now limited by the lack of

[42]Note that the 17% share of government expenditure in Singapore today is below what it was in the 1990s (over 20%), and much lower than the OECD average of 34%.

[43]In the "start-up nation" of the U.S., for example, taking a second mortgage on one's home is a very common means by which individuals fund entrepreneurial ventures, and housing also consumes a much smaller share of income, savings and wealth than it does in Singapore.

[44]See Lee (2015b) in this volume.

land and people, causing rising costs, economic inefficiencies, infrastructure bottlenecks, growing income disparities and social tensions that, if not contained, could compromise the prosperity, stability and identity of the nation-state, and its ability to meet the needs and aspirations of its citizens. There are inherent tensions between being a global city and a nation state. From a labor market perspective, a global city is characterized by two-way labor mobility, especially of the highly-skilled, which would include Singaporeans lacking economic and cultural roots and interests in Southeast Asia being readily pulled or pushed to leave the nation-state for more attractive career opportunities and lifestyles in distant developed locations.[45]

REFERENCES

Abeysinghe, T and KM Choy (2004). The aggregate consumption puzzle in Singapore. *Journal of Asian Economics*, 15(3), 563–578.

Abeysinghe, T and J Gu (2011). Lifetime income and housing affordability in Singapore. *Urban Studies*, 48(9), 1875–1891.

Asher, MG, AS Bali and YK Chang (2015). Public financial management in Singapore: Key characteristics and prospects. A fifty-year retrospective on Singapore's economy. *Singapore Economic Review*, 60(3). DOI: 10.1142/S0217590815500320.

Au Yong, H (2014). Singapore's Productivity Challenge, Part 1–3. Available at http://lkyspp.nus.edu.sg/wp-content/uploads/2014/05/Productivity-challenges-in-Singapore-Part-1.pdf; http://lkyspp.nus.edu.sg/wp-content/uploads/2014/08/Productivity-challenges-in-Singapore-Part-2.pdf; http://lkyspp.nus.edu.sg/wp-content/uploads/2014/11/Productivity-challenges-in-Singapore-Part-3.pdf.

Basu, R (2015). Make Foreigners, PRs Count in Income Data. Straits Times, 26 February.

Cabuyao, P (2015). The Singapore Jobs Market: Data vs Discontent. RSIS Commentary No. 002/2015, 3 February. Rajaratnam School of International Studies, Nanyang Technological University, Singapore.

[45]For example, Hooi (2012) reports on a Mindshare survey showing that 56% of Singaporeans "would like to emigrate", 65% did not believe they would be able to retire comfortably in Singapore, 73% thought that public housing prices are "getting out of hand", 73% agreed that "I should not be spending my entire working life paying off my housing loan", 72% said they "could not afford to get sick due to high medical costs", and 69% said that "there are too many foreign workers taking up job opportunities in our society today." According to the World Bank, there are 300,000 Singaporeans living and working abroad (about 9% of the total native population, although government figures put the number at 200,000 or 6%, a third of whom left in the last 10 years), with Malaysia the top destination, followed by Australia, the UK and USA, all countries with lower per capita incomes than Singapore.

Chang, R (2015). Liak Teng Kit: 5 Million People, 70,000 Cleaners... That's Ridiculous. Straits Times, 16 February.

Chia, SY (2011). Foreign Labour in Singapore: Trends, Policies, Impacts and Challenges. Discussion Paper Series No. 2011–24. Philippine Institute for Development Studies. December.

Chia, YM (2015). Investments Down as S'pore Chases Quality. Straits Times, 3 February.

Choy, KM (2010). Singapore's changing economic model. In *Management of Success: Singapore Revisited*, T Chong (ed.). Singapore: Institute of Southeast Asian Studies.

Choy, KM (ed.) (2012). Introduction. In *Studies on the Singapore Economy*. Singapore: World Scientific.

Economist (2013). Has the Ideas Machine Broken Down? 12 January.

Economist (2015). The Economy and Productivity: Bargain Basement. 14 March.

Hooi, J (2012). Singapore's Emigration Conundrum. Business Times, 6 October.

Hoon, HT (2013). The Future of Wages in Singapore. Straits Times, 8 February.

Huang, S and BSA Yeoh (2003). The difference gender makes: State policy and contract migrant workers in Singapore. *Asia and Pacific Migration Journal*, 12(1–2), 75–98.

Huff, WG (1999). Singapore's economic development: Four lessons and some doubts. *Oxford Development Studies*, 27(1), 33–55.

Hui WT and R Toh (2014). *Growth with Equity in Singapore: Challenges and Prospects*. Conditions of Work and Employment Series No. 48. Geneva, Switzerland: International Labour Office.

Jun, K (2015). Seoul Swallows Tough Medicine for Economy. Wall Street Journal, 4 March.

Krugman, P (1994). The myth of Asia's miracle. *Foreign Affairs*, 73(6), 62–78.

Lee, M (2015). Top SMEs' Revenue "Hit by Labour Woes". Straits Times, 30 January.

Lee, SA (2015). Governance and economic change in Singapore. *Singapore Economic Review*, 60(3). DOI: 10.1142/S0217590815500289.

Lim, J (2015). Fresh Ingredients Needed to Fix Eatery Troubles. Straits Times, 19 February.

Lim, LYC (1983). Singapore's success: The myth of the free market economy. *Asian Survey*, 23(6), 752–764.

Lim, LYC (1987). The state and private capital in Singapore's economic development. *Political Economy, Studies in the Surplus Approach*, 3(2), 201–222.

Lim, LYC (1989). Social welfare. In *Management of Success: The Moulding of Modern Singapore*, KS Sandhu and P Wheatley (eds.). Singapore: Institute of Southeast Asian Studies.

Lim, LYC (2010). Rebalancing in East Asia. In *Rebalancing the Global Economy: A Primer for Policymaking*, S Claessens, S Evenett and B Hoekman (eds.). London: Centre for Economic Policy-Making.

Lim, L (2014). How land and people fit together in Singapore's economy. In *Hard Choices: Challenging the Singapore Consensus*, D Low and ST Vadaketh (eds.). Singapore: NUS Press.

Lim, LYC (2015a). Beyond gender: The impact of age, ethnicity, nationality and economic growth on women in the Singapore economy. *Singapore Economic Review*, 60(2). DOI: 10.1142/S0217590815500204.

Lim, LYC (2015b). Beyond the "global city" paradigm. In *Singapore Perspectives 2015: Choices*, S Hoe and C Soon (eds.). Singapore: World Scientific for the Institute of Policy Studies.

Lim, LYC and SA Lee (2010). Globalizing state, disappearing nation: The impact of foreign participation in the Singapore economy. In *Management of Success: Singapore Revisited*, T Chong (ed.). Singapore: Institute of Southeast Asian Studies.

Lim, L, EF Pang and R Findlay (1993). Singapore. In *Five Small Open Economies*, R Findlay and S Wellisz (eds.). New York: Oxford University Press for the World Bank.

Low, D (2015a). Focus on Welfare, Not Wages, of Foreign Workers. The Straits Times, 23 January.

Low, D (2015b). Foreign Worker Issues: Rethinking Assumptions. The Straits Times, 10 February.

Low, D and ST Vadaketh (2014). *Hard Choices: Challenging the Singapore Consensus*. Singapore: NUS Press.

Magnier, M (2015). China Chooses a Long, Slow Road to Reform. *Wall Street Journal*, 5 March.

Mahtani, S and G Raghuvanshi (2012). Singapore Restricts Foreigners. *Wall Street Journal*, 10 July.

Ministry of Finance, Singapore (2015). Singapore Budget 2015. Available at www.singaporebudget.gov.sg.

Ministry of Manpower, Singapore (2014). Comprehensive Labour Force Survey. Available at http://stats.mom.gov.sg/Pages/Labour-Force-Summary-Table.aspx.

Ministry of Manpower, Singapore (2015a). Employment Situation 2014, 30 January.

Ministry of Manpower, Singapore (2015b). Job Vacancies 2014, 27 January.

Ministry of Trade and Industry, Singapore (1986). Report of the Economic Committee.

Ministry of Trade and Industry, Singapore (2010). Report of the Economic Strategies Committee. Available at www.mti.gov.sg.

Ministry of Trade and Industry, Singapore (2014). Drivers of Labour Productivity Growth Trends in Singapore. Available at http://www.mti.gov.sg/Research Room/SiteAssets/Pages/Economic-Survey-of-Singapore-2014/FA_AES2014.pdf.

Monetary Authority of Singapore (2010). Sources of Singapore's economic growth 1990–2009. *Macroeconomic Review*, 9(1), 66–81.

Nomura, K and T Amano (2012). Labor productivity and quality change in Singapore: Achievements in 1974–2011 and prospects for the next two decades. KIEO Discussion Paper No. 129 (September). Available at http://www.sanken.keio.ac.jp/publication/KEO-dp/129/KEO-DP129.pdf.

Noorashikin Abdul Rahman (2010). Managing labour flows: Foreign talent, foreign workers and domestic help. In *Management of Success: Singapore Revisited*, T Chong (ed.). Singapore: Institute of Southeast Asian Studies.

Pang, EF (1975). Growth, inequality and race in Singapore. *International Labour Review*, 111(1), 15–28.

Pang, EF (1977). Capitalising on labour. *Singapore Business*, 1(9), 14–16.

Pang, EF (1988). Development strategies and labour market changes in Singapore. In *Labour Market Developments and Structural Change: The Experience of ASEAN and Australia*, EF Pang (ed.), pp. 195–242. Singapore University Press.

Pang, EF (1994). An eclectic approach to turning points in migration. *Asian and Pacific Migration Journal*, 3(1), 81–92.

Pang, EF and L Lim (1981). Singapore's Foreign Workers: Are They Worth the Cost? *Asian Wall Street Journal*, August 4.

Pang, EF and L Lim (1982a). Foreign labor and economic development in Singapore. *International Migration Review*, 16(3), 548–576.

Pang EF and L Lim (1982b). Political Economy of a City-State. Singapore Business Yearbook 1982, pp. 7, 13–33.

Pang, EF and PL Quek (1980). Is the national wages council necessary to Singapore's economic progress? *ASEAN Business Quarterly*, 4(3), 35–37.

Png, I (2015). PIC: Move from Subsidy to Root Cause. Straits Times, 7 February.

Tan, KY (2015). Managing Singapore's globalization and its discontents: A long-term perspective. In *Singapore Perspectives 2015: Choices*, S Hoe and C Soon (eds.). Singapore: World Scientific for the Institute of Policy Studies.

Tay, K (2015). More redundancies in 2013 Due to Restructuring. Business Times, 31 January.

Teh, KP (2014). Globalisation and Singapore's Discontent. Talk given at the Asia Pacific Real Estate Association (APREA) Chairman/CEO Series, 5 September.

Teng, A (2015). Fewer Skilled Jobs Expected to be Created This Year. Today, 3 February.

Toh, MH and L Low (1990). *An Economic Framework of Singapore: Principles and Issues*. Singapore: Mc-Graw-Hill.

Tsao, Y (1982). Growth and Productivity in Singapore: A Supply Side Analysis. Ph.D. Dissertation in Economics, Harvard University.

Tsao, Y (1985). Growth without productivity: Singapore manufacturing in the 1970s. *Journal of Development Economics*, 19(1–2), 25–38.

Vasil, R (1989). Trade unions. In Management of Success: The Moulding of Modern Singapore, KS Sandhu and P Wheatley (eds.). Singapore: Institute of Southeast Asian Studies.

Vu, MK (2011). Sources of Singapore's economic growth, 1965–2008: Trends, patterns and policy implications. *ASEAN Economic Bulletin*, 28(3), 315–336, ISSN: 0217–4472.

Wong, D (1997). Transience and settlement: Singapore's foreign labour policy. *Asia and Pacific Migration Journal*, 6(2), 135–167.

Wong, T (2013). Most Support Curbs on Foreigner Inflow. Straits Times, 19 March.

Yap, MT and C Gee (2015). Singapore's demographic transition, the labour force and government policies: A fifty-year retrospective on Singapore's economy. *Singapore Economic Review*, 60(3). DOI: 10.1142/S0217590815500356.

Yeoh, B and W Lin (2012). Rapid Growth in Singapore's Immigrant Population Brings Policy Challenges. Migration Information Source (April).

Available at http://www.migrationpolicy.org/article/rapid-growth-singapores-immigrant-population-brings-policy-challenges.

Young, A (1992). A tale of two cities: Factor accumulation and technical change in Hong Kong and Singapore. *National Bureau of Economic Research (NBER), Macroeconomics Annual 1992.* Cambridge, Massachusetts: MIT Press.

Young, A (1994). The Tyranny of Numbers: Confronting the Statistical Realities of the East Asian Growth Experience. NBER Working Paper 4689 (March).

Chapter 7

BEYOND GENDER: THE IMPACT OF AGE, ETHNICITY, NATIONALITY AND ECONOMIC GROWTH ON WOMEN IN THE SINGAPORE ECONOMY*,†

LINDA Y. C. LIM

This paper examines trends in women's labor force participation, sectoral and occupational distribution, and wage incomes relative to men, including by age and education. Since 1980, gender disparities in virtually all categories have substantially narrowed; those remaining result from women's continued disproportionate responsibility for family care, and additional factors affecting women at the highest levels of the labor force and income distribution. There are some areas of concern for women's economic future in Singapore, including the impacts of ageing, foreign labor and immigration, and wage stagnation experienced by low-income families under Singapore's economic development model.

1. INTRODUCTION

In 1982, I published an Occasional Paper on *Women in the Singapore Economy* for the Economic Research Centre at the National University of Singapore (Lim, 1982). My paper was based on national statistical data up to 1980, and employed an economic framework of labor force analysis common in international academic and public policy journals. It (i) showed that women then occupied an inferior labor market status relative to men

---

*This is a revised version of a paper presented at the 25th Anniversary Forum of the Association for Women in Action and Research (AWARE), organized in conjunction with the National University of Singapore Society (NUSS) Singapore, March 5, 2011. Thanks are due to Bernadette Tan and Yuchen Lu for research assistance, and to many colleagues for their thoughtful comments.

†This paper first appeared in *Singapore Economic Review*, Vol. 60, No. 2, 2015, pp. 1550020-1–1550020-16. Reprinted with permission from World Scientific Publishing, Singapore.

in the Singapore economy and (ii) attributed this to the primacy of their reproductive role in the family relative to their productive role in the labor force. I argued that women's lower labor force earnings reflected their lower labor productivity, itself the result of their (i) lower average educational attainment levels than men, (ii) concentration in low-wage, low-productivity labor-intensive manufacturing, and (iii) shorter/interrupted working-lives and hence lesser work experience. These factors themselves reflected women's differential educational, industrial and occupational choices as influenced by differential sex roles and stereotypes which also contributed to sex discrimination in the workplace.

At the same time I was somewhat optimistic that gender inequality in the labor force would diminish (though not disappear) as a result of (i) narrowing in the male-female educational gap, (ii) technological upgrading and industrial restructuring minimizing female disadvantages in the workplace, (iii) narrowing in the male-female seniority gap (in part because of higher female educational attainment increasing the opportunity costs of not working given the increased opportunities and rewards for higher-skilled, higher-wage employment), (iv) human resource needs in a tighter labor market where labor scarcity would undermine the rationale for employer discrimination, and (v) changes in social and cultural attitudes in the direction of greater gender equality. In other high-income developed economies like the U.S., these presumptions have generally been validated (U.S. Bureau of Labor Statistics, 2013).

2. WOMEN IN THE SINGAPORE LABOR FORCE 2013[1]

2.1. Labor Force Participation

In 2013, women accounted for 44.4% of the Singapore labor force, a marked increase from their 35% share in 1980. The female labor force participation rate (LFPR) — the proportion of women who are economically active (employed or unemployed and looking for work) — was 58.1% (versus 40% in 1980), compared with 75.8% for males.

Fewer females than males were in the labor force in every age-group, with the smallest gap in the 25–29 age cohort, when 89% of males and 88% of females were economically active. Between the prime working-age years of 25 and 64, 89.3% of men and 69.2% of women were economically active. Single, widowed or divorced males had lower LFPRs than married males, whereas

[1]Except where otherwise noted, data for this paper are from Ministry of Manpower (2013), *Labor Force in Singapore 2013*.

single, widowed or divorced females had higher LFPRs than married females; for example, among females aged between 30 and 45, 90% or more of the single, widowed or divorced were in the labor force, compared with between 71.6% and 79.4% of married females.[2]

Among economically inactive persons aged 25 to 54, 65% were females, and most cited "housework" and "childcare" as the main reasons for being economically inactive. In contrast, economically inactive males cited "poor health/disability", "schooling/taking courses" and "taking a break" as their main reasons for not being in the labor force. For both males and females in this age-group, "employers' discrimination" (relating mainly to age discrimination) was negligible.

For both males and females, LFPRs are higher for those with higher educational attainment: among those whose highest educational qualification is secondary school, 66.1% of males and 54.3% of females are in the labor force; among post-secondary (non-tertiary) graduates it is 78.1% of males and 61.8% of females; among those with polytechnic diplomas, 86.6% of males and 78.4% of females are economically active; while among those with university degrees, 93.4% of males but only 82.5% of females are in the labor force. Economically active males and females tend to be equally well-educated, measured by the proportion with post-secondary or better qualifications (61.7% for males and 61.3% for females), though slightly more economically active females have university degrees (32.6%) than males (30.6%).[3]

Unemployment rates in Singapore are low by international standards; in 2013 it was 2.9% for males and 2.5% for females.

LFPRs by ethnic group which were available for 1980 are no longer provided. The implications of this, and of the now large proportion of non-residents and foreign-born residents in the Singapore labor force, will be considered in the discussion below.

2.2. Sector, Occupation and Incomes

The changed sectoral distribution of the female labor force since 1980 reflects changes in the composition of GDP, specifically a relative shift from

[2] As a comparison, in the U.S. in 2011, 74.9% of unmarried mothers with children under 18 years old were in the labor force, compared with 69.1% of married mothers (U.S. Bureau of Labor Statistics, 2013).

[3] *Ibid.*, Tables 8 and 90. These results conform to the higher wage elasticity of labor supply for females than for males, and its positive association with educational level, found in Kim (2012) for 12 emerging Asian countries, including Singapore.

manufacturing to services, and within manufacturing, from labor-intensive, female-intensive low-skill, low-wage manufacturing to more capital-intensive, male-intensive, higher-skill, higher-wage manufacturing. In 1980 manufacturing employed 40.5% of all females in the labor force (24.7% of all males) and females accounted for 46.3% of all manufacturing workers, as compared with 34.4% of the labor force as a whole.[4] By 2013 manufacturing employed only 11.4% of all females (but 15.4% of all males), and females accounted for 37.3% of all manufacturing workers, as compared with 44.4% of the labor force as a whole (Table 1).

Women instead flocked to the expanding services sector, where 85.1% of female workers (76.1% of males) were employed in 2013, accounting for 47.2% of total employment, slightly more than their 44.4% share of the labor force as a whole. While women are spread throughout the different services — most heavily in wholesale and retail trade, and in public administration and education — they are now particularly disproportionately represented among workers in health and social services (76.1%), financial

Table 1. Sector Distribution of Resident Labor Force 2013.

Sector	% of Total	% of Males	% of Females	Female % of Total
Manufacturing	13.6	15.4	11.4	37.3
Construction	5.0	6.8	2.6	23.6
Services	80.1	76.1	85.1	47.2
Wholesale & Retail	14.7	13.6	16.1	48.7
Transport & Storage	9.4	12.7	5.2	24.9
Accommodation & Food	6.6	5.2	8.2	55.7
Info & Communications	4.5	4.9	4.0	39.5
Financial & Insurance	7.2	6.0	8.7	53.7
Real Estate	2.4	2.2	2.7	49.1
Professional	6.9	6.6	7.4	47.2
Administrative & Support	4.8	4.9	4.8	44.0
Public Admin & Education	13.8	13.6	14.1	45.4
Health & Social	4.6	2.0	7.9	76.1
Arts, Entertainment & Rec	1.8	1.7	1.9	46.5
Other Comm, Soc & Personal	3.4	2.7	4.1	54.5
Others	1.3	1.7	0.9	28.7
Total	100.0	100.0	100.0	44.4

Source: Ministry of Manpower, *Labor Force in Singapore 2013*, Table 42.

[4] *Census of Population 1980*, cited in Lim (1982), p. 6. At the time of this revision (July, 2014), the *Economic Characteristics* section of the *Census of Population 2010* has not been released.

services (53.7%), accommodation and food (57.7%), and other community, social and personal services (54.5%).

While occupational segregation or "the tendency for men and women to be in different occupations" has declined over time, as of 2000 "females' representation in higher-skilled occupations in Singapore still lagged that in the developed countries." (Ministry of Manpower, 2000), For the working population as a whole, this situation persisted in 2013, with women workers under-represented relative to their overall share in the labor force (44.4%) in the higher-skill job categories of management, administrators and working proprietors (33.7%, or 12.9% of all female relative to 19.9% of all male workers), and professionals (43.1%, or 13.6% of all female relative to 14.4% of all male workers) (Table 2). Females were over-represented in the middle-level categories of associate professionals and technicians (49%, or 23.9% of all female versus 19.8% of all male workers), clerical workers (76.9%, or 22.4% of all female versus 5.5% of all male workers), sales and service workers (52.3%, or 14.7% of all female versus 10.7% of all male workers), and in the lower-skill category of cleaners, laborers and related workers (55.2%, or 9.1% of all female versus 5.9% of all male workers).

Among government employees, females outnumbered males in higher-level jobs in Division I (72% more females) and Division III (22% more females), while males outnumbered females in lower-level jobs in Division IV (25% more males) while Division II was roughly equal (7% more males).[5] The Division I discrepancy probably reflects female domination of

Table 2. Occupational Distribution of Resident Labor Force 2013.

Occupation	% of Total	% of Males	% of Females	Female % of Total
Man, Admin & Proprietors	17.0	20.3	12.9	33.7
Professionals	14.1	14.4	13.6	43.1
Associate Prof & Technicians	21.6	19.8	23.9	49.0
Clerical Support	13.0	5.5	22.4	76.5
Sales & Service	12.5	10.7	14.7	52.3
Craftsmen & Related Trades	4.0	6.6	0.8	8.9
Plant/Machine Op & Assembly	7.2	10.9	2.5	15.8
Cleaners, Laborers & Related	7.3	5.9	9.1	55.2
Others	3.3	5.9	0.1	1.6
Total	100.0	100.0	100.0	44.4

Source: Ministry of Manpower, *Labor Force in Singapore 2013*, Table 28.

[5]Department of Statistics (2013), *Yearbook of Statistics Singapore 2013*, Table 5.8.

the ranks of teachers in government service, and the greater preference of women high-level professionals such as doctors, lawyers and accountants for more stable government employment than higher-earning private practice, while the Division III discrepancy probably reflects female dominance in clerical ranks.

Disaggregating by age-cohort yields some potentially interesting results (Table 3). In the 20 to 29 age group, where women are 44.4% of all workers, females outnumber males in the higher-skill categories of professionals (56.5% of all workers), and associate professionals and technicians (56.5% of all workers versus 50.1%in the 30-39 age cohort); they account for more than half (53.5%) of managers, administrators and working proprietors. At the same time, their disproportionate share of clerical workers (70.1%) is less

Table 3. Occupational Distribution by Gender and Select Age-Group 2013.

Occupation	% of Total	% of Males	% of Females	Female % of Total
Man, Admin & Proprietors				
age 20–29	4.2	3.8	4.6	53.5
age 30–39	18.8	20.9	16.4	41.9
Professionals				
age 20–29	14.9	12.6	17.3	56.5
age 30–39	23.8	26.2	21.2	42.8
Assoc Prof & Technicians				
age 20–29	29.9	25.3	34.8	56.5
age 30–39	28.4	27.2	29.7	50.1
Clerical Support				
age 20–29	18.1	10.2	26.5	71.0
age 30–39	11.3	4.2	19.0	80.7
Sales & Service				
age 20–29	13.6	13.0	14.4	51.3
age 30–39	9.6	9.0	10.2	51.2
Craftsmen & Related Trades				
age 20–29	1.7	2.9	0.4	10.5
age 30–39	0.2	3.8	0.2	5.0
Plant/Machine Op & Assembly				
age 20–29	1.9	3.1	0.6	15.2
age 30–39	2.9	4.5	1.2	19.6
Cleaners, Laborers & Related				
age 20–29	1.9	2.4	1.4	34.8
age 30–39	1.9	1.9	1.9	47.4
Others				
age 20–29	14.0	22.6	0.2	0.6
age 30–39	1.2	1.9	0.1	3.3

Source: Ministry of Manpower, *Labor Force in Singapore 2013*, Table 32.

than in the 30 to 39 age cohort (80.7%), and they account for only 34.8% of cleaners, laborers and related workers, as compared with 47.4% among those aged 30 to 39.

There are many possible explanations for this apparent trend toward increased female representation in higher-skill job categories and their lesser representation in lower-skill categories among those aged 20 to 29. (i) Women's increased (and possibly superior) educational attainment levels, particularly at younger ages, qualify more of them for higher-skilled occupations (see Table 5). (ii) Women in their 20's are more likely to have completed their higher education and training, and to have had more years of work experience, then men in the same age cohort whose labor force participation would have been delayed by two years of compulsory military service in their late teens. (iii) Highly-educated women in their 20's are more likely to be single and childless, which are positively correlated with labor force participation, whereas mothers in their 30's may have lost some seniority by temporarily dropping out of the labor force, or accepting less-responsible jobs, due to childcare obligations. Thus it is possible, even likely, that when the present 20 to 29 age cohort of highly-educated women moves into their 30's, their representation in higher-skilled jobs might also decrease.

(iv) The shift in Singapore's economic structure toward post-industrial status with a greater GDP and employment share for services, especially relatively female-intensive services like finance, health, education, retail trade, accommodation and food, would over time result in more higher-skill jobs in these sectors, and more women in these sectors reaching those job levels. This would be accompanied by a corresponding decline in the GDP and employment share of relatively male-intensive sectors like manufacturing, and hence in the share of highly-skilled jobs in these sectors which are more likely to be occupied by men. Further disaggregation and the passage of time are necessary to ascertain the likely relative weight of each of these potential explanations.

This pattern of greater gender equity/lesser disparity among those in their 20's holds also for income. The ratio of female to male median gross monthly income in full-time work is 82.5%, but for those in the 25 to 29 cohort it is over 90% at all educational levels, reaching 98% for those with post-secondary education and polytechnic diplomas and 100% among those with university degrees.[6] The female-to-male income ratio at all educational

[6]Ministry of Manpower (2013), Table 18.

attainment levels drops for those in their 30's and above, but with rough parity at the secondary and post-secondary (non-tertiary) levels between the ages of 35 and 60; thus, gender income gaps are larger at the low and high ends of the educational distribution.

Employed resident women earn less than men with the same educational qualifications, and in the same occupations and sectors. For example, in 2013 only 7.6% of women whose highest educational qualification was secondary school earned over $5,000 a month, compared with 14.8% of men; among those with post-secondary (non-tertiary) education, 11.3% of women but 14.1% of men earned over $5,000; among those with a polytechnic diploma, the ratio was 18.4% of women and 31.5% of men; and among those with a university degree, the ratio was 47% for women and 67% for men.[7]

By occupation, the proportion of managers and administrators earning $5,000 or more a month was 83.4% for males and 75.1% for females, with 44.8% of males, and 30.4% of females, earning over $10,000. Among professionals, 63.7% of men, and 52.8% of women, earned over $5,000, with 17.3% and 10.0% respectively earning over $10,000. Among associate professionals and technicians, 25.7% of males and 19.8% of females earned over $5,000.[8]

Within particular sectors, the income distribution for female workers is also lower than it is for males. For example, in financial services, where women represent 53.7% of all workers, 42.5% of males earn over $5,000 and 23.3% earn over $10,000, while the corresponding proportions for females are 36.4% over $5,000 and 13.5% over $10,000. In health and social services, where women are 76.1% of all workers, only 17% of them earn over $5,000 and 4.0 percent over $10,000, whereas 42.3% of males in this sector earn over $5,000 and 22.0% over $10,000. In the public administration and education services sector, 46.5% of males and 30.1% of females earn over $5,000.[9]

The *Labor Force in Singapore 2013* report does not provide median income by gender and occupation, or by gender and industry. But Table 4 shows that women workers, who form 46.5% of the labor force, are under-represented in the upper income brackets and over-represented in the lower income brackets.

[7] *Ibid.*, Table 27.
[8] *Ibid.*, Table 22.
[9] *Ibid.*, Table 23.

Table 4. Gross Monthly Income from Work of Employed Residents by Gender.

Gross Monthly Income	% of Males	% of Females	Females as % of Total
<$500	1.3	3.5	68.2
$500–$999	5.5	11.3	63.4
$1,000–$1,499	9.4	11.7	51.0
$1,500–$1,999	10.8	10.2	44.4
$2,000–$2,499	10.1	10.3	46.0
$2,500–$2,999	7.9	7.7	45.0
$3,000–$3,999	13.4	14.4	45.5
$4,000–$4,999	9.4	9.4	45.1
$5,000–$5,999	7.6	6.7	42.4
$6,000–$6,999	4.6	3.8	40.7
$7,000–$7,999	3.4	2.6	38.8
$8,000–$8,999	3.1	2.0	36.1
$9,000–$9,999	1.9	1.3	36.7
$10,000 and over	11.6	5.3	27.5

Source: Ministry of Manpower, *Labor Force in Singapore 2013*, Table 25.

3. DISCUSSION: GAINS, LAGS, CAUTIONS AND UNKNOWNS

3.1. Gains

The 2013 Labor Force data, compared with Labor Force and Census of Population data for 1980, show that women's labor force status in Singapore has improved substantially over the past thirty-plus years. With respect to many variables, it is today probably on par with if not superior to that in most other developed countries at similar income levels. Though parity with men has not been achieved, most gender disparities in the labor force have been substantially reduced.

A higher proportion of women residents in Singapore now participate in the labor force, and they account for a higher proportion of the working population, comparable to other developed countries like the U.S. Women workers in Singapore are now more evenly distributed across more occupational categories and sectors than previously, and they earn 82.5% of the overall male median employment income, again, similar to the U.S. In younger age groups, female workers' occupational status and income levels are much closer to those of males, possibly suggesting that gender differentials are continuing to narrow.

These improvements are due primarily to (i) consistently rapid GDP growth generating strong demand for labor that exceeds the domestic supply (Hui and Hashmi, 2007), (ii) restructuring and diversification of the Singapore economy from male-intensive sectors (e.g. manufacturing) to more female-intensive services (e.g. finance, health and education) as economic development has proceeded and incomes have risen, (iii) women's rising educational attainment levels and the diminution of gaps with men, especially among younger age cohorts. For example, among the citizen population in 2005, males were more likely than females to have university degrees, but the gap in the 25 to 29 age group (33.2% of males versus 31% of females) was much smaller than that in the 30 to 34 age group (24.2% of males versus 18.8% of females). Among those without tertiary education, 18% of males but only 9.9% of females continued their education to acquire technical, commercial or vocational qualifications.[10]

Table 5 shows that females accounted for just over half of all university students, and just under half of all polytechnic students graduating in 2012. Interestingly, in both types of institutions, they form the majority — in many cases a large majority — of graduates in most fields of study, including professional fields like accountancy, architecture, business and law, with the notable exceptions of engineering and information technology, which have larger intakes of mostly male students, though the 56.2% of natural, physical and mathematical sciences university graduates who are female is a higher ratio than typically found in other developed countries.

3.2. Lags

At the same time, occupational and sectoral segregation by gender persists, as does women's relative over-representation in lower-skill occupations and lower-income levels of the labor force, and their corresponding under-representation at higher occupation and income levels. Even within the same occupational category or sector, women are disproportionately clustered at lower levels, and under-represented at higher levels, with the notable exception of government service. After 30 years of more-or-less "equal opportunity" in education and the labor market, this is no longer explicable by the "pipeline problem", i.e., the fact that women are only recent entrants to the labor force and thus disproportionately clustered in its lower ranks due to lack of seniority.

Instead, today continued occupational and sectoral segregation most likely reflect differences in seniority and job choices constrained by

[10]Department of Statistics, Ministry of Trade and Industry (2005), *General Household Survey 2005 Statistical Release 1: Socio-Demographic and Economic Characteristics*, Chapter 2, "Education and Language".

Table 5. University and Polytechnic Graduates (Full-Time) in 2012.

Courses	Females as % of All Graduates
UNIVERSITY	52.0
Accountancy	56.9
Architecture & Building	60.9
Business & Administration	59.1
Dentistry	50.0
Education	81.9
Engineering Sciences	30.0
Fine & Applied Arts	57.7
Health Sciences	78.1
Humanities & Social Sciences	67.0
Information Technology	36.6
Law	59.7
Mass Communication	78.2
Medicine	48.8
Natural, Physical & Mathematical Sciences	56.2
Services	54.8
POLYTECHNIC	49.0
Applied Arts	54.8
Architecture & Building	52.9
Business & Administration	62.0
Education	91.8
Engineering Sciences	24.9
Health Sciences	77.6
Humanities & Social Sciences	60.6
Information Technology	43.4
Legal Studies	65.8
Mass Communication & Information Science	69.2
Science & Related Technologies	60.7
Services	44.7

Source: Ministry of Education, *Education Statistics Digest 2013*, Tables 17 and 18.

child-raising responsibilities or preferences, including for women at higher educational, occupational and income levels, where some residual discrimination likely persists, as it does in other developed countries. In addition to cultural factors, until relatively recently there were de facto restrictions on women's admission into particular courses of tertiary education (e.g., medicine, abolished in 2002). There remain other policy inequities which discourage or limit women's careers. It was only in 2005 that married women civil servants received the health care benefits for dependents always available to men. Also, statutory provisions for maternity but not for paternity leave (before 2013) may have caused women to disproportionately drop out of the labor force temporarily or permanently, and could have led to some unwillingness among employers to recruit, train and retain women workers especially at more expensive higher levels of the labor force. Nearly three decades of government pro-natalist policies, though apparently ineffective in reversing the precipitously declining birth-rates characteristic of all rapidly-industrializing East Asian countries (Economist, 2010), may also contribute to such discriminatory employer behavior.[11]

Given Singapore women's high educational attainment levels, their relatively greater under-representation at the highest levels of the labor force remains to be explained. For example, women have dropped from 27% to 23% of top corporate leaders (Mok, 2014), and are particularly thinly-represented at the board level (The Straits Times, 2013). At least one study (Dimmovski *et al.*, 2010) argues that women middle managers in Singaporean (and Malaysian) organizations face a "glass ceiling" which inhibits their promotion to senior management ranks.[12] Women are also under-represented in government (e.g., as parliamentarians) and the civil service (e.g., as Permanent Secretaries), compared with their relative educational attainment levels and proportions in the civil service, and with the situation prevailing in other developed countries, particularly other small (and thus presumably more talent-scarce and therefore less discriminatory) nations like those in Scandinavia.

3.3. Cautions

Higher female labor force participation rates and reduced gender gaps in occupational and sectoral distribution do not necessarily reflect an improvement in the economic status and well-being of low-income Singaporean families. The stagnation of individual wage incomes at the lower end of the income distribution (Dhamani, 2008) may simply mean that both husband and wife must work because a single income is insufficient to support the family, thereby increasing female LFPRs. Economic restructuring and wage stagnation may also mean that low-skilled men can increasingly find

[11]Yip and Wong (2014) find for Hong Kong, a territory more similar to Singapore than most, "unequivocal evidence that age-specific fertility rates exert negative impact on female wages, after controlling for other observable characteristics the negative effects of fertility on women's earnings are notably greater in female dominated occupations, whereas similarly situated men are unaffected. Since fertility rates tend to be increasing with age during the early stage of women's work careers, our theory partially explains why the gender gap rises with age."

[12]In a different context, Narayanan *et al.* (2014) attribute very senior women executives' much lower gains from insider trading to gender differences in access to information, due to network inequalities.

jobs only in previously "female-dominated" low-skilled occupations such as "Cleaners, Laborers and Related Workers", where they form two-thirds of such workers in the 20 to 29 age cohort (Table 3), thereby reducing previous male-female occupational and income gaps i.e. "downward leveling" rather than "upward leveling".

The labor market is also only one — albeit the most important — way in which women participate in the economy. Disproportionately represented among the economically inactive because of family care responsibilities (which contribute indirectly to spousal and family income), and at the lower-end of the income distribution, and with a lower labor force participation rate, women are at risk of having inadequate personal savings (e.g., through CPF accounts) to support themselves in the event of family break-up (e.g., marital abandonment) and given their greater longevity than males. Presumably because of the rapid ageing of the population, there are already just 974 males per 1000 females in Singapore's population, and this gap is likely to grow. Population ageing is also likely to make disproportionate demands on the family care-giving responsibilities of women workers, forcing some of them to leave the labor force to supervise or provide elder care at the very ages where their own seniority-enhanced income (and thus saving-for-retirement potential) is likely to be greatest (in the 40 to 65 age cohort). It therefore poses a major risk to women retaining the labor force gains they have made in the past 30 years, "squeezing" or "sandwiching" them between the twin obligations of child- and elder-care.

3.4. Unknowns

Incompleteness in the Ministry of Manpower's *Labor Force* data may conceal pockets of vulnerability among particular groups of women, especially ethnic minorities, since no such information is provided for 2013, in contrast to 1980. While by 1980 LFPRs had ceased to differ among women by ethnicity, there are ethnic differences in educational attainment. For example, in 2010, the proportion of Singapore residents with tertiary (diploma, professional or university) qualification was 38.1% for Chinese, 16.7% for Malays and 49.1% among Indians (a large jump from 20% in 2000 due partly to the inflow of Indian permanent residents).[13] There are thus likely to be ethnic differences by industry and occupation, as well as discrimination against minorities (e.g., in some service professions where there may be — however

[13] *Census of Population 2010 Statistical Release* 1: *Demographic Characteristics, Education, Language and Religion*, Key Indicators of the Resident Population, p. ix.

unjustified, and perceived rather than real — consumer preferences for being served by individuals from the same ethnic group as oneself), and unequal access to social capital and networks (Chua, 2010). Fertility rates do differ by ethnicity, with women from the Malay and Indian minorities having more children, which could result in their suffering disproportionately in the labor market from the constraints resulting from childcare responsibilities (e.g. more interruptions and thus shorter working lives and accumulated experience), and associated employer discrimination.

But the biggest unknown in Singapore labor force data is the impact of recent immigrant labor on the employment status of Singapore citizens and residents, including women. Labor force data refer (without breakdown) to Singapore residents, who in 1980 accounted for 94.5% of the total population, while 96% of all residents were Singapore citizens. But in 2010, residents were only 74.2% of the population, and only 85.7% of residents were citizens, such that citizens accounted for 63.6% of the total population. Among residents, 22.8% were born outside of Singapore. Non-residents accounted for 25.7% of the population; together with permanent residents, they accounted for 36.4% of the total population. Since permanent residents accounted for 14.3% of the resident population, it appears that 8.5% of the population were Singapore citizens born outside of Singapore, for a total of 44.9% of the population being foreign-born.[14]

All these are extremely high ratios of the foreign- to domestic-born, non-residents to residents, and non-citizens to citizens, which must have a significant impact on employment and incomes.[15] Non-resident workers are likely to be disproportionately temporary migrant labor, i.e., work-permit or employment pass holders. Given the ease with which highly-skilled persons in working-age cohorts (presumably those aged between 30 and 60 years) and their family dependents can get permanent residence, and subsequently citizenship, they should have an impact on the labor force in middle- to higher-level occupational and income categories. For example, the influx of better-educated Indian migrants has resulted in Indian households having the highest median monthly income by ethnic group, or $5,370 compared with $5,300 for Chinese and $3,844 for Malay households.[16]

---

[14] *Census of Population 2010*, "Key Demographic Trends".

[15] Non-residents accounted for 29 percent of the labor force in the 2000 census, the highest such ratio in Asia, and since then the influx of foreign workers has accelerated (Yeoh, 2007).

[16] *Census of Population 2010 Statistical Release 2: Households and Housing*, cited in Ong (2011).

How both temporary foreign labor and permanent immigration impact women, especially citizen and locally-born women, in Singapore cannot be ascertained without disaggregated longitudinal data. Given the size of the phenomenon, and the fact that it is government-regulated and not purely market-determined, it is improbable that it has no impact on women's labor market status. Here are some a priori ways the increased foreign labor supply might affect women in the labor force.[17]

(i) The import of foreign female labor to provide domestic services could reduce the family care obligations and thus labor force disruptions otherwise incurred by women workers, helping to maintain their LFPRs through the child- and elder-care years.

(ii) At the same time, the ready supply of foreign female domestic help may (a) depress wages in this sector, making employment in it unattractive or unaffordable for resident/citizen females, and (b) discourage private and social investment in alternative institutional mechanisms especially for elder-care (e.g., collective housing arrangements by state, non-profit and for-profit providers such as occur in other developed countries). There are also well-known issues with regard to the status and welfare of foreign female domestic helpers themselves (Huang, 2003; Devasahayama, 2010).

(iii) Wages may be depressed and upward mobility channels reduced by the import of foreign labor in other female-intensive sectors and occupations such as hotels and restaurants, and health and social services, where there is an inadequate supply of low- to medium-skilled citizen and resident female labor (e.g. in nursing, clerical services and retail sales) at the prevailing wage.[18]

(iv) The import of highly-skilled foreign labor may reduce channels of occupational upward mobility and depress incomes beyond what they otherwise might be for locally-born women, who are more likely than men to be affected if they interrupt their working lives and careers for child- and family-care reasons (to be substituted for in the interim by long-staying foreigners, especially male foreigners).

(v) Highly-skilled foreign workers are more likely to be male, both because this reflects labor force structures and opportunities in their

---

[17]See Yeoh *et al.* (1999) for an early analysis of the multifaceted impacts of migrant female domestic workers.

[18]Anecdotally, the nursing profession in Singapore is particularly lower in wages, education and status than in other affluent developed countries, with a much higher ratio of foreign nurses from lower-wage less-developed countries.

foreign home countries—particularly those in Asia, from which most of Singapore's foreign-born population comes—and because in every society women are more likely to relocate/sacrifice their own careers to follow male spouses in their career advancement, resulting in expatriate labor force participants in every country being disproportionately male. This could help explain the under-representation of women in higher occupational and income categories (e.g., in financial services) despite the equalization of educational and employment opportunities for women in Singapore itself.[19]

(vi) Foreign workers and immigrants from countries where women's educational and labor force status relative to men's is inferior to that of the domestic labor force in Singapore may import cultural patterns and habits, including among foreign-born employers, that could undermine the socio-cultural advances and labor force achievements of women in Singapore. Alternatively, different family structures (e.g., multi-generational extended versus single-generation nuclear models) could give foreign-born women from these cultures a competitive advantage over locally-born women in the labor market.

(vii) Employer, co-worker and consumer prejudices against foreign-born residents and temporary workers could have a negative impact on locally-born ethnic minority women of the same ethnic heritage.

4. CONCLUSION

The rapid growth, diversification and restructuring of the Singapore economy since 1980, together with expanded and increasingly gender-neutral educational and employment opportunities, and reduced policy and market discrimination, have greatly improved women's relative labor force status. These have resulted in reduced gender disparities in education, labor force participation, occupational and industrial distribution, and incomes. The gender disparities which persist reflect the continued, if diminished, constraints of family-care responsibilities on women's career choices and advancement. These are universal and unlikely to be completely eliminated even if there were to be innovative institutional developments for elder-care in particular.

More interesting and potentially concerning are three major demographic and labor market trends. The first is the ageing of the population,

[19] Ye (2014) argues that social and cultural capital linked to gender and class condition labor recruitment practices for both Bangladeshi male migrants and (high-end) transnational financial professionals in Singapore's segmented labor market.

particularly the native-born population, which is likely to add elder-care to the child-care constraints on women's labor force participation and career and income advancement. In Singapore, as in other developed economies, women are disproportionately the care-givers not only because of cultural norms of the recent past, but also because their lower incomes mean lower opportunity cost for the family if women rather than men withdraw from or reduce their participation in the labor force. Because of women's greater longevity and lesser savings, they are expected to experience more financial insecurity and poverty in old age (Dhamani, 2008).

The second factor, more unique to Singapore, is the impact of the large foreign-born population on both resident and non-resident women in the labor force. This cannot be gauged without access to the relevant data. But foreign labor and immigration policy are intrinsic to Singapore's overall economic development strategy (Lim and Lee, 2010; Ng, 2010), and its impact on the domestic labor force, including any distinctive impacts on female labor, needs to be studied to discern any problems and issues that might require remediation through adjustment of government policy or business practice.

The third factor is the peculiar nature of Singapore's recent economic growth model — characterized as it is by high volatility and inequality (Li and Hussain, 2010; Low and Yeoh, 2014), very low shares of consumption and of wage income in GDP (Abeysinghe and Choy, 2004; Choy, 2010; Lim, 2010; Lim and Lee, 2010), long working hours[20] and wage stagnation for the low-wage workers who constitute the bottom third of the domestic labor force, such that per capita GDP (on which Singapore has performed well) is a relatively inferior indicator of individual, family and worker well-being.[21] This reduces the beneficial effects of reduced gender differences.

[20]For example, in 2010 full-time resident male workers worked an average of 50.7 h a week, with 43.4% working more than 48 h; sales and service workers worked 52.5 h (54.2 h for those aged 50-59) and plant and machine operators 52.1 h (54.7 h for those aged 50-59). Females worked fewer hours. *Report on Labor Force in Singapore 2010,* Tables 16 and 18. These data are not provided in subsequent *Labor Force in Singapore* reports but the new *Singapore Yearbook of Manpower Statistics 2013* Tables C.6 and C.7 report that in 2012 full-time resident male workers worked 49.6 h a week (females 46.4 h), with 39.3% (females 25.7%) working more than 48 h; sales and service workers worked 51.7 h, and plant and machine operators worked 52.5 h (no breakdown is available by age group).

[21]Jones and Klenow (2010) found that Singapore has the greatest (negative) gap between per capita GDP and well-being of any of the 134 countries studied. In particular Singapore has a welfare score less than half that of Hong Kong despite a slightly higher GDP per capita — the cumulative effect in their model of a slightly lower life expectancy, much lower share of consumption in GDP, greater income inequality, and less leisure (more hours worked). There are also indications of declining social mobility through the education system, as reported in Ng (2011).

In sum, gender is inextricably inter-related with other economic, demographic, social and cultural phenomena that need to be considered as we look into women's future in the Singapore economy. Challenges for gender equity, and strategies to meet these challenges, must also be determined in the larger context of national economic development and social change.

REFERENCES

Abeysinghe, T and KM Choy (2004). The aggregate consumption puzzle in Singapore. *Journal of Asian Economics*, 15, 563–578.

Choy, KM (2010). Singapore's changing economic model. In *The Management of Success: Singapore Revisited*, T Chong (ed.), pp. 123–138. Singapore: Institute for Southeast Asian Studies.

Chua, VKH (2010). Social capital and inequality in Singapore, Ph.D. dissertation, University of Toronto.

Department of Statistics (2010). Census of Population 1980.

Department of Statistics (2010). Census of Population 2010 Statistical Release 1: Demographic Characteristics, Education, Language and Religion.

Department of Statistics (2013). Yearbook of Statistics Singapore 2013.

Devasahayama, TW (2010). Placement and/or protection? Singapore's labour policies and practices for temporary women migrant workers. *Journal of the Asia-Pacific Economy*, 15(1), 45–58.

Dhamani, I (2008). Income inequality in Singapore: Causes, consequences and policy options. http://www.mas.gov.sg/resource/eco_research/eco_education/Esss2007/uni_%201st_%20Ishita.pdf.

Dimmovski, V, M Skerlavaj and MKM Mok (2010). Comparative analysis of mid-level women managers' perceptions of the existence of "glass ceiling" in Singaporean and Malaysian organizations. *The International Business and Economics Research Journal*, 9(8), 61–77.

Economist (2010). An exercise in fertility. September 18, 2010.

Huang, S (2003). The difference gender makes: State policy and contract migrant workers in Singapore. *Asian and Pacific Migration Journal*, 12(1–2), 75–97.

Hui, WT and AR Hashmi (2007). Foreign labour and economic growth, policy options for Singapore. *Singapore Economic Review*, 52(1), 53–72.

Jones, CI and PJ Klenow (2010). Beyond GDP? Welfare across countries and time. NBER Working Paper No. 16352.

Kim, J (2012). Past and future of the labor force in emerging Asian economies. *Japan and the World Economy*, 24(2), 87–100.

Li, X and Z Hussain (2010). Widening wage gap: Does it matter? *The Straits Times*, 11 December 2010.

Lim, LYC (1982). *Women in the Singapore Economy*, Occasional Paper No. 5, Economic Research Centre, University of Singapore. Singapore: Chopmen Publishers.

Lim, LYC (2010) Rebalancing in East Asia. In *Rebalancing the Global Economy, A Primer for Policymaking*, S Claessens, S Evenett and B Hoekman (eds.), pp. 32–35. London: Center for Economic Policy-Making.

Lim, LYC and SA Lee (2010). Globalizing state, disappearing nation: The impact of foreign participation in the Singapore economy. In *The Management of Success: Singapore Revisited*, T Chong (ed.), pp. 139–158. Singapore: Institute for Southeast Asian Studies.

Low, D and LK Yeoh (2014). Beware the inequality trap. In *Hard Choices: Challenging the Singapore Consensus*, D Low and S Vadaketh (eds.), pp. 113–119. Singapore: National University of Singapore Press.

Ministry of Manpower (2000). Occupation Segregation: A Gender Perspective.

Ministry of Manpower (2013). Labour force in Singapore 2013.

Ministry of Manpower (2013). Singapore yearbook of manpower statistics 2013.

Ministry of Trade and Industry (2005). General household survey 2005 statistical release 1: Socio-demographic and economic characteristics, Chapter 2, "Education and Language".

Mok, FF (2014). Survey shows fewer women in top corporate roles in Singapore. March 10, 2014.

Narayanan, MP, N Seyhun and AC Inci (2014). Gender differences in executives' access to information. http://www.bus.umich.edu/NewsRoom/ArticleDisplay.asp?news_id=26677.

Ng, IYH (2010). Globalization intentions in tension: The case of Singapore. *International Social Work*, 53(5), 671–685.

Ng, IYH (2011). Growing worry of social immobility. *The Straits Times*, 16 February 2011.

Ong, A (2011). Households smaller but more affluent. *The Straits Times*, 16 February, 2011.

Straits Times (2013). More women for Singapore boardrooms, December 27, 2013.

U.S. Bureau of Labor Statistics (2013). Women in the labor force: A databook (2012 edition).

Ye, J (2014). Labour recruitment practices and its class implications: A comparative analysis of constructing Singapore's segmented labour market. *Geoforum*, 51, 183–190.

Yeoh, BSA (2007). Singapore: Hungry for foreign workers at all levels. Migration information source, January 2007. http://www.migrationinformation.org/Profiles/display.cfm?ID=570.

Yeoh, BSA, S Huang and J Gonzalez III (1999). Migrant female domestic workers: Debating the economic, social and political impacts in Singapore. *International Migration Review*, 33(1), 114–136.

Yip, CM and RSK Kwok (2014). Gender-oriented statistical discrimination theory: Empirical evidence from the Hong Kong labor market. *Research in Social Stratification and Mobility*, 37, 43–59.

Chapter 8

POVERTY, IDEOLOGY AND WOMEN EXPORT FACTORY WORKERS IN SOUTH-EAST ASIA[1]

GILLIAN H. C. FOO and LINDA Y. C. LIM

INTRODUCTION

The women who work in Asia's export-oriented industries are frequently presented and treated in the scholarly and popular literature as dual victims of poverty and ideology. Poverty, it is argued, causes women's employment in export factories because it results in the low wages which are necessary for competitiveness on the world market, and forces poor women to take exploitative jobs in export factories in order to survive; at the same time, their low wages keep them poor. Traditional ideology, on the other hand, is thought to conflict with women's wage employment, such that even if they are economically better off as a result of their employment, they may suffer socially and psychologically from it. This chapter will take issue with these two popular hypotheses, thereby questioning the contention that factory work has primarily a negative impact on women workers' lives. We argue that both poverty and ideology as they relate to these workers are in reality more complex than the prevailing hypotheses allow for. Since poverty has been extensively though incompletely explored elsewhere (e.g. ILO, 1985; Maex, 1983; Lim, 1986a; Lim, 1987b; Addison and Demery, 1988), it will be treated only briefly here. Most of our discussion will concentrate on the more complex and under-studied issue of ideology, drawing heavily on the case of Malaysia (Foo, 1987; Lim, 1987a).

---

[1]This chapter first appeared in Women, Poverty and Ideology in Asia, Haleh Afsar and Bina Agarwal (eds.), 212–233, 1989. Reprinted with permission from Macmillan, London.

An earlier version of this paper was presented at the panel on Export-Oriented Industrialization at the annual meeting of the Association of Women in Development, Washington, DC, 15 April 1987.

POVERTY

Simplistic and inadequate definitions of poverty, and the considerable diversity which exists among different Asian countries, bedevil attempts to generalise about the income status of women export factory workers. For example, there is the problem of defining what constitutes poverty in a particular country, given its specific historical and cultural circumstances, and the different results obtained, depending on whether absolute or relative, statistical or subjective standards are used. If poverty is defined as existence at or below the subsistence level within a country, then clearly the majority of women export factory workers in Asia are not poor, simply by virtue of their employment in the relatively privileged modern wage sector. The poor are usually the unemployed or underemployed. If poverty is defined as belonging to the lowest income group in a country, then the women may or may not be poor, depending on the country, but this tells us little about their absolute living standards.

Generally speaking, the poorer a country, the less likely women factory workers are to be poor relative to their fellow citizens, but the more likely they are to be poor in absolute terms, while the reverse is true in richer countries. Thus, for example, women export factory workers earning the legal minimum wage in Thailand and the Philippines are relatively well-off compared to most of their fellow citizens — especially the majority residing in rural areas where there is no minimum wage. But their absolute standard of living may seem poor to an observer from a developed country. On the other hand, women export factory workers in Singapore and Hong Kong may be among the lowest-paid workers in their countries, but their absolute standard of living may be high even to an observer from a developed country. In Singapore, for example, the typical female electronics factory worker's household belongs to an income group where in 1983:

> ...96.2% of the households, had a refrigerator, 95.9% had a television set, 23.1% a video cassette recorder, 12.8% a motor-car, 17.5% a motor-cycle, 44.7% a washing-machine, 3.6% an air-conditioner and 3.8% a piano/organ. (Lim, 1986b)

As early as 1975 in Singapore, even a lowly-paid garment factory worker whose costs of employment exceeded 80 per cent of her monthly income could afford to employ a domestic servant (Salaff and Wong, 1984: 203). In 1981, a Singapore garment factory worker whose own wage was below the national average had with her husband purchased a three-room flat with 'marble floors, an iron-wood desk, large colour and smaller black-and-white television sets, and other house fixtures that cost over S$6,000' (Salaff and

Wong, 1984: 205). Studies done in other countries like Hong Kong, Taiwan and Malaysia also show a high level of consumption of consumer durables among women export factory workers' families.

The picture is further complicated by workers' subjective view of their own relative income status. Among electronics factory workers in Malaysia, for example, urban workers considered themselves to be from poor families, while rural migrants did not consider their families to be poor (Foo, 1987), despite the statistical reality that, on the whole, urban families have higher incomes than rural families. This anomaly might be explained by the fact that in urban areas, factory labour may be a low-income and low-status occupation entered only by women from the poorest urban families. But the same urban factory employment offers women from rural areas a definite step up in income and status, and may be accessible only to those from relatively well-to-do rural families who have the requisite education and contacts to obtain these jobs. Thus while objectively the urban workers may be more well-off than the rural workers, subjectively they may consider themselves to be poor, whereas the rural workers do not.

Despite these definitional problems, we may attempt some brief generalisations about women export factory workers' income status, based on our own fieldwork and our reading of the extensive literature (see also ILO, 1985; Lim, 1986a; Lim, 1987b). First, in terms of their *origins*, the women who work in Asia's export factories are mostly not the poorest of the poor, who are typically uneducated and labour in rural occupations. Rather, most of them belong to urban or established rural–urban migrant families with better-than-average resources, although this may vary by country and over time (Lim, 1987b). Women who work in multinational electronics factories are particularly well-off, since they must possess educational qualifications considerably higher than the local male or female average.

Second, in terms of their *motivation*, while most women work out of economic need, this is usually not absolute poverty or minimum physical subsistence. Rather, there is a strong desire to improve their consumption standards, and to contribute to the upward mobility of their families. That is, the women work not for rice but for colour TVs and other consumer 'luxuries', as indicated by the following representative statements of a young single Malay factory worker in Malaysia:

> I wanted to work [in a Penang factory] because working in the village I won't earn much . . . and I felt I couldn't have anything of my own. If I wanted things like beautiful dresses, cosmetics, and so on, the income that I earned in the village didn't allow me to afford any of these, so I wanted to find a job outside the village. (Foo, 1987: 191)

and an older married Chinese factory worker in Singapore:

> By working I can afford to pay people to do things for me, and I have a little left over for pocket money. (Salaff and Wong, 1984, p. 203)

Salaff's and Wong's study found that low-income women workers in Singapore

> ...spent their wages first to buy clothes and toys for their children and next to maintain the families' enveloping networks of kinship connections, such as allowances to the members of the older generation and gifts on the occasion of visits, marriages, birthdays and religious festivities. (Salaff and Wong, 1984, p. 205)

They also purchased 'a public sector flat, appliances and furnishings for the new home, tuition for their children' (Salaff and Wong, 1984: 198).

In addition to these economic motivations, the women cite many non-economic motivations for working in export factories. Young single women say they welcome the opportunity that factory work provides to delay marriage and childbearing, to enjoy the companionship of their peers and lead independent lives, and to 'broaden their horizons' through new experiences (e.g. Snow, 1975; Lin, 1986; Foo, 1987). Married women say they feel bored staying at home and miss the companionship of colleagues (e.g. Lim, 1986b). Among both single and married women are many who say they would choose to work even in the absence of economic need (e.g. Lin, 1986; Foo, 1987), and Salaff and Wong quote one Singapore woman forced to quit work because of competing family demands as saying: 'This [not working] is a sacrifice I must make for my family' (Salaff and Wong, 1984, pp. 212–13).

Third, in terms of the *consequences* of export factory labour, women workers are clearly economically better off as a result of their jobs than they were before. They are also better off compared to other, much more numerous, female wage workers employed as domestic servants, agricultural labourers, helpers in small local shops, and unpaid family labour (e.g. Palabrica-Costello, 1984). Those employed in multinationals are usually the most well off.[2]

In sum, the evidence from the Asian countries which account for most of the female employment in export factories suggests that many if not

[2]A partial exception would be workers employed in third world multinationals from other developing countries, whose wages and working conditions would approximate those of local firms.

most of these women do not start out poor by local standards. If they are poor, their employment lifts their families out of poverty and enhances their living standards. There are of course differences by country and industry, by individual worker, and over time, but these are readily explained, as we have done elsewhere (e.g. Lim, 1986a; Lim, 1987b).

IDEOLOGY

In much of the literature on women export factory workers, consideration of ideology largely focuses on ideologies governing gender and class. While these are important, we contend that a comprehensive assessment of the implications of ideology must also include consideration of ideologies concerning family and self. In this section, we discuss aspects of ideology as it relates to familial values, individual aspirations, gender and class — all of which interact with factory work in shaping its impact on women workers' lives. Our discussion incorporates individual-level, qualitative data from Foo's (1987) study of women export factory workers in Penang, Malaysia. It aims to demonstrate that when 'traditional' and 'modern' ideologies intersect within the context of factory employment for women, contradiction and conflict do not necessarily result.

Family Ideology: Parent Repayment

It is frequently assumed that ideologies which emphasise the primacy of women's reproductive role and, at the extreme, recommend their confinement to the domestic sphere, are in fundamental conflict with women's participation in modern factory wage-labour, which is conducted in the public sphere. It follows that women would engage — or be permitted to engage — in such wage-labour only where severe economic need dominates any ideological concerns.[3] Hence the assumption that poverty must be the motivating factor for Asian women's employment in export factories. But we have suggested above that women export factory workers are generally not poor in their respective local contexts, nor are they necessarily or primarily motivated by poverty. This implies that their employment directly challenges traditional ideologies about women's proper roles, without the mitigation afforded by economic need.

[3]See, for example, Siraj (1984), which presents the views of various Islamic authorities on Malay women's work in multinational export factories. All recognised that economic need provides valid justification for women's wage employment; only the most extreme fundamentalist interpretation called for home-work as the preferred alternative.

In fact, studies of women export factory workers, their families and communities in many Asian countries show that traditional ideologies do not conflict with women's wage employment as much as is often assumed, and in many cases they in fact provide the motivation for such employment. It is important to note first that in nearly all countries, women, both daughters and wives, participated actively in production in the pre-capitalist 'family economy', as unpaid family labour on farms or other family economic enterprises, such as handicraft production. It is thus not their engagement in productive activities *per se* which represents any change from traditional norms and practices, but rather their engagement in such activities outside of the family or village context, as in an impersonal modern factory, which sometimes requires that they leave the family before marriage, migrating to distant cities for employment. Women export factory workers have merely exchanged contributions in cash or commodities for what in an earlier era would have been a contribution of labour to their families' livelihood. In the process, their economic contribution to the family increases, and despite initial ideologically-derived apprehensions or opposition from male or female family authorities, their employment in export factories is therefore generally welcomed by their families.[4]

Indeed, several studies argue that Asian women's families not only encourage but practically compel daughters to work in export factories because of the very considerable economic benefits which accrue to the family as a result of this employment. It has been suggested that the women are thereby exploited by their own families, and their personal interests sacrificed for the family's good (e.g. Elson and Pearson, 1981; Salaff, 1981; Greenhalgh, 1983; McLellan, 1985, etc.). If correct, this interpretation suggests that economic interests (not necessarily absolute need, since most of the families studied were not poor, but rather interested in upward mobility) readily dominate ideology where women's wage-employment is concerned — not only in the women's own families, but also among others in the community who benefit from their employment. Mather (1983), for example, has shown that the religiously conservative Islamic patriarchy in an Indonesian village not only supported, but even promoted, women's factory employment, because they benefited directly from it. (In Malaysia, on the other hand, the Islamic patriarchy tends to oppose such employment because they do not benefit from it (Lim, 1987a).) In the context of the family, export factory work does

[4]Evidence for this comes, for example, from studies in Taiwan (Kung, 1983; Greenhalgh, 1983), Hong Kong (Salaff, 1981), Singapore (Salaff and Wong, 1984); Malaysia (Ackerman, 1984; McLellan, 1985; Foo, 1987, etc.) and Indonesia (Wolf, 1984).

not seem to be viewed differently from other forms of wage-employment, except possibly more favourably than lower-income, lower-status jobs in the service, informal and agricultural sectors, and less favourably than higher-status white-collar jobs. Where not complicated by migration and residence away from the family, it has even increased women's desirability as marriage partners and the 'bride price' paid to their parents, e.g. in Malaysia (Ackerman, 1984).[5]

Foo (1987) advances a different interpretation of the relationship between daughters employed in export factories and their parents. Her study of women export factory workers in Penang, Malaysia, shows that *it is the women themselves* who decide and choose to work in the export factories, and that they do so even in the absence of obvious family economic need. In most cases it is also the women themselves who decide and choose to give their parents a portion of their earnings, whether or not they are living with them, and whether or not the parents ask for, expect or need such a contribution. Very often the desire to give money or goods to their parents is a major reason why the women seek employment in export factories in the first place, regardless of their parents' approval or economic need.

Ideology, rather than poverty, is the motivating factor here, and the women in Foo's study express this in terms of the traditional concept of 'parent repayment', which is strongly held in all three of the ethnic communities represented in this study — Muslim Malays, Confucianist Chinese, and Indians who include Muslims, Hindus and Christians — as well as in other countries in the region such as Hong Kong and Taiwan (inhabited by Confucianist Chinese), Thailand (Buddhist) and Indonesia (Muslim — Foo, 1987, pp. 194–8). 'Parent repayment' is not viewed by the women or their families as coercive or exploitative; rather, it is voluntary, natural, logical, and a rational act of reciprocity — repaying one's parents for all that they have expended on one during one's childhood and growing years, including affection. As one of Foo's respondents put it: 'Well, our parents raised us. We should give something back to them. It's only right' (Foo, 1987, p. 198). Factory employment enables women to make this repayment before they marry and are caught up in family expenses of their own. They expect to be on the receiving end of this reciprocal relationship when their own children are grown.

[5]Even in the case of women prostitutes in Thailand, Phongpaichit (1982) has clearly shown that not only the women's families, but their home communities in general, readily accept economic need as a justification for prostitution, and the women are not discriminated against in marriage when they eventually leave this occupation.

The ideology of 'parent repayment' is not peculiar to women only, but they appear to adhere to it more strongly than men: the anecdotal evidence presented in most studies suggests that daughters tend to contribute more to their parents than sons. From the viewpoint of traditional ideologies, this asymmetry is again seen to be rational, rather than unfair. Because of their greater participation in the domestic sphere, and lesser freedom to participate in the public sphere of social life, daughters tend to be closer to their parents, especially their mothers, than sons. They are more likely to live with their parents until marriage, and to spend more time at home and thus to share in the consumption of possessions that their monetary contributions help acquire for the family. Since the expectation is that men will later support their wives, their spending most of their incomes on themselves while still unmarried is accepted. On the other hand, daughters' independent income is likely to cease when they quit work to marry and raise their own children, making parent repayment more difficult later. For those women who continue working after marriage, cash contributions to their own and even their husbands' families continue (e.g. Salaff and Wong, 1984).

Individual Ideology: Consumer Autonomy and Independence

Family ideology is not the only reason why women export factory workers do not view their wage-employment as a coercive or unpleasant obligation which diminishes their personal autonomy, as suggested by some Western writers (e.g. Elson and Pearson, 1981). They additionally see the ability to work as an opportunity to exercise and express their personal autonomy, especially in the sphere of consumer purchases, and to acquire economic independence and valued life experiences, both of which are radical departures from the lives of women in traditional society. In the words of respondents from Foo's (1987) study:

> When we earn our own money, we don't have to depend on others. We have the freedom to spend it as we wish, and I like it this way...I feel this freedom is very important. Everyone must stand on their own two feet rather than being dependent on someone else. (p. 329)
>
> Whatever I want, I can buy because I have a job and can earn a living of my own. Whenever I was at home, whatever I wanted, I couldn't get because I didn't have my own money, and I had to ask my parents...I have more freedom now because I don't have to ask from my father for money. I can buy whatever I need. (p. 175)
>
> Yes, I enjoy being able to make money on my own and decide what I myself want to spend it on, because being able to make money on my own, 1 can buy anything that I like such as clothes and jewelry, and can go anywhere for tour that I desire, (p. 329)

> Now that I have economic independence, I can do anything and learn anything I want without asking from my parents. But last time, not only did I have to ask permission to do anything, I had to ask money from them as well. So I dared not tell my mother that I was taking up 'L' license. [A learner's licence for operating a scooter or motorbike.] Now I need simply inform them that I want to learn how to operate a motorbike, and that's it. (p. 174)

Although consumer purchases are the main arena in which factory wage-employment enables young women workers to exercise personal autonomy, it is not the only one, and they are not only materialistic in their goals and desires. They also appreciate independence, experience and broader horizons, from which they derive greater confidence and self-esteem.

> The main reasons for my working here are first, to be independent; second, to try to gain experience outside; third, to lessen my parents' burden, (p. 194)
>
> I've gained experience in my working life mixing with people. I've learnt how to interact with others. I feel that I've lots more friends now and am more daring and not so shy — I'm more independent and more mature. I have my own money so I'm more independent. If I stayed at home, it'd be boring, and there'd be nothing to do. I'd also be more dependent, especially on my mother. (p. 334)
>
> Before I started working, I was very timid, whatever I did, I was scared. I was scared of the supervisor, of my work, and so on. Now, I'm brave enough to speak up, to explain and to clarify my mistakes, to speak my objections and to lead the society that I'm a member of.... After working in a factory, I've met a lot of friends and got to know a lot of people so I'm not scared of asking questions and making my points to others. I'm not shy about doing whatever I think is right. I'm brave enough to be a party leader in politics too. (pp. 335–6)

Note that the women's values of independence and individualism revealed here are clearly at odds with those of their traditional cultures and society — rural Muslim Malay and urban Confucianist Chinese — yet they appear to be firmly and universally[6] entrenched without causing conflict. These values presumably derive from the women's relatively high level of education (mid-secondary or better) and the pervasiveness of modern media in Malaysia, even in rural areas.

[6]In addition to in-depth interviews, Foo's study includes a survey of 385 women factory workers.

Gender Ideology: Women's Roles

Scholars have been most interested in gender ideology as it affects women's employment in export factories. Ideologies about women's roles do play an important role in structuring the female labour market. On the demand side of the labour market, employers hire young women for assembly work in labour-intensive export factories in part because of their presumed feminine characteristics. These include manual dexterity, experience with precise manual tasks such as sewing and food processing, conscientiousness, docility, and an expected short working life due to voluntary quits at marriage or childbearing. These characteristics make women efficient, productive, well-behaved and low-cost workers. Their short working life, for example, ensures low average seniority and hence low wages, as well as a weak commitment to the labour force and high group turnover, making labour organisation difficult (e.g. Lim, 1978). Ideology also causes sex discrimination by employers in the structuring of the labour force, e.g. restricting managerial and supervisory positions in female-intensive industries to males (e.g. Wong and Ko, 1984). Asian export factories, especially multinationals, are also well known for factory social and cultural practices and fringe benefits designed to appeal to young women, such as fashion and make-up classes, beauty contests and dinner-dances (e.g. Lim, 1978; Grossman, 1979).

On the supply side of the female labour market, ideologies which emphasise the primacy of women's role in reproduction and the domestic sphere, and the secondary importance of their role in production, reduce the supply price of female labour (i.e. the wage at which women are willing to work). These ideologies restrict women to relatively short working lives between school-leaving and marriage (perhaps followed by lower-paid homework and informal sector employment later), and to jobs considered suitable for women: mainly 'light', low-skilled, sex-segregated female occupations and industries. The resulting low seniority of female workers and 'overcrowding' in the segregated female industries also contribute to the low supply price of female labour. Women both have few job opportunities and do not view themselves as either primary or long-term breadwinners for their families; they are therefore willing to work for relatively low wages.

Although there are variations by country and over time, these effects of gender ideology on women's employment in export factories are found virtually everywhere, and the traditional ideologies themselves remain fairly intact. This does not, however, mean that women workers' 'gender subordination' has merely been modified or even intensified by their factory employment, as claimed by some Western writers (e.g. Elson and Pearson, 1981). On the contrary, there is evidence that wage employment for women has lessened, though not completely undermined or eliminated, traditional patterns of gender subordination. For example, the women become less dependent on their families, especially if their jobs require migration:

> Now, girls who move to the city and live away from their families learn to manage their lives by themselves and learn how to be independent. Once in a while, they may consult their elders, but they are not totally dependent on their opinions. When one stays away from the family, one begins to do anything for oneself, making her own decisions and being independent on oneself. As time goes by, you begin to enjoy making your own decisions and don't want to consult your parents. Just like me, I don't like to ask my mother's opinion about a lot of things because some of the things I want to do are beyond the knowledge of my mother. (Foo, 1987, pp. 220–1)

Both urban Chinese and rural Malay women in Foo's (1987) Malaysian sample clearly view their life circumstances as an improvement over those of their mothers:

> In our mothers' time girls married young, were narrow-minded, restricted by their parents, were less knowledgeable, and had no experience of life. There were no advantages at all. In our generation, we shoulder the same responsibility as a man in the family, we get a good job, we have the opportunity to learn, (p. 339)
>
> We are better than our mothers' time — We have greater job opportunities, we are free to do what we want, we can choose our own husbands, we have better educational opportunities, we have the chance of'travelling and seeing the world outside. My mother's — they had less freedom, they had to obey the elders and submit to arranged marriage and marrying at a very young age. They could only stay at home doing housework, looking after their husband and children for their whole life. They couldn't wear whatever clothes they wanted to and they couldn't associate with boys freely. They had little chance of education and working outside. But they are better than us in certain ways. They are fantastic cooks and domestic workers. They've spent their entire lives cooking so they are very good cooks now. They are less complicated. (p. 339)

In virtually all the Asian countries, factory employment has resulted in or contributed to a later age of marriage, and to a switch from arranged to self-made marriages.[7] The evolution of a dating culture (which is not,

[7]Most studies cite these developments, which have been noted in the Philippines (Snow, 1975), Hong Kong (Salaff, 1981), Taiwan (Kung, 1983), Malaysia (Ackerman, 1984; Foo, 1987), Singapore and other countries.

however, peculiar to women employed in export factories) represents a clear change from traditional patterns of mate-selection (by parents) and relations between the sexes (non-existent outside the family). In most cases it has not produced any pronounced conflicts for the women or their families (but see the discussion on Malaysia below). Rather, self-selection of one's marriage partner through dating is seen by the women themselves as a progressive development, one which reflects a further exercise of personal autonomy, choice and freedom by young women, rather than their 'commoditization' on the 'marriage market' as suggested by Elson and Pearson (1981). To quote one of Foo's (1987) respondents:

> Our generation is marrying a lot later than our mothers' generation. I think we are luckier because our mothers' generation followed arranged marriage and we don't have to. Our generation wouldn't agree to the idea of meet once and then get married. Our generation has a lot of new ideas, not like our mothers' generation. They are simple and less complicated. Our generation's involvement in economic activities and education is more common than in our mothers' time. So we are more conscious about our rights and the gap between male and female is not as great among the present generation. So a girl won't be happy following an arranged marriage, (p. 425)

Although this and similar comments were made by Muslim Malay women in Malaysia, many of them do face a conflict between the proper — modest and chaste — conduct expected of young unmarried females in traditional ideology, and behaviour such as dating which results from their exposure to more 'modern' ways through factory work and urban living. At an extreme, this conflict has led to outbreaks of 'mass hysteria' among factory workers — an affliction peculiar to Muslim Malay women in Malaysia which does not affect their Chinese or Indian colleagues but is also found in other (non-industrial) Malay female group settings (Lim, 1987a).

It should be noted here that young Asian factory women's concerns with beauty, sexual attractiveness and relationships with men (e.g. Fatimah, 1985) do not necessarily originate with the emphasis in some factory social activities on fashion, beauty, romance and intermingling between the sexes, as many writers have claimed. On the contrary, beauty and sexual attractiveness are important in traditional Asian cultures, with the exception of those which practise feminine seclusion. In South-East Asia especially there has long been a cult of feminine beauty involving among other things the use of traditional cosmetics and herbal treatments; the weakness of the marriage bond (with traditionally high divorce and remarriage rates) may be one reason for this. In any event, export factory women are not the only young women in these societies to wear fashionable Western dress and make-up, patronise cinemas and discos, and date men — all of which are common in the urban areas and have even been disseminated to rural areas through the mass media. Most of the workers do not even participate in factory social and cultural activities (e.g. Lim, 1987a), and remain fairly traditional in their beliefs and behaviour (e.g. Foo, 1987).

Despite the primacy of marriage in their own ideology, the factory women's views on this institution are not altogether traditional. The rural–urban migrants voice their reluctance to marry men who are less educated than they are or who have rural occupations. And here are what two of Foo's (unmarried) respondents, a Chinese and a Malay respectively, have to say about the relationship between husband and wife:

> I think it's a partnership. The couple must have equal say in discussions — for example, about the children's education. When you have a child, you'll talk to the husband about how many you want. One can't agree with everything he says. He should respect you too. Nobody is perfect. Even if he is the head of the family, I don't think you have to follow whatever he demands. (p. 429)
>
> Family heads are both husband and wife. They both must plan and discuss all issues and problems. Both must respect each other and understand. Man has the right to be the main head because he has to earn for the family as a whole. And it's also traditional. (p. 429)

In Foo's larger sample of 385 women, the majority of Chinese respondents disagreed with the statement that 'The husband is the head of the household and it is the wife's duty to obey him', while the majority of Malay and Indian respondents agreed, revealing the importance of ethnic and cultural differences in influencing gender ideology, despite similar objective circumstances. Salaff and Wong's (1981) study of married Chinese women in Singapore shows a similar pattern of preference for joint decision-making between husband and wife in the working-class family.

Class Ideology

Factory women's ideology and behaviour related to class consciousness and action varies considerably from situation to situation, and over time, a subject which cannot be fully discussed here.[8] The Malaysian case is usually presented as an extreme example of docility and lack of class consciousness, compared, for example to the highly-unionised and often militant female and

[8]See ILO (1985) and Lim (1986a) for more discussion.

female-led unions found in export industries in South Korea, the Philippines and even Thailand. The reasons for this have been explored elsewhere (e.g. Blake, 1984; Lim, 1987a), and here we will merely present in their own words the Malaysian women's views of factory work (Foo, 1987), which suggest why class ideology is underdeveloped among them.

Firstly, as predicted by Marx and Engels, the women clearly regard their employment in capitalist factories as a progressive development over their pre-capitalist circumstances:

> I prefer working in a factory because with relatives there is not much freedom. (p. 332)
>
> ...Working for a member of the family, I wouldn't be able to earn much money. (p. 332)
>
> I still prefer factory work. It's not so nice working for the family. If they pay less, I wouldn't dare to complain. With factory work, if I'm not satisfied, I can quit and change jobs. (p. 332)
>
> I prefer working outside. If you work in the family, it's very difficult... If you work in the factory, you have some form of independence. (p. 332)

Second, most of the workers see the exchange of their labour for wages as a fair one:

> I feel that it's quite fair that they pay certain wages in the hopes that we'll work hard, produce better quality cloth. And it's still fair that even though they earn a lot of income, they still pay us salary. It doesn't mean that they earn profit and they don't give salary to workers. (p. 301)
>
> I think it's fair enough for them to pay us certain wages that are worth our work. Everywhere it's the same — that the workers will get certain wages. So long as we do our part, I feel they should pay us accordingly. (pp. 301–2)

They also see the necessity for factory rules and regulations:

> ...those rules and discipline are necessary. Example, we can't talk while we are working and we can't move around while we are in the factory... All this is quite reasonable for we need to concentrate on our work... these rules and regulations are necessary to ensure that the work will be carried out smoothly and efficiently. (p. 307)

Third, at least some workers take pride in .their job-related skills and the outcome of the tasks they perform:

> Yes, I'm certainly proud of the work I do. Using scope (microscope) and bonding requires a lot of skill and speed. It's not easy, you know. (p. 320)
>
> ...at Intertech, we say that our work puts men on the moon! The management told us that at one point one of the buyers was using our chips for building something with the space program in U.S. It's quite amazing to think that something as small from us is used for something so big. (p. 320)

The workers did have complaints about various aspects of their factory jobs, but these were usually targeted at individual supervisors or employers who were seen to be 'unfair'; the complaints did not translate into objections to wage-labour in general or into any sense of class antagonism.

THE RATIONALITY OF IDEOLOGY

Women factory workers subscribe to the various traditional and modern ideologies which condition their attitudes and behaviour, largely because these ideologies are rational in their given socioeconomic context, and not because they are victims of so-called 'false consciousness'. Where family ideology is concerned, parent–child reciprocity provides for social security where the State does not, and where traditional forms of social security, such as patron–client relationships in rural areas, are breaking down with development and 'modernisation'. For the women in Foo's study, parent–child reciprocity is particularly important in guaranteeing them emotional and financial security in a situation where marriage bonds are weak.[9]

Where gender ideology is concerned, the traditional division of labour between husband and wife is also rational in a situation where men have more and better employment opportunities and earn higher wages. Women are additionally restricted by their responsibilities for child care, especially since in urban areas traditional extended family and kin networks are less readily available to assist with child care. Working-class women's jobs are also intrinsically unsatisfying, and so hold little long-term attraction compared with the traditional élite ideal of full-time wife and mother.

As for class ideology, in a situation where modern factory wage-labour represents an improvement over alternative forms of capitalist or pre-capitalist employment, where workers because of their acceptance of the traditional sexual division of labour within marriage do not have a lifelong commitment to the labour force, and where an individualist ideology is in the ascendancy, it is not surprising that a collective proletarian consciousness and class antagonism do not develop.

Whereas women factory workers' ideology as it relates to family, gender roles and class may be typified as a variant of the 'traditional', the same cannot be said of their adherence to the distinctly non-traditional ideology of individual freedom and independence. Historically, this ideology has evolved

[9]Polygamy is permitted among the Muslim Malays, while the immigrant origins of the Chinese have weakened traditional extended family/kin/village relationships enforcing the permanence of marriage.

as a concomitant of the rise of free labour markets and the demise of pre-capitalist forms of labour organisation. But in the situation of women export factory workers in Asia today, gender is an additional, and central, underpinning of this and the other ideologies to which the women subscribe. The onerous nature of women's traditional confinement within the home and family causes them to appreciate greatly the independence and experience that wage-employment affords for an at least temporary escape from such confinement, and therefore to accept the terms and conditions on which such employment is offered. The importance of children as social security, especially where marriage bonds are weak and men cannot be relied on for lifelong maintenance, also results in women's strong support of the ideology and practice of parent–child reciprocity, a major motivation for their desire for factory jobs. Women's disadvantaged position in the labour market, because of the constraints imposed on them by traditional gender roles within the family (that is, responsibility for housework and child care), causes them to accept the role of the husband as primary breadwinner and therefore the temporary nature of their own employment. This in turn results in a relatively weak commitment to the labour force and an underdeveloped proletarian consciousness.

In short, the ideology of women workers which so conditions their employment in export factories in Asia is a product of gender inequality within their societies. Factory employment does not create or worsen such inequality, nor does it destroy it. It does, however, alleviate, at least temporarily, the subordination that women suffer as a result of gender inequality. But these 'liberating' effects are the combined result of education, migration and wage-employment *per se* rather than of export factory jobs in particular. Factory employment contributes by making available the wage-employment, necessitating the migration, and motivating the education. This last point is illustrated by one of Foo's (1987) respondents:

> Before, parents in the *kampong* (Malay village) would only educate their daughters up till Primary Standard Four — they felt there was no point in giving girls further schooling since daughters were married off at 13 or 14. They are now willing to educate daughters for longer and then let them go and work. (p. 212)

Factory employment is significant because it is generally superior to other forms of wage-employment for women (Lim, 1986a, 1987b). Export factories are important because, unlike many other industries, they employ a high proportion of women and in some countries include many multinationals, which have better terms and conditions of employment than local firms.

It remains to consider if the Malaysian women's attitudes presented here differ significantly from those of women working in export factories in other Asian countries. Studies done in the other middle- and upper-income Asian developing countries where export manufacturing is concentrated and has been long-established reveal considerable similarities in the factory women's attitudes and motivations.[10] The Malaysian case itself is more representative than most because it includes women of different cultures and backgrounds: Muslim Malays, Confucianist Chinese and Hindu, Muslim and Christian Indians, from both urban and rural backgrounds. The greatest difference among women in different countries appears to be in class ideology, which depends on a host of economic, legal, political and cultural factors which vary considerably from case to case (e.g. Blake, 1984). The Malaysian women appear to be more underdeveloped in their class ideology than women in other Asian locations, particularly Thailand, the Philippines and South Korea (e.g. Lim, 1987a).

The Asian countries not considered here, which may turn out to be significantly different even after export manufacturing has matured in them as it has in the more established countries, are those of South and West Asia, from Bangladesh to Turkey. These countries are much poorer than the East and South-East Asian countries discussed here, have very conservative traditional cultures which are much more oppressive of women (e.g. which practise feminine seclusion), and a much smaller and more recent experience with export manufacturing and with modern wage-employment for women. They are mostly involved in textile and garment exports undertaken by local or other developing-country firms, rather than in electronics manufacture by developed-country multinationals. More systematic research needs to be done on these 'newer' countries before we can attempt to assess their situation.

CONCLUSION

This chapter has made the following arguments about poverty, ideology and women export factory workers in Asia, drawing on the existing literature and our own research. First, in the context of their own countries, these women are mostly not poor by origin, or as a consequence of their employment, which is motivated by reasons other than absolute poverty or desperate

[10]See, for example, Kung (1983) on Taiwan, Salaff (1981) on Hong Kong, Wong and Ko (1984) on Singapore, Snow (1975) on the Philippines, and the various articles in Jones (1984) on these and other Asian countries such as Thailand and Indonesia. Similar findings have also been reported from Latin America and North Africa.

economic need, and in fact lifts the women and their families out of poverty, substantially enhancing their living standards. Second, the sexual division of labour, pre-existing gender inequality, and prevailing ideologies about women's proper roles, constrict their labour market opportunities and participation, thereby determining the pattern of their employment in female-intensive export factories. Third, although they emphasise women's reproductive role in the domestic sphere, traditional ideologies do not necessarily conflict with and may even foster women's productive role in the public sphere, such as their employment in export factories. Many women welcome this employment as an opportunity to fulfil certain traditional obligations, even in the absence of economic need, and ideology — such as the ideology of parent repayment — may be more important than poverty in motivating their employment. Fourth, wage-employment in modern export factories does not drastically change women's ideologies with respect to the family and women's roles within it, but it does endow them with greater personal autonomy which they value and exercise, as in independent living and the choice of a marriage partner. Some of them also expect more shared responsibility between husband and wife than is common in traditional society. This perhaps partial embrace of 'modern' values of independence, individualism and equality represents the biggest break with traditional values resulting from modern wage-employment for women and its concomitants of higher education and rural-urban migration. Fifth, at least in the Malaysian case, class ideology remains underdeveloped among the women factory workers, as a result of gender-specific ideologies and role constraints, and the locally- and historically-specific circumstances of export manufacturing in this country (Lim, 1987a).

In short, the existing evidence from the Asian countries which have the longest experience in female-intensive export manufacturing and the largest number of women employed in such manufacturing strongly challenges the common assumption that women export factory workers in Asia suffer from poverty, backward ideology and a hypothesised conflict between the two.[11] We suggest instead that poverty is both less serious than is often assumed, and less important than ideology in motivating women's factory employment. Women factory workers' ideology itself is both rational and facilitates rather than conflicts with their employment. Factory employment, by improving the economic status of women workers and their families, and by contributing to

[11]This contradiction between theory and reality is itself a notable feature of scholarship on the subject of women export factory workers in Asia, and has been explored and explained elsewhere (Lim, 1987b).

changes in ideology in a more individualistic and egalitarian direction, may also be seen as a historically progressive development for the women and their societies.

REFERENCES

Ackerman, S (1984). Impact of Industrialization on the Social Role of Malay Women. In Yun, HA, NS Karim and R Talib (eds), *Women in Malaysia* (Kuala Lumpur: Pelanduk Publications) pp. 40–60.

Addison, T and L Demery (eds) (1988). *Wages and Labour Conditions in the Newly-Industrialising Countries of Asia* (London: Overseas Development Institute).

Blake, ML (1984) 'Constraints on the organization of women industrial workers', in Gavin W. Jones (ed.) (1984), pp. 149–62.

Elson, D and R Pearson (1981). The subordination of women and the internationalization of factory production, in Young, K, C Wolkowitz and R McCullagh (eds), *Of Marriage and the Market: Women's Subordination in International Perspective* (London: CSE Books) pp. 144–66.

Fatimah, D (1985). '*Minah Karan*', *The Truth About Malaysian Factory Girls* (Kuala Lumpur, Malaysia: Berita Publishing Sdn. Bhd).

Foo, GHC (1987). 'Work and Marriage: Attitudes of Women Factory Workers in Malaysia', PhD dissertation in population planning, University of Michigan, Ann Arbor.

Greenhalgh, S (1983). 'Sexual Stratification: The Other Side of "Growth with Equity" in East Asia', Center for Policy Studies Working Papers no. 111 (New York: The Population Council).

Grossman, R (1979). 'Women's place in the integrated circuit', *Southeast Asia Chronicle*, no. 66, Jan.–Feb., pp. 1–17.

ILO (International Labour Office) (1985). *Women Workers in Multinational Enterprises in Developing Countries* (Geneva: ILO, prepared by Linda Y. C. Lim).

Jones, GW (ed.) (1984). *Women in the Urban and Industrial Workforce: Southeast and East Asia* (Canberra: Development Studies Centre Monograph no. 33, Australian National University).

Kung, L (1983). *Factory Women in Taiwan* (Ann Arbor, Michigan: University Microfilms Inc. Research Press).

Lim, LYC (1978). 'Women Workers in Multinational Corporations: The Case of the Electronics Industry in Malaysia and Singapore', Michigan Occasional Papers no. 9 (Ann Arbor, Michigan: Women's Studies Program, University of Michigan).

Lim, LYC (1986a). 'Export-Oriented Industrialization and Asian Labor', Paper presented at the Conference on Origins and Consequences of National Development Strategies: Latin America and East Asia Compared, Duke University, Durham, NC, 31 March-1 April 1986.

Lim, LYC (1986b). 'Export-Led Industrialisation, Labour Welfare and International Labour Standards in Singapore', paper prepared for Addison, T and L Demery (eds), *Wages and Labour Conditions in the Newly-Industrialising Countries of Asia* (London: Overseas Development Institute, 1988).

Lim, LYC (1987a). 'Women industrial workers: the specificities of the Malaysian case' in Ariffin, J and W Smith (eds), *Malaysian Women in the Urban and Industrial Labour Force* (Singapore: Institute of Southeast Asian Studies), forthcoming.

Lim, LYC (1987b). 'Women's work in export factories: a review and critique'. Manuscript later published as 'Women's work in export factories: the politics of a cause' in Irene Tinker (ed.), Persistent Inequalities, Women and World Development'. New York: Oxford University Press (1990), pp. 101–119.

Lin, V (1986). 'Health, Women's Work, and Industrialization: Women Workers in the Semiconductor Industry in Singapore and Malaysia', Women in International Development Working Paper no. 130 (East Lansing, Michigan: Women in International Development Program, Michigan State University).

Maex, R (1983). *Employment and Multinationals in Asian Export Processing Zones*, Multinational Enterprises Programme Working Paper no. 26 (Geneva: ILO).

Mather, C (1983). 'Industrialization in the Tangerang Regency of West Java: women workers and the Islamic patriarchy', *Bulletin of Concerned Asian Scholars*, vol. 15, no. 2, pp. 2–17, and in H. Afshar (ed) (1985), *Women, Work and Ideology* (London: Tavistock) pp. 153–80.

McLellan, S (1985). 'Reciprocity or Exploitation? Mothers and Daughters in the Changing Economy of Rural Malaysia', Women in International Development Working Paper no. 93 (East Lansing, Michigan: Women in International Development Program, Michigan State University).

Palabrica-Costello, M (1984). 'Female domestic servants in Cagayan de Oro, Philippines: social and economic implications of employment in a 'premodern' occupational role', in Jones, GW (ed.) (1984), pp. 235–50.

Phongpaichit, P (1982). *From Peasant Girls to Bangkok Masseuses*, Women, Work and Development no. 2 (Geneva: ILO).

Salaff, J (1981). *Working Daughters of Hong Kong: Filial Piety or Power in the Family?* (New York: CUP).

Salaff, J and A Wong (1984). 'Women's work: factory, family and social class in an industrializing order', in Gavin W. Jones (ed.) (1984), pp. 189–214.

Siraj, M (1984). 'Islamic attitudes to female employment in industrializing economies: some notes from Malaysia', in Jones, GW (ed.) (1984), pp. 163–74.

Snow, RT (1975). 'Dependent Development and the New Industrial Worker', PhD dissertation in sociology, Harvard University.

Wolf, DL (1984). 'Making the bread and bringing it home: female factory workers and the family economy in rural Java', in Jones, GW (ed.) (1984), pp. 215–31.

Wong, AK and Y-C Ko (1984). 'Women's Work and Family Life: The Case of Electronics Workers in Singapore', Women in International Development Working Paper (East Lansing, Michigan: Women in International Development Program, Michigan Stale University).

Chapter 9

WOMEN'S WORK IN EXPORT FACTORIES: THE POLITICS OF A CAUSE*

LINDA Y. C. LIM

One of the most popular new areas of research on women in development since the mid-1970s has been research on women factory workers in export industries in the Third World, especially those women employed by multinational corporations. The extensive literature on this subject needs to be explained, since it is disproportionate to the relative importance of such employment for Third World women, the vast majority of whom are employed in agriculture, services, and nonexport, nonmultinational manufacturing activities. In the mid-1980s no more than half a million women worldwide were employed in export-oriented multinational factories in developing countries (ILO, 1985, pp. 27–28). If nonmultinational export factories were included, this number would at most triple to 1.5 million women, a total that is still minute compared to the several hundred million working women in the Third World. Yet this handful of women have captured the disproportionate attention and imagination not only of scholars and students, but also of journalists, film makers, religious groups, feminist organizations, and the labor movement, especially in the Western industrial countries.

The reason for the widespread interest in this subject is the historical coincidence of growing interest in women's changing roles worldwide with the expansion of export manufacturing in Third World countries. Both of these trends were new in the early 1970s. The then newly popular dependency theory seemed to explain the scattered data available, producing a widely accepted stereotype of poverty-stricken Third World women suffering low wages, wretched working conditions, and ruthless exploitation

*This chapter first appeared in Persistent Inequalities. Women and World Development, Irene Tinker (ed.), 1990, pp. 101–119. By Permission of Oxford University Press, USA.

by multinationals located in export-processing free trade zones in Asia and Latin America.

The prominence of this stereotype was enhanced by the proclivity of many scholars and political activists to blame multinational corporations for the world's economic problems. Manufactured exports from the developing countries challenge powerful protectionist vested interests in the industrial countries. They are equally condemned by vested interests in developing countries, which oppose the accompanying trade liberalization and modern factory employment for women. Longstanding nationalist critics of multinationals thus broadened their coalition to include both feminists and patriarchs.

This chapter will examine the empirical validity of this negative stereotype in the light of more recently accumulated data on the life and work of women workers in both national and multinational export factories in the Third World. It will then consider the methodological and political reasons behind the persistence of the stereotype in popular opinion and much of the current literature.

WOMEN AND EXPORT MANUFACTURING

Manufacturing employment for women, even in multinationals, is not new in the Third World (e.g., Chincilla 1977), but manufacturing for export began only in the late 1950s, first in local and then in multinational firms. It has been concentrated in labor-intensive industries, which tend to be female-intensive in all countries, since these industries are sensitive to wage costs and female labor is typically cheaper than equivalent male labor. The job characteristics of these industries also fit well with the needs and characteristics of female labor constrained by the sexual division of labor. Readily learned skills requiring manual dexterity and patience with tedious tasks make women appropriate workers, conditioned as they are by culture and extensive experience with sewing, food processing, and other household tasks. The difficulty of combining factory labor with rearing children also ensures a labor force that is largely unmarried, and therefore young and healthy, with high turnover and a low average wage, without jeopardizing productivity because of the short learning curve. Since labor-intensive industries tend to have low capital requirements, relatively simple technologies, and low skill content, barriers to entry are low. Even in developed countries they are highly competitive industries with low profit margins which exert continuous pressure on production costs and especially on wages, reinforcing the necessity of employing cheap female labor.

Labor-intensive, female-intensive industries in the developed countries thus were the most vulnerable to low-wage competition from newly industrialized developing countries. In the 1950s Hong Kong became the first developing country to export manufactures because of the small size of its domestic economy and disproportionate industrial capacity.[1] By the 1960s, Taiwan (also endowed with refugee Chinese capitalists) and South Korea had established locally owned import-substituting industries for their somewhat larger domestic markets and were looking for export outlets to expand volumes and lower costs through economies of scale. Local firms in these countries could penetrate developed country markets because the low wages characteristic of preindustrial and newly industrializing economies made them competitive in labor-intensive, female-intensive industries such as textiles, garments, footwear, and toys. This competition from emerging private capital in developing countries and from Japan eventually forced developed country firms in these industries to relocate in Third World countries to take advantage of cheaper labor, becoming "multinational" in the process.

Across the Pacific, Mexico in the mid-1960s was also already embarked on import-substituting industrialization for its domestic market. It then established a new industrialization program along its border with the United States hoping to generate much-needed employment and foreign exchange, as Puerto Rico had done earlier by exporting manufactures to the mainland. This attracted many relocating U.S. firms, some of whom soon joined other firms in migrating to Asia as well.

Most of the early export-manufacturing countries set up special industrial estates for their new industries, which, like established domestic market-oriented industries, were heavily dependent on imported inputs. But unlike the tariff-protected domestic industries, which could raise their output prices to pay for import costs, export industries faced a competitive world market and so needed free trade (i.e., inputs imported at world prices) to succeed. Thus was born the "free-trade zone" or "export-processing zone," where export industries are exempt from import and export duties, often also eligible for tax holidays, and permitted to have 100 percent foreign ownership (Lee 1984). The zones thus allow developing country governments to promote export manufacturing and foreign investment without dismantling tariff-protected, nationally owned domestic industries. In socialist countries like

[1]The 1949 Communist revolution in China cut the British colony off from its natural hinterland, sending capitalist industrialists from cities such as Shanghai fleeing with their capital and expertise to Hong Kong.

China (and, reportedly, soon Vietnam as well), they allow segregated capitalist sectors to develop without disrupting the rest of the economy.

Today, about a third of all export factory workers in the Third World, male and female, work in these zones. This proportion would rise if "bonded factories," not located in zones but enjoying the same privileges, were included; it may also be somewhat higher for female workers alone, since many male-intensive export industries (e.g., steel, shipbuilding, automobiles) are heavy industries also producing for the domestic market. Analytically, there is little to distinguish export industries located in export-processing zones from the majority not located in these zones; my analysis will therefore not distinguish between them, concentrating instead on export-manufacturing industries in general.

Once the success of export manufacturing became evident, developing country governments began aggressively to promote this development strategy. They did so to generate income and employment and earn foreign exchange required to service import-dependent domestic market industries, which for most governments remained their priority in industrial development. Some, but not all of these governments promoted export manufacturing under the persuasion and even pressure of international development lending agencies like the World Bank and International Monetary Fund, which wanted them to earn foreign exchange in part to repay the debts they had earlier incurred to establish import-substituting industries. Exporting manufactures was considered more desirable than exporting commodities, as developing countries had traditionally done, because of better market prospects and higher productivity, skills, and income. Encouraging multinationals also provided an inflow of foreign capital, which could support broader industrial development efforts.

The success of developed country firms that relocated production in lower cost developing countries to enhance their competitiveness and preserve market share inspired imitation from other firms. Traditional labor-intensive industries with relatively simple technologies, such as textiles, garments, footwear, toys, sporting goods, and accessories, were soon followed by electrical household products and consumer electronics, often manufactured by large multinationals such as Philips from the Netherlands and General Electric and RCA from the United States. American firms in particular were encouraged to engage in offshore production by Items 806.30 and 807.00 of the U.S. Tariff Schedule, which imposed tariffs only on the foreign value added of imports containing duty-exempt U.S.-made inputs.

Beginning in the late 1960s the semiconductor industry expanded rapidly; though high-tech and capital-intensive, it was also highly competitive and included very labor-intensive processes employing female labor. Because of the advanced technology involved, it was not competition from Third World producers which forced the semiconductor manufacturers to locate in the Third World, but rather competition among themselves. Heavy research and development expenditures and short product life cycles made it important to produce the largest volumes at the lowest possible costs to forestall competition and recoup investment before imitation or obsolescence of new products set in. This peculiar characteristic of high-tech industry — now including computers — remains an incentive for selecting developing countries today (Lim, 1987a), despite the rapid progress of automation.

European and American multinationals were soon joined by Japanese competitors, as rapid development raised wages in Japan, protectionist trade policies in Western countries restricted imports of goods from Japan, and other developed countries offered trade preferences for manufactured exports from developing countries.[2] By manufacturing for export in developing countries, Japanese multinationals could thus enjoy both lower labor costs and freer and even privileged trade access to Western markets. In recent years the strong yen has encouraged even more production in Third World countries by Japanese firms exporting back to their home market as well as to third-country markets.

These factors explain the demand-side causes of women's employment in export factories in developing countries. It is women who are predominantly employed in these factories because female-intensive industries, being labor-intensive and sensitive to wage costs, are the first to lose their international competitiveness in high-wage developed countries when low-wage developing countries industrialize. This shift of manufacturing capacity from developed to developing countries, initiated by market forces and Third World firms, soon becomes encouraged by Third World government development policies and the corporate strategy of First World multinationals.

WOMEN WORKERS IN EXPORT INDUSTRIES

The supply-side cause of women's employment in export factories in developing countries is more simple and universal: like men, they need and want to work. This is shown by the fact that even women not previously in

[2]This is mainly the generalized system of preferences (GSP), which allows for the duty-free import into developed country markets of manufactures from developing countries, subject to annual country and product quotas and a minimum local content requirement.

the labor force flock to the export factories when they are established. Their reasons for wanting to work are primarily economic —to enhance individual and family income — but there are also social and cultural factors involved (e.g., Foo and Lim, 1989). In most developing countries, the structure of the economy does not provide many modern wage jobs for women, most of whom are concentrated in inferior employment in farming, domestic service, and the informal sector. Modern factory jobs, whether in the export or domestic sector, are thus much desired.

Altogether there are probably about 1.5 million women directly employed in export manufacturing in developing countries, between a third and half of them in wholly or partly foreign-owned enterprises, which include not only multinationals from industrialized countries but also firms from other Third World nations. There is considerable variation by country; for example, in South Korea, Taiwan, and Hong Kong most employers are local, whereas in Singapore and Malaysia most are foreign. Third World multinationals are more common in the less developed countries such as China, Bangladesh, Sri Lanka, and the Philippines. In each country, the number of women working in export factories is small relative to the total female labor force, with the important exception of small, heavily industrialized, heavily export-oriented countries like Hong Kong and Singapore.

In Asia, where the bulk of the women are employed, most of them are young and unmarried, although this varies by country and industry and over time, according to economic and cultural factors. For example, in the four Confucianist Asian NICs (newly industrialized countries) which enjoy full employment and relatively high incomes, married women's income is not essential for working-class family survival, though it enhances standards of living. Cultural pressures as well as the limited availability of child care discourage mothers from working outside the home. There is also age discrimination by employers against women reentering the labor force after spending some years bearing and rearing children. In Malaysia, similar factors operate, with Islam being the dominant cultural influence. In neighboring Thailand and the Philippines, however, women's income is much more important for family survival because of low male incomes and high unemployment. In these countries local traditions have always accorded women a strong and independent economic role, and child care is more readily available because of an existing rural labor surplus and the persistence of the extended family. Thus many more older married women enter or stay in the labor force, including export factory jobs. By industry, the textile and garment industry has more older and married women than the electrical and electronics industry, while over time, the proportion of older married women workers increases in all countries and industries.

In Latin America and the Caribbean, export industries include more older and ever-married (including separated and divorced) women than in Asia. Locally specific economic and cultural factors appear to be at work here, including a tradition of female breadwinners in the Caribbean and a high proportion of female-headed households along the Mexican border, where many men are absent because they are working illegally in the United States. One may also speculate that the difficulty of remarriage in Catholic societies which forbid divorce produces many older separated women who must work outside the home to support themselves and their children.[3]

Besides age and marital status, the educational levels of women export factory workers also differ by country, industry, and over time. Average educational levels tend to be lower in the textile/garment, and probably also toy and footwear industries, and higher in the electrical/electronics, computer, and other high-tech industries. In part this is simply a function of vintage: the textile/garment industry is longer established than the electrical/electronics industry, thus employing older women who tend to have had less normal education than younger women, given the relative recentness of the spread of mass modern education for girls in developing countries. Textile/garment and similar industries utilizing relatively simple technologies and manual processes do not require a high level of education, or even literacy; in the electrical and especially electronics and computer industries, on the other hand, literacy and numeracy are important, especially for operation of sophisticated machines. Education has become more important over time as more advanced technologies have been transferred, especially to the Asian NICs; short product life cycles in high-tech industries also require constant retraining, which is easier for more highly educated workers.

The educational differences by country are more complex. On the one hand, average educational levels and technological and skill levels are higher in the more advanced NICs than in less advanced developing countries. On the other hand, the NICs also have tight labor markets, so that workers with more education have access to better jobs than factory work, which tends to attract only lowly educated workers. In contrast, the less advanced developing countries tend to have labor surpluses, and factory work attracts more highly educated workers who do not have better job alternatives. Thus, for example, I have seen similar tasks in multinational electronics factories

[3]This is not as much of a problem in East Asia, where the divorce rate is very low, or Southeast Asia, where the divorce rate is high but so is the remarriage rate.

being performed by primary school dropouts in Singapore, where labor is scarce, and by high school graduates and even part-time college students in the Philippines, where unemployment rates are high. This makes it difficult to predict changes in factory workers' educational status over time. As development and industrialization proceed, production workers in a given export industry may become more highly educated, due to improved public education and technological upgrading requiring more highly skilled workers; or they may become less well-educated, as the more highly educated move into better (e.g., white-collar) occupations, vacating production jobs, which then go to the lowly educated.

In general, women workers in export industries in the Third World tend to be better educated than the average worker in their countries, especially in the less developed countries. Workers in multinational electronics factories in Thailand, Malaysia, the Philippines, and Mexico, for example, usually have at least a mid-secondary school education, several years more than the average worker. Workers in local textile and garment factories, however, tend to have average or lower levels of education. In the NICs, on the other hand, women export factory workers tend to be among the least educated in the urban labor force, though they are still better educated than most rural workers.

The social origins of women export factory workers are similarly diverse. In poor countries with high unemployment and low wage rates, these factory jobs are highly desirable. Especially in multinational electronics factories requiring higher levels of education, the jobs tend to be occupied mainly by urban residents or established rural-urban migrants, who have both the qualifications and the contacts to obtain these jobs, and who reside in the urban locations where most factories are found. They belong to the more fortunate upper strata of the urban working class. The poorest, least educated rural women usually would not be competitive for these jobs, except in the Asian NICs, especially South Korea and Taiwan with their substantial rural populations, where better qualified urban workers can afford to shun these low-level production jobs in favor of better paid, higher skilled occupations. Malaysia is another important exception where government political priorities, specifically the imposition of ethnic employment quotas, ensure the employment in export factories of rural women who are required to fill the quotas, and who therefore migrate to the city to work in these jobs. Ethnically oriented development policies have also ensured that rural women in Malaysia have higher levels of educational attainment than is the case for rural women in most other developing countries (Lim 1989a).

Overall, then, there is considerable diversity among women export factory workers in developing countries in terms of their age, marital status, education, and social origins. But this diversity is readily explained, being determined primarily by local labor market conditions in each country and by the varying needs of employers in different industries. Occasionally labor market forces may change the sex composition of the labor force. In high-tech industry in both California and Massachusetts, for example, previously predominantly female production work forces have been partially supplanted by nonwhite immigrant males, particularly from Latin America and Southeast Asia, who are willing to work for the same low wages as native women. And in more geographically remote locations along the Mexican border, more and more men are being employed by newly established *maquiladoras* (export-oriented factories), which are unable to recruit sufficient women due to the export industry boom and resultant tightening labor market in this region.

WOMEN'S WORK IN EXPORT INDUSTRIES

The existing literature on women's work in export industries is full of complaints about low wages, poor working conditions, frequent layoffs, and lack of union protection. This section draws on recent empirical studies (e.g., Addison and Demery 1987; Foo and Lim 1989; ILO 1985; Lim 1987b) to examine these complaints.

The wages earned by women workers in these industries are typically lower than average wages for the manufacturing sector as a whole. There are many reasons for this. Export industries are typically of more recent vintage than the import-substituting industries that dominate most Third World manufacturing sectors; thus their workers are younger, have less seniority, and receive lower wages. Export industries are also usually labor-intensive and must be competitive on the world market; they consequently can afford to pay less than tariff-protected, monopolistic, often capital-intensive and high-profit (if inefficient) industries supplying the domestic market, which can always raise prices to cover higher wages. The preponderance of female workers in export industries also means a lower average wage in these industries than in the predominantly male-intensive domestic market industries; this is because domestic role conflicts mean that women usually have a much shorter working life and thus less experience, less training, less seniority, and lower productivity and wages than male workers. Sex and age discrimination by employers, which affects women who seek to reenter the labor force after rearing children, and a sometimes lower rate of unionization due to higher turnover and weaker commitment to the labor force, also contribute to a lower wage for female workers.

Lower wages in export industries than in manufacturing as a whole do not, however, mean that these workers are poorly paid relative to all others in the economy. Manufacturing wages in general are typically higher than incomes earned in the much larger agricultural, service, and informal sectors. In Mexico, for example, women working in the *maquiladoras* along the U.S. border typically earn at least the legal minimum wage; in a country where unemployment runs as high as 40 percent and barely half of those who have jobs earn the minimum wage, this puts them in the top quartile of the national income distribution. The same is true in Bangkok and Manila, where some estimates are that no more than 10 percent of the urban labor force earn the minimum wage, which is, however, paid by virtually all multinational export factories.

Wages earned by women in export factories are also usually higher than what they could earn as wage laborers in alternative low-skilled female occupations, such as farm labor, domestic service, most informal sector and other service sector activities, small-scale local industry, and, in some countries, even white-collar and so-called pink-collar jobs such as a hairdresser, beautician, or sales clerk.[4] The disparities are sometimes great. One multinational electronics factory in Indonesia paid its workers four times the local manufacturing wage (already higher than the prevailing agricultural wage), while wages in China's export-oriented special economic zones are two and a half times higher than wages outside these zones. Though it may be inferior by developed country standards, work in modern export factories also generates more income, with shorter working hours and better working conditions, than traditional housework, home-based work, and unpaid family labor. This is partly because factory employment is more heavily and readily regulated by governments than, for example, agricultural labor or domestic service, where 16-hour workdays seven days a week are common.

The local purchasing power of women's export factory wages is not inconsiderable. Although these wages, like wages in most urban working-class occupations — including male occupations — in the Third World, are often inadequate to support typically large extended families, they are almost always more than adequate to support the individual worker herself. Especially in poorer countries with high male unemployment and low wages,

[4]In some countries prostitution is a high-paying exception. See, for example, Phongpaichit (1982).

the woman factory worker may even be the largest income earner in her family, earning more than her husband, father, or brother. When added to other incomes in multiple-income households, which are the norm in the Third World, these wages are often sufficient to raise women factory workers' family living standards to comfortable and even middle-class levels. For example, in Singapore, where women export factory workers are among the lowest paid workers in the economy, usually earning less than the men in their families, their total family income puts them in an income bracket where, in 1983, "96.2% of the households had a refrigerator, 95.9% a television set, 23.1% a video cassette recorder, 12.8% a motor-car, 17.5% a motorcycle, 44.7% a washing-machine, 3.6% an airconditioner, and 3.8% a piano/organ" (Lim 1987c). Singapore, like Hong Kong, may be an exceptional case because of high average wages, publicly provided housing, and low consumer prices due to free trade. But in many if not most countries — especially the NICs and near-NICs like Malaysia — women export factory workers earn enough to save for themselves and/or contribute a large proportion of their incomes to family expenses, even where they are rural-urban migrants who live on their own and not with their families.

It also cannot be assumed that the working conditions and living standards of women export factory workers in the Third World are inferior in every case to those of similar workers in the developed countries. This is certainly true in the majority of cases, and in absolute as well as relative terms, wages, working conditions, and living standards leave much to be desired, especially in very poor countries. Working conditions in small locally owned garment factories in Bangladesh, for example, are abysmal even if they are marginally better than the poor conditions prevailing throughout that economy, which has the second lowest per capita income in the world. At the other end of the spectrum, however, workers in large modern garment factories in Singapore and Hong Kong probably enjoy better working conditions and higher living standards than immigrant sweatshop and home workers in the U.S. garment industry, who toil long hours in unprotected conditions yet are not as well off or secure as the Singapore and Hong Kong workers, who earn half their wages in dollar terms.

Beyond the obvious economic benefits of working in export factories, especially those owned by multinationals where wages and working conditions are better, women in developing countries often cite various non-economic benefits to explain why they work and appreciate, without necessarily enjoying, their work in these factories. These include the ability to earn independent income and spend it on desired consumer purchases or save for marriage or a further education; the ability to help support their families and "repay" their debt to parents; the opportunity to delay marriage and childbearing and to exercise personal choice of a marriage partner; the opportunity to enjoy some personal freedom and the companionship of other women and to experience more of what life has to offer, such as a "widening of horizons" (Foo and Lim, 1987; Lin, 1986). For example, in Malaysia, a relatively rich country where low status and a strong social stigma attach to factory women, they still consider themselves better off than they would be had they not chosen to work outside the home, and especially better off than their mothers (Foo, 1987).

Export factory employment is often considered to be insecure because of frequent layoffs resulting from vulnerability to the world market. But vulnerability to layoffs varies considerably by country, industry, and firm and is determined by both world market and host country factors. Export industries are not necessarily more vulnerable to layoffs than other sectors of the economy, such as export-oriented mining and agriculture and manufacturing for the domestic market. In fact, workers in multinational export factories may be more insulated from economic problems than workers in small local firms, because of the greater strength and resilience of their employers in a recession. Workers in large modern enterprises, whatever their market orientation, are usually also better protected by labor legislation and unions than workers in the traditional sector or unorganized enterprises and are more likely to receive retrenchment benefits. When women are laid off in a recession, this is not necessarily due to their being women but rather to their being employed in industries or firms adversely affected by the recession. (For further elaboration see Lim, 1987b.)

Whether women workers in export industries are more or less likely to be unionized than workers in other industries varies considerably by country. On the one hand, employment in the formal sector, especially in large industrial enterprises, provides a better opportunity for organization than most other forms of employment, and in many countries female-intensive export industries are more heavily unionized than other sectors of the urban-industrial as well as rural economy. This is true, for example, of the electronics industry in Singapore and the textile industry in South Korea. On the other hand, the shorter working life and higher turnover rate of women workers makes them more difficult to unionize than comparable male industries. This is true in developed as well as developing countries; in fact the female-intensive electronics industry is more heavily unionized in the Third World than it is in the United States. Some developing countries do restrict union organization in new industries, but export industries are not necessarily singled out for more restrictive treatment than domestic market-oriented industries (Lim, 1987b).

WOMEN EXPORT FACTORY WORKERS: STEREOTYPE VERSUS REALITY

We have seen that the empirical reality of women export factory workers in developing countries is varied and complex, with significant differences in their situation by country, industry, and period of time. Yet the stereotypical view of these women presented in the feminist literature and popular media is remarkably homogeneous — and generally negative. The predominant stereotype is that First World multinational factories located in Third World export-processing zones employ mostly young, single, female rural-urban migrants, who are ruthlessly exploited in harsh factory environments where they suffer long hours, poor working conditions, insecure, unhealthy, and unsafe jobs, and wages so low that they are not even sufficient to cover individual subsistence (Frobel, Heinrichs, and Kreye, 1977/80; Ong, 1983). This, together with discriminatory practices by employers and disruptive world market forces, results in a high turnover rate, as women are "exhausted" by their employment, or are forced to resign when they marry, or are laid off in frequent recessions. They face constant harassment by employers, supervisors, and even the government, especially if they attempt to unionize or take any labor action. The women are forced to work by poverty and are exploited by their families, who claim a disproportionate share of their wages yet do not accord them more power or status within the family. They thus suffer a double oppression — that of imperialist/capitalist exploitation on the one hand and of gender subordination on the other — and benefit little if at all from their employment (Elson and Pearson, 1981a, 1981b).

The foregoing discussion suggests that while there may be *some* situations characterized by this stereotype in some or all of its details, it is by no means the norm in *all* or even *most* situations where women are employed in export factories in the Third World. A majority of these women are employed not by multinationals but by local firms, and most are not located in export-processing zones; they include a significant and growing proportion of older married women. Although in most, but not all cases wages, working conditions, and job security in the export factories are inferior to those in the developed countries, they are comparable if not superior to those found in women's (and even men's) jobs in most other sectors of these still poor, underdeveloped local economies. The length of time that women work in these factories varies by country, individual, and over time, and is usually truncated by the mounting domestic responsibilities women face when they marry and have children, rather than by employer compulsion or market disruption. The women working in these large modern factories are better able to organize in unions than are women in most other sectors of the economy and forms of employment, and despite obstacles they have in many cases become more unionized than sections of the male labor force in their countries or than the female labor force in similar industries in the developed countries. They have also not hesitated to undertake sometimes militant labor actions, such as strikes and work slowdowns, and in countries like the Philippines and South Korea, they have even been involved in wider political actions. Women textile workers are considered to be among the most militant workers in South Korea's labor unions.

Women export factory workers typically do not come from the poorest segments of society, who are usually found in the rural areas, but from families located in or near more prosperous urban areas, or those who had the resources to educate them more than the average male or female in their societies and/or to finance their migration to cities from rural locations. Although some women do work because they would otherwise be destitute, most do so in order to improve their own living standards and those of their families, even where families object to their working or have no pressing need for their income. They are motivated by social and cultural as well as economic factors, and they typically are accorded more respect and more say in their families and households because of their employment and contribution to family income, though this is insufficient to completely undermine the traditional sexual division of labor and its cultural constructs (Foo and Lim, 1989).

This is not to say that women export factory workers form the elite of the working class in Third World countries, though in some cases (e.g., Mexico) this may be close to the truth. But they are unambiguously better off than they would have been without these jobs. In absolute terms they are best off in the Asian NICs, the countries most heavily involved in export manufacturing for the longest time. Conditions are worst in very poor countries where there are few export factories and where high unemployment and low wages mean that employers do not have to compete for labor. But where there are so many export factories that they dramatically increase the demand for female labor, and full employment exists — as in some of the Asian NICs — workers' market bargaining power is greater, skill levels increase with capital investments and capital/labor ratios, and wages and working conditions are higher as employers have to compete for increasingly scarce but productive workers.

METHODOLOGICAL PROBLEMS IN THE LITERATURE

The great discrepancy between the stereotype and the reality of women export factory workers' work and lives in the Third World needs to be explained. Much of the literature on the subject is methodologically flawed in a number of ways. There is a tendency to employ a static, ahistorical approach to the subject despite the dynamism of developing economies. Authors tend to generalize from their observations in one particular location at one time. This is usually in the earliest stages of the establishment of export factories, when they attract the greatest attention, especially from journalists, and when wages and workers' tolerance of their new working conditions are lowest and labor turnover is highest. This is because the labor market is still slack, workers lack job experience and skills, have unrealistic expectations and problems adjusting to the regimentation of modern factory employment,[5] and often are still earning low "probationary" wages since they have not yet reached minimum productivity. Foreign employers, in particular, may have problems adjusting to a culturally different work force, so that many frictions and tensions arise. Over time, many of these problems are smoothed out, wages rise, conditions of work and employer-worker relations improve, and workers themselves adjust to their jobs. Thus labor turnover rates are always highest for newly hired workers in newly established factories and lowest for experienced workers in long-established factories, even in the same location. A particularly dramatic example of adjustment over time is the sharply declining incidence of mass hysteria among women export factory workers in Singapore and Malaysia as this form of employment has become more widespread and entrenched.[6]

Lack of a dynamic historical approach seriously distorts perspectives on this subject. For example, dated information from the mid-1970s is still quoted today as if it were current, despite enormous changes since

[5]This is found in all factories, regardless of their market orientation, the sex composition of their labor force, and operation by capitalist or socialist principles.

[6]Mass hysteria outbreaks have traditionally been fairly common among young Malay (Muslim) girls in all-female environments such as girls' schools, dormitories, and more recently, factories. Such outbreaks do not affect young women of other ethnic groups in the same situations. Though traditionally attributed to spirit possession, a more likely cause of the hysteria is conflict between traditional and modern gender identities. See Lim (1989a).

then, particularly in the rapidly changing electronics industry (e.g., Fuentes and Ehrenreich, 1983; Mies, 1986; Ward, 1986). And information from an "abnormal" period is often presented as if it were a typical or representative situation. Thus, for example, large layoffs in female-intensive export industries in Malaysia and Singapore during the post-OPEC recession of 1974–75 are still cited today as "evidence" of the instability of export factory employment (e.g., Heyzer, 1986, pp. 108–9), despite the fact that recovery was achieved in less than a year. The next round of widespread layoffs in these two countries did not occur until 1985–86, when recovery was also relatively swift. This is a record much superior to that of most agricultural employment in developing countries, where, for example, women harvesters lose their jobs after each harvest or are permanently displaced by machinery.

A second common methodological problem in the literature is the frequent absence of a comparative standard by which to judge conditions in female-intensive export factories. Very few studies evaluate the circumstances of women workers in export factories in direct comparison with control groups of women, or even men, working in other industries or occupations, or who do not work at all. Where comparison is made, it is implicitly or even explicitly made with prevailing conditions in developed countries, which is not helpful in evaluating the developmental impacts of export manufacturing in the developing countries.

For example, to know that women export factory workers in a Third World country earn $2 an hour or $2 a day tells us nothing about the "worth" of this employment to the workers themselves or to their country. To assess this, we need to know how $2 a day or $2 an hour compares with the average wage in the country, with wages earned in other female occupations, and with what the women were earning before they took up their factory jobs or would earn without these jobs. We also need to know the standard of living that this wage will purchase in that country; for example, it may well be that $2 an hour in Singapore buys a better standard of living than $5 an hour in Boston or Los Angeles. The same comparative standard goes for hours of work and other working conditions; for example, 10 hours a day for 6 days a week is an improvement if the local norm is 12 hours a day for 7 days a week. The impacts of their employment on women workers' lives and their position in and relations with their families must all also be assessed in comparison with what these would be in the absence of employment. For example, for a young woman in a developing country, how does living on her own, earning an independent wage in an export factory, and marrying when and whom she chooses compare with the alternative of staying at home with her parents, performing unpaid labor in a family farm or shop or working as a domestic servant, then being married off while still in her teens to a man of her parents' choice?

A third methodological problem with much of the literature on this subject is the absence of a normal multivariate approach to causality. For example, there is the tendency to attribute all the observed impacts of women's export factory employment in developing countries to the designs and practices of multinationals, which do not even constitute the majority of employers. It is frequently asserted that these employers grossly exploit their workers by paying them low wages and extracting intensive labor effort in order to earn maximum profits for themselves. In fact, wages and working conditions are set primarily by the prevailing norms and regulations of the host country, which multinational employers especially tend to match if not better. Women's typically high turnover and short working life is due less to employers' exploitative tactics than to the traditional sexual division of labor, which makes it difficult for women who have primary responsibility for housework and child care to work outside the home, forcing many of them to "voluntarily" leave their jobs when they marry or have children.

These and other methodological weaknesses in the literature on women export factory workers in the Third World are explained by several factors. First, many if not most of the writers on this subject are inadequately informed about the facts of the situation, frequently basing their analyses on only a handful of outdated, empirically inadequate studies. These studies are rarely the product of serious and systematic scholarly research; most consist of anecdotal accounts prepared by journalists and activist groups which are often deliberately selective, focusing on extreme rather than representative situations (e.g., *Asian Women Workers Newsletter*, various years; Christian Conference of Asia, various years; Fuentes and Ehrenreich, 1983; Grossman, 1979; ISIS, 1985; Karl, 1983). Even writers who attempt to be scholarly use these limited sources almost exclusively (e.g., Mies, 1986). It is true that much of the more serious and recent empirical research done by Third World scholars is relatively inaccessible in the West, being mostly locally published or unpublished and only rarely finding its way into international academic journals. But these sources need not elude the committed researcher. In recent years more comprehensive, systematic, balanced, and up-to-date studies have also appeared in the West (e.g., Fawcett, Khoo, and Smith, 1984; ILO, 1985: Ch. 5; Jones, 1984; North-South Institute, 1985), but they have so far been either ignored or only selectively cited by writers attempting "theoretical overviews" of the subject (e.g., Ward, 1986).

Second, many writers lack sufficient knowledge and understanding of export manufacturing, the world economy, the workings of labor markets, and simple economics. In particular, the field is dominated by anthropologists, who are used to working intensively with, and generalizing from a single case. They lack the data, the analytical tools, and the macro perspective with which to accurately locate individual cases in their national or international context, yet they frequently aspire to do so (e.g., Mies, 1986; Nash, 1983; Ong, 1983). Errors of fact, omission, and analysis consequently abound.

A third cause of methodological weaknesses is the willingness of many writers, anthropologists in particular, to embrace global political-economic theories that they cannot accurately evaluate, yet they allow to determine their gathering and interpretation of data. The flawed and dated work of Frobel, Heinrichs, and Kreye (1977/80) on the new international division of labor, which I have criticized elsewhere (Lim 1987b), has been particularly influential here. The feminist analysis of Elson and Pearson (1981a, 1981b), linking this new international division of labor with gender subordination, has also become widely accepted despite its many flaws (Lim 1987b). Besides inadequate information and analytical tools, political and ideological predilections appear to be responsible for this uncritical acceptance of questionable theories, which in almost any other field would stimulate many challenges and much theoretical discussion.

IDEOLOGY AND POLITICS

On the ideological level, anti-imperialists committed to a view of the Third World as being relentlessly dominated and exploited by the First World reject any suggestion that at least some developing countries and their workers could benefit and have benefited from export manufacturing, especially where undertaken by multinationals.[7] The work of Frobel, Heinrichs, and Kreye (1977/80) and other sympathizers of world-system analysis supports this view.

Also on the ideological level, feminists who see patriarchy and gender subordination as crucial underpinnings and inevitable consequences of all capitalism refuse to recognize any benefits to women in the Third World from employment in export factories, insisting that such employment intensifies rather than alleviates their gender subordination. The works of Elson and Pearson (1981a, 1981b) are popular with this group.

[7]The larger picture of export manufacturing in general has been especially inadequately considered in studies of women workers, though it has been treated in other areas of development studies, especially development economics.

Ironically, these anti-imperialists and feminists both frequently consider themselves to be Marxist, yet their beliefs conflict with the theoretical predictions of Marx and Engels. Marx clearly considered capitalism to be a historically progressive mode of production, superior to precapitalist modes in its technological and economic achievements and liberating for workers previously subject to feudal bondage. Engels, his close colleague, saw women's participation in factory wage labor as emancipating them from domestic slavery. Both incorporated the concepts of dialecticism and contradiction into their thought, predicting the simultaneous existence of positive and negative, exploitative and liberating features and consequences of capitalist development, as are found in the situation of women export factory workers in the Third World (Lim, 1983). In contrast, some feminists have stood Marx and Engels on their heads by claiming that instead of the proletarianization of women, export factories in the Third World contribute to the "feminization" (Fernandez-Kelly, 1983d) and "housewifization" (Mies, 1986) of industrial production, with negative consequences for women.

On this subject, ideology is given a powerful boost by politics. In the industrial countries, there exists a strong political constituency, a coalition of industry, labor, and local communities, which is opposed to export manufacturing in the Third World because it threatens its own economic and political interests. In the United States, for example, anti-import protectionist fervor is strongest in the textile states of the South, under the leadership of some of the most conservative Republican political leaders (such as Strom Thurmond and Jesse Helms). Yet liberal and even radical social activists in the labor, feminist, and church movements often support protectionism, feeling that it is necessary to support the women who work in labor-intensive import-competing industries in industrial countries. Disparaging the effects of export industries in the developing countries is important to this protectionist effort because it minimizes the negative impact of the resultant loss of women's jobs in the Third World.

In fact this narrow nationalism ultimately undermines not only poor Third World workers, but also industrial country consumers, particularly poorer consumers, who are forced by import restrictions to pay much higher prices to support the monopolistic profits of inefficient domestic manufacturers. This is the "new imperialism," where capital and labor in the First World combine to protect their common interests and industrial domination of the Third World by preventing both capitalist and socialist Third World economies from industrializing for export and thereby providing better jobs and incomes for their workers, especially women.

Feeding this political self-interest is a simple ethnocentrism that values jobs in the developed countries much more highly than the same jobs in the Third World, defending them in the former while devaluing them in the latter, an ethnocentrism that does not oppose the centuries-old export of manufactures from developed to developing countries but does oppose the recent export of manufactures from developing to developed countries. Ethnocentrism also causes writers and activists in the West to judge conditions in the Third World by their own Western standards rather than from the Third World worker's perspective. It leads to the stereotyping of developing countries, resulting in failure to discern their considerable differences from one another in women's indigenous position and the consequences of their export factory employment.

Feminist ethnocentrism is revealed in the common assumption that Third World women workers are introduced to concepts of "bourgeois femininity" by multinational employers' factory cultural practices, which, for example, encourage Western dress, beauty and fashion consciousness, dating and romance among women workers (Grossman, 1979; Lim, 1978). In fact such feminine values, habits, and practices are already common elsewhere in contemporary developing country societies, where concern about beauty and sexual attractiveness is long-established in traditional society and culture. At the same time, many Western and Western-oriented feminists assume, often incorrectly, that Third World cultures are more oppressive of women than Western culture. This leads them to ignore, for example, the traditionally strong economic and even entrepreneurial role of women in some societies where they seek out wage work in order to fulfill traditional obligations of family support, and consequently appreciate the opportunity to work in export factories.

Political opposition to women's work in export factories also exists in the developing countries themselves. Domestic industrialists dependent on protected home markets and a cheap labor force for their monopoly profits frequently oppose both the trade liberalization that accompanies manufacturing for export and the participation of multinationals, which compete with them for labor and other productive resources, thereby raising costs (e.g., Lim, 1989a). Opposition based on such vested self-interest is readily cloaked in nationalist rhetoric. Never popular in developing countries, multinationals also provide a convenient target for political oppositionists and even labor activists, who find it easier to mobilize nationalist rather than class sentiment in support of their struggles against employers. Large, wealthy multinational enterprises also afford a more promising target for union organization than myriad small, marginal local enterprises, which employ substantially more workers under much worse conditions. Even so, unlike domestic capitalists, few labor leaders in the Third World aim to eliminate multinationals from their home economy, since workers would suffer the most from this; their goal is rather to enlarge union membership by organizing export factories and to obtain employment-based benefits for workers.

Finally, traditionalists and religious and cultural conservatives in some Third World countries — for example, Catholics in Latin America and Islamic fundamentalists in the Middle East and Asia — object to women working in export factories, particularly multinationals, because it gives them greater personal freedom and removes them from patriarchal control (often disguised as "protection"), including control of their previously home-based, often unpaid labor (Lim, 1989a). Because of this opposition, in some countries women do manufacture for export, not in modern, much less multinational factories, but from the "protection" (or confinement?) of their own homes, subcontracting to male middlemen (as in Turkey), or in cottage industries and small factories run by local male elites (as in parts of Indonesia). Needless to say, under such circumstances labor organization is impossible, and wages are lower and hours of work longer than they would be in modern multinational factories, confirming Marx's belief in the progressivity of capitalist over precapitalist production.

CONCLUSION

In studies of women in development, it has become commonplace to note that women tend to gain disproportionately less, and lose disproportionately more, from most forms of economic development, which, it is argued, destroy more jobs than they create for women. Export manufacturing, which still accounts for only a small part of most Third World economies, and an even smaller proportion of developed countries' manufactured imports, is one exception that creates employment disproportionately for women. Despite a decade of pessimistic forecasts that have not come true, it has continued to grow, and market prospects are good, or at least better than prospects for most other sectors of developing countries' economies (Lim, 1989b).

Yet this form of development, despite or perhaps because of its benefit to women, continues to be disparaged by most writers on the subject, who ignore its diversity and complexity to focus on negative aspects that will validate their theories. The policy implication of this negativity is that export manufacturing and the employment it creates for women should not be encouraged, and perhaps should even be actively discouraged.

A powerful coalition of political interests — especially patriarchal, capitalist, and nationalist interests — in both the developed and developing countries advances this position, which regrettably is directly or indirectly supported by many feminists and radicals.

In this chapter I have pointed out the methodological weaknesses of the literature, which feed and sustain this opposition to women's employment in export factories in the Third World. These weaknesses result primarily from biases introduced by ideology, ethnocentrism, and vested political interests. Obviously, my own past and present work is not immune from these and other, criticisms. But feminist solidarity should not preclude diversity, disagreement, and mutual criticism, the processes by which scholarly and political advances are made. My hope is that this chapter and works like it will contribute to more careful and objective scholarship and more open and balanced debate, especially by and within the feminist scholarly community, on what is still a very important, if often exaggerated, topic of research in the field of women in development.

REFERENCES

Addison, T and L Demery (eds.) (1987). *Wages and Labour Conditions in the Newly-Industrialising Countries of Asia.* London: Overseas Development Institute.

Asian Women Workers Newsletter, n.d. Hong Kong: Committee for Asian Women, Urban-Rural Mission of the Christian Conference of Asia.

Chincilla, NS (1977). Industrialization, Monopoly Capitalism, and Women's Work in Guatemala. *Signs* 3(1), 38–56.

Christian Conference of Asia (1981a). *In Clenched Fists of Struggle.* Report of the Workshop on the Impact of Transnational Corporations in Asia. Hong Kong: Urban-Rural Mission of the Christian Conference of Asia.

Christian Conference of Asia (1981b). *Struggling to Survive: Women Workers in Asia.* Hong Kong: Urban-Rural Mission of the Christian Conference of Asia.

Christian Conference of Asia (1982). *The Plight of Asian Workers in Electronics.* Hong Kong: Urban-Rural Mission of the Christian Conference of Asia.

Christian Conference of Asia (1984). *Our Rightful Share.* Hong Kong: Urban-Rural Mission of the Christian Conference of Asia.

Elson, D and R Pearson (1981a). Nimble Fingers Make Cheap Workers: An Analysis of Women's Employment in Third World Manufacturing. *Feminist Review* (Spring), 87–107.

Elson, D and R Pearson (1981b). The Subordination of Women and the Internationalisation of Factory Production. In *Of Marriage and the Market: Women's Subordination in International Perspective*, Young, K, C Wolkowitz and R McCullagh (eds.). London: CSE Books.

Fawcett, JT, S-E Khoo and PC Smith (eds.) (1984). *Women in the Cities of Asia: Migration and Urban Adaptation.* Boulder, Colorado: Westview Press.

Foo, GHC (1987). Work and Marriage: Attitudes of Single Women Factory Workers in Malaysia. Doctoral Dissertation in Public Health, University of Michigan.

Foo, GHC and Lim, LYC (1989). Poverty, Ideology and Women Export Factory Workers in South-East Asia. In *Women, Poverty and Ideology in Asia*, Afsar, H and B Agarwal (eds.). London: Macmillan.

Frobel, F, J Heinrichs and O Kreye (1977/80). *The New International Division of Labour*. Cambridge: Cambridge University Press.

Fuentes, A and B Ehrenreich (1983). *Women in the Global Factory* (Institute for New Communications Pamphlet No. 3). Boston: South End Press.

Grossman, R (1978/79). Women's Place in the Integrated Circuit. Joint issue of *Southeast Asia Chronicle* No. 66 and *Pacific Research*, 9(5–6), 2–16.

Heyzer, N (1986). *Working Women in South-East Asia: Development, Subordination and Emancipation*. Milton Keynes, UK: Open University Press.

ILO (International Labour Organisation) (1985). *Women Workers in Multinational Enterprises in Developing Countries*. Geneva: ILO. Prepared by Linda Y.C. Lim.

ISIS International (1985). Industrial Women Workers in Asia. *ISIS International Women's Journal* No. 4, published with the Committee for Asian Women of the Urban-Rural Mission of the Christian Conference of Asia.

Jones, GW (ed.) (1984). *Women in the Urban-Industrial Workforce: Southeast and East Asia*. Development Studies Centre Monograph No. 33. Australian National University, Canberra.

Karl, M (1983). Women and Multinationals. In *ISIS, Women in Development: A Resource Guide for Organization and Action. Geneva: ISIS International Women's Information and Communication Service.*

Lee, E (ed.) (1984). *Export Processing Zones and Industrial Development in Asia*. Bangkok: Asian Employment Program of ILO.

Lim, LYC (1978). *Women Workers in Multinational Corporations: The Case of the Electronics Industry in Malaysia and Singapore*. Michigan Occasional Papers No. 9, Women's Studies Program, University of Michigan.

Lim, LYC (1983). Capitalism, Imperialism and Patriarchy: The Dilemma of Third World Women Workers in Multinational Factories. In *Women, Men and the New International Division of Labor*, Nash, J and MP Fernandez-Kelly (eds.). Albany, NY: SUNY Press.

Lim, LYC (1987a). Capital, Labor and the State in the Internationalization of High-Tech Industry. In *Transnational Corporations and Urbanization in the Pacific Rim: Proceedings of a Conference*, Douglass, M and J Friedman (eds.). Center for Pacific Rim Studies, University of California, Los Angeles.

Lim, LYC (1987b). Export-Oriented Industrialization and Asian Labor. Paper presented at the Conference on the Origins and Consequences of Development Strategies: Latin America and East Asia Compared, Duke University, March 31–April 1.

Lim, LYC (1987c). Export-Led Industrialization, Labour Welfare and International Labour Standards in Singapore. In Addison and Demery.

Lim, LYC (1989a). Women Industrial Workers: The Specificities of the Malaysian Case. In *Malaysian Women and the Urban-Industrial Labor Force*, Ariffin, J and W Smith (eds.). Singapore: Institute of Southeast Asian Studies.

Lin, V (1986). Health, Women's Work and Industrialization: Women Workers in the Semiconductor Industry in Singapore and Malaysia. Women in International Development Working Paper No. 130, Women in International Development Program, Michigan State University.

Mies, M (1986). *Patriarchy and Accumulation on a World Scale: Women in the International Division of Labour*. London: Zed Books.

Nash, J (1983). The Impact of the Changing International Division of Labor on Different Sectors of the Labor Force. In *Women, Men and the New International Division of Labor,* Nash, J and MP Fernandez-Kelly (eds.). Albany, NY: SUNY Press.

North-South Institute (1985). *Women in Industry: North-South Connections*. Ottawa, Canada: North-South Institute.

Ong, A (1983). Global Industries and Malay Peasants in Peninsular Malaysia. In Nash, J and MP Fernandez-Kelly (eds.). *Women, Men and the New International Division of Labor*. Albany, NY: SUNY Press.

Phongpaichit, P (1982). *From Peasant Girls to Bangkok Masseuses*. Bangkok, ILO.

Ward, KB (1986). Women and Transnational Corporation Employment: A World-System and Feminist Analysis. Women in International Development Working Paper No. 20, Michigan State University.

Part III

BUSINESS-GOVERNMENT RELATIONS AND SOUTHEAST ASIAN CHINESE IN ECONOMIC DEVELOPMENT

Chapter 10

THE EVOLUTION OF SOUTHEAST ASIAN BUSINESS SYSTEMS*

LINDA Y. C. LIM

This paper considers how the changing regional economic, political, and cultural environments and the actions of national governments, Western and Japanese multinationals, and ethnic Chinese and indigenous capitalists, have contributed to shaping the business systems of developing market economies in Southeast Asia. It argues that as the region's enterprises, economies, political and legal systems mature, the entrepreneurial family businesses and ethnic networks heavily dependent on personal relationships and government linkages that currently dominate business systems here will change and become less dominant, but only gradually and incompletely.

INTRODUCTION

The task of articulating what constitutes "Southeast Asian business systems" is made difficult by several factors. Firstly, unlike Japan, Korea, China, or Taiwan, Southeast Asia consists of many countries, not one. Secondly, these countries are extremely heterogeneous both among and within themselves in terms of level of economic development, political system, ethnicity, and culture. Thirdly, unlike Western countries and, arguably, Japan, business systems in Southeast Asia are very dynamic, i.e., constantly evolving due both to "immaturity" or incomplete development and to extremely rapid economic growth. Fourthly, a long history of colonization by Western powers, early integration into the world economy, and continuous openness to foreign trade and investment have resulted in a high degree of penetration by and absorption of external forces and players. The result is a highly complex, diverse, and ever-changing hybrid "system" which does not lend itself easily to analysis.

*This chapter first appeared in Journal of Asian Business, vol. 12. No. 1 (1996), pp. 51–74. Reprinted with Permission.

Nonetheless, an attempt to do so is worthwhile, in my judgment, for a number of reasons. Firstly, despite their heterogeneity, the different national business systems in Southeast Asia are systematically similar in many ways that make an attempt to analyze them in common, both feasible and useful. Secondly, Southeast Asia's above-mentioned characteristics arguably make it a potentially more representative "model" of business system development for other developing regions of the world than either "Western" or "East Asian" models. Thirdly, the area's extremely rapid growth sustained over many decades suggests that conformity to either set of established models is not necessary for economic and business success. Fourthly, Southeast Asia's already significant and rapidly increasing integration into both "Western" and "East Asian" business systems makes the continued development of its own business systems of growing global as well as regional importance.

In this paper I will attempt to describe and explain existing business systems in the developing capitalist market economies of Southeast Asia,[1] and to suggest the directions that their future evolution is likely to take. I will do so by discussing, first, the regional economic, political, and cultural environments, then the evolving roles of different regional business actors, before providing an integrative overall analysis. My aim is to consider whether and why Southeast Asian business systems may or may not distinctively differ from Western and East Asian systems and if any distinctiveness is likely to persist over time as economies, enterprises, and political systems mature, global business linkages proliferate, and the influence of "internationalization" on local cultures intensifies.

THE ECONOMIC ENVIRONMENT

The economic environment facing business in Singapore, Malaysia, Thailand and Indonesia over the past thirty years has been one of rapid export-led growth with relatively low inflation, and high savings and investment rates (Hill 1993). Dependence on foreign investment has also been high, and there is continued though diminishing relative reliance on the export of primary commodities. Growth has led to sectoral diversification and movements up

[1]Southeast Asia consists of the six market economies of ASEAN–Brunei, Indonesia, Malaysia, Philippines, Singapore and Thailand — with a total population of 330 million, now joined by Vietnam's 70 million, and the three other reforming socialist economies of Myanmar (Burma), Cambodia and Laos, with a total population of another 50 million.

the value chain and technology ladder, impelled by both market-led adjustments and government policy. This developmental progression has led from subsistence through export-oriented primary production, to labor-intensive export manufacturing, capital-intensive and high-tech manufacturing, and labor- and skill-intensive services, for world and domestic markets. Such sectors coexist within given countries, with newer sectors displacing older ones only when resource constraints are reached.

The regional division of labor in Southeast Asia is based on differences in national comparative advantages, and on the special role of Singapore. Singapore is a commercial and financial intermediary and provider of capital, skilled labor and infrastructure services for its neighbors. It is also the location of many "high-end" manufacturing functions linked to "lower-level" activities in neighboring economies, including linkages through the internal division of labor within multinational corporations, based on comparative advantage and facilitated by the existence of free trade zones (Lim and Pang, 1991; Lim, 1994b). As national comparative advantages change, trade and investment also shift activities among different Southeast Asian countries e.g. by relocating labor-intensive manufacturing from Singapore to Indonesia and land- and labor-intensive agriculture from Malaysia to Vietnam (Lee Tsao, 1994; Lim, 1995a). Trade and investment flows also link Southeast Asia with Northeast Asia. Japan is cumulatively the region's largest trade partner, foreign investor and aid donor, with Taiwan, Hong Kong and Korea ranking close behind as sources of foreign investment (Doner, 1993; Wells, 1993).

Except for Singapore, the countries of Southeast Asia are still "developing", though Malaysia, and sometimes Thailand, are occasionally classified as "newly-industrializing". They are thus characterized by market imperfections and underdeveloped market institutions. As we shall see, this condition gives rise to particular organizational responses on the part of business actors to access resources and information, assess and reduce risks, and minimize transactions costs. At the same time, resource abundance, the rapid growth of markets, and new market opportunities encourage and reward opportunistic, entrepreneurial and risk-taking business behaviors, rather than the productivity enhancing, static profit-maximizing behaviors characteristic of more mature, resource-scarce and slower-growing industrial economies like those of the West and, arguably, Japan.

Underdevelopment and rapid export-led growth in Southeast Asia mirror conditions in Northeast Asia at an equivalent stage of development, and thus might be expected to elicit somewhat similar organizational and behavioral responses from the business community. Two other aspects — resource abundance[2] and the active, often dominant, participation of foreign business actors — distinguish the Southeast Asian cases from their Northeast Asian neighbors. They introduce different forms and stronger external influences into local business systems. Thus, for example, resource-extracting multinationals like oil-and-gas companies, and plantation-based agribusiness are two prominent forms of business enterprise in Southeast Asia that are generally not found in Northeast Asia. Both import-substituting industrialization and labor-intensive export manufacturing have been led by foreign business actors. Both regions began industrializing under protective trade and investment regimes, then liberalized over time, but Southeast Asia has received much larger sums of foregin direct investment. And among "domestic" business actora, the dominant commercial role of the ethnic Chinese immigrant minority in Southeast Asia has no parallel in Northeast Asia.

THE POLITICAL ENVIRONMENT

National political systems in the capitalist market economies of Southeast Asia have been for the most part authoritarian, though there is considerable diversity among countries and over time. To varying degrees, emerging nation states in the region, with the exception of Thailand, embraced nationalist ideologies in the aftermath of Western colonialism. Military-backed regimes have dominated most of the post-colonial era in Indonesia, the Philippines, and Thailand, while dominant-party governments characterize the electoral systems in Malaysia and Singapore.

Authortarianism and militarism have been legitimated on grounds of national security concerns, given internal political tensions caused by ethnic diversity, the widespread existence of communist insurgencies and ethnic separatist movements in the immediate post-colonial period, and the triumph of socialist regimes in nearby Indochina and Myanmar. National security concerns, particularly the Vietnam War, also provided the motivation for the pursuit of national economic development, and for regional cooperation within the ASEAN grouping, as politically stabilizing forces. They also encouraged the maintenance of external economic, political and military links with Western powers, long after the end of colonialism.

[2]Southeast Asia has a greater relative abundance of labor than Northeast Asia and, unlike Northeast Asia, also has an abundance of land and natural resources. Capital has been readily available through domestic savings and foreign investment.

Nationalism and authoritarianism both imply interventionist government in the economic sphere, which will be discussed below. In Southeast Asia there is the additional element of indigenism, which differentiates between immigrant-origin ethnic Chinese and peoples of heterogeneous indigenous origins — called *bumiputra* in Malaysia and *pribumi* in Indonesia, for example. The Chinese — now locally-born and - domiciled, and partially culturally assimilated, but still in most places a small minority[3] — dominate local private business, particularly in the modern urban-industrial sector. This is a source of internal political tension which has been managed in part by discriminatory policies designed to restrict Chinese business activities and/or to advantage their indigenous counterparts through affirmative action (Golay *et al.*, 1969).

In response, segments of the Southeast Asian Chinese business community developed personal "clientelistic" relationships with politically powerful individuals, or the military, to protect, maintain, and advance their business interests, most notably with the Suharto regime in Indonesia. Chinese business interests thus benefitted from both the political stability engendered by, and the connections they had with, authoritarian indigenous regimes. In more "democratic" countries, they organized collectively to achieve the same end, most notably in ethnic-based business associations (e.g., the Chinese Chamber of Commerce) and political parties (e.g., the Malaysian Chinese Association) in Malaysia. In either case, political involvement has been necessary to Chinese business success, if not survival, in Southeast Asia.

Recently, democratic regimes have begun to emerge in Southeast Asia after decades of authoritarian rule. Improved information flows and popular demands for more transparency and fairness in government and business actions (relating, for example, to issues of corruption and the environment) may induce some changes in local business practices. But the position of the Chinese in Southeast Asia makes the implications of political democratization for business more complex. On the one hand, their slight representation in Southeast Asian electorates suggests that Chinese political influence is likely to decline with the rise of democratically elected governments. On the other hand, their economic power and established clientelistic relationships might enhance their political influence through the funding of sympathetic political parties or candidates (Lim and Gosling, 1997).

[3]Apart from Singapore, which is 75 percent Chinese, their relative numbers are 2 percent in the Philippines, 4 percent in Indonesia, 10 percent in Thailand, and 30 percent in Malaysia.

THE CULTURAL ENVIRONMENT

Southeast Asia's extreme cultural diversity contrasts vividly with Northeast Asia's ethnic and cultural homogeneity, which has occasionally been advanced as one of the reasons for the latter's economic success, based on the presumption that inter-group conflicts are minimized and a "sense of common purpose" is easier to marshall among people with a common heritage. High savings and investment rates, high levels of education, and tolerance for and high standards of bureaucratic intervention, have been associated with Northeast Asia's Confucian culture, which is also found among ethnic Chinese commercial minorities in Southeast Asia.

Yet the Southeast Asian countries have virtually matched the economic achievements of Northeast Asia without the aid of cultural homogeneity or Confucian values. Indonesia, for example, has more than 300 ethno-linguistic groups and is the world's largest Islamic country, with Chinese accounting for only 4 percent of its population, yet it. has had savings and investment rates of around 35 percent of GDP, and annual GDP growth rates of over 6 percent, for more than two decades. Thailand, where Theravada Buddhism is the major religious and cultural influence, has enjoyed even more rapid growth for a longer period of time. Malaysia's three ethnic groups — Muslim Malays, Confucian Chinese, and predominantly Hindu Indians — have achieved social harmony as well as rapid economic growth over many decades. Only in the predominantly Catholic Philippines has economic performance been lagging until recently.

One may argue from this that capitalist economic development is compatible with many different cultures, or that all Asian cultures contain elements that are conducive to capitalism. Malaysia's Deputy Prime Minister Datuk Seri Anwar Ibrahim has even argued that "collaboration between Muslim-Malay and Confucian-Chinese communities has made Southeast Asia into a prosperous region" (*The Straits Times*, 14 March 1995). Our interest here is in whether culture shapes aspects of the business system. Certainly the political ramifications of cultural diversity play a role, as noted in the case of ethnic Chinese business dominance. Certain elements common to all Asian cultures, such as the importance of family, gift-giving, relationships, and respect for age and education, are also reflected in regional business behaviors. Whether specific cultural attributes result in distinctive business systems and practices in different ethnic and cultural groups will be discussed below.

REGIONAL BUSINESS ACTORS

National Governments

National governments have arguably been the dominant players in the evolution of modern Southeast Asian business systems to date (Maclntyre 1994). There have been many differences among countries and over time in government economic policy, but also some similarities. The early adoption and maintenance of sound macroeconomic management and realistic exchange rates by Malaysia, Singapore, and Thailand was eventually emulated in Indonesia and the Philippines, especially from the 1970s on. In the microeconomic area, policies have been more varied and variable.

Like most other developing countries, Southeast Asian governments pursued policies of import-substituting industrialization in the post-independence period, motivated economically by latecomer disadvantages and politically by nationalist aspirations. This required the erection of trade barriers, and occasionally overvalued exchange rates, but the distortions here were relatively mild by developing country standards. In most periods and places (the Philippines being the most notable exception), the competitiveness of primary commodity exports was never seriously threatened. Later, the push to export manufactures in the 1970s resulted in partial trade liberalization. Economic reforms in the wake of external debt problems and recession in the mid-1980s included more unilateral trade liberalization that continues to this day, bolstered by similar initiatives at the regional, sub-regional, and multilateral levels. (Regional policy initiatives include the ASEAN Free Trade Area (AFTA) to be completed by 2003, and the Asia Pacific Economic Cooperation (APEC) free trade area to be completed by 2020; the sub-regional policy development is the "growth triangle" linking contiguous territories of neighboring countries in limited local freedom of goods, capital, services and labor flows; and the multilateral influence is the GATT Uruguay Round agreement and the establishment of the World Trade Organization).

Most countries imposed at least some restrictions on foreign investment (Singapore being the exception here), mostly by requiring majority local ownership in resource exploitation and domestic market-oriented sectors, and/or phase-ins to increased local ownership over time (most notably in Indonesia). By the 1970s, 100 percent foreign ownership was permitted in export-oriented manufacturing, and the economic reforms of the 1980s resulted in further investment liberalization. This continued into the 1990s, with the most dramatic example being Indonesia's lifting of local ownership phase-in requirements in May 1994, which led to a record US$24 billion of new foreign investment commitments in that year, and an additional $10 billion in the first two months of 1995 alone. There have even been suggestions that Southeast Asia may be receiving "too much" foreign capital (*Wall Street Journal* 23 January 1995, p. 1).

Some governments in the region have been open to foreign direct investment not only for the usual reasons of access to capital, technology and foreign markets, but also because of their desire to secure a counterweight to the private sector dominance of local ethnic Chinese business. This was most clearly the case in Malaysia, where employment created in multinational subsidiaries for bumiputras and equity ownership for them in foreign-owned companies helped achieve the ethnic redistribution objectives of the Malay-dominated government's New Economic Policy (Jesudason 1989). In Indonesia, joint ventures with foreigners provided a channel of entry into business for aspiring pribumi businessmen, particularly the politically well-connected.

The dominant business presence of minority ethnic Chinese in Southeast Asia helps explain the relatively weak support provided by the indigenous-dominated state for local private business. This lack of support for, and in some cases even antagonism toward, local Chinese private business arguably existed even in Singapore, where an English-educated bureaucracy held the reins of political power. State-owned enterprise sectors were developed, largely in infrastructure and resource-based industry, for political (nationalism, indigenism) as well as economic (public goods, externalities, contribution to government budget) reasons. They provided an alternate economic space for the development of indigenous bureaucrat-managers, and in the case of Malaysia, of economic assets explicitly held "in trust" for the bumiputra community at large. Privatization, when it came in the 1980s and 1990s, often involved privileged distributions of such state-owned assets to politically well-connected members of this community, partly as a means of ethnic redistribution (Jomo 1995). A somewhat similar situation prevails in Indonesia, where privatization is much less advanced than in Malaysia, while in Thailand more limited state enterprises remain in the hands of the Thai bureaucracy.

Beyond policies to attract foreign investment and promote exports generally, the governments of Singapore, Malaysia, and Indonesia have also undertaken strategic industrial policy to channel resources into specific key industrial sectors or industries, most notably electronics and other high-tech industries in Singapore, automobiles, steel, and other heavy industry in

Malaysia, and aircraft in Indonesia (Lim, 1994a, pp. 205–238; Jomo, 1993; Bowie, 1991; Lim, 1995c). Foreign multinationals have played a key role in these strategic ventures, primarily as suppliers of technology, but also as joint-venture partners with state-owned enterprises. Similar policies have not been enacted in Thailand or the Philippines.

Western Multinationals

Western multinationals are the oldest-established "modern" enterprises in Southeast Asia, beginning with colonial-era multinational trading companies and export plantations. Some of these "traditional" enterprises survive today (e.g., Dole pineapple plantations in the Philippines), but most have been taken over by nationals in both ownership and management (e.g., former British rubber and palm-oil plantations in Malaysia). Some are being transformed (e.g., from trading companies into manufacturers, and from plantations into property development companies). Other Western multinationals include oil and gas companies, import-substituting "brand name" industrial enterprises established in the 1960s and 1970s, export-manufacturing enterprises established since the 1970s, financial services companies, and most recently, manufacturing ventures oriented simultaneously to both domestic and foreign markets.

Thus, even before the investment liberalizations of the late 1980s and 1990s, Western multinationals occupied a major, if not dominant, role in the modern sectors of Southeast Asian economies. They included both 100 percent foreign-owned and joint-venture companies, and in Malaysia and Singapore many were publicly listed on the local stock exchanges. Since the 1970s, the presence of Western multinationals has steadily increased as these economies have grown and developed new sectors, and barriers to foreign trade and investment have been progressively reduced (Lim 1995b).

Until the 1990s, Western investment in Southeast Asia was most attracted by the region's abundant physical resources and cheap labor, and the possibilities they provided for competitive exports to world markets. In resource-based activities such as oil and gas extraction, partnership with state-owned enterprises was required, and production-sharing agreements took the place of foreign ownership. In export-oriented manufacturing, 100 percent foreign ownership was allowed, in part because foreign technology and global sourcing and marketing networks were essential. Western enterprise was least represented in manufacturing for protected local markets, where joint ventures with local partners, often with only a minority foreign stake, were usually required. In consumer products, however, licensing to local manufacturers was common.

The 1990s surge of Western multinational investments in Southeast Asia includes both continued resource extraction and export manufacturing projects, now of a more capital-intensive, and often regionally-integrated, nature. Companies increasingly practice a regional division of labor, locating different stages of production, or producing different products, in different countries according to their respective comparative advantages. But there is also new interest in production for the rapidly growing local and regional markets. These are now either of a sufficient size to attract the interest of global companies in their own right, or are perceived as "strategic" in companies' struggle for global market share, including the need to block or counter competitors' first-mover advantages or to penetrate their profit sanctuaries. Most such projects still involve the participation of local joint-venture partners, whose contributions of capital, manpower, local market knowledge and government and business connections balance the technological, managerial and global market access contributions of the foreign investors.

Japanese Multinationals

If Western companies were the earliest foreign investors in Southeast Asia, they were soon overtaken by Japanese multinationals supplying protected local markets through minority joint-venture partnerships, and exporting labor-intensive manufactures to world markets from often 100 percent-owned subsidiaries (see Phongpaichit, 1990; Yamashita, 1991; Tokunaga, 1992; Dobson, 1993; Doner, 1993). The relocation of Japanese export industry to Southeast Asia accelerated in the 1980s and 1990s with the appreciation of the yen. Much more so than in the case of Western firms, manufacturing investments by major Japanese multinationals were accompanied or followed by investments by other, smaller, firms in their home-country supplier networks. This helped to multiply and integrate Japanese investments, which are arguably in the process of integrating Southeast Asia into Japanese multinationals' global production networks. The Japanese influence on Southeast Asian business systems is spread through their local joint-venture partnerships with ethnic Chinese businesses and indigenous state-owned enterprises, and their growing relationships with local suppliers.

Ethnic Chinese Capitalists

Ethnic Chinese account for only a small proportion of Southeast Asia's population as a whole, but they dominate its private business sector (Wu and

Wu 1980; Lim and Gosling 1983; Limlingan 1986; McVey 1992; Chan and Chiang 1994; Lim and Gosling 1997). Estimates typically have the Chinese accounting for roughly 4 percent of Indonesia's population but 75 percent of its modern private sector, with equivalent figures for the Philippines of 2 percent (40 percent), for Thailand of 10 percent (85 percent), and for Malaysia of 30 percent (65 percent).

This phenomenon has its roots in the pre-colonial and European colonial era, when trade-oriented immigrants from southeastern coastal China came to Southeast Asia. Here they were favored by both local rulers and European colonialists as tax-collectors and commercial intermediaries ("compradors") with indigenous peasant populations because, being a small immigrant minority, they did not constitute a political threat to their patrons. Their status as "outsiders", and their political vulnerability, also led the Chinese to cultivate relationships with those in power as a means of assuring political protection, accessing business opportunities in a controlled environment, and reducing risk.

Besides the sponsorship of local authorities, the Chinese had several other advantages over indigenous populations in entering into trading ventures. They were not subject to existing local cultural sanctions against trade, or indeed to any discouragement posed by the low status of the merchant in the Confucian social hierarchy in China itself. As migrants, they were not only arguably self-selected for risk-taking, ambition and entrepreneurialism, but also maintained international links with their home country and with fellow countrymen who had migrated to other countries in the region. These links facilitated trade. In their host countries, the Chinese immigrants were not tied to conservative established social orders, but were rather excluded from traditional modes of livelihood such as agriculture. Trade was thus often their only means of subsistence and upward mobility, and one which fit in with the migrant's short-term horizon and preference for liquid investments and quick returns. In addition, many of the early Chinese migrants to Southeast Asia had been traders at home and were motivated by trade to emigrate.

Chinese migrants set up clan, village, occupational, school, temple and other associational networks for mutual assistance in Southeast Asian host countries. These ethnic networks, which often had cross-national extensions, provided them with privileged access to scarce capital and information, and cheap loyal labor from within the Chinese community itself. This helped them to find business opportunities, assess and reduce risks, minimize transactions costs and ensure collective security to advance their business interests in economies with underdeveloped markets and institutions and imperfect information and price signals. Migrants also tended to save much of their income for repatriation to the mother country as well as for reinvestment in the host country.

After independence, Chinese communities in some Southeast Asian countries were subject to nationalist government policies which discriminated against them on the basis of race, in some cases reducing the scope of their business activities (Golay *et al.*, 1969). This reinforced the need to develop clientelistic relationships with politically powerful local patrons, who often included the military. The erection of trade and investment barriers by new nation-states in Southeast Asia, and the isolation of China after the communist revolution in 1949, further restricted the previously "borderless" reach of Chinese businesses in the region. Chinese communities lost their migrant or "sojourner" characteristics but not their minority status in their adopted lands. Even before this, permanent settlement had increased and with it, varying degrees of assimilation to indigenous Southeast Asian cultures.

With the assistance or at least tolerance of indigenous patrons and their communities, Chinese businesses took advantage of import-substituting policies (which otherwise hurt their import trade) to enter the industrial sector. This was sometimes done at the behest of national governments which wished to develop particular key industries and relied on their Chinese clients to take the risk and the initiative (e.g. steel and cement in Indonesia). In import-substituting industries, the external relationships that Chinese traders had with foreign suppliers helped provide the foreign joint venture capital, technology and expertise required in modern manufacturing for the domestic market. Chinese businesses themselves contributed some capital, local political connections, and market knowledge, and distribution networks.

Chinese businesses in Southeast Asia had long been involved in the export of primary commodities. But export manufacturing for industrial country markets in the West (since regional markets were themselves protected) required different skills and connections. These had been developed by Chinese in Hong Kong and Taiwan, who established themselves as subcontractors to, and original equipment manufacturers for, foreign buyers. They were the first to bring such labor-intensive export manufacturing to Southeast Asia in the 1970s, as foreign investors escaping third-country import quotas (as in textiles and garments), or chasing cheaper local labor and tax incentives. Some of them entered into partnerships with Southeast Asian Chinese, more because they were often the only local partners available, rather than because they were Chinese (for example, dialect-group differences existed between Chinese from Taiwan and Hong Kong, on the one hand, and those in Southeast Asia on the other, some of whom by now spoke little or no Chinese of any kind). Western and Japanese multinationals also invested in export manufacturing, but since 100 percent foreign ownership was allowed in this sector, they rarely took on local partners. However, they played a major role in developing local suppliers, who were overwhelmingly drawn from the ranks of Chinese entrepreneurs (Lim, 1983; Lim and Pang, 1982; Lee Tsao and Low, 1990; Doner and Ramsay, 1993).

Two developments since the late 1980s have increased the public profile of ethnic Chinese capitalists in Southeast Asia. The first is the increased presence of foreign Chinese investors from Taiwan, Hong Kong, and Singapore as shifting comparative advantage has caused them to relocate labor-intensive export manufacturing to the cheaper ASEAN countries. The second is the economic rise of China, which has attracted large investments from Chinese business domiciled in Southeast Asia. For example, the Sino-Thai Charoen Pokphand group of Thailand is considered to be the largest single foreign investor in China, and other cumulatively large investments in China have been made by the Salim, Lippo and other Chinese-Indonesian business groups, and by Chinese-Malaysian and Chinese-Filipino tycoons, as well as Singaporeans. These two developments have arguably led to a "re-Sinification" of otherwise partially-locally-assimilated Chinese business groups in Southeast Asia.

The "typical" Chinese business enterprise in Southeast Asia is a diversified family-owned conglomerate headed by the founder-patriarch or his immediate descendants. It is tempting to see ethnic cultural characteristics embedded in this enterprise form — particularly the Confucian family system and the inclination toward individual entrepreneurship resulting in the proliferation of autonomous business units. But it is at least equally likely that this form is dictated by environmental conditions — specifically the underdevelopment of markets and the consequential importance of relationships. These relationships then become the core competitive asset of the firm which is leveraged to provide new business that is likely to be in different sectors, given relatively small markets and rapid growth. The minority status of the Chinese, rather than their ethnic cultural characteristics (which are arguably "diluted" in the Southeast Asian context), may make relationships both within and outside the group more important to them. Similarly, the family nature of the enterprise and the use of family members to manage its different branches may simply reflect the youthful stage of enterprise development, the inadequacy of capital markets, the scarcity of skilled labor in fast-growing economies, and underdeveloped human resource management systems.

Indigenous Capitalists

My discussion here will refer only to indigenous capitalists in Malaysia and Indonesia. Thailand is excluded not only because of the overwhelming dominance of ethnic Chinese and Sino-Thai business at the medium- and large-scale enterprise levels, but also because Sino-Thai ethnic admixture makes separate identification of an indigenous capitalist class difficult.[4] In the case of the Philippines, most non-Chinese local capital is of Spanish-Chinese-mestizo, rather than indigenous Malay, origin (Yoshihara 1985).

In Malaysia and Indonesia, on the other hand, the development of bumiputra and pribumi business communities has been promoted by indigenous-dominated governments which, for example, have given them privileged access to government contracts and credit allocations. Malaysia's New Economic Policy from 1970–1990 also included ethnic quotas favoring Malays in higher education, employment and equity ownership in larger companies, and provided scholarships to train Malays in business skills. State-owned enterprises were set up that were run by Malay managers, and subsequently privatized into the hands of privileged members of the Malay business elite. Some of these enterprises, particularly agribusiness plantations and mining companies, were taken over from foreign shareholders in "market nationalization" moves by the Malaysian government in the 1970s. The Malay ruling party UMNO has also been very active in business, generating further opportunities for its members. The result of these developments has been the rapid emergence of a class of Malay capitalists (Gomez 1994). Malay-Chinese joint business ventures are also evolving.

Access to higher education, especially in the pre-NEP era when it was dominated by non-Malays, has been a crucial element of the success of Malay, but not Chinese, business leaders in Malaysia. Political connections have been important to both groups, but for the Chinese these have often been connections with Chinese political leaders, who exist because of Malaysia's electoral democracy, its racially-based parties, and the large proportion (about one-third) of the electorate who are ethnic Chinese. Despite their common educational background, senior Malay business leaders are themselves a heterogeneous group. They include "products of the conservative boardroom" in publicly-listed diversified conglomerates like Sime Darby and Golden Hope, which retain a "Western organisational face" *(Far Eastern*

[4]The most prominent Thai company not founded and primarily owned by Sino-Thai capital is the Siam Cement group, which was established by the Thai government and whose main shareholder is the Thai royal family through its Crown Properties Bureau. For more on the relationship between Sino-Thai capital and the Thai state, see Hewison (1989).

Economic Review 3 March 1994: 48–52; *Asiaweek* 14 December 1994: 51); entrepreneurial managers of state-owned corporations like Petronas (*Asiaweek* 5 October 1994: 46–49); UMNO party members or supporters involved in party-based "money politics"; politically well-connected private entrepreneurs (*Far Eastern Economic Review* 25 August 1994: 77–78); as well as other independent enterpreneurs who have made little if any use of political connections (*Far Eastern Economic Review* 1 December 1994: 72–76 and 6 October 1994–77). Note that for this last group, even without explicit use of political connections, ethnicity as well as education has been an important asset in an environment where bumiputra partners or contractors are considered desirable if not officially required. Malays are also not the only non-Chinese local businessmen — there are also prominent Indian business leaders who, like the Chinese and Malays, may also make use of political connections. Probably the most prominent example here is spot oil trader and property developer, Ananda Krishnan.

Political connections are even more important to pribumi business in Indonesia, which has a less-developed, more heavily-regulated and less-transparent market economy than Malaysia, and is not an electoral democracy. Here the strategic alliance between Chinese conglomerates and members of President Suharto's immediate family as well as other individuals close to him has been oft noted as a source of monopolization of lucrative sectors of the Indonesian economy (*Far Eastern Economic Review* 30 April 1992: 54–58 and 25 August 1994: 47–49). Suharto himself has defended his children's involvement in business as both their individual right and a means of increasing pribumi participation in the otherwise Chinese-dominated private sector. More recently, some observers argue that Suharto is beginning to distance himself from the Chinese, whose unpopularity is a political liability in a potentially liberalizing political environment (*Far Eastern Economic Review* 22 December 1994: 21). At the same time, non-Suharto-linked, non-Chinese-linked pribumi groups are on the ascendancy, and will provide more competition for the Chinese, particularly as economic liberalization proceeds. The most prominent of these is the Bakrie group (*Asiaweek.* 5 October 1994: 48–49; *Wall Street Journal.* 18 April 1994: A5A). Note that pribumi firms account for only five of the twenty-five largest conglomerates in the country, the rest being Chinese.

In terms of their structure and operations, indigenous Southeast Asian businesses greatly resemble the ethnic Chinese enterprises which operate in the same countries. They are family-based enterprises which rely heavily on personal relationships, including political connections, to access business opportunities. Using these relationships as their core competitive asset to attract foreign and local Chinese partners, they can thus access external sources of capital, technology, managerial and marketing expertise. As in the case of Chinese business, a diversified conglomerate enterprise form is the natural result.

The major differences are that indigenous Southeast Asian businesses are more likely to be directly involved in politics or state-owned enterprises, and to rely on education and previous occupational experience as secondary or even primary assets in launching and expanding their business ventures. Ethnic and village-based networks, while they exist, are probably less significant for the indigenous Southeast Asian capitalist than for the Chinese, and international connections are weaker. But the "minority" effect may be similar. Ethnic minorities have traditionally had an advantage in indigenous Southeast Asian trade (Foster 1974), and many pribumi businesses in Indonesia are drawn not from the majority Javanese community but from outer island minority groups, such as the Malay, the Bugis and the Minahasa. Further, since Chinese dominate the business community, indigenous enterprises operate as a minority within the private sector. This arguably encourages them to seek a competitive edge through privileged access to state resources, to form strategic alliances with the "majority" community and with foreigners to bolster their own position, and to network among themselves.

A SOUTHEAST ASIAN BUSINESS SYSTEM?

The discussion in this paper has outlined several distinctive features of Southeast Asian business systems. They are located in underdeveloped economies, which encourages the development of private institutional mechanisms such as networks and relationships to access information and reduce costs and risks. Rapid economic growth additionally rewards opportunistic, risk-taking behavior, thereby encouraging an entrepreneurial mode of operation. This, together with the development of relationships as core competitive assets, leads to a conglomerate form of enterprise. The recentness of market economic development and the youthfulness of most firms in these economies also makes family enterprise the most common enterprise form. In addition, for historical reasons the state plays an important role in economic development as the major initiator and regulator of economic activity, and as a participant in such activity in its own right.

Thus far, there would seem to be little to distinguish business systems in Southeast Asia from those in Northeast Asia. Distinctiveness comes from the presence of an important natural resource and agricultural exporting sector, from long-established openness to international trade and foreign business participants, and from the dominant presence of an ethnic Chinese minority business community.

Control of the natural resources sector has arguably strengthened the economically interventionist role of the state. The Southeast Asian countries' long-established involvement in international trade and with foreign traders also began with the export of natural resources and agricultural products. Locally-domiciled ethnic Chinese played an important role in this trade as middlemen or agents of European colonial import-export houses. In the post-colonial period, many foreign-owned companies in the agricultural and mining sectors were taken over by the state, creating a base of Western-derived organizations run by indigenous bureaucrat-managers who themselves eventually formed the nucleus of an indigenous business class. New state-owned enterprises were also set up to develop newly discovered natural resources like oil and natural gas, and these have remained in state hands.

Western business organizations are prevalent in the modern manufacturing and services sectors too. Western organizational forms and business practices are disseminated through their hiring of mostly local employees, including managers, and their active development of local suppliers — both of which groups incubate local, particularly ethnic Chinese, business entrepreneurs. Japanese enterprises, on the other hand, have been frequently criticized for inadequate localization of both managers and suppliers. This, together with the lower turnover of local managers in Japanese subsidiaries, might be expected to limit the dissemination of Japanese business practices. But this effect is countered by the strong Japanese influence through numerous joint ventures with local partners, their position as the most important suppliers to industrial firms of all nationalities, and their increasingly proactive development of local suppliers (Doner, 1997).

Local ethnic Chinese enterprises are differentiated from those in Chinese-majority territories like Hong Kong, Taiwan, and Singapore by the specific nature of their relationships with the indigenous state, and with both Western and Japanese business organizations which supply them with technology and world market contacts. The Southeast Asian Chinese enterprises are arguably more likely to include both conglomerates and very large firms, and to be concentrated in trade, services, and property development, than in manufacturing on their own account without foreign joint venture partnerships. This is because they are less likely to develop internal firm competitive advantages based on technology or marketing assets, and more likely to rely on privileged external relationships. Since the numbers of ethnic Chinese are few, and many prefer to be entrepreneurs rather than employees,[5] Southeast Asian Chinese companies must employ many non-Chinese, who also form the bulk of their customers. Thus they need to develop ethnically-neutral business practices.

I have argued above that the differences between local Chinese and indigenous business enterprises in Southeast Asia are relatively minor and historically-specific. Rather, their considerable similarities are based on adaptations to similar environmental conditions, particularly the abundant opportunities for entrepreneurship, the utility of networks and relationships, and the natural evolution of family-based enterprise, in fast-growing under-developed but newly industrializing economies. Both groups also share a common need for state support or patronage as a response to government regulation and minority status. These politically-based relationships then become part of their competitive asset base and may be leveraged to access technology (e.g. from foreign partners) in many different sectors. This gives rise to the diversified conglomerate, which is also a means of economizing on scarce entrepreneurial and managerial skills.

Beyond shared economics and politics, it is also arguable that cultural differences between local Chinese and indigenous business enterprises are minimal, and much less than the differences that exist between Southeast Asian and Western cultural systems, (Deyo 1983; Ismail 1988; Abdullah 1992). Certainly the diversity of business cultures found in Southeast Asia, and their close interaction with each other over long periods of time, makes it difficult to argue that a single ethnic business culture dominates overall, though this may be the case in particular sectors of individual countries (e.g. indigenous state enterprise in petroleum in Malaysia and Indonesia). Rather, there is mutual adaptation by the various business actors, both to each other and, more fundamentally, to shared underlying economic and political conditions. This readiness to adapt to and include foreign and minority participants in the local business system has been characteristic of Southeast Asia throughout its long and very active trading history. It has certainly underlain the region's openness to foreign trade and investment, which has contributed substantially to its rapid economic growth, and may

[5]This is a rational choice in fast-growing economies where new market opportunities are plentiful and competition often limited, and where upward mobility as an employee is limited either because monopoly of top management by family owners, or government-mandated ethnic quotas, impose a "glass ceiling" on the career advancement of ethnic Chinese employees.

deliver a particular advantage in competing in the increasingly liberalized, diverse and "globalized" business world of the future.

CONCLUSION AND CONTINUING EVOLUTION

As described in this paper, Southeast Asian business systems are characterized by a diversity of business actors operating in rapidly-growing, underdeveloped, and politically-controlled market economies. Among local private — as distinct from foreign and state — enterprises, there is a preponderance of family firms which operate in an entrepreneurial and opportunistic mode, with many ending up as large diversified conglomerates. Closely linked to government and politics, these enterprises are heavily networked and dependent on personal relationships, which are maximized by extension to all ethnic groups and foreigners. Southeast Asian Chinese enterprises rely more heavily on ethnic and familial networks, while indigenous enterprises rely more heavily on education and the state. For both groups of firms, government and private sector connections comprise a key competitive asset that enables them to access information, capital, and specific business opportunities, and to reduce risks and transactions costs.

This business system is continuing to evolve in response to major changes that are under way in the Southeast Asian environment. In the economic arena, market liberalization policies since the 1980s are both increasing competition from new foreign and domestic entrants, and reducing the importance of government connections given deregulation and privatization. With economic development, market imperfections diminish and new legal and financial institutions become established, again reducing the need to resort to non-market institutions such as relationships and networks to access capital or guarantee contracts.

Some countries are also experiencing shifts in comparative advantage which, together with the emergence of newly hospitable investment locations in other developing countries, has reduced their international competitiveness in labor-intensive industry and agriculture. Labor scarcity makes retaining workers and increasing their productivity a matter of high priority. At the same time, new business opportunities elsewhere — e.g. in China, India, Vietnam and Myanmar — are enticing overseas investment by Southeast Asian companies. These developments make it necessary to compete on the basis of new firm competitive advantages — based, say, on technology, management, or marketing — that are transferable to different locations, which increases the value of alliances with foreign companies relative to local governments and ethnic networks.

In the political arena, slow but steady movements toward more participatory democracy and institutions such as a free press and free labor organization also increase popular demands for greater transparency in business operations and reduce tolerance of close business-government relationships which are perceived as having anti-competitive, rent-seeking effects. As previously discussed, democratization is also likely to reduce the influence of the ethnic Chinese minority business community on government and politics.

At the same time, the growing size and complexity of Southeast Asian enterprises increases their need for public sources of capital — e.g. through emerging local equity and bond markets, and participation in global financial markets — and professional management, both of which will lead to a loss of family ownership and control. Outside capital providers especially will demand more transparency in business practices and better management, just as family-based businesses face the challenge of succession from their founder-entrepreneurs to a new generation. Whether the new company leaders come from the ranks of family members or from unrelated professional managers, their ways of doing business are likely to differ from those of the founder-patriarchs. For both groups, and even for new-generation entrepreneurs, these ways are perhaps more likely to resemble those of the West due to the spread of Western managerial training and experience (*Far Eastern Economic Review* 17 November 1994: 78–86; *Asiaweek* 14 December 1994: 42–51; *Economist.* 23 Dec. 1995: 85–86). Education is likely to become a more important competitive asset to the firm.

In short, the maturing of enterprises, economies, and political and legal systems is already initiating significant changes in Southeast Asian business systems. These changes may progress more rapidly here than in Northeast Asia, given that the established systems are less entrenched than they are in Japan and Korea.

Change is likely to encounter both less resistance and fewer problems of transition, especially given continued rapid growth. The already high degree of market and foreign penetration of the Southeast Asian systems, their cultural diversity, the presence of many different cooperating and competing business actors,'and the political weakness of the ethnic Chinese commercial minority, also weaken resistance to change.

At the same time, change is unlikely to occur overnight, or to be complete. First, except for Singapore, the Southeast Asian economies have a long way to go before they become "developed", thus the "old ways" of doing business will retain their utility for a long time to come. Second, the "old ways" will be maintained because of their continued usefulness in neighboring underdeveloped economies like China and Vietnam, in which Southeast Asian companies are increasingly involved. Third, indigenist policies are unlikely to be completely eliminated given concerns about business domination by the ethnic Chinese minority and/or foreigners, so market liberalization is unlikely to be complete.

Fourth, there is considerable utility in the "old ways" even in an advanced modern economy. For example, high-tech industry is characterized by rapid growth, the proliferation of multiple new opportunities, imperfect information, high risk and uncertainty, short product-cycles, and first-mover advantages rewarding speed to market. Trust based on long-term relationships can help in accessing information and patient capital, encouraging risk-taking, and permitting flexibility and speed in operations. The entrepreneurial mode of operation, conglomerate form of enterprise, and international strategic alliance so familiar in Southeast Asian business systems, all retain their utility under these circumstances. But high-tech industry of this type, already increasingly common in East Asia, particularly Taiwan, has yet to make its appearance in Southeast Asia outside of Singapore, where local ethnic engineer-entrepreneurs invented the computer sound-card and dominate the world market for it.

REFERENCES

Abdullah, A (1992). Influence of Ethnic Values at the Malaysian Workforce. *Understanding the Malaysian Workforce.* Kuala Lumpur: Malaysian Institute of Management. 2–17.

Bowie, A (1991). *Crossing the Industrial Divide.* New York: Columbia University Press. Chan, K-B and C Chiang (1994). *Stepping Out: The Making of Chinese Entrepreneurs.* Singapore: Simon and Schuster.

Deyo, FC (1983). Chinese Management Practices and Work Commitment in Comparative Perspective. in L.A.P. Gosling and L.Y.C. Lim (eds.). *The Chinese in Southeast Asia.* Vol. II. Singapore: Maruzen Asia. 215–230.

Dobson, W (1993). *Japan and East Asia: Trading and Investment Strategies.* Singapore: Institute for Southeast Asian Studies.

Doner, RF (1993). Japanese Foreign Investment and the Creation of a Pacific Asian Region. in J.A. Frankel and M. Kahler (eds.). *Regionalism and Rivalry: Japan and the United States in Pacific Asia.* Chicago: University of Chicago Press for the National Bureau of Economic Research. 159–216.

Doner, RF (1997). Japan in East Asia: Institutions and Regional Leadership. in P. Katzenstein and T. Shirashi (eds.), *Japan in Asia.* Cornell University Press: Ithaca.

Doner, RF and A Ramsay (1993). Postimperialism and development in Thailand. *World Development* 21(5), 691–704.

Foster, BL (1974). Ethnicity and Commerce. *American Ethnologist* 1(3), 437–448.
Golay, F *et al.* (1969). *Underdevelopment and Economic Nationalism in Southeast Asia.* Ithaca: Cornell University Press.
Gomez, ET (1994). *Political Business: Corporate Involvement of Malaysian Political Parties.* Townsville, Australia: Centre for South-East Asian Studies, James Cook University of North Queensland.
Hewison, K (1989). *Bankers and Bureaucrats, Capital and the Role of the State in Thailand.* New Haven: Yale University Southeast Asia Studies Monograph Series 34.
Ismail, NAR (1988). Value Systems of Malay and Chinese Managers. *Economic Performance in Malaysia.* New York: Professors World Peace Academy. 95–109.
Jesudason, JV (1989). *Ethnicity and the Economy: The State, Chinese Business, and Multinationals in Malaysia.* Singapore: Oxford University Press.
Jomo, KS (ed.) (1993). *Industrialising Malaysia.* London/New York: Routledge.
Jomo, KS (ed.) (1995). *Privatizing Malaysia: Rents, Rhetoric, Realities.* Boulder, Colorado: Westview Press.
Lee Tsao, Y (1994). "Overseas Investment: Experience of Singapore Manufacturing Companies." Singapore: McGraw-Hill for the Institute for Policy Studies.
Lee Tsao, Y and L Low (1990). *Local Entrepreneurship in Singapore, Private and State.* Singapore: Times Academic Press for the Institute of Policy Studies.
Lim, LYC (1983). Chinese Business, Multinationals and the State: Manufacturing for Export in Malaysia and Singapore. in Lim and Gosling. 245–274.
______. (1994a). Foreign Investment, the State and Industrial Policy in Singapore. in H. Stein (ed.), *Asian Industrialization and Africa.* New York: St. Martin's Press. 205–238.
______. (1994b). The Role of the Private Sector in ASEAN Regional Economic Cooperation. in L. Mytelka (ed.), *South-South Cooperation in a Global Perspective.* Paris: OECD Development Centre. 125–168.
______. (1995a). "Models and Partners: Malaysia and Singapore in Vietnam's Economic Reforms". Unpublished manuscript.
______. (1995b). "Southeast Asia: Success Through International Openness" in Barbara Stallings, ed., *The New International Context of Development.* Cambridge: Cambridge University Press, 238–271.
______. (1995c). "Technology Policy and Export Development: The Electronics Industry in Singapore and Malaysia". Unpublished manuscript.
______ and Pang EF (1982). Vertical Linkages and Multinational Enterprises in Developing Countries. *World Development.* Vol. XX, 7. 582–595.
______ and Pang EF (1991). *Foreign Direct Investment and Industrialisation in Malaysia, Singapore, Taiwan and Thailand.* Paris: OECD Development Centre.
______ and LAP Gosling (eds.) 1983. *The Chinese in Southeast Asia,* Vol. 1, *Ethnicity and Economic Activity.* Singapore: Maruzen International.
Lim, LYC and LAP Gosling (1997). Strengths and Weaknesses of Minority Status for Southeast Asian Chinese. In Daniel Chirot and Anthony Reid, eds., *Essential Outsiders: Chinese and Jews in the Modern Transformation of Southeast Asia and Central Europe*, Washington: University of Washington Press, 1997, 285–317.

Limlingan, VS (1986). *The Overseas Chinese in ASEAN: Business Strategies and Management Practices.* Manila, Philippines: Vita Development Corp.

Maclntyre, A (ed.) (1994). *Business and Government in Industrialising Asia.* Australia: Allen and Unwin.

McVey, R (ed.) (1992). *Southeast Asian Capitalists.* Ithaca: Southeast Asia Program, Cornell University.

Phongpaichit, P (1990). *The New Wave of Japanese Investment in ASEAN.* Singapore: Institute of Southeast Asian Studies.

Tokunaga, S (ed.) (1992). *Japanese Foreign Investment and Asian Economic Interdependence.* Tokyo, Japan: University of Tokyo Press.

Wells, LT (1993). "Mobile Exporters: New Foreign Investors in East Asia" in Kenneth A. Froot, ed., *Foreign Direct Investment.* Chicago: University of Chicago Press. 173–196.

Wu, Y-L and CH Wu (1980). *Economic Development in Southeast Asia, the Chinese Dimension.* Stanford, California: Hoover Institution Press.

Yamashita, S (ed.) (1991). *Transfer of Japanese Technology and Management to the ASEAN Countries.* Tokyo, Japan: University of Tokyo Press.

Yoshihara, K (1985). *Philippine Industrialization, Foreign and Domestic Capital.* Manila: Ateneo de Manila University Press.

Chapter 11

STRENGTHS AND WEAKNESSES OF MINORITY STATUS FOR SOUTHEAST ASIAN CHINESE AT A TIME OF ECONOMIC GROWTH AND LIBERALIZATION*

LINDA Y. C. LIM and L. A. PETER GOSLING

Southeast Asia is distinguished from other ethnically diverse, economically developing regions by the coincidence of extreme ethnic and religious diversity with relative interethnic peace and rapid economic growth over three decades.[1] Stability and prosperity have been achieved, even though small minorities of ethnic Chinese dominate the region's private-sector economies while once-colonized indigenous majorities control the modern nation-state.[2]

---

*This chapter first appeared in *Essential Outsiders: Chinese, Jews in the Modern Transformation of Southeast Asia and Central Europe*, Daniel Chirot and Anthony Reid (eds.), 1997, pp. 285–317. Reprinted with permission from University of Washington Press, USA.

[1]Regarding ethnic and religious diversity, Indonesia alone, for example, contains between 80 and 250 ethnolinguistic groups (depending on how they are defined). who practice variants of Islam (90 percent of the population), Christianity, Hinduism, and indigenous animistic religions. Muslims are the largest religious minority in the predominantly Catholic Philippines and in Buddhist Thailand. The European colonial era saw the immigration of Indians and especially Chinese into the region and the superimposition of European languages and cultures (Spanish, Dutch, British, French). Regarding interethnic peace, there have been occasional outbreaks of ethnic violence during this period, particularly anti-Chinese riots in Indonesia, but these have not been frequent, prolonged, sustained, or disruptive of the general polity and social order, nor have they involved large numbers of deaths. Ethnic tensions and frictions and ethnic separatist movements do exist, but for the most part they have not resulted in widespread or persistent interethnic violence. And regarding rapid economic growth, among the capitalist ASEAN countries, Indonesia, Malaysia, Singapore, and Thailand — but not the Philippines — have enjoyed real GDP growth rates averaging 6 to 7 percent annually for the past twenty-five years.

[2]For example, ethnic Chinese in 1991 accounted for 3.5 percent of the Indonesian population but had a 73 percent share of listed equity. Equivalent figures for Malaysia were

In this essay we seek to analyze, in a comparative regional context, the complex interplay between economic growth, ethnicity, and national policy in determining the state of interethnic relations between the entrepreneurial minority and the majority populations. The central question we address is the extent to which the particular character of Southeast Asia's contemporary economic growth is likely to assuage or aggravate ethnic tensions.

In theory, economic growth improves ethnic relations because it removes the tensions caused by potential interethnic competition over scarce resources, jobs, and business opportunities. The growth in absolute shares of an expanding economic pie reduces concern over relative shares. This is, arguably, what has happened in Southeast Asia, where sustained economic prosperity has minimized the economic basis for interethnic rivalry. Ethnic conflict has been most entrenched in Myanmar, with its poor record of economic growth, whereas Malaysia — with potentially the most volatile ethnic mix, resulting from a colonial-era ethnic division of labor — has not exploded in ethnic violence because economic growth, aided by state policy, has delivered material benefits to all groups.[3] In southern Thailand, a Malay-based ethnic separatist movement disintegrated as Thailand's economic growth accelerated in the 1980s, whereas the similar Moro nationalist movement in the southern Philippines has persisted in part because of a weaker national economy.

But economic growth also has the potential to undermine ethnic harmony: first, if the growth is unevenly distributed across ethnic groups, or if it is predicated on or generates occupational or class distinctions that correlate with particular ethnic groups; second, if economic success leads to the enhancement of ethnic identity and a resurgence of ethnic pride among ascendant groups, which others resent; and third, if economic growth increases interethnic contact between previously segregated ethnic groups, giving rise to more opportunity for ethnic friction. All of these developments have also occurred in Southeast Asia as part of its recent rapid economic

29 percent and 61 percent, respectively; for the Philippines, 2 percent and 50 percent; and for Thailand, 10 percent and 81 percent. See Sakura Bank — Nomura Research Institute, cited in *Asiaweek*, "A Taxing Dilemma," October 20, 1993, p. 58. Listed equity refers to only a small proportion of the total private-sector wealth in these countries, where most Chinese companies are family owned and not publicly listed. But respected estimates for the private sector as a whole tend to parallel these figures.

[3]Malaysia did experience one post-independence incidence of interethnic violence, the May 1969 riots, but they occurred before Malaysia's take-off into rapid industrial growth and have not been repeated in the quarter-century since.

growth, which has enhanced the historically dominant role of ethnic Chinese in the business sector.[4]

To the local Chinese business families domiciled in the region for generations have been added, since the late 1980s, foreign Chinese investors from Hong Kong, Taiwan, and Singapore. Growing intraregional flows of goods, capital, and labor increasingly involve interethnic exchanges, occurring as they do within the larger geographical context of Asia-wide rapid economic growth, including the spectacular rise of the People's Republic of China (PRC).[5] And it is not only overseas Chinese capital and capitalists who have been flooding into Southeast Asia, but also overseas and PRC Chinese tourists and PRC Chinese labor. Even PRC businesses are starting to trickle in.

The increasingly visible Chinese dominance of Southeast Asia's modern economic life, interwoven as it is with cultural and political divisions, could indeed exacerbate underlying ethnic tensions, despite the counteracting effects of economic growth.

THE EVOLVING CHINESE ECONOMIC ROLE IN SOUTHEAST ASIA

Chinese immigrants and their descendants have played a disproportionate role in the commercial life of Southeast Asia since (and even before) the European colonial era.[6] In the postcolonial era, nationalistic indigenous

[4]Lim, LYC "The New Ascendancy of Chinese Business in Southeast Asia: Political, Cultural, Economic, and Business Implications" (paper presented at the annual meeting of the Association for Asian Studies, New Orleans, Louisiana, April 1991); Wells, LT, Jr., "Mobile Exporters: New Foreign Investors in East Asia," in Kenneth Froot, ed., *Foreign Direct Investment* (Chicago: University of Chicago Press, 1993), pp. 173–96; Stoltenberg, CD and Lim, LYC (1994). Investment in Southeast Asia, in Mitchell Silk, ed., *Taiwan Trade and Investment Law* (Hong Kong: Oxford University Press, 1994), pp. 247–68.

[5]See Lim, LYC (1992). The Emergence of a Chinese Economic Zone in Asia? *Journal of Southeast Asia Business*, 8(1) (Winter 1992), pp. 41–46; Lim, LYC "The Role of the Private Sector in ASEAN Economic Cooperation," in Lynn Mytelka, ed., *South-South Co-operation in a Global Perspective* (Paris: OECD Development Centre, 1994), pp. 125–68.

[6]There is a voluminous literature on this subject. For recent overviews, see Wang Gungwu, *China and the Chinese Overseas* (Singapore: Times Academic Press, 1991), and Yeu-Farn Wang, "Chinese Entrepreneurs in Southeast Asia: Historical Roots and Modern Significance" (Stockholm University, Center for Pacific Asia Studies, Working Paper no. 34, May 1994). For various attempts to explain Chinese economic competitiveness in the region, see Yuan-li Wu and Chun-Hsi Wu, *Chinese Development in Southeast Asia: The Chinese Dimension* (Stanford, California: Hoover Institution Press, 1980); Lim, LYC and LAP Gosling, eds., *The Chinese in Southeast Asia*, vol. 1, *Ethnicity and Economic Activity*, and vol. 2, *Identity, Culture and Politics* (Singapore: Maruzen

governments acted to curtail the economic role of Chinese and foreign enterprises and to promote indigenous commercial activity.[7] Restrictive licenses, protective tariffs, ownership limitations, preferential credit allocations, and outright bans on Chinese commercial activity in particular sectors were typical policies. This discriminatory infrastructure elicited a range of adaptive responses from the Chinese, including so-called Ali-Baba ventures with indigenous "sleeping partners" in whose names enterprises were registered, direct and indirect payments to local and national government officials to circumvent restrictions or secure protection, and cultivation of powerful indigenous political patrons and sponsors, particularly where there were ruling military regimes.[8]

Through these and other means, Southeast Asian Chinese businesses succeeded in maintaining the bulk of their operations intact, thereby retaining their dominance of the local private sector. In many cases, they even emerged as the main beneficiaries of nationalist restrictions on foreign-owned enterprises, since these restrictions limited the competition they faced in domestic markets. When foreign enterprises were "localized" in response to national ownership requirements, Chinese were often the only established private-sector parties with the capital and expertise to acquire and operate them. When import-substituting industrialization programs were launched, local ownership requirements helped Chinese acquire foreign technology, because foreign investors often turned to them as the only local partners with the requisite capital and connections. Further "local content" requirements in industries such as automobiles also created new business opportunities for local Chinese enterprises.

International, 1983); Limlingan, VS, *The Overseas Chinese in ASEAN: Business Strategies and Management Practices* (Manila: Vita Development Corp, 1986); Mackie, J, "Chinese Businessmen and the Rise of Southeast Asian Capitalism," *Solidarity* 123 (July–September 1989), pp. 96–107; Mackie, J, "Changing Patterns of Chinese Big Business in Southeast Asia," in Ruth McVey, ed., *Southeast Asian Capitalists* (Ithaca, New York: Southeast Asia Program, Cornell University, 1992), pp. 161–90; Redding, SG, *The Spirit of Chinese Capitalism* (Berlin: Walter de Gruyter, 1990); L. A. Peter Gosling, "Analysing the Chinese 'Edge' in Business in Southeast Asia" (paper presented at the annual meeting of the Association for Asian Studies, New Orleans, Louisiana, April 1991); and Kraar, L, "Overseas Chinese: Lessons from the World's Most Dynamic Capitalists," *Fortune*, October 31, 1994, pp. 91–114.

[7]Golay, F, R Anspach, R Pfanner and Ayall, R, *Underdevelopment and Economic Nationalism in Southeast Asia* (Ithaca, New York: Cornell University Press, 1969).

[8]Many of these adaptive business practices would likely have characterized Chinese business operations in the immigrant traders' home provinces of coastal southern China as well, given the often parasitic control that Chinese officialdom was wont to exert over private enterprise, and still does in China today.

Because the ASEAN (Association of South East Asian Nations) governments were anticommunist and ideologically committed to private enterprise and capitalism (albeit often with an equally strong commitment to state enterprise in key sectors), they were limited in their ability and willingness to completely disenfranchise the Chinese, who constituted the main private-enterprise actors in the local modern sector.[9] Chinese control of distribution networks ensured that disenfranchisement would severely disrupt the economic growth to which postcolonial nationalist governments were committed, partly as a component of their strategy for fighting communism. The authoritarian, even military, nature of most of these governments protected Chinese business interests by keeping in check any potential grassroots disaffection. The governments themselves were easily paid off for their tacit support of Chinese economic interests. Continued local Chinese investment and reinvestment in their Southeast Asian home economies also propelled economic growth.

In the 1980s, the ASEAN economies embarked on structural adjustment and liberal market-oriented economic reform programs involving trade and investment liberalization, financial reforms, deregulation, and privatization of state-owned enterprises. Such policies — including fiscal and monetary restraint and reduced protection from foreign competition — hurt the local private sector by increasing its costs, reducing subsidies, and increasing competition. These policies, arguably, were more readily effected in Southeast Asia than in other developing countries because the politically weak (or at least politically dependent) Chinese dominated local private sector could not and did not resist them. Ethnic distinctions rendered the Southeast Asian state sufficiently "autonomous" from local capital that it could effect necessary policies which hurt business without encountering serious resistance. The persistence of an ethnic division of labor may thus be considered to have been conducive to the enactment of macroeconomic policies required for sustained economic growth.

These policies may indeed have inflicted temporary pain on the Chinese-dominated private sector. But it is equally arguable that in the longer run the Chinese have benefited disproportionately, since they are the best endowed and most competitive members of the private sector and thus are best placed to take advantage of new market opportunities created by economic liberalization, including opportunities for the establishment of joint ventures with new foreign investors. Chinese enterprises, especially

[9]In the PRC, the Chinese motherland, Chinese private enterprise was more seriously disenfranchised by communism than it was by ethnic discrimination in Southeast Asia.

the larger ones, are also better insulated than indigenous enterprises against the tight money policies, credit rationing, and high interest rates characteristic of macroeconomic stabilization policies. This is because they have disproportionate access to alternative sources of (often, ethnic Chinese) capital abroad, to informal ethnic-based credit networks at home, to internal financing in Chinese conglomerates (many of which own their own banks), and to preferred customer status among other local banks (most of which are Chinese owned).

Investment liberalization permitted a huge influx of overseas Chinese capital and enterprise into Southeast Asia in the late 1980s, responding to currency realignment, labor shortages, and capital surpluses in the source economies of Taiwan, Hong Kong, and Singapore. This capital influx accelerated economic growth, particularly in labor-intensive, export-oriented manufacturing industries. It also increased the ethnic Chinese share of the booming private sector and linked the Southeast Asian economies closer to those of the ethnic Chinese homelands of their new foreign investors.[10]

At the same time, China's spectacular market-based economic growth has attracted profit-seeking and sentimentally motivated investments from overseas Chinese businesses in Southeast Asia. For example, the Charoen Pokphand (CP) group of Thailand is reported to be the largest single foreign investor in China, and many Indonesian and Filipino Chinese conglomerates are investing heavily in their founders' home provinces in China, most notably Fujian.[11] The prime ministers of Singapore, Malaysia, and Thailand and the president of the Philippines all led large delegations of mostly ethnic Chinese businesspeople to China in 1993. China itself is becoming a major growth market for Southeast Asian commodity and manufactured exports, while competing with the region both for international (including overseas Chinese) investments and in world export markets. Some Chinese enterprises are starting to invest in Southeast Asia, and all countries in the region are increasingly concerned about burgeoning flows of illegal Chinese foreign labor.

In short, rapid regionwide economic growth has turned Southeast Asia into a "South China Sea" of ethnic Chinese capital and labor movements, greatly increasing the visibility and the actual presence of both foreign

[10]New foreign investments into Southeast Asia from Taiwan and Hong Kong declined in the early 1990s as investors diversified and responded to the competing attractions of China, but they are now recovering.

[11]On the Charoen Pokphand group, see Goldstein, C, "Full Speed Ahead," *Far Eastern Economic Review*, October 21, 1993, pp. 66–70, and Chapter 10 in this volume, by Gary G. Hamilton and Tony Waters.

and local Chinese in regional economies. As the ASEAN countries move toward closer regional economic integration through the newly established ASEAN Free Trade Area (AFTA), and as they accord a greater role to the private sector both domestically and in the process of regional integration, cross-national links between ethnic Chinese businesses in the region are likely to increase further.[12] It remains for us to consider what impact this Chinese economic role has had and is likely to have on ethnic relations in Southeast Asia.

THE IMPACT ON ETHNIC RELATIONS

In traditional Southeast Asian culture and society, profit-seeking trade (as opposed to barter or exchange for use) was regarded as an activity involving tension between buyer and seller and therefore connoting high social cost. It was thus best undertaken by "outsiders," persons not intimately involved in the social fabric of a particular village society.[13] Throughout the region, trade beyond the simplest level of local exchange (conducted primarily by peasant women and often "disguised" as a social activity) tended to be the terrain of alien groups, including migrants from elsewhere in Southeast Asia. The Chinese are only the most recent, most widespread, and most successful of these ubiquitous "middleman minorities" — originally tolerated as simply one more variant of an established and socially accepted pattern. Social tension generated by trade, which could be internally disruptive in cohesive village societies and cultures that traditionally avoided confrontation, could be dissipated by being turned into ethnic tension directed against "outsiders."

But this ethnic tension, in turn, was held in check by factors including cultural predispositions against violence, the recognized, if also resented, social service provided by the trader, and, later, the power and protection of European colonial authorities. The Europeans not only sanctioned but also encouraged the spreading commercial activities of Chinese middlemen, because they fulfilled a necessary role as intermediaries in the colonial export economy and, being a numerically small group of aliens, did not pose a potential political threat to European colonial rule. In the immediate postcolonial era, resentments against Chinese traders did occasionally erupt into violence, particularly in Indonesia, but it was rarely long-lasting or generalized throughout individual countries or the region as a whole. Military

[12]Lim, "The Role of the Private Sector in ASEAN Economic Cooperation."
[13]Foster, BL (1974). Ethnicity and Commerce. *American Ethnologist*, 1(3), pp. 437–48.

protection and patronage became a factor in the survival and prosperity of Chinese business.

At the same time, the Chinese themselves adopted a partly coerced, partly voluntary strategy of overt assimilation, which earned them a degree of tolerance in host societies historically used to the accommodation of diverse ethnic groups. This assimilation involved the diminution of ethnic Chinese characteristics and expressions such as language, names, the public practice of Chinese religion and culture, and even personal behavior. Southeast Asian Chinese in Thailand, Indonesia, and the Philippines took pains to assimilate local cultural characteristics and norms of behavior, publicly displaying their commitment to their countries of domicile by becoming outwardly more "Thai" or "Indonesian" than "Chinese."[14]

Part of this process occurred naturally through long residence, which included birth, upbringing, and education in the local host society and, especially after the communist takeover of China in 1949, distance and prolonged separation from the "mother country." Intermarriage played a role wherever religion was no barrier, as was the case in Thailand and the Philippines but not in Muslim Malaysia and Indonesia. Many Southeast Asian governments also forbade the learning or use of the Chinese language and of Chinese names, which forcibly accelerated the pace of cultural assimilation. Other than in Chinese-dominated Singapore, the least assimilation occurred in Malaysia, because of its proportionately large Chinese population, the presence of another significant though smaller alien minority, the Indians, and a national philosophy of multiracialism in a largely immigrant population.

Thus, traditional practice, government policy, and voluntary assimilation as a strategy of ethnic accommodation all combined with continuous economic growth to ensure relative interethnic peace and stable ethnic relations in postcolonial Southeast Asia.

But this situation has changed to some degree with the heightened economic presence and cultural profile of both foreign and local Chinese in the region since the late 1980s. Further, state policies throughout the region have encouraged these changes. Governments eager to attract foreign

[14]The "dual ethnicity" of Southeast Asian Chinese has long fascinated scholars. Some recent studies are those of Lim and Gosling, *The Chinese in Southeast Asia*; Jennifer Cushman and Wang Gungwu, eds., *Changing Identities of the Southeast Asian Chinese since World War II* (Hong Kong: Hong Kong University Press, 1988); Wickberg, E (1990). Some Comparative Perspectives on Chinese Ethnicity in the Philippines. *Asian Culture*, 14, pp. 23–37; and Ang 'See, T (1990). Integration and Identity: Social Changes in the Post-World War II Philippine Chinese Community. *Asian Culture* 14, pp. 38–46.

investment not only liberalized investment rules, bringing an influx of foreign Chinese investors, but also relaxed domestic restrictions on expressions of Chinese culture. In Indonesia, a twenty-five-year-old ban on the importation and use of written Chinese characters has been lifted, and Chinese language schools are now allowed to operate. In Malaysia, Chinese cultural activities such as lion dance performances, once a red flag signaling ethnic chauvinism and a refusal to assimilate, have blossomed, and Chinese schools and community groups have been the beneficiaries of donations from Taiwan investors. The Malaysian government has relaxed permanent residence requirements for ethnic Chinese, extending eligibility to Taiwan investors and their families. In Thailand, the willingness of Sino-Thais and Chinese to acknowledge their ethnic identity has increased, as have the use of Chinese languages, the number of Chinese language schools, and public celebrations of Chinese festivals such as the Chinese New Year. Even in Indonesia, the most restrictive country, public celebrations of Chinese New Year were permitted for the first time in 1993.

In short, after decades of adapting their ethnicity to local political requirements and cultural norms — practicing "situational ethnicity" — the hitherto bicultural Chinese of Southeast Asia are suddenly reverting to open expressions of their original Sinic culture and flaunting rather than hiding their commercial success. It is now not only socially acceptable but even socially and certainly economically desirable to be Chinese.[15] The ascent to power of democratically elected ethnic Chinese political leaders such as President Aquino of the Philippines, who, while president, made a highly publicized visit to her family's ancestral village in China's Fujian province, and Prime Minister Chuan Leekpai of Thailand appears to set the official seal of approval on overt Chinese ethnic identity.

At the same time, the establishment of official relations with China — once isolated from its Southeast Asian neighbors — has led to vastly expanded trade and investment links, mainly mediated by locally domiciled Chinese firms, and to greatly increased travel by Southeast Asian Chinese to China. Increasingly affluent Chinese from Taiwan, Hong Kong, Singapore, Malaysia, and China have become the largest group of tourists in Southeast Asia. Even Vietnam and Myanmar receive a few hundred thousand tourists from neighboring southern Chinese provinces every year. Approximately the same number of illegal Chinese migrant workers are believed to be in Thailand, with smaller but increasing numbers in Malaysia and the

[15]See Chapter 3 in this volume, by Kasian Tejapira.

Philippines.[16] Thus, Chinese visibility, customer and employer contact, and even labor-market competition with indigenous ethnic groups have increased.

The continued rise of China as a world political and economic power increases both the prestige and the value of being Chinese.[17] Historically, in the precolonial era, China was acknowledged as an "overlord" by many of the smaller stales of Southeast Asia; in the postcolonial era it provided material and moral support to pro China and often ethnic Chinese-dominated communist insurgency movements in the region. This support was dropped in the 1980s, effectively killing these movements, as China sought to become economically involved with the successful capitalist countries of Southeast Asia, transforming itself from a security threat into an economic partner.

So far, the increased economic presence and cultural profile of both foreign and local ethnic Chinese in Southeast Asia does not appear to pose a threat to continued harmonious ethnic relations with the indigenous populations. In a region accustomed and committed to economic growth, the Chinese are seen as bringers of prosperity rather than as competitors for scarce resources. But this does not mean that there are no underlying or potential sources of ethnic tension. There is, first, understandable jealousy and resentment of an alien ethnic minority seen to benefit disproportionately from economic growth. There is a perception that an increasingly unequal class structure correlates with ethnicity. This resentment is exacerbated when increased Chinese wealth is accompanied by conspicuous consumption and the "flaunting" of Chinese ethnic pride, and when there is the perception that the Chinese have not always "played fair" in their economic ascendancy, particularly when they have resorted to corrupt practices and political influence to advance their business interests. As political liberalization and pressures for greater democracy increase in Southeast Asia, the willingness of Chinese businesses to ally with and support corrupt authoritarian regimes becomes both better known and less tolerable to the general population.

[16]Pang, EF and LYC Lim, "Economic Growth, Structural Change, Regional Integration and International Labor Migration in Asia" (paper presented at a seminar on "Migration and the Labour Market in Asia in the Year 2000," organized by the OECD, the Japanese government, and the Japan Institute of Labour, Tokyo, January 19–20, 1995).

[17]Currently the world's third largest national economy after the United States and Japan, China is projected to be the largest within twenty years — about 40 percent bigger than the second largest, the United States, by the year 2020.

A second source of potential ethnic tension generated by Chinese-led economic growth in Southeast Asia is the perception of diminished "loyalty" on the part of local Chinese to their countries of domicile and their correspondingly greater attachment to pan-Asian Chinese economic interests and ethnic identity. In the Philippines, many Chinese-Filipino big business families have been criticized for establishing dual residency in Taiwan and the Philippines. In Indonesia, there are grumblings about the large outward investments that Chinese-Indonesian business groups are making in China, out of the proceeds of their often privileged Indonesian ventures, and at a time when Indonesia itself expects to face a shortage of capital. The resentment is greater when these outward investments are seen to fuel China's competitiveness with Southeast Asia, especially in labor-intensive manufactured exports to the world market, a sector in which the two already compete for capital and technology, including that from overseas Chinese sources. Southeast Asian investments in China are a consequence partly of domestic financial liberalization, partly of the business diversification strategies of Southeast Asian Chinese enterprises, partly of China's attraction as a competitive and profitable investment location, and partly of sentiment for the motherland, especially the home provinces of the investors.

But Southeast Asian Chinese enterprises also invest in neighboring countries, including both the ASEAN and the socialist countries, especially Vietnam.[18] The push of the ASEAN private sector for a regional free trade area and for regional investment projects can be seen as an initiative of ethnic Chinese business leaders, who are the most able to compete outside of their home countries without government protection but with the assistance of their considerable ethnic business networks.[19] Both these outward investments by Southeast Asian Chinese businesses and the increased dependence of Southeast Asian economies on inward investments from foreign-domiciled overseas Chinese businesses reduce the capacity of Southeast Asian governments to control Chinese economic activity in their own territories.

Besides complaints about the outflow of Chinese capital, there have been complaints about an influx of Chinese labor, particularly in Thailand and

[18]Lim, "The Role of the Private Sector in ASEAN Economic Cooperation"; Linda Y. C. Lim. Unpublished manuscript.

[19]Hamilton, GG, ed. (1994). *Business Networks and Economic Development in East and Southeast Asia* (Hong Kong: Centre of Asian Studies, University of Hong Kong, 1991); Kraar, "Overseas Chinese"; Tanzer, A, "The Bamboo Network," *Forbes*, July 18, 1994, pp. 138–144.

the Philippines, where there are tens if not hundreds of thousands of illegal migrant workers from the PRC, most of whom are likely to be employed in small, Chinese-owned enterprises. Local workers resent the competition and the resulting downward pressure on their wages. A small but growing cadre of PRC skilled and professional workers is also emerging in the region, but generally not to an enthusiastic welcome by local fellow-workers, even in Singapore.[20]

A third and related factor that could lead to heightened ethnic tension in Southeast Asia's increasingly Chinese-led growth economy relates to the uncertain role of China in the region. In the post-cold war world, China is emerging as an increasingly assertive and potentially belligerent regional power, staking territorial claims to islands in the South China Sea, far from its shores, and rapidly building up its military capabilities in ways that potentially threaten its Southeast Asian neighbors. China already competes with Southeast Asia for international, and especially overseas Chinese, capital and technology and in world export markets. It clearly sees the extensive networks of capital-rich overseas Chinese businesses as part of its strategy for achieving not only domestic development but also international economic power.[21]

China's own economic participation in Southeast Asia is increasing through expanding two-way trade, direct investments, and multicountry joint regional development projects, such as the "Golden Quadrangle" and Mekong River projects, with mainland Southeast Asian states. Such economic relations are likely to presage greater political and cultural influence, especially when military links are also involved, as in the case of Myanmar, which is reportedly being "taken over by China" to the discomfiture of its neighbors and its own leaders.[22] Insofar as Southeast Asian countries feel threatened by China, they will feel threatened by its increasing links with and potential patronage of locally domiciled Chinese. Competition between the PRC and Taiwan for the allegiance of Southeast

[20]The influx of mostly illegal migrant labor from the PRC is a cause of concern in lapan, Korea, and Taiwan as well, but ethnic tensions are most likely to result in Southeast Asia. Note that intraregional labor flows also include indigenous Southeast Asians. See Pang and Lim, "Economic Growth, Structural Change."

[21]For analyses of China's changing relations with the overseas Chinese, see Godley, MR, "Reflections on China's Changing Overseas Chinese Policy," *Solidarity* 123 (July–September 1989), pp. 108–12; Tan, C-B, "People of Chinese Descent and China," *Solidarity* 123 (July–September 1989), pp. 113–20; and Wang, *China and the Chinese Overseas.*

[22]*The Economist*, "China takes over Myanmar," October 8, 1994.

Asian Chinese can also, on occasion, affect domestic politics and policies in the region.[23]

Linked to all these factors is the changing cultural behavior of Southeast Asian Chinese themselves. To the extent that adaptiveness and assimilation to indigenous Southeast Asian cultures contributed to the social acceptability of the Chinese minority and tolerance of its dominant business activities in the past, any reversion to explicitly Sinic cultural patterns as a result of recent Chinese-led economic growth could pose a threat to the continuation of this ethnic tolerance. Increased ethnic pride and expression based on economic supremacy could lead to chauvinism on the part of the Chinese themselves, while highlighting their separateness from local communities. This could induce anti-Chinese resentment on the part of the indigenous populations. As one observer put it:

> The transformation of China, the achievements of the newly industrializing economies of East Asia and the growth of intra-Pacific trade and investment, in which the overseas Chinese are key players, are all working together to reduce incentives for the Chinese to assimilate in Southeast Asian societies.
>
> They are also encouraging the Chinese minorities to identify more closely with China. Although profitable in the short run, this is a very dangerous trend for the Chinese in Southeast Asia, where an obsession with profit is matched only by insensitivity towards the feelings of their host nations.
>
> The economic success of China and the overseas Chinese in exploiting regional and international links that are beyond the reach of many indigenous businessmen is breeding an arrogance — and a countervailing force of ethnic nationalism — that the Chinese may live to regret.[24]

Even Lee Kuan Yew, Singapore's former prime minister and a vocal advocate for China and expanded overseas Chinese links with China, has warned that such links could adversely affect race relations in the ASEAN countries, and he has cautioned ethnic Chinese businessmen from the region to "be sensitive" to indigenous feelings on this issue. Speaking in Hong Kong to a gathering of Chinese entrepreneurs from around the world in 1993, he said:

> We are all ethnic Chinese. We share certain characteristics through a common ancestry and culture. We can build up trust and rapport more easily between ourselves. But we must be honest and recognize the fact that

[23]Natalia Soebagjo, "Chinese Power Play in Indonesia and the Role of the Ethnic Chinese" (paper presented at the annual meeting of the Association for Asian Studies, New Orleans, Louisiana, April 1991).

[24]Hicks, G, Developments that Reduce Incentive for Overseas Chinese to Assimilate, *International Herald Tribune* (reprinted in the *Straits Times*, Singapore, January 30, 1993).

at the end of the day, our fundamental loyalties are to our home country, not to our ancestral country.[25]

How does this interplay of domestic and regional, economic, political, and cultural factors affect ethnic relations between the Chinese minority and indigenous majorities in particular ASEAN nations? We turn now to the contemporary peculiarities of the individual national situations, focusing especially on the likely impact on interethnic relations of ongoing political and economic liberalization.

THAILAND

Economic liberalization naturally favors private business while reducing the role and influence of bureaucrats and the state. In Thailand, the rapid, export-oriented growth of the economy since the 1980s, led by the private sector, has greatly increased the wealth and relative power of the urban-based, Sino-Thai-dominated business community while limiting that of the rural-based, Thai-dominated military and provincial bureaucracy. Local and sector-specific business associations — mostly dominated by ethnic Chinese but motivated by business rather than ethnic concerns — have played an important role in influencing government economic policy during this period.[26]

Political democratization has accentuated the trend. The Chatichai Choonhavan government elected in 1988 gave top priority to business-led economic growth, and the antimilitary "pro-democracy movement" of 1992 was essentially based in Bangkok (a disproportionately Sino-Thai city) and led by educated middle-class youths, including many from the business community. Both groups are also disproportionately Sino-Thai.

Electoral politics, too, have led, arguably, to the growth of "money politics," because funds are important for the establishment and maintenance of political parties and the mounting of political campaigns. Most Thai parties must therefore have backers from the business community. Even in provincial cities, political influence is increasingly wielded not by government officials but by local businesspeople, who tend to be of ethnic Chinese origin.[27]

[25] *Straits Times Weekly*, November 27, 1993, p. 1.

[26] Anek Laothamatas, *Business Associations and the New Political Economy of Thailand* (Boulder, Colorado: Westview Press for the Institute of Southeast Asian Studies, Singapore, 1992).

[27] Kevin Hewison and Maniemai Thongyou, "The New Generation of Provincial Business People in Northeastern Thailand" (Murdoch University, Asia Research Centre, Working Paper no. 16, 1993).

Economic influence at the top of the political pyramid thus compensates for the limited influence that Sino-Thais can exert on national polls, given their small proportion (10 percent) of the electorate.[28]

The coincidence of increased political and economic influence for a small ethnic minority might be expected to generate some ethnic tension. Furthermore, this shift in the domestic balance of power is occurring within a larger regional context in which nearby China is flexing its enhanced economic and military muscles, in which Sino-Thai business families are making huge, high-profile investments in developing China's economy, which competes with Thailand's, in which large inflows of overseas Chinese (especially Taiwan) capital have now slowed because of this competition, and in which inflows into Thailand of illegal PRC migrant labor have increased. These developments might be expected to cause at least some indigenous Thais to resent the disproportionate benefit the Sino-Thai business community has derived from economic growth, to doubt the "loyalty" to Thailand of some in this community, to chafe at the potential costs to Thai workers of China's competitive economic growth and illegal migrant streams, and, especially in the case of the conservative, anticommunist Thai military, to fear China as a potential security threat.

That ethnic tension based on such sentiments does not appear to have developed yet in Thailand reflects the influence of several factors. First, despite unequal distribution, the sustained, very rapid rate of growth of the Thai economy has led to some "trickle-down" diffusion of prosperity, even to rural areas, which might tend to diffuse ethnic-based tensions. Second, the relatively high rate of cultural and biological "assimilation" of ethnic Chinese to the Thai population obscures the distinction between Thai and Sino-Thai, dampens awareness of the latter's disproportionate economic power, and wins Thai acceptance of Sino-Thais as fellow nationals whose economic power is not resented the way that of "aliens" might be.

Third, there is no organized opposition to the business ascendancy of Sino-Thais on either ethnic or class grounds. On the political "left," this is because of the demise of communist-led or communist-leaning grassroots protest movements such as the worker-farmer-student coalitions of the 1970s. On the political "right," the Thai military has been weakened by both economic and political reform and by its cooptation by segments of the Chinese business community. Indeed, the military itself might become

[28]Note, however, that the electoral weight of Sino-Thai voters is disproportionately concentrated in urban constituencies, particularly Bangkok, that carry disproportionate weight in national politics.

increasingly dependent on Chinese business for financial support, because of declines in government budget allocations and in U.S. military aid following the end of the cold war and the establishment of peace in Indochina.

Heightened ethnic tension and anti-Chinese sentiment are likely to result only if these three conditions change — if economic growth and its trickle-down slow dramatically, if there is a reversal in the process of Chinese cultural assimilation toward "re-Sinification," and if organized opposition to ethnic Chinese economic dominance develops. But the Thai economy has not experienced a single year of negative GDP growth for forty years, through times of internal and external economic and political turmoil alike, and it is difficult to envisage the specific circumstances that would reverse this trend. Growth, in turn, keeps potential organized opposition in check.

The question of a possible evolution in Sino-Thai ethnic identity is a more difficult one. The long historical experience of the Chinese in Thailand and their high degree of prior assimilation to Thai culture and society make it unlikely that they will suddenly embrace a heightened Chinese ethnic identity. Hewison and Thongyou's study of Sino-Thai provincial business elites suggests that the new generation is much more "Thai" than its parents and likely to remain so.[29] But various forms of Chinese ethnic identification, including education in the Chinese language, remain deep-rooted in Sino-Thai society and have already been given a boost by increasing Sino-Thai domestic political and economic power and by increased linkages with China through expanded two-way travel and growing use of the Chinese language in business communications.[30]

At the same time, the greater freedom of expression resulting from political democratization, along with the disproportionate representation of Sino-Thais in urban consuming populations and in intellectual and artistic communities, has resulted in a shift toward "re-Sinification" in the blossoming Sino-Thai urban popular culture and in consumption patterns that are being diffused throughout the country by the media and market forces. Possible resentment among indigenous Thais may be muted to the extent that they accept this new culture as "Thai" rather than as "Chinese" — that is, to the extent that Sino-Thai culture, as propagated by Sino-Thai-controlled media and consumer outlets, succeeds in "taking over" or "absorbing" indigenous Thai culture.

[29]Hewison and Thongyou, "The New Generation."

[30]Chan, KB and Tong, CK (1993). Rethinking Assimilation and Ethnicity: The Chinese in Thailand. *International Migration Review*, 27(1) (Spring 1993), pp. 140–68.

INDONESIA

In Indonesia, a nation of great indigenous ethnic diversity, the Chinese constitute a small minority, less than 4 percent of the population. They have not intermarried with indigenous Indonesians to a significant degree, largely because of their reluctance to convert to Islam. They are characterized by more diverse patterns of cultural assimilation, and they are scattered throughout Indonesia's vast archipelago rather than concentrated in a single primate city like Bangkok, as the Sino-Thais are.[31]

Partly as a consequence of these special characteristics, the ethnic Chinese business community in Indonesia has had to develop closer ties with the military regime that has ruled the country since 1966. These personalistic ties have served to protect the Chinese from potential harassment as a distinctive, nonindigenous ethnic minority identified with commercial monopoly power at many levels of the economy. They have also provided the Indonesian ruling regime with a degree of control over the private sector, which, because it is Chinese dominated, does not pose a political threat to the military's rule in the way an independent indigenous, or *pribumi*, business class might. The Indonesian state has thus been able to use the Chinese business community to effect certain state developmental goals and has benefited from patronage opportunities created by the dependence of Chinese business on its protection.

An oft-cited example is the case of the Salim group, whose rise to business prominence began with the ascent to power of General Suharto in 1966. Salim's founder, Liem Sioe Long, an immigrant from China's Fujian province, established a relationship with Suharto when he was still a provincial general that paid off handsomely when Suharto became president. Capitalizing on this relationship and the related ability to secure licenses and subsidies and generally "get things through" the labyrinthine Indonesian bureaucracy responsible for overseeing the highly regulated economy, Salim grew by forming alliances with foreign industrial and commercial enterprises. From them it obtained the technology and market expertise, connections, and information that it has used to become, reportedly, the world's largest Chinese-owned conglomerate, accounting for an estimated 8 percent of the Indonesian GDP.

In return, Salim has entered into various strategic sectors of the economy, such as steel, that the Indonesian government wished to see developed, and

[31]Leo Suryadinata, *Pribumi Indonesians, the Chinese Minority and China* (Singapore: Heinemann Asia, 1992, 3d ed.), provides an excellent overview of the situation of ethnic Chinese in Indonesia.

it has assisted or participated in the business ventures of various of President Suharto's children.[32] It is not the only Chinese-Indonesian conglomerate that has established such a pattern of mutual reciprocity in relations with both the ruling regime and the first family of Indonesia. The government's *pribumi* policy, which is supposed to favor indigenous Indonesian businesses over "alien" Chinese and foreign enterprises, often reduces to Chinese businesses taking *pribumi* partners from ruling elite circles, in part to ensure the political and bureaucratic influence often necessary to operate successfully in Indonesia's complex business environment.

Chinese business in Indonesia has done extremely well for itself under the Suharto regime, owing both to its privileged access to sectoral business opportunities and to the growth generated by the regime's economic policies. Economic reforms in the 1980s gave Chinese business growth a further disproportionate boost, resulting in murmurings of dissatisfaction among indigenous opposition groups and intellectuals. Continued perceptions of unequal benefit from the fruits of economic growth and liberalization could pose a threat to further economic reforms. To forestall this, Suharto held a much-publicized "summit" meeting with the nation's biggest Chinese tycoons in May 1991, at which he exhorted them to distribute equity in their enterprises to indigenous cooperatives — to date, apparently with little effect.

Since then, new controversies have added to growing indigenous and foreign criticisms of Chinese-Indonesian business practices.[33] Expanding economic linkages with China are the major precipitating force in this

[32]For an account of the Salim family enterprises, see Adam Schwartz, "Empire of the Son" and related articles, *Far Eastern Economic Review*, March 14, 1991, pp. 46–50, 52–53. For more general analyses of Chinese business and politics in Indonesia, see Andrew McIntyre, *Business and Politics in Indonesia* (Sydney: Allen & Unwin for the Asian Studies Association of Australia, 1990); and Richard Robison, "Industrialization and the Economic and Political Development of Capital: The Case of Indonesia," in McVey, ed., *Southeast Asian Capitalists*, pp. 65–88.

[33]Foreign criticisms of Chinese-Indonesian business practices come from two main sources: (1) non-Chinese, particularly Western, multinationals, which, like indigenous Indonesian entrepreneurs, find it difficult to compete with Chinese enterprises in the supposedly "newly open" Indonesian market because they lack their established personal connections; and (2) international donor agencies, particularly the World Bank, which are concerned that the market-oriented reforms they propose and help to engineer are being subverted by monopolistic private-sector practices that reduce competition, discourage foreign investment, and undermine political support for continued reforms. International donors, however, were not in favor of Suharto's May 1991 equity-distribution proposal because they felt it interfered with the market mechanism and went against the grain of the economic reforms up to that time.

regard. Chinese-Indonesian conglomerates have been criticized for "capital flight" because of their reportedly massive investments in China, especially in infrastructure, which Indonesia also desperately needs. In 1993, one company was criticized for importing PRC construction workers for a power plant, when creating employment was a major public policy concern and many Indonesians needed wage jobs.[34] So far, the Indonesian government has defended the right of its Chinese citizens to invest abroad freely, insisting that the benefits from such investments will come back to Indonesia because "we can make them come back" — an allusion, no doubt, to the control it still wields over the politically dependent and vulnerable Chinese business community.

It has not helped that the most prominent Indonesian businessmen investing in China are *totok* Chinese, the less-assimilated recent immigrants whose command of the Indonesian language is imperfect and who are suspected of having stronger sentimental ties to their home provinces in China than to Indonesia. It is precisely in these parts of China that their foreign investments are concentrated. Observed increases in the expression of Chinese culture, use of the Chinese language, lavish celebrations of Chinese New Year, and so on by some in this group have also heightened doubts about their "loyalty." The behavior of the *totok* big business conglomerates even causes apprehension among the more assimilated *peranakan* Chinese, including those in business, who fear that, being smaller-scale, less politically protected, and more confined to the Indonesian home economy, they are the ones who will bear the brunt of any violent anti-Chinese backlash.

At the same time — in contrast to Thailand, where Sino-Thais are officially accepted as being fully Thai nationals — the Indonesian government itself does not always accept even *peranakan* Chinese, whose ancestors have lived in Indonesia for generations, as full Indonesians. Separate treatment of them continues in many spheres, including insistence on the preservation of Chinese names for official recording purposes. This adds to the insecurity the Chinese feel, driving them to seek protection from influential indigenous political leaders and to diversify their economic assets abroad.

Eventual political democratization in Indonesia — which has yet to proceed very far — poses a potential threat to the Chinese business

[34]The company, which was eventually forced to repatriate the Chinese workers, claimed in mitigation that they possessed skills that were absent in the native Indonesian work force. This in turn led to the charge that the company should provide training to Indonesians rather than rely on a foreign work force.

community there. Because their very small numbers are widely dispersed throughout Indonesia, the Chinese would have no electoral voice in a democratic political system, in contrast to the disproportionate influence they have in the current regime. Democracy would also be likely to reduce public tolerance for "corruption" or for the patronage networks that have been developed between the Chinese and members of the current indigenous ruling regime.[35] By reducing the power of the military, democracy would also undermine the political protection it has long afforded to the Chinese community. The close alliance of some of the largest Chinese business conglomerates with the authoritarian, military-backed regime — specifically with the Suharto family's politically favored and increasingly extensive and monopolistic business interests — makes the situation of both parties potentially highly insecure when Suharto's tenure as president ends and there is an eventual transition to democracy.[36]

For the moment, two factors are likely to hold back any major outbreak of anti-Chinese sentiment or policy in Indonesia. The first is the continued trickle-down effect from Indonesia's rapid economic growth, to which the Chinese business community and the Suharto regime have positively contributed. The second is the probability that Indonesia's movement toward democracy will be slow. The government crackdown against an increasingly contentious press in 1994 is evidence of this.[37] Other factors that could contribute to the staving off of ethnic tension include de-monopolization of the Indonesian private sector through further economic reforms and greater sensitivity on the part of the Chinese business community to indigenous concerns about its activities at home and abroad. It is likely that what the Chinese do as businessmen — that is, whether they adhere to corrupt business practices or exploit their workers — is much more important than what they do as Chinese. Ariel Heryanto has argued that the violent labor unrest in Medan in April 1994, which led to the destruction of Chinese commercial property and the death of a Chinese businessman (and which, significantly, drew an official protest from China), reflected anti-employer

[35]A case in point is the public uproar over unsecured bad loans made by a state bank to Chinese businessman Eddie Tansil, who was subsequently sentenced to seventeen years in jail as a result of the 1994 Bapindo scandal.

[36]Paul Jacob, "Anti-Chinese Moves Targeted at Indonesian Leadership" and "Chinese Indonesians Reaffirm National Identity," *The Sunday Times* (Singapore), June 26, 1994.

[37]A potentially significant development here is the establishment by Bob Hasan, a Chinese timber tycoon with close links to the Suharto regime, of a new magazine following the closure of several pro-democracy journals. It may signal an attempt to control the media through private ownership rather than through public censorship.

class conflict rather than anti-Chinese ethnic conflict.[38] Ethnic Chinese leaders themselves reportedly met after this incident:

> They agreed that there was a need to ensure greater adherence to labour requirements, including prompt payment of wages, overtime and other work benefits... giving greater attention to workers' welfare. Greater attention would also be paid to their obligations to society through community development projects and the like.[39]

A week later, anti-Chinese pamphlets circulated in several major Indonesian cities.

PHILIPPINES

"Pure" ethnic Chinese account for less than 2 percent of the Philippine population, but Chinese have long intermarried with the country's "indigenous" Spanish mestizo elite, and it is estimated that about 10 percent of the population has some Chinese ancestry. As in Indonesia and Thailand, Chinese in the Philippines range in cultural identity from highly assimilated, long-domiciled Chinese mestizos to relatively recent immigrants who retain most of their original ethnic characteristics and culture. Both groups, particularly the latter, are disproportionately represented in the private business community. But unlike in the other ASEAN countries, in the Philippines they have to contend with competition from a dominant, entrenched, indigenous mestizo business class with agrarian and urban-industrial business interests. This class has traditionally relied on the Philippine state to protect it from foreign competition and occasionally to restrict domestic Chinese competition as well.

During the Marcos military government of the 1970s and early 1980s, Chinese business flourished, owing in part to the many patronage opportunities provided by the regime. Also, as Marcos sought to dismantle the rival business empires of members of the old "landed oligarchy," who posed an economic barrier and potential political threat to his ambitions and those of his "crony capitalists," the established indigenous businesses lost ground. The "apolitical" Chinese, on the other hand, were willing to work with the military regime so long as they could continue their businesses largely undisturbed. The Chinese community in general also benefited from Marcos's liberalization of immigration laws.

[38] Ariel Heryanto, "A Class Act," *Far Eastern Economic Review*, June 16, 1994, p. 30.
[39] Jacob, "Chinese Indonesians Reaffirm National Identity."

With the fall of Marcos, the Chinese transferred their support to his elected successor, Corazon Aquino, who freely acknowledged her ethnic Chinese heritage. During her administration (though more because of the opportunity for sustained growth rather than for ethnic reasons), the Philippines received a wave of domestic and foreign Chinese investment from nearby Hong Kong and Taiwan. Unlike other investors, the Chinese were not discouraged by repeated attempted military coups during the Aquino administration, seeing them merely as opportunities to acquire assets at bargain prices. Often with the assistance of external sources of capital, Chinese businesses also took advantage of new market opportunities provided by the government's economic reform policies, thereby expanding their control over the Philippine economy.[40]

The increasingly visible business dominance of the Chinese has resulted in some ethnic tensions. Filipinos were outraged at an immigration corruption scandal involving large numbers of illegal Chinese immigrants, and criticism has been voiced of Chinese-Filipino tycoons who move their capital freely between multiple domiciles in the Philippines, Taiwan, Hong Kong, and China. The anticorruption public fervor that developed after the collapse of the Marcos regime also bred resentment against the corrupt practices that had long been virtually routine in Chinese-Filipino business as a means of getting around often discriminatory government regulations. But only since the election of General Fidel Ramos as Aquino's successor in 1992 has the Chinese business community in the Philippines faced more serious problems.

Ramos's election coincided with a downturn in the Philippine economy and signaled the continued progress of democratic politics and institutions, including moves to "clean up" government. Yet there followed a spurt of violent kidnappings and murders of members of Chinese business families, which the government seemed powerless to stop. The kidnappings have been variously attributed to, among other things, local military and police groups' attempting to acquire alternate sources of income as their national political and economic power waned with democratization, and international Chinese criminal gangs' targeting the Philippines because of its laxer and more corrupt public security environment. Even if the kidnappings were not ethnically motivated, the ensuing protests from the governments of China and Taiwan threatened to increase ethnic tension by seeming to put the Chinese in the Philippines under the protection of foreign powers whose interests they might even be serving.

[40]Roberto Tiglao, "Gung-ho in Manila," *Far Eastern Economic Review*, February 15, 1990, pp. 68–71.

In late 1993, a further chill descended on the ethnic Chinese business community in the Philippines when the Ramos administration targeted its six richest tycoons for investigation for massive tax evasion.[41] This move came just six months after the six had accompanied Ramos on a state visit to China, and shortly after they had agreed to his request to form consortia to invest in infrastructural development in the Philippines. The government said its motive was merely to "promote fair competition," including the dismantling of monopolies obtained through political connections. According to this interpretation, the six tycoons were being investigated not because of their ethnicity but simply because of the sheer size of their business operations. Government investigators looking for large potential revenue gains for the overstretched government budget, according to this explanation, felt that this is where there was the greatest opportunity for a windfall.

Whatever the case, it is likely that the Chinese business community was targeted not only because of its ability to pay but also because, as part of a tiny ethnic minority under a democratic political regime, it lacked both the electoral clout and the state protection to fight back. This made the Chinese more popular, lucrative, and vulnerable targets than their rivals from the indigenous mestizo business community, who were strongly represented in Congress. It remains to be seen whether the Philippine Congress's periodic consideration of legislation to end monopoly licenses, quotas, and other such arrangements is even indirectly aimed at undermining the business empires of Chinese-Filipino tycoons, to the advantage of their now politically more powerful indigenous mestizo rivals, as some suspect it is. These rivals may seek to use the instruments of the democratic state to recover market positions lost to the Chinese over the past two decades.[42]

The kidnappings and the tax investigations contributed to a steep drop in 1993 of both domestic and foreign Chinese investment, which was already being reduced by competition for capital from China and Vietnam. But the kidnappings ended, the economy recovered and for the first time in two decades seemed poised for sustained growth, and investment from Taiwan began pouring back in, especially for the industrial conversion of the former

[41] *Asiaweek*, "A Taxing Dilemma," October 20, 1993, pp. 57–62.

[42] For example, the first target of the tax commissioners was Lucio Tan, head of the Asia Brewery company, which had aggressively and successfully challenged — including in bitter lawsuits — the long-held near-monopoly of the mestizo-controlled San Miguel company in the domestic beer market. The tax commissioner was a former employee of a company also headed by San Miguel's chairman, and Tan was a major funder of one of Ramos's opponents in the 1992 presidential campaign. See *Asiaweek*, "A Taxing Dilemma," p. 62.

U.S. naval base at Subic.[43] It now seems likely that the trickle-down from increased growth to which the Chinese contribute will serve to stifle any elite- or mass-based anti-Chinese actions in the near future.

MALAYSIA

Although ethnic Chinese also dominate private business in Malaysia, the situation there is strikingly different in several respects. First, the Chinese make up a third of the Malaysian population, and the degree of assimilation of most of them to indigenous culture and society is significantly less than it is in Thailand, Indonesia, or the Philippines. A second minority, descendants of immigrants from India, accounts for more than 10 percent of the population, leaving the indigenous Malays, many of them also of immigrant origin, with only a slight majority. Second, Malaysia has been an electoral democracy since independence in 1957, with dominant, ethnic-based political parties and without a politically powerful military. Third, the Malay-dominated government has undertaken affirmative action policies to increase the representation of ethnic Malays in the modern sector of the economy. A twenty-year New Economic Policy (NEP) established in 1971 imposed ethnic quotas for corporate equity ownership, public and private sector employment, and university admission. State enterprises were set up to develop sectors of the economy by and for Malays, and policies were enacted to create both a Malay bourgeoisie and a Malay industrial proletariat.[44]

Conventional wisdom in economic thinking posits a trade-off between growth and distribution. In the Malaysian case, this suggests that ethnic redistribution should result in some reduction of economic growth, since ethnic discrimination might be expected to reduce investment, especially by the Chinese who dominate the private sector. Also, according to economic theory, this trade-off should reduce productivity because of interferences with

[43]Lim, LYC "Economic Outlook ASEAN 1995–1996," in *Regional Outlook: Southeast Asia 1995–1996* (Singapore: Institute of Southeast Asian Studies, 1995), pp. 34–50.
[44]The NEP has been extensively studied. For a selection of references, see Donald R. Snodgrass, *Inequality and Economic Development in Malaysia* (Kuala Lumpur: Oxford University Press, 1980); Tat-Wai Tan, *Income Distribution and Determination in West Malaysia* (Kuala Lumpur: Oxford University Press, 1982); Ozay Mehmet, *Development in Malaysia* (London: Croom Helm, 1986); James Jesudason, *Ethnicity and the Economy: The State, Chinese Business and Multinationals in Malaysia* (Singapore: Oxford University Press, 1989); K. S. Jomo, *Growth and Structural Change in the Malaysian Economy* (New York: St. Martin's Press, 1990); K. S. Jomo, "Whither Malaysia's New Economic Policy?" *Pacific Affairs* 64:4 (Winter 1990–91), pp. 469–99.

market mechanisms — for example, preferential access to jobs and business opportunities is given to less-competitive groups, or the less-efficient public sector is favored over the private. Yet the record indicates that economic growth in Malaysia actually accelerated during the 1970s and 1980s, when the NEP was in force. Ethnic redistribution and poverty reduction goals were also largely met by 1990, even though some criticism of the NEP's achievements has continued because of claims that it distributed its benefits unevenly and led to a distortion of the class structure.

This apparently anomalous result may be explained in several ways. First, the NEP sought to achieve "distribution through growth" by changing the distribution of an expanding economic pie to increase the relative Malay share without diminishing the absolute shares of other ethnic groups. Second, a successful overall economic growth strategy emphasizing industrialization and export diversification more than outweighed any diminution of growth resulting from ethnic redistribution policies.

Third, specific components of the redistributional policy itself had growth-enhancing effects. Extensive public investment in infrastructure and education for the Malay community contributed to the development of physical and human capital. The policy of attracting foreign multinationals to create mass industrial employment opportunities for Malays contributed to capital inflows, technology transfers, productivity growth, and export market demand far greater than could have been generated by the mostly small-scale Chinese domestic private sector alone.

Fourth, market forces and private enterprise were allowed to provide alternative educational, employment, and entrepreneurial opportunities for the non-Malay population. Chinese unable to secure public- or private-sector wage and salary employment because of ethnic quotas could still become self-employed in entrepreneurial ventures, and small businesses were exempt from following NEP ownership and employment rules. Private schools and colleges opened up to provide higher education at affordable rates for those unable to secure desired public university places owing to ethnic quotas.

Fifth, even NEP requirements were flexibly and pragmatically enforced in order not to conflict with the prior objective of economic growth. In response to recession in the mid-1980s, for example, the government relaxed NEP ownership requirements to attract more foreign investment. The resultant influx of capital, including much from non-Malaysian Chinese, pushed economic growth to record levels, with the subsequent achievement of full employment. Upon termination of the NEP in 1990, the government substituted a New Development Policy (NDP), which pursues NEP goals in a more "flexible" manner, without explicit numerical quotas.

Thus, Malaysia's policy of ethnic redistribution has not adversely affected, and may even have promoted, economic growth. There has been no return to the ethnic violence of 1969, and the economic position of Malays has improved greatly both in absolute terms and in relation to that of the Chinese. Malay dissatisfaction with Chinese economic success has thus diminished considerably. The Chinese, too, have benefited from economic growth: their share of the modern sector of the economy has actually doubled since 1970 (from 23 percent to 46 percent of the total), because Chinese capitalists and rentiers were in the best position to take advantage of the declining share of foreign corporate stockholders and, to some extent, of the gradual privatization of state enterprises. The Malay ownership share of the corporate sector increased from 2 percent to nearly 20 percent over the same period.

Besides economic advancement, Chinese Malaysians can take satisfaction in the growing liberalization afforded to Chinese cultural expressions of ethnic identity, now that ethnic relations are more "relaxed." This is the result of three separate developments. The first is the government's move toward greater economic liberalization and its emphasis on the private sector. This move includes continuing deregulation and the promotion of a more supportive attitude toward local Chinese business, as well as official attempts to attract foreign Chinese investment. The government has even emphasized the presence of a sizable local Chinese population as an attraction for new Chinese capital. The second development is the political split in the ruling Malay party, UMNO, that occurred in the late 1980s and made it necessary for both factions to court non-Malay votes at the ballot box. The Chinese threw their electoral support largely behind the government faction, and this has been appreciated. A third development is the Malay-dominated government's enthusiasm for expanded business relations with China, which has resulted in many Malay-led official business missions to China, unprecedented government financial support for Chinese schools, and the encouragement of Chinese language learning among all ethnicities.[45]

[45]Even before the economic, political, and cultural liberalizations of the late 1980s, the Chinese had signaled some satisfaction with their position in Malaysia by the lack of large-scale capital flight or sustained emigration. The earlier 1980s outflow of Chinese professionals from Malaysia, mostly to Australia and chiefly in response to declining higher education opportunities for their children in Malaysia, has since stopped. With the excellent performance of the Malaysian economy and liberalization of the education system, many Chinese migrants to recession-ridden Canada and Australia are reportedly interested in returning to Malaysia.

Deputy Prime Minister Anwar Ibrahim, a Malay nationalist, has successfully cultivated the Chinese community, and in a highly symbolic gesture at a recent public event, he personally wrote in Chinese characters, "We are all one family."[46]

Overall, Malaysia appears to have achieved both rapid economic growth and ethnic harmony. Progressive liberalization of the private enterprise market economy, along with an electoral system in which the Chinese community's one-third share of the electorate gives it some influence over voting outcomes, has provided sufficient opportunities for Chinese economic prosperity despite distributive policies favoring Malays in education and business. The NEP's twin goals of "eliminating the identification of race with economic function" and "eradicating poverty" are close to being achieved, and strong economic growth is expected to continue.

But, as in other diverse societies (such as the United States), ethnic tensions are unlikely to disappear completely. The entrenchment of ethnicity as a dominant variable in public policy has resulted in an ethnic polarization of Malaysian society, with the various ethnic groups tending to lead ethnically separate and distinct rather than racially integrated social lives. In the process, particularistic ethnic social and cultural characteristics and behavior have been enhanced.

For the Chinese, ethnic identification has increased, and cultural assimilation may have declined — for example, with the spread of Chinese education and use of Mandarin, a development encouraged by greater economic opportunities and interaction with an external Chinese trading world. The sheer size of the ethnic Chinese community also reduces both the need and the incentive for interaction and hence integration with the majority Malay population. The increasing economic prosperity and self-sufficiency of the Malays may also feed a heightened sense of ethnic identification on their part. For some, this identification has taken a religious, Islamic form. It is conceivable, therefore, that ethnic integration could be gradually rejected by both groups as the economic necessity for it declines. The end result would be a society divided ethnically, not on horizontal (class) lines but on a vertical (purely ethnic) basis.

Yet there are forces working to counter such a division. A major one is the homogenizing influence of the "international" secularistic and materialistic culture that comes with modern industrial growth. It has an impact on lifestyles, consumption patterns, and values. Already studies have shown

---

[46]Cited in *Asiaweek*, "Wealth and Worries," August 24, 1994, pp. 38–42; see also *Asiaweek*, September 7, 1994.

that the values of Malays and Chinese are converging along occupational lines.[47] There is also evidence of increased cross-ethnic cultural sharing motivated by commercial purposes.[48] In other words, neither increasing ethnic cleavage nor a move toward greater integration is precluded, because there are countervailing forces working simultaneously in both directions.

SINGAPORE

Singapore, the only Southeast Asian country with a Chinese majority, is 75 percent Chinese. This has, on occasion, been a sensitive issue in relations with its neighbors. The Singapore economy itself still functions very much as a "middleman" in intraregional flows of commercial, industrial, and financial services as well as merchandise trade. Statistics on Singapore's trade with Indonesia remain an undisclosed "state secret," presumably because they might reveal the extent of giant Indonesia's trade dependence on its tiny neighbor. Being much richer than its neighbors, just as the Chinese community as a whole is vis-à-vis indigenous majorities in the other ASEAN countries, Singapore may be similarly vulnerable to their envy, resentment, and charges of exploitation.

This structural vulnerability is increased by Singapore's own past admiration for, and emulation of, the Israeli model of an armed-to-the-teeth small state set amid larger, potentially hostile Muslim neighbors (the "Jews in a sea of Arabs" analogy). Singapore still maintains close military and diplomatic links with Israel, despite the hostility of Malaysia and Indonesia toward that nation, a hostility echoed in the sentiments of many among Singapore's own sizable (15 percent) Malay Muslim minority. The country's relationship with Israel has occasionally even led to diplomatic friction between Singapore and its neighbors, as was the case when an Israeli prime minister paid a controversial visit to Singapore in the 1980s.

---

[47]Frederic Deyo, "Chinese Management Practices and Work Commitment in Comparative Perspective," in Lim and Gosling, *The Chinese in Southeast Asia*, vol. 1, pp. 215–65; Nik A. Rashid Ismail, "Value Systems of Malay and Chinese Managers," in Manning Nash, ed., *Economic Performance in Malaysia* (New York: Professors World Peace Academy, 1988), pp. 95–110.

[48]Examples are the sponsoring of Malay dance and cultural troupes by Chinese businesses catering to Malay customers and the proliferation of Chinese lion dance troupes whose members are non-Malays performing for remuneration at Chinese business events. See Mohd Nor Mohd Anis, "Dances for Hire: Performances for the Inauguration of Chinese Business Premises in Malaysia" (paper presented at the annual meeting of the Association for Asian Studies, New Orleans, Louisiana, April 1991); also, personal communications from Anis.

Despite, or perhaps because of, Singapore's Chinese majority, Chinese ethnic identity has been a public policy issue subject to periodic manipulation by the state to suit its changing purposes. After independence, the 1960s and 1970s saw the decline of Chinese media and educational institutions, which had been identified with left-wing politics and opposition to the mostly English-educated leadership of the ruling People's Action party (PAP).[49] This period also coincided with Western hegemony in the world economy and the dominant role of Western multinationals in Singapore itself, particularly in the manufacturing sector.

Later in the 1970s and into the 1980s, the PAP began reconstituting a state-sanctioned version of Chinese ethnicity. It centered on stamping out use of the southern Chinese dialects that were the mother tongues of most Chinese Singaporeans and the foundations for dialect-based Chinese social organizations that could be politicized. The use of Mandarin was promoted instead, for purposes that were social (to "unify the Chinese community"), cultural (to transmit "traditional values"), and economic (to facilitate trade with China). This period coincided with the rediscovery and propagation, in Western, particularly American, academic and intellectual circles, of "Confucian values" (favoring education, savings, and hard work, not to mention obedience to central state authority) as an explanation for East Asia's spectacular economic success. It also coincided with China's embrace of outward-oriented market economic reforms.

By the 1990s, official policy had reaccorded legitimacy to the use of Chinese dialects, to dialect-based names, and to "home province" affiliation. This was the product of three concurrent developments. First, the growing regional and global economic presence of Taiwan (whose native dialect is a version of Fujianese, the dominant Chinese dialect in Singapore and the rest of Southeast Asia) led to the expressed recognition that "same dialect helps business." Second, the policy was reinforced by the spectacular economic growth of southeastern coastal China and recognition of the importance of provincial links to Southeast Asian Chinese investments there — Singapore aspires to compete with Hong Kong as the middleman for these capital flows. Third, within Singapore itself, electoral opposition to the PAP apparently

[49]For example, the government closed down Southeast Asia's only Chinese-language university, the privately funded Nanyang University, and clamped down on Chinese newspapers. But the closure of Chinese and other vernacular (Malay, Tamil) schools had as much to do with economics (in an English-language-dominated modern economy) as with politics (fears that these schools would be breeding grounds for ethnically based political discontent).

shifted from the English-educated middle class to the dialect-speaking working class, which had a hard time learning two foreign languages (English and Mandarin) simultaneously, as required by the state school system. Ostensibly because speaking in dialect had helped an opposition candidate win election to parliament, Prime Minister Goh Chok Tong himself spoke in Hokkien during a 1992 by-election.

In the mid-1990s, although dialect use has declined in Singapore, it is accepted and even celebrated as one of the few things that "touches the heart" in a supermodern urban situation where most traces of the Chinese population's migrant history have been obliterated, reconfigured, or sanitized by progress. But Mandarin remains supreme in its role as transmitter of cultural values conducive to the Confucian ideal of the patriarchal family and authoritarian state. The government considers the transmission of this ideal important to counter any tendencies toward political liberalization and weakened family cohesion that Singaporeans might develop as a consequence of their current affluence, Westernized education, modern life-style, and extensive contact with the rest of the world (including newly democratic Taiwan and South Korea).

Mandarin is also an invaluable aid to Singapore's ambition to play an important role in China's economic development by extending state as well as private enterprise links with the PRC and acting as a middleman and bilingual-bicultural intermediary between China and the rest of the world, including other Southeast Asian and Western countries. China's apparently inexorable economic ascendancy and the relative economic decline of the West have even caused Lee Kuan Yew to speculate on the need for Singaporeans to adapt their established business practices (which, for example, eschew corruption) to what is acceptable and necessary in China today.

CONCLUSION

The foregoing analysis supports our a priori contention that economic growth has indeed contributed to more harmonious ethnic relations between the Chinese minority and indigenous majority populations in Southeast Asia. Without growth benefiting indigenous Southeast Asians, it is unlikely that the disproportionate economic benefit to local and foreign Chinese would be so readily accepted. The national benefits to be gained from more economic engagement with "greater China" (the PRC, Taiwan, and Hong Kong) have also enhanced the value of local Chinese business communities to their Southeast Asian home nations.

For the Chinese in Southeast Asia, even those in Chinese-dominated Singapore, ethnicity has always been historically constituted in response to social, political, and economic circumstances. But recent developments are themselves predicated on a historical base, and it appears that the commitment of most Chinese to their Southeast Asian home countries is stronger today than it has ever been. It is grounded not only in economic but also in affective, social, and cultural roots. As Lee Kuan Yew has put it (on several occasions):

> After two or three generations away from China, we have become rooted in the country of our birth.... The Chinese-Thai is a Thai, and in the end he wants Thailand to prosper so that his assets in Thailand can grow and his children's future in Thailand can be secure. So, too, Chinese-Singaporeans, Chinese-Indonesians, Chinese-Malaysians and Chinese-Filipinos. They may invest and visit China frequently, but few want to make China their homes.[50]

Yet Lee goes on to argue that ethnic Chinese should nonetheless build and maintain worldwide networks, or *guanxi*, among themselves as a valuable tool for business advancement.[51] Certainly, ethnic links can enhance intraethnic economic relations, but, as Philip Bowring has noted, they are a "two-edged sword" that, if not handled with care, could undermine interethnic relations.[52] No doubt aware of this, Chinese-Indonesian tycoons, significantly, did not attend the international gathering of Chinese entrepreneurs at which Lee spoke.

So, despite the greater commitment to their home countries noted by Lee, increased domestic tolerance and expanded external economic linkages are contributing to the re-Sinification of the Southeast Asian Chinese as they discover that enhancing their Chinese characteristics and behavior is now both possible at home and desirable, even profitable, abroad.

From the perspective of indigenous Southeast Asians, national economic growth is more than ever intertwined with, and even dependent on, the business activity of local and foreign Chinese. It is against their national economic self-interest to act in any way that might jeopardize this growth. But because the growth process itself is unequal, it could nevertheless

[50]Quoted in Hicks, G and Mackie, JAC, "A Question of Identity," *Far Eastern Economic Review*, July 14, 1994, pp. 46–51.

[51]In China, the term *guanxi* connotes a network of clientelistic relationships based on mutually beneficial exchanges, and more than a hint of what Westerners might consider corruption.

[52]Philip Bowring, "Chinese Minorities in South-East Asia Have Reason to Be Careful," *International Herald Tribune* (reprinted in the *Straits Times*, Singapore, January 30, 1993).

generate frictions that, although not ethnic in origin, might be ethnic in manifestation, as suggested by the Medan incident of anti-employer labor unrest.[53] In places where most of the employers who offer unsatisfactory working conditions happen to be Chinese, it might even be in the economic self-interest of particular indigenous worker groups, as a bargaining tactic, to contest with them on an ethnic as well as on a class basis. Similarly, where illegal Chinese migrant workers exert downward pressure on the wages and working conditions of low-skilled indigenous workers, the latter's economic self-interest might add an ethnic element to class-based conflict with the foreign workers and their mostly Chinese employers.

Whether the enhanced ethnic pride, cultural assertiveness, and pan-Chinese ethnic identification of Chinese minorities in Southeast Asia will generate or exacerbate ethnic, class, or other tension depends on the local political economy. Malaysia, for example, has the most "unassimilated" Chinese population in the region, yet an outbreak of ethnic violence is probably least likely there. Successful economic development has drawn most Malays out of poverty, Malays control the state and have made major inroads into the private sector as capitalists in their own right, the employer class includes many other foreign nationalities in addition to Chinese and Malays, wages and working conditions are rather good and improving, and there are few illegal Chinese migrant workers.

In Indonesia, the Chinese are more culturally assimilated, but their perceived economic monopoly and close association with the authoritarian regime, which is seen as favoring and protecting them while restricting the freedoms of the indigenous workers they are accused of exploiting, have already led to anti-Chinese reactions. In Thailand, acceptance of an evolving Sino-Thai cultural identity as legitimately Thai and even as representative of Thai urban cultural identity, which it dominates, may make anti-Chinese reactions unlikely, but the long-term impact of Sino-Thai capital outflows to China and illegal migrant worker inflows from China is uncertain. In the Philippines, the long-standing acceptance of culturally assimilated Chinese-Filipinos may be challenged by re-Sinification and the growing foreign, as well as local, Chinese economic presence — but this too may be counterbalanced by accelerating economic growth.

Ultimately, three major developments hold the key to the future evolution of ethnic relations involving the Chinese in Southeast Asia: the progress of market capitalism, the progress of political democracy, and the role of

[53]Heryanto, "A Class Act," p. 30.

China in the region. If continued economic liberalization entrenches market capitalism, sustaining economic growth, reducing Chinese monopoly power, raising indigenous incomes, and improving wealth and income distribution, it will help ensure interethnic peace. But market capitalism also brings attendant inequalities that could be correlated with ethnicity and thus become a threat to interethnic peace. Political democratization could reduce the political influence of the Chinese business elite and increase awareness and resentment of their corrupt business practices. Or it could, equally, increase Chinese political influence because of the importance of money and fund-raising to party politics in contemporary democracies (the United States and Japan, for example), and this in turn could limit indigenous enthusiasm for democracy. Finally, whether China emerges as a belligerent or a benign power in the political-security sphere, and whether it emerges primarily as a competitor or as a partner in the economic sphere, could influence indigenous attitudes toward the local and foreign Chinese in their midst.

In short, the current situation of the Chinese in Southeast Asia suggests that economic growth eases but does not eliminate ethnic tensions. Improvement of interethnic relations has not eliminated forces that might reverse the trend. The ultimate outcome depends on much more than economics, even though we have argued that economic influences have predominated until now. The complex and dynamic interplay of domestic and international cultural and political variables with economic ones will ultimately determine the state of interethnic relations in any particular historical situation. These will almost certainly vary both between countries in Southeast Asia and over time in the entire region in a manner that is responsive to individual, group, and state actions. This is why it is so important to keep track of the situation in each country as it develops, and to be aware that both desirable and undesirable outcomes remain possible.

Chapter 12

WHOSE 'MODEL' FAILED? IMPLICATIONS OF THE ASIAN ECONOMIC CRISIS*

LINDA Y. C. LIM

The Asian economic crisis is cause for rethinking the long-established consensus among mostly Western and Western-trained economists about the causes of the region's "miracle" economic growth and industrial development. Most recently restated in the Asian Development Bank's 1997 study *Emerging Asia: Changes and Challenges*, essentially an update of the World Bank's 1993 study *The East Asian Miracle*, this consensus interpretation among mainstream economists goes as follows:

Asian economic success is the product simply of the application of orthodox Western textbook economic principles — external "openness" to trade and foreign investment on the one hand, and domestic "good government" with small, balanced, or surplus government budgets and conservative monetary policy leading to low inflation and high savings rates, on the other. For these reasons, Asian countries typically rank relatively high on the "economic freedom" indices annually produced by think tanks such as the Fraser Institute in Canada[1] and the Heritage Foundation in Washington, D.C.[2] Of the countries currently in crisis, South Korea has been less open than the various countries of Southeast Asia, but nonetheless has subjected its firms to the discipline of the international marketplace through export manufacturing.

*This chapter first appeared in *The Washington Quartely*, Vol. 21, No. 3, 1998, pp. 25–36. Reprinted with permission.

[1]Gwartney, J, R Lawson and W Block (1996). *Economic Freedom of the World 1975–1995.* Canada: Fraser Institute.

[2]Johnson, BT, KR Holmes and M Kirkpatrick (Eds.) (1998). *1998 Index of Economic Freedom.* Washington, D.C.: Heritage Foundation and the Wall Street Journal.

But mainstream economists are not the only Western or Western-trained scholars who have sought to dissect the Asian economic miracle through the lens of their particular discipline. Political scientists and political economists have also had their play with the subject, usually concluding that the "developmental state" — focused on promoting economic development in the national interest — and statist industrial policy — government protection and subsidies targeted at developing specific "strategic" industrial sectors — have been essential to the rapid industrialization of the East Asian newly industrialized economies.[3] South Korea is the classic case, but it is harder to identify "developmental states" and successful statist industrial policy in Southeast Asia outside of Malaysia and Singapore. Rather, state development policy in Thailand, Indonesia, and the Philippines is more likely to be viewed as having been captured by crony capitalists with close personal relations with governments, thereby violating the developmental state principle of state autonomy from special interests.[4]

Notwithstanding this, and despite the contradiction between the economist and the political scientist/political economist views, the Southeast Asian countries are always included as part of the so-called Asian economic miracle or "Asian model" that has been promoted by advocates of free-market economics. These include both conservative Western think tanks like the Heritage Foundation and more liberal multilateral institutions like the World Bank and the International Monetary Fund, whose Washington consensus of liberal economic policies has been foisted on emerging economies around the world.

Although economists like these generally did not care for the industrial policies and microeconomic state interventions pursued by Asian governments, they did praise the latter's practice of conventional macroeconomic policy embracing both openness and fiscal and monetary conservatism. It is not an exaggeration to say that the Asian economies became showcases for

[3]Deyo, FC (1987). *The Political Economy of the New Asian Industrialism.* Ithaca, NY; Cornell University Press; Alice Amsden, *Asia's Next Giant: South Korea and Late Industrialization* (New York: Oxford University Press, 1989); Stephan Haggard, *Pathways from the Periphery: The Politics of Growth in Newly Industrialized Countries* (*Ithaca: Cornell University Press, 1990*); Robert Wade, *Governing the Market: Economic Theory and the Role of Government in East Asian Industrialization*(Princeton, N.J.: Princeton University Press, 1990); Karl Fields, "Strong States and Business Organization in Korea and Taiwan," in Sylvia Maxfield and Ben Ross Schneider, eds., *Business and the State in Developing Countries*, (Ithaca, N.Y.: Cornell University Press, 1997), pp. 122–151.

[4]Andrew Maclntyre, ed., *Business and Government in Industrializing Asia* (*Ithaca: Cornell University Press, 1994*); K. S. Jomo, ed. *Southeast Asia's Misunderstood Miracle* (Boulder, Colo.: Westview Press, 1997).

the success of a policy prescription that is being peddled to other newly liberalizing emerging economies in Latin America, East Central Europe, Central Asia, and Africa.

When the Philippines, Taiwan, South Korea, and Thailand became politically democratic as well in the late 1980s, this completed the picture of triumph for the Western liberal model of free-markets-with-democracy that Francis Fukuyama proclaimed ushered in *The End of History*[5] or the end of the ideological political-economic conflict between East and West that defined the Cold War. In Asia, for example, it was proclaimed that the United States "lost the Vietnam war (against communism) but won the peace," as reflected in the economic prosperity and political stability enjoyed by its capitalist allies in the region, and the subsequent embarkation of their socialist neighbors, particularly China and Vietnam, on the path of market-oriented economic reform.[6]

Culture as an element in the Asian economic miracle has largely been neglected or dismissed by both Western economists and political scientists, although the former might occasionally acknowledge that the highly entrepreneurial, economically responsive populations in the region, themselves the product of market forces, might have spurred the development of private-enterprise economies. The latter sometimes note that Confucian cultures may have lent moral authority and political legitimacy to interventionist developmental states. Western and some Asian anthropologists and sociologists, on the other hand, have identified kin and ethnic networks, or "culturally embedded network capitalisms," as locally efficient means of mobilizing capital and industrial growth in the Asian miracle economies.[7]

Culture has also played a much larger role in explaining the Asian miracle by Asian intellectuals who hail mostly from the political establishment

---

[5]Fukuyama, F (1993). *The End of History and the Last Man*. New York: The Free Press.

[6]About the only sour note in this triumph was sounded by Samuel Huntington's *Clash of Civilizations*, which warned that the cessation of the Cold War's ideological conflicts would usher in an era of mounting cultural conflict between the West on one side and the competing civilizations of Islam and Confucianism on the other. See Samuel Huntington, *The Clash of Civilizations* (New York: Simon and Schuster, 1996).

[7]Redding, SG (1990). *The Spirit of Chinese Capitalism*. Berlin: Walter de Gruyter; Hamilton, GG ed. (1991). *Business Networks and Economic Development in East and Southeast Asia*. Hong Kong: Center of Asian Studies, University of Hong Kong; Hefner, R (1998). *Market Cultures: Society and Morality in the New Asian Capitalisms*. Boulder, Colo.: Westview Press. Whitley, R (1992). *Business Systems in East Asia: Firms, Markets and Societies* (London: Sage Publications); World Bank, *The East Asian Miracle: Economic Growth and Public Policy* (New York: Oxford University Press, 1993).

in patriarchal-authoritarian and semi-authoritarian states like Singapore, Malaysia, China, and Indonesia. They argue that "Asian values" — emphasizing the primacy of order over freedom, family and community interests over individual choice, and economic progress over political expression, together with thrift, ambition and hard work — were largely responsible for the fortunate public sector policies and private sector actions that resulted in the Asian miracle.

WHOSE MODEL FAILED?

The "Asian values" school was unpopular among many Western commentators for suggesting, among other things, that capitalism and democracy need not go hand-in-hand. So it was predictable that when the Asian economic crisis hit during a period of unprecedented economic strength in the United States and economic recovery in Western Europe, opponents of the "Asian values" school were out in full swing (chiefly in the editorial pages of the *Wall Street Journal*), crowing over its assumed demise and the concomitant assumed triumph of the "American way."

The Asian miracle was particularly attacked for its reliance on industrial policy and cronyism, or relationships between big business and government, both of which contributed to moral hazard in the inefficient financial sector and the resultant over-investment in a classic asset bubble. Paul Krugman, the MIT economist who had some years earlier pronounced the Asian miracle a "myth" based on low total factor productivity growth,[8] is one of those who favor the moral hazard argument that "crony capitalism" or Asian reliance on *guanxi* (relationships) is what caused the crisis, which in this view is essentially a crisis of bad investments in both the public and private sectors.[9] This line of argument directly challenges both the praise of statist industrial policy by mostly Western political scientists and of "culturally embedded networks" favored by mostly Western anthropologists and sociologists.

There is no question that crony capitalism did play a role in the over-inflation and subsequent deflation of economic growth and asset prices in Asia. But this is far from the only or most plausible interpretation for the crisis and it is certainly not the whole story. Indeed, in the affected Asian countries and other emerging economies around the world, another interpretation is taking hold, one that is much less favorable to the liberal orthodoxy favored by Western economists. In this view, it is the Western

[8]Krugman, P (1994). The Myth of Asia's Miracle. *Foreign Affairs* 73, 62–78.
[9]Krugman, P (1998). What Happened to Asia?, Mimeo, January.

model of free-markets-with-democracy that has failed along with the collapse of its prime success stories in Asia — or a case of "the West won the Cold War, only to lose the peace."

THE PERILS OF OPENNESS

First, if openness was an essential ingredient of the Asian economic miracle, too much openness too fast was responsible for its downfall. In particular, rapid and sweeping (although not yet complete) capital market liberalization that began in the late 1980s led to a massive influx of foreign capital, especially short-term loan and equity capital, which contributed to the boom economy and over-investment bubble of the 1990s. Without this influx of foreign funds — which in some cases amounted to as much as 75 percent of the equity capital on local stock markets — domestic crony capitalism alone could not have fed a boom and bubble of such proportions. Even without crony capitalism, high growth and the expectation of continued uninterrupted high growth, fed in large part by foreign capital, might have led to excessive risk-taking and overleveraging of local businesses believing that their economies were immune from the business cycle.

High domestic growth and investment in turn contributed to ballooning current account deficits, with imports (mostly of machinery and equipment required by the flood of new investments) constantly exceeding exports by a wide margin. This was further fueled by overvalued exchange rates, the result both of more or less fixed exchange-rate regimes, established to attract foreign capital by removing currency risk, and of large inflows of capital. Open capital markets and capital-account convertibility also increased these economies' vulnerability to currency speculation that could, at the appropriate moment, trigger a sudden massive exit of foreign funds as easily as these funds had previously entered.

Financial market liberalization in Asia also occurred before there were appropriate state or collective institutions to monitor and regulate financial institutions or local expertise to manage them. The region's much-vaunted entrepreneurialism led to the establishment of a horde of new banks and finance companies — Indonesia alone had more than 200 banks — within a short span of time and with inadequate experience in money management. Even without crony capitalism, excess capacity in the financial sector and intense competition to lend and invest among these neophyte institutions would have led to a fair proportion of "bad investments." It was aggravated by the easy availability of cheap capital from abroad, in many cases pressed on local borrowers by overeager foreign lenders who should have known better, but faced intense competition among themselves and were attracted by the returns presented by higher interest rates and by rosy projections of continued rapid growth.

With or without the moral hazard presented by local crony capitalism, the resultant excess supply of capital was bound to lead to some bad investments as capital started flowing to more and more marginal projects. Unlike their local borrowers, foreign lenders and investors from Western countries and Japan possessed the requisite expertise in risk assessment and credit evaluation. But they apparently chose not to apply this knowledge, yielding instead to herd instinct[10] and, as Alan Greenspan characterized the sentiments toward the booming U.S. stockmarket, "irrational exuberance." This exuberance contributed first to the overvaluation of assets, then reversed course and with "irrational pessimism"[11] led to the current undervaluation, as the following quotes indicate.

> All banks are under certain competitive pressure. If the market is attractive, you go with the herd. Even if you have doubts, you don't stop lending.[12] — *Ernst-Mortiz Lipp, member of the board of managing directors of Dresdner Bank AG*
>
> There was a huge euphoria about Asia and Southeast Asia. It was the place to be.[13] — *Dennis Phillips*, Spokesman *for Commerzbank*
>
> All the banks would be standing in line — J.P. Morgan, Deutsche Bank, Dresdner. We were all standing in line trying to help these countries borrow money. We would all see each other at the same places. We all knew each other.[14] — *Klaus Friedrich, chief economist, Dresdner Bank* AG
>
> There are problems in Asia now because investors and bankers were overly optimistic about the Asian economies, and then they panicked,[15] — *Anonymous American banker*

Openness and the dominance of private enterprise in the Asian economies also severely limited their governments' ability to intervene to control these flows. Given domestic excess demand and external imbalance (huge

---

[10]Jeffrey, AF (1996). How Well Do Foreign Exchange Markets Function? In Mahbub ul-Haq, Kaul, I and I Grunberg (Eds.), *The Tobin Tax: Coping with Financial Volatility*, (New York: Oxford University Press, 1996), pp. 41–81.

[11]"Irrational pessimism" is how Japanese finance ministry official Eisuke Sakakibara's characterized sentiment toward the depressed Japanese stockmarket.

[12]Chanda, N (1998). Rebuilding Asia. *Far Eastern Economic Review*, February 12, pp. 46–50.

[13]O'Brien, T (1998). Covering Asia With Cash, Banks Poured Money Into Region Despite Warning Signs. *New York Times*, January 28, p. Dl.

[14]Ibid.

[15]Ibid.

current account deficits), governments should have allowed their currencies to depreciate or raised taxes and interest rates and cut government spending to reduce domestic demand and correct the imbalance. But in very open economies such as these, with high import shares of GDP, currency depreciation would increase costs, including offshore loan servicing costs, and cause inflation from higher import prices, while higher domestic interest rates would be ineffective so long as businesses could resort to cheaper borrowing in accessible offshore markets — that is, they may as well have *increased* rather than reduced external borrowing.

> We could have borrowed locally, something like 14 percent per annum, or borrowed overseas, where we could get (dollar) loans for 8 percent or 9 percent. If I had borrowed locally, the analysts would be saying that we were being foolish for not taking advantage of lower rates overseas... We could have bought insurance, but that would only be adding to the cost. Our government, our bankers, economists, even foreigners were telling us that the baht was stable... We never imagined that the baht would be devalued.[16] —*Chumpol Nalamlieng, CEO of Siam Cement, a blue-chip Thai company on their $4.2 billion dollar debt*

At the same time, public sectors were small and mostly in balance, and governments had little control over overborrowing in the private sector. This reduced the effectiveness of raising taxes and cutting expenditures as is typically required, for example, in IMF programs in countries that have large fiscal deficits and loose money policies. In short, the dominance of private enterprise reduced the influence that governments had over the macroeconomy.

THE PERILS OF DEMOCRACY

The nascent democracies that since the late 1980s had taken hold in Korea, Thailand, and the Philippines also caused a loss of government control over the macroeconomy. Whereas previous authoritarian regimes could impose higher interest and taxation costs on local business communities almost at will, and had done so to maintain currency stability for decades prior, this became difficult with the increased political influence of businesses over elected legislatures whose members were either business persons themselves, or required business support to get elected.

---

[16] Shameen, A (1997). Biting the Bullet: Siam Cement Tackles its Debts. *Asiaweek*, October 24, p. 62.

As *Wall Street Journal* reporter George Melloan commented on the American political process,

> Practicing politics costs money, and all politicians, unless they are fabulously wealthy, depend on campaign contributions. The more generous donors usually would like a favor or two. Quid pro quo, dating back at least to the steps of the Roman Forum, is alive and well in the U.S., as in most other corners of the world.[17]

Thailand's short-lived coalition governments (five in six years), frequent general elections, and extensive vote-buying ($1.1 billion in the November 1996 general election alone) made it particularly vulnerable to vested interest opposition to the fiscal and monetary contraction necessary to correct an external imbalance — as suggested by the parade of four finance ministers and three central bank governors in the year before the July 2, 1997, devaluation of the baht. Democracy has also contributed to the expansion of crony capitalism, as exemplified by the favoring of businesses with ruling political party connections in Malaysia's joint public-private sector infrastructure projects, who naturally would oppose both interest rate increases and cuts in public expenditures from which they benefit.

By contrast, Hong Kong — which does not have an elected government — and Singapore — which has a single-party-dominated parliament — have done relatively well through the economic crisis. Like the authoritarian governments of the past in Korea and Thailand, both administrations maintain strong central economic control and can impose economic hardship on their populations or take politically unpopular measures when necessary for economic stabilization. Thus the Singapore government cooled off the domestic property market when it was still booming in 1996, and the Hong Kong authorities were able to ignore domestic business leaders' complaints about the currency peg hurting their businesses and were able to raise local interest rates to beat back an attack by currency speculators in 1997. In the terminology of political scientists, both states have an autonomy from business interests that their newly democratic neighbors do not have.

IN DEFENSE OF THE WESTERN MODEL

Proponents of the Western liberal model do not, of course, see things this way. Instead, they assert that open markets and democracy have worked and that instead it is the "Asian" parts of the Asian economic model that have

[17]Melloan, G (1998). Influence Peddlers Have a Growing Global Clientele. *Wall Street Journal*, February 17, p. A23.

failed — particularly statist industrial policy in Korea (beloved though it is of some Western political scientists); crony capitalism in Thailand, Malaysia, and Indonesia (a reflection of both statist industrial policy and culturally embedded networks); and political mismanagement everywhere — from the virtual absence of government in Thailand, to persistent authoritarianism in Indonesia, and an idiosyncratic strong leader in Malaysia. They further argue that the excessive lending and investment by domestic and foreign financial institutions resulted from information gaps caused by inadequate local government regulation, monitoring, and disclosure requirements, not from mistakes made by financial markets. They believe that financial restructuring along Western lines and the takeover of troubled local financial institutions by more experienced and expert foreign counterparts would increase efficiency in the channeling of local savings to investments, reduce the risk of bad investments, and forestall a recurrence of the present crisis.

The IMF occupies a peculiar position in the Western economic policy canon. On the one hand, the multilateral agency is seen and has operated as an instrument of Western policy orthodoxy that advocates free trade and capital flows together with fiscal austerity and monetary conservatism. The IMF typically requires policy deregulation and liberal economic reforms, including financial sector liberalization and restructuring, in exchange for low- interest emergency loans of foreign exchange for client countries facing balance of payments difficulties and inability to meet their external liabilities. At the same time, it is recognized that the availability of IMF "bailouts" creates another moral hazard problem, by encouraging governments and private borrowers, lenders and investors to take excessive risks in emerging markets, secure in the knowledge that their risk is minimized by the likelihood of an IMF rescue should things go really bad. The result is periodic overinvestment and overlending bubbles such as characterized Mexico in 1994 and Southeast Asia and Korea in 1997.

THE ASIAN RESPONSE

For Asians, disillusionment with market openness has set in. At worst, they see themselves as the victims of a massive conspiracy of Western governments, the IMF, financial markets, and industrial corporations to first deliberately inflate and then deflate the asset values of Asian banks and corporations, and then to subsequently take control of them at post-crisis fire sale prices under forced liberalization by the IMF.[18] At best, Asians

[18]I have analyzed and dismissed such "conspiracy theory" in Linda Lim, "Economic Crisis and Conspiracy Theory in Asia" (mimeo, February 1998).

view the current crisis as a case of massive market failure, particularly on the part of globally unregulated foreign financial market actors who, despite their greater expertise and global experience, still indulge in excess lending and investment to Asian markets and so cannot be trusted to better manage the local financial institutions that they may take over.

One of Thailand's most respected economists, Ammar Siamwalla, former president of the Thailand Development Research Institute, has been very critical of his own government's errors that led to the crisis, but still expresses extreme doubts about the policy of financial liberalization.

> The currency market is really crazy... we are receiving all the punishment because we have opened our currency markets to the forces of globalization (which) in retrospect has been far too rapid.[19]

> Others share his views:
> The West has pushed us to open our markets, but what are we getting in return? Through globalization we have created a monster.[20] — *Park Yung Chul, President of Korea Institute of Finance*

Already, China and Vietnam have postponed capital market liberalization that would expose their currencies to speculation, and there have been calls for regional and global cooperation in the monitoring and possibly regulation of international capital flows. This idea was first raised by Malaysian prime minister Mahathir and supported by his nemesis, currency trader George Soros, who has said:

> Financial markets are inherently unstable, and international financial markets are especially so. International capital movements are notorious for their boom-bust pattern...The recent turmoil in Asian markets raises difficult questions about currency pegs, asset bubbles, inadequate banking supervision, and the lack of financial information which cannot be ignored. Markets cannot be left to correct their own mistakes, because they are likely to overreact and to behave in an indiscriminate fashion.[21]

Today, even the World Bank has lent its support to some forms of capital controls for small open economies that can be severely disrupted by massive inflows and outflows of foreign capital. There is a growing consensus that, at

---

[19] Scherer, P (1998). Distrust of Western Economics Grows in Thailand Amid Crisis. *Wall Street Journal*, p. A14.

[20] Bremmer, B and P Engardio (1998). What to Do about Asia. *Business Week*, January 26, pp. 26–30.

[21] Soros, G (1998). Toward a Global Open Society. *Atlantic Monthly*, January, pp. 20–24.

a minimum, some international monitoring and perhaps risk-insuring agency is necessary to oversee these currently largely unregulated flows.

At the same time, some Asians may also lose their enthusiasm for the chaos, corruption, and weak and unstable government that political democracy has ushered in to different degrees, in countries like Korea, Thailand, and the Philippines, which contributed to the crisis both by weakening government macroeconomic control in some cases and by increasing financial markets' perception and punishment of political risk in these countries.

CONCLUSION

Clearly, both the Western economists' and Western political scientists' competing open and statist models have, in some sense, failed with the crisis in their showcase economies in Asia. On the one hand, market openness without the requisite institutional infrastructure and expertise — including political infrastructure and managerial expertise — to manage it can be a recipe for economic disaster. Even the normal workings of global financial markets themselves can be disruptive to small open economies. On the other hand, statist industrial policy can lead to crony capitalism, excess capacity, over-leverage, and bad investments (as can Western sociologists' "culturally embedded networks" of ethnic business relationships or *guanxi*). Both openness and statism have contributed not only to the Asian miracle, but also to the Asian meltdown.

What about "Asian values"? At first glance, the indictment of openness and democracy in the crisis, and the evident need for more state-led institution building, state monitoring if not control of private sector financial transactions, and state autonomy from private interests in the political sphere, might seem to be a confirmation of the wisdom of the Asian values school. Too much freedom too fast in both markets and politics can lead to downfall, suggesting a continued need for a strong, benevolent, central state authority.

But at the same time, Asian government involvement in industrial policy and Asian cultural networks may also be indicted for fostering the crony capitalism that led to overinvestment in bad projects—ranging from Indonesia's Timor "national car" project[22] (of President Suharto's son), to Malaysia's privatization of huge public infrastructure projects favoring

[22]This project gave special tariff privileges to a new car company started by Tommy Suharto in a joint venture with Kia Motors of Korea, enabling their product, the Timor, to be sold on the local market for a price far below that of established competitors (mainly Japanese) and aspiring new entrants (from U.S. and European carmakers).

politically well-connected businesses and individuals, and the overextension of credit by overseas Chinese-owned banks to overseas Chinese industrial conglomerates with the presumed security of "relationships" substituting for modern risk assessment. The fact that the authoritarian regime and Indonesia's policy errors have compounded both the economic crisis and its adverse social and political consequences also undermines the belief of some Asian values advocates that authoritarianism might be superior to democracy in economic policy management. The Indonesian case contrasts vividly with the market confidence inspired, at time of writing, by the policy statements and actions of newly elected President Kim Dae Jung of Korea.

In short, the Asian economic crisis does not provide unqualified support for *either* the Western open-markets-and-democracy model *or* the Asian strong-government-and-cultural-values model. Both need some adjustment for global and national capitalisms to work smoothly. Certainly, the paths to capital market liberalization and democracy should be carefully planned, and perhaps staged to occur only in line with the concomitant development of supportive state and civil institutions. At the same time, governments need to resist the pressures of would-be crony capitalists to interfere with their fiscal, monetary, and regulatory autonomy, while private sector business networks need to be adjusted to adequately account for risk and to reduce purely rent-seeking behavior.

The Asian crisis does expose the futility of applying simplistic and essentially ideological models to the messy practical business of public and private sector economic management in developing countries whose political, economic, and business systems are not only diverse and complexly intertwined, but also still evolving. Far from yet another presaging of the end of history — in this case the presumed triumph of "Western" over "Asian" models — the crisis suggests that it is time to *return* to history, that is, to each country's particular configuration of economic, political, social, and cultural forces, to discern both the complex, multifaceted causes of the crisis and its eventual solutions. This is a task too important to allow to be jeopardized by those who would approach it only through the limited lenses of partial, monocausal theories and models of one or the other cultural-ideological predilection.

Chapter 13

SOUTHEAST ASIAN CHINESE BUSINESS: PAST SUCCESS, RECENT CRISIS AND FUTURE EVOLUTION*

LINDA Y.C. LIM

University of Michigan

Much has been written about the so-called "Overseas Chinese" — ethnic Chinese communities long domiciled outside the Chinese mainland — including their dominance of private business sectors in Southeast Asia. This essay will not attempt a comprehensive review of the voluminous literature in this area, but instead will draw selectively on the more recent literature to outline the stereotypical features of local Chinese enterprise in Southeast Asia alone (i.e. not including Hong Kong, Taiwan or lands further afield), to highlight the causes of its past success and recent crisis experience, and the likely prospects for its future evolution.

THE REGIONAL CONTEXT: HISTORY AND POLITICS

Southeast Asia is a region "made by trade", and Chinese traders have been a fixture of its numerous cosmopolitan trading ports for centuries. But migrants from the south-eastern coastal provinces of China came to Southeast Asia in large numbers only during the era of colonization by western powers, primarily in the late nineteenth and early twentieth centuries. The expanding colonial economy — specialized in primary commodity exports to world markets, and superimposed on self-sufficient and subsistence-oriented indigenous peasant economies — created a strong demand for immigrant (mostly Chinese, some Indian) wage labor in plantations and mines, and provided opportunities for migrant entrepreneurs (Chinese, Indian and others) in commerce and services as intermediaries and services providers, and as competitors, for western enterprises. While "push" factors in the deteriorating Chinese mainland economy also contributed to the out-migration, like all migrants the Chinese were to some extent self-selected

*This chapter first appeared in *Journal of Asian Business*, Vol. 16, No. 1, 2000, pp. 1–14. Reprinted with permission.

(or in some cases, selected by sponsors) for ambition, energy and risk-taking propensity. Many had urban or semi-urban origins, and a few had prior commercial experience and access to capital in China.

"Minority middlemen" were already common both within the region's indigenous societies and its external trading communities; Chinese immigrants were only the most recent and, given the large population and market base provided by immigrant Chinese wage-labor, most numerous of these. Their success was predicated on a number of favorable factors. First, indigenous populations arguably had a cultural preference for trading with "outsiders," because of the threat to group social harmony posed by the tensions inherent in the trading relationship itself (bargaining over prices, extension of credit, etc.) (e.g. Foster, 1974). The difficulty that demands by related parties for "special treatment" (e.g. more favorable prices or credit terms) pose for the trader persist to this day (Li, 1998). Second, colonial and in some cases even pre-colonial governments favored the Chinese and other ethnic minorities in "comprador" or intermediary roles such as tax-farming and commercial crop brokering — both because of the arms-length relationship they could bring to such unpopular tasks, and because it inhibited the rise of indigenous people to positions of greater prosperity and power which could pose a future political threat to the ruling authority. Alien minorities like the Chinese lacked demographic clout and so were politically vulnerable and more likely to do the bidding of ruling authorities rather than to challenge or compete with them. This practice of favoring Chinese business at the expense of indigenous business (Brown, 1994) continued into the post-colonial period (Griffin, 1998).

But local governments not only favored Chinese businesses, they also discriminated against them, particularly in the post-colonial period when nationalist governments took office and embarked on policies of economic indigenism (Golay *et al.*, 1969). Such discrimination may have had the perverse effect of enhancing rather than reducing Chinese competitiveness:

> Lack of access to political power has contributed to the development of strategies to gain political protection and patronage.... Limitations on access to government sources of credit have resulted in increased solidarity and efficiency in marshaling credit within the Chinese community, or increased use of foreign capital resulting in beneficial foreign linkages. Restrictions on entry to many forms of salaried modern employment have slowed the normal progression of the third generation into secure professions, bureaucratic positions and other salaried employment, serving instead to keep the Chinese in the rough-and-tumble world of competitive business. Restrictions on the kinds of businesses Chinese are allowed to

> undertake... has tended to make them more efficient and competitive in the business niches where they are permitted to compete, and more innovative in subverting the restrictions on their activities... limiting Chinese access to higher education has induced them to increase their investment in human capital by sending their children abroad for quality education, thereby acquiring a further edge in new knowledge, skills, technology and foreign contacts... government restrictions... have encouraged the Chinese to become even more risk-taking, innovative and entrepreneurial in developing new activities not yet or not as easily subject to restriction. (Gosling, 1991, p. 7)

CULTURE AND COMPETITIVENESS: VALUES, FAMILY AND NETWORKS

Beyond migrant origins, minority status, and government favor or discrimination, Chinese business in Southeast Asia has drawn many resources from its own cultural heritage and social organization. Unlike traditional Southeast Asian societies, where there are negative attitudes toward trade, at least within the same community, and despite the formal Confucian denigration of merchant activity, trade or business was a preferred occupation in overseas Chinese communities. This probably resulted from: the lesser stigma attached to trade in southern Chinese origin communities, which had historically engaged in international trade even when it was forbidden by the imperial regime in the north; the value of accumulation in Chinese culture, and trade as a very efficient method of accumulating wealth in a relatively liquid form, including for return to and reinvestment in the "mother country"; and exclusion of Chinese from land-owning and hence from agriculture in many host locations in Southeast Asia, making commerce the only viable channel for upward economic mobility. Associated with this "inclination toward trade" is the high value attached to entrepreneurship, or "being your own boss" — which is essential for economic survival and family advancement in this regional context.

The family is also a key competitive asset for Chinese business. The Chinese family is patriarchal and hierarchical, with power centralized in the father or parents who have the authority to command members of the family, including extended family, to pool their labor and capital (savings), and to allocate these resources for collective security and benefit, for example through the use of unpaid family labor and reinvestment of earnings in the jointly-held family business. In contrast, the Southeast Asian family characterized by bilateral descent and strong horizontal (same-generation) rather than vertical (multi-generational) family relationships can make it difficult to concentrate family resources to expand the family business (Hefner, 1998), particularly within a traditional village context of resource abundance where distribution rather than accumulation is the route to power. The allocation of scarce labor, capital, management and entrepreneurial resources is internalized within the Chinese family and its decision dynamics, with the goal of maximizing long-term wealth accumulation for the group as a whole. Centralization of decision-making power in the patriarch or the family holding company facilitates quick decision-making and implementation, as well as flexibility and risk-taking, since corporate governance or consultation with minority shareholder representatives is not an issue.

Besides the family, Chinese business is embedded in dense ethnic social networks which provide the "social capital" that help enhance its competitiveness and profitability in underdeveloped market environments which lack established market institutions to provide information, allocate resources, assess and insure against risk. Chinese belong to a wide range of formal organizations and informal networks — from dialect-group, surname, home-village and professional associations to religious, cultural, educational and philanthropic groups — which can fulfill these functions. Constant interaction provides channels of communication for accessing and assessing information and business opportunities, obtaining capital and credit, and employing trustworthy skilled labor. Social networks also help to reduce risk and guarantee the security of one's investments, by providing social as well as economic sanctions for "dishonorable" behavior which will diminish one's personal reputation and social status as well as "creditworthiness" (ability to raise capital) in business. For overseas Chinese, the social capital provided by ethnic networks may cross national borders, providing links which can facilitate international expansion (Lim, 1996).

Finally, colonial history, minority status and political vulnerability require that Southeast Asian Chinese develop multi-cultural traits and capabilities, or what anthropologists have called "situational ethnicity" in navigating their diverse business environments, which require dealing with indigenous populations, governments and political patrons who are themselves ethnically, linguistically, culturally and religiously heterogeneous, with other Chinese also of different dialect-groups and from different countries, and with foreign partners. customers and suppliers. In its middleman function, Chinese business must serve as both cultural and economic intermediary, and thus acquires multi-cultural skills and trans-national connections which provide additional valuable resources for business success.

Figure 1 summarizes the factors which have led to the past business success of Southeast Asian Chinese, while Figure 2 illustrates the relationship

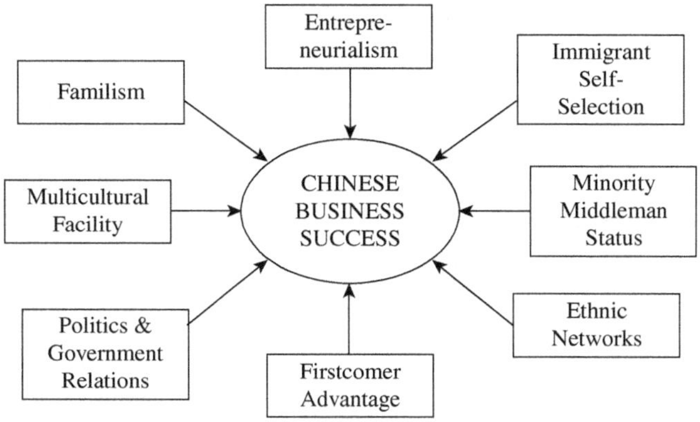

Figure 1. Sources of Chinese Business Success

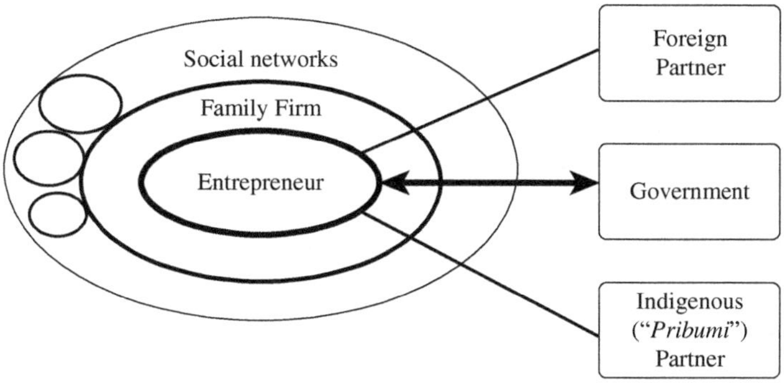

Figure 2. External Relationships and Social Networks

of the Chinese enterprise to local governments, foreign and indigenous partners on the one hand, and with the Chinese family and ethnic social networks on the other. The entrepreneur in Figure 2 leverages his core asset, a government relationship, to access technology, capital and marketing expertise from foreign partners, and also forms relationships with indigenous partners, in part for political "cover" and "ethnic disguise." The family firm provides the entrepreneur with capital, labor and managerial resources, while ethnic social networks provide access to more capital, labor, information, customers, suppliers and business opportunities more generally.

ENTERPRISE ECONOMICS: CONGLOMERATE DIVERSIFICATION AND VERTICAL INTEGRATION

In Southeast Asia, as in other developing economies, imperfect markets (e.g. for capital, labor and information), underdeveloped market institutions (e.g. a legal infrastructure supporting property rights and contract), periodic political uncertainty if not unrest, and substantial government intervention in the economy, result in high information costs, transaction costs, and risks for businesses. Chinese social networks and the personalistic patron-client relationships that individual Chinese businesses develop with governments and indigenous business partners to secure their enterprises and avoid or evade discriminatory restraints, help to reduce these costs and risks, giving them a competitive advantage (Gomez and Jomo, 1997; Robison, 1997; Unger, 1998; Gomez, 1999). But because patron-client linkages are unevenly distributed (or they would have little value), in each country the privileged access they procure for those who possess them is concentrated in a handful of favored firms.

Together with first-comer advantages, small markets and scarce resources, privileged government relationships have contributed to the development and market dominance of large diversified conglomerates in Southeast Asia. Fisman (1999), for example, found that political connections enhanced firm value on the Jakarta Stock Exchange. Strong government ties become a competitive asset for the local firm, which is then sought-after as a joint-venture partner or supplier/distributor by foreign companies possessing capital, technology and market assets (e.g., brand name) but in need of local (land or labor) resources, market knowledge and distribution channels — all of which are facilitated by government connections. Firms which possess valuable connections then leverage this core asset to seize new business opportunities and enter new markets by partnering with foreign or other local companies possessing the requisite technology arid expertise. Diversification thus provides a welcome outlet for growth, especially where initial business segments quickly become saturated due to small market size. Monopoly rents earned by the domination of protected or otherwise restricted markets provide capital for such horizontal diversification. Governments which provide the privileged market access to their "cronies" may also demand that they expend some of their rents on developing new industries and sectors seen as essential for national economic development, but lacking in national comparative or competitive advantage. An example would be the expansion of the Salim group in Indonesia into steel-making, at the behest of the Suharto regime. Conservation of scarce resources like capital, managerial and technical expertise also make it efficient to share such resources over a diverse family of jointly-held enterprises. Horizontal diversification further provides an outlet for perhaps culturally-induced entrepreneurial instincts, by allowing individual family members and long-term professional managers to start or run separate businesses of their own, drawing upon the capital-raising abilities, facilities and contacts of the parent business — for example, through cross-guarantees of new loans, cross-subsidized affiliate investments, and the sharing of overhead costs. And diversification may reduce the risk that one line of business or another might at some time be closed off to Chinese participation for strategic national reasons, such as the promotion of state-owned or indigenous private enterprise, as has happened in the past to rural crop brokers in many countries.

Underdeveloped markets also provide the incentive for vertical integration, which enables the internalization of many market functions within the firm, increasing its efficiency and competitiveness, and enhancing market power in buying from suppliers and selling to customers. Often it is vertical integration which provides the rents that are invested in horizontal diversification, as in the case of Thailand's Charoen Pokphand group (Australian Department of Foreign Affairs, 1995), whose domination of the value chain in chicken production enabled it to diversify into telecommunications ventures. Both horizontal diversification and vertical integration are not peculiar to Chinese firms only, but have also been entered into by indigenous private enterprises with government connections, such as the Suharto family enterprises in Indonesia, and Renong and other conglomerates led by politically-connected Malay as well as Chinese tycoons in Malaysia.

Figure 3 presents a schematic of a Chinese family-owned conglomerate whose organizational structure — a core firm or family holding company owning many diverse subsidiaries and allocating resources among them paralleling the structure of the extended family, with family members and

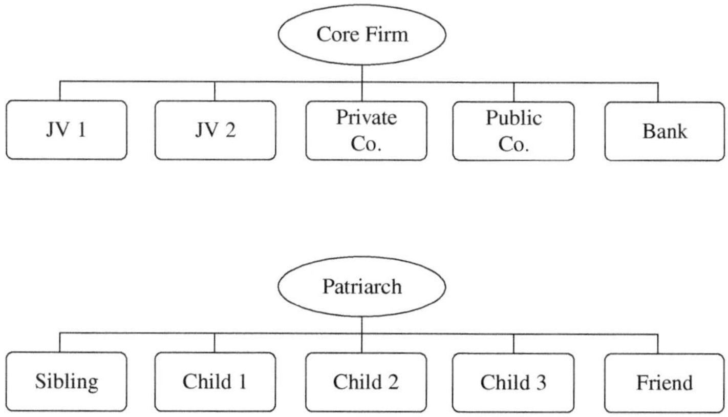

Figure 3. Family-Owned Conglomerate

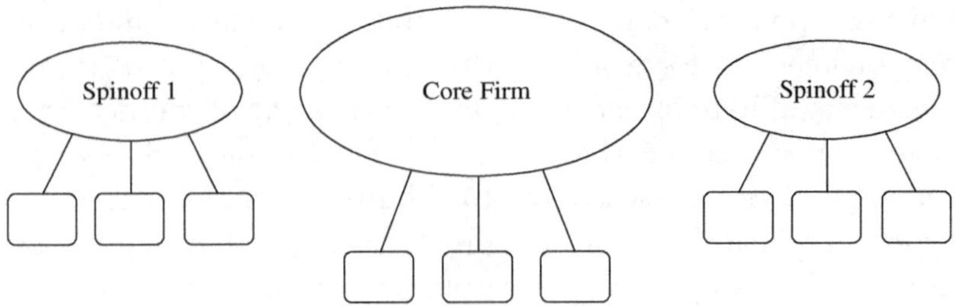

Figure 4. Related Entrepreneurial Spinoffs

close associates managing the different affiliates, illustrating the ease of exchanging resources and information among the affiliates, some of which are joint ventures with different foreign partners, in different industries or sectors. A family-owned bank and a publicly-listed affiliate provide access to more external capital, which can be internally leveraged to grow privately-held companies within the group.

It is also typical for Chinese conglomerates to spawn spin-offs of related and even competitive firms that are led by former employees, whose ventures may well be set up with initial assistance from the original employer — in terms of loans, loan guarantees and even guaranteed orders from the firm itself or its other customers. The belief that good managers will ultimately depart to set up their own businesses results in what can be interpreted as a preemptive move to keep them "within the family" while operating on their own. The trend of conglomeration then raises the possibility that eventual expansion and diversification of the "spun-off" enterprise might generate future profitable partnering possibilities with the original "core" firm, in new or different sectors. Such spin-offs, though they may immediately reduce the size of the original firm's business, in the long run will contribute to its growth in more directions than can be handled internally. Figure 4 illustrates spin-offs which generate their own conglomerate structure and potential partners for affiliates of the "core" firm.

SOUTHEAST ASIAN CHINESE BUSINESS AND REGIONAL ECONOMIC GROWTH

The structure and operations of Southeast Asian Chinese family firms are clearly geared toward growth and the maximization of both business opportunity for individual family members and of family assets for future generations. This results in the constant reinvestment of profits into growing and diversifying the original enterprise, based on the ability to raise funds both internally and from ethnic social networks and foreign and state partners, even in the absence of developed capital markets. Though the reasons are primarily demographic and macro-economic, Chinese family businesses have contributed to the high savings and investment rates which propelled Southeast Asian growth over the past two to three decades. Their growth-oriented, entrepreneurial and risk-taking nature, government relationships, conglomerate structure and openness to foreign business partners, arguably made them highly responsive to economy-wide developments, as the rapid state- and market-led growth and diversification of Southeast Asian economies provided many opportunities for enterprise growth and diversification which would not have been available in slower-growing national economies or exploitable by firms without these resources. Cross-border ethnic Chinese networks also increased bilateral international trade within Southeast Asia (Rauch and Trindade, 1999) and facilitated international investment by overseas Chinese (Lim, 1998a), further stimulating regional growth and integration. At the same time, excessive monopolistic rent-seeking by Chinese firms with privileged government connections was held in check by relatively open trade and investment regimes which introduced external competition and foreign partners into domestic production and markets, and by the inability of this entrepreneurial minority to distort domestic economic policy in its self-interest, i.e., by relative state autonomy in macro-economic and industrial policy and the existence of ethnic competition which helped to reduce rents (Lim, 2000).

SOUTHEAST ASIAN CHINESE BUSINESS AND THE FINANCIAL CRISIS

But the operations of Southeast Asian Chinese business which contributed to the region's rapid economic growth also played a role in contributing to the excessive borrowing and over-investment which contributed to the regional financial crisis of 1997–99. The widespread practice of related-party lending contributed to the build-up of excessive leverage and domestic asset-bubbles, and bad loans and investments due to a neglect of risk management. Common bank and corporate practices included: loans from banks to corporate affiliates, and between corporate affiliates, within a family-owned conglomerate; affiliate cross-guarantees and cross-subsidization; deployment of the same group-held collateral for multiple loans; the siphoning of capital from publicly-listed units to privately-held ones within a family-owned group; and extension of credit based on "trust" and individuals' "creditworthiness" alone. Corporate governance and accounting transparency were weak or non-existent, and over-reliance on government privilege and patronage networks created a "moral hazard" problem which fed excess borrowing and lending, including by international banks (Lim, 1998b). The very practices which contributed to rapid growth when macro-economic fundamentals were strong led to financial collapse when they weakened, creating excess capacity in the industrial and property sectors along the way.

Financial crisis was not, however, necessary for corporate collapse. The collapse of Thailand's previously high-flying Alphatec Electronics preceded the collapse of the Thai baht by at least a year, as did the earlier collapse of the Bangkok Bank of Commerce.

> The stark absence of corporate controls at Alphatec — the mingling of funds among listed and closely held companies run by the same family, the use of multiple sets of accounting books and misleading accounting methods, the highly paid, rubber-stamp board — mirrors the problems at other Thai companies that have brought this country's economy to the brink of collapse (Waldman and Sherer, 1997).

Earlier notable examples include the mid-1980s collapse of Pan-Electric, the business empire of Malaysia's leading Chinese politician of the time, Tan Koon Swan, which was so inter-woven with other companies that the authorities closed the Malaysia and Singapore stock exchanges for three days. In the early 1990s, the Indonesian Chinese Soedradjaya family lost their publicly-listed but majority family- owned company Astra, otherwise a model of good professional management, because the family's holdings had been mortgaged to support the eldest son's wish to establish a bank, which was over-extended and subsequently collapsed. Backman (1999) provides other examples.

Individual cases aside, recent World Bank research on the Asian corporate sector suggests that family and bank relationships "provide insurance against likelihood of bankruptcy during bad times" (Claessens, Djankov and Klapper, 1999, p. 17), while close family control of publicly-listed companies results in "expropriation of minority shareholders by controlling shareholders" (Claessens, Djankov, Fan and Lang, 1998, p. 21). Ownership and control are most highly concentrated in Southeast Asia (Claessens, Djankov and Lang, 1998), where most publicly-listed companies are held by overseas Chinese families. Ownership concentration in the Thai corporate sector was associated with lower profitability and higher leverage in the period just prior to the financial crisis, and the researchers suggest that risk-preference and growth aspirations led unprofitable companies with concentrated ownership and links to the banking system to borrow heavily to finance their losses (Alba, Claessens and Djankov, 1998).

Not all Southeast Asian Chinese companies suffered during the financial crisis. Those which weathered it well tended to be focused rather than diversified, concentrated in resource-based export-oriented sectors whose competitiveness increased with currency devaluation, and with low debt burdens. These characteristics suggest that they are not reliant on political connections — which are necessary largely to access protected domestic markets — and do not have favored access to bank funds, both of which tend to lead to diversification.

THE FUTURE EVOLUTION OF SOUTHEAST ASIAN CHINESE BUSINESS

Even before the financial crisis, Southeast Asian Chinese businesses faced many changes which should accelerate in the aftermath of the crisis. The limitations of family sources of capital, labor and management as their enterprises grew in size and complexity had already led to increased reliance on external sources of capital — through public listings and international loans with unaffiliated financial institutions, which played a role in the soaring stock-market valuations and large debt burdens which financed over-expansion and increased vulnerability to the crisis. Now, more outside capital is required to fund debt repayment and corporate restructuring, and the crisis experience will make these unrelated lenders and investors demand more transparency, accountability and attention to risk management and shareholder value, than was typical of traditional Chinese family businesses. This need to satisfy external partners and markets will also increase reliance on professional managers, and reduce the influence of family members in the enterprise.

With institutional development, and further market liberalization, including foreign investment liberalization following the crisis, traditional ethnic social networks on the one hand, and personalistic patron-client linkages with governments and politicians, on the other, should become a less important source of competitive advantage for Chinese business. Not only did network linkages play a role in exacerbating the effects of the crisis on firms — for example, through the extension of unsecured loans and guarantees to network-related enterprises and individuals — but banks and firms within the networks themselves have also been weakened by the crisis, requiring a search for new, unrelated sources of capital and credit. At the same time, greater disclosure and corporate governance requirements, and new accounting standards, may make some network relationships unworkable. Political patronage will be diminished both by post-crisis economic deregulation reducing the importance of the state as a source of subsidies and protected market access (monopoly licenses, permits, etc.), and by political democratization, including a free press, especially in Indonesia, where "KKN"— "corruption, collusion, nepotism" — will no longer be so readily tolerated.

The shift in leadership of Chinese family-owned businesses from their founder-patriarchs to a new generation should also introduce changes.

> Younger members of Chinese family firms often have less emotional attachments to the family's traditional businesses; have a better grasp of new technology and how it can be used; are better at dealing with non-Chinese partners; are willing to loosen family control so the company can expand; manage business more openly and fairly, making their firms more acceptable to investors (Gilley, 2000, 44 box).

Rapid developments in technology — particularly the rise of e-commerce and internet businesses which will transform traditional businesses, reduce entry barriers and monopoly rents, and introduce more competition and new business entrants — should accelerate this transformation of Southeast Asian Chinese business.

But this transformation will by no means be rapid, or total. With macro-economic recovery, weak government implementation of bankruptcy laws and restructuring procedures, and even government support to rescue troubled but politically well-connected firms, regional businesses have been able to resist asset sales to outsiders. There have been few bankruptcies or foreign takeovers of local companies, and the state, far from withering away, has become a large owner of domestic assets in state asset management companies — the disposition of which may not be entirely transparent or competitive. Politically, Chinese business has actually become more powerful — in Malaysia, where its support was crucial in the electoral victory of the weakened UMNO ruling party, in Indonesia, where the recently elected government is friendly to Chinese interests and includes Chinese cabinet ministers and economic advisers, and in Thailand, where Sino-Thai businessman still dominate the ranks of parliamentarians. Even the new internet businesses tend to be dominated by large conglomerates which still have readier access to financial resources, and need to both defend their traditional businesses and carve out new sources of growth in the world of e-commerce.

Two examples will serve to illustrate the opposing trends in the post-crisis evolution of Southeast Asian Chinese business. In the first, Alphatec Electronics of Thailand was forced into bankruptcy under the country's new bankruptcy laws, despite the attempt of its "new generation" Sino-Thai founder, Charn Uswachoke, to forestall them from his seat in parliament. Alphatec became the subject of the country's first court-supervised restructuring plan, eventually being bought by two foreign investor groups from the U.S. and Sweden, who installed new foreign management and will presumably turn the semiconductor exporter into a "world-class" company devoid of its previous "Chinese" characteristics.

In the second case, the Soedradjayas, the ethnic Chinese former owners of Indonesia's Astra, teamed up with two American investor groups to bid for the Indonesian Bank Restructuring Agency's large share of the company. But they were thwarted by the *pribumi* (native Indonesian) CEO who had restructured the company's huge external debt, reportedly because she was supported by Suharto-era and Muslim political interests who wanted to see the company end up in *pribumi* hands. The Indonesian President Wahid, a decades-long close associate of the Soedradjayas (who had never been in the Suharto camp, and were believed to have suffered for it when they lost their company in the early 1990s), apparently concurred with IBRA's decision to fire the CEO, replacing her with her predecessor, a cousin of the Soedradjayas. There will be renewed bidding for the conglomerate — whose main asset is its majority share of the protected domestic automobile market — with additional foreign and local bidders and, presumably, an investigation into its accounts which the fired ex-CEO had refused to reveal, (McCawley and Hammond, 2000, Murphy, 2000a, 2000b). While the outcome is uncertain at the time of writing, it indicates the possible durability of the model sketched in Figure 2 above.

These two examples may be extremes, in that Alphatec represents a complete transformation from "very Chinese" to "not Chinese at all" in its ownership and operations, whereas Astra began as a very professionally run company with extensive non-Chinese involvement (external investors and foreign joint venture partners) but may now be re-taken by the original Chinese founding family. More representative examples may be the Charoen Pokphand (Biers and Vatikiotis, 1999) and Kanajanapas (Gilley, 1999) family empires in Thailand, where the crisis has led to some restructuring, including some asset sales, re-focusing on core businesses and reduction of related lending and cross-holding among affiliates and extended networks, but without changing the essential conglomerate structure and family ownership and management — which is now moving to a younger generation. In the Philippines, large Chinese conglomerates appear to be still dependent on protected markets and government linkages (Paras, 1999), while Malaysia's particular response to the crisis has required few changes of those Chinese businesses with the "right" connections (Gomez, 1999).

Both the Alphatec and Astra models indicate an underlying continuity in the structure and operations of Southeast Asian Chinese business — its inevitable integration into multinationals' global supply chains and market networks (Alphatec contract manufactures semiconductors for Texas Instruments, Compaq and others while Astra essentially assembles Toyota and other Japanese auto makes), and its need to partner with foreign capital, technology and management (both companies) because of a lack of any firm-specific "core competence" in technology, manufacturing or marketing. Whether Southeast Asian Chinese businesses will survive as independent entities in the long run will depend on their continued ability to be multi-cultural managers of and for others, providing sufficient value that multinationals will continue to see partnerships with them as necessary assets. But the more developed the Southeast Asian economies become, the less value that this intermediary function will have, as shown in Daimler-Chrysler's recent effort to reduce the role of its long-term Singapore distributor, Cycle and Carriage, while still searching for local partners in other, less-developed Asian countries. In the long run, Southeast Asian Chinese companies will need to develop firm-specific competitive advantages that extend beyond their location-specific market knowledge, network assets and political connections to survive and prosper in the increasingly globally-integrated regional economy.

REFERENCES

Alba, P, S Claessens and S Djankov (1998). "Thailand's Corporate Financing and Governance Structures: Impact on Firms' Competitiveness" Paper presented at the Conference on Thailand's Dynamic Economic Recovery and Competitiveness, UNCC, Bangkok, May 20–21.

Australian Department of Foreign Affairs and Trade (1995). *Overseas Chinese Business Networks in Asia*, Commonwealth of Australia: East Asian Analytical Unit.

Backman, M (1999). *Asian Eclipse: Exposing the Dark Side of Business in Asia.* Singapore: John Wiley & Sons (Asia)

Biers, D and M Vatikiotis (1999). "Back to School", *Far Eastern Economic Review.* 8 April: 10–14.

Brown, RA (1994). *Capital and Entrepreneurship in Southeast Asia.* London: Macmillan.

Claessens, S, S Djankov and LHP Lang (1998). "Who Controls East Asian Corporations?" Working Paper, The World Bank.

Claessens, S, S Djankov, JPH Fan and LHP Lang (1998). "Expropriation of Minority Shareholders: Evidence from East Asia." Working Paper, The World Bank.

Claessens, S, S Djankov and L Klapper (1999). "Resolution of Corporate Distress: Evidence from East Asia's Financial Crisis," Working Paper, The World Bank.

Fisman, R (1999). "It's Not *What* You Know... Estimating the Value of Political Connections", manuscript, mimeo, The World Bank.

Foster, B (1974). "Ethnicity and Commerce," *American Ethnologist*, I (3): 437–448.

Gilley, B (1999). "Crawling Back," *Far Eastern Economic Review* 21 October: 56–60.

———, (2000). "Pulling Away," *Far Eastern Economic Review*. 20 February: 42–45.

Golay, F *et al.* (1969). *Underdevelopment and Economic Nationalism in Southeast Asia*. Ithaca: Cornell University Press.

Gomez, ET (1999). *Chinese Business in Malaysia: Accumulation, Accommodation and Ascendance*, UK: Curzon Press.

Gomez, ET and KS Jomo (1997). *Malaysia's Political Economy: Politics, Patronage and Profits*, Cambridge: Cambridge University Press.

Gosling, LAP (1991). "The Chinese 'Edge' in Business in Southeast Asia," paper presented at the panel on Chinese Business in Southeast Asia: The Changing Dynamics of Dominance, Part I, 43rd Annual Meeting of the Association for Asian Studies, New Orleans, manuscript.

Griffin, PJ (1998). "Reconsidering the Role of Tollgates and Tax Farms in the Indonesian Economy: The Rise of the Chinese Entrepreneur and the Decline of the *Pribumi* Entrepreneur," M.A. thesis. Center for South and Southeast Asian Studies, University of Michigan, manuscript.

Hefner, RW (ed.) (1998). *Market Cultures: Society and Morality in the New Asian Capitalisms*, Boulder, Colorado: Westview Press.

Li, TM (1998). "Constituting Capitalist Culture: The Singapore Malay Problem and Entrepreneurship Reconsidered," in Hefner, ed., *Market Cultures: Society and Morality in the New Asian Capitalisms*, Boulder, Colorado: Westview Press: 147–152.

Lim, LYC (1996). "Social Capital and Foreign Direct Investment by Newly-Industrializing Countries: A Perspective from Southeast Asia," paper presented at the NBER Workshop in Social Capital in Developing Countries, Stanford, California, March 1996, manuscript.

———, (1998a). "Relations: Trade and Investment between Southeast Asia and Greater China, 1980s and 1990s," in Lynn Pan, ed., *The Encyclopedia of the Chinese Overseas*, Singapore: Chinese Heritage Center: 110–112.

———, (1998b). "Whose 'Model' Failed? Implications of the Asian Economic Crisis," *The Washington Quarterly* XXI (3):25–36.

———, (2000). "Southeast Asia," in Eleanor Westney, ed., *The Future of Asian Business Systems*, Unpublished manuscript.

McCawley, T and A Hammond (2000). "The Revenge of Cronyism," *Asiaweek* 18 February: 58.

Murphy, D (2000a). "Stalled Deal," *Far Eastern Economic Review*, 10 February: 10–13.

———, (2000b). "New Clout," *Far Eastern Economic Review*, 17 February: 57.

Paras, W (1999). "Growing Pains," *Asiaweek* 19 February.

Rauch, JE and V Trindade (1999). "Ethnic Chinese Networks in International Trade," Working Paper 7189, National Bureau of Economic Research, Cambridge, Massachusetts.

Robison, R (1997). "Politics and Markets in Indonesia's Post-Oil Era," in Rodan, Hewison and Robison, eds., *The Political Economy of South-East Asia: An Introduction*. Melbourne: Oxford University Press.

Unger, D (1998). *Building Social Capital in Thailand: Fibers, Finance and Infrastructure*. Cambridge, UK: Cambridge University Press.

Waldman, P and PM Sherer (1997). "High-Tech Trauma: A Company's Travails Show Why Economy in Thailand is Shot," *Wall Street Journal*, 8 Sept.: Al.

Chapter 14

SOUTHEAST ASIAN CHINESE BUSINESS AND REGIONAL ECONOMIC DEVELOPMENT*

LINDA Y.C. LIM

Ethnic Chinese minorities in Southeast Asian countries have attracted most of the scholarly and popular attention on the Chinese diaspora worldwide. This is due to their large absolute and relative numbers in this region, and to their observed disproportionate role in the economies of which they are nationals, particularly as owners of private sector businesses. Most of the literature in the economic realm has concentrated on the reasons for the business dominance of ethnic Chinese minorities.

My own, hardly unique, work has explored the specific roles of ethnicity (Lim and Gosling, 1983) and minority status (Lim and Gosling, 1997) in explaining this dominance. I, like many others, attribute this to a combination of location-specific market knowledge, family culture, network assets and political connections (Lim, 2000), added to the migrant and "middleman minority" characteristics found among other ethnic populations and in other geographical locations, such as Jews in Europe and Indians in East Africa and the Caribbean. With other scholars (e.g. Mackie, 1995), I also attribute the significance of these ethnic Chinese competitive advantages to market imperfections at transitional stages of development in Southeast Asia's emerging economies, expecting such "Chineseness" to diminish in importance as modernization and corporatization of the private business sector proceed with economic development (Lim, 1996). Others see the "success" of Chinese business in the region deriving primarily from macroeconomic and structural developments in their host economies, without ethnic characteristics being particularly salient (e.g. Go, 1996; Lee, 2002), while yet others reasonably caution against the dangers of generalization and

*This chapter first appeared in Handbook of Chinese Diaspora, Chee-Beng Tan, (ed.), 2013, pp. 249–260. Reprinted with Permission from Routledge London.

cultural reification given the historical and contemporaneous diversity of the Southeast Asian Chinese business experience (e.g. Chan and Ng, 2002), and its ongoing contextual evolution (e.g. Yeung, 2007). Some scholars even argue that traditional cultural explanations for Chinese business success are neither unique to them nor necessarily beneficial in economic impact (e.g. Hodder, 1996). However, more recently, some scholars have explored the contribution of "Chineseness" to specific management practices in Asian business (e.g. *Asia-Pacific Business Review*, 2005; *Journal of Asian Business* 2006/7), suggesting that cultural relevance may persist even in advanced modem economies.

This chapter has a different focus. Rather than revisiting the influence of (in this case, diasporic) ethnic Chinese characteristics on business structure, organization and practice in Southeast Asia, it discusses the role and impact of ethnic Chinese business on national and regional economic development in the region, which has been somewhat less considered (Mackie, 2000).

COLONIALISM AND INDEPENDENCE

Historically, Chinese minorities occupied particular niches in the colonial and early post-colonial economies of Southeast Asia. Their activities were propelled by typical migrant motivations and organizational networks, and circumscribed by discriminatory local and colonial regulations which both excluded them from land ownership and hence agriculture, and favored them as tax-farmers and rural crop-brokers (e.g. Cribb, 2000). Ethnic Chinese merchants and laborers thus helped to develop the commodity export sectors of Southeast Asia, as middlemen, traders, bankers and processors of agricultural commodities, linking indigenous peasant economies to world markets, usually in *comprador* (agent) relationships with Western colonial trading houses (e.g. Khanh, 1996). They also served as manual labor and small business owners in mining, construction and other sectors of the colonial economy.

Chinese immigrants thus contributed to the increase in productivity and output growth of Southeast Asian economies under Western colonization in the nineteenth and twentieth centuries. But in so doing they were also part of a pattern of colonial exploitation of the region's natural resources and associated ethnic division of labor which arguably disadvantaged segments of the indigenous population even as GDP and exports expanded and average incomes rose. This happened with the diversion of arable land and labor from subsistence to export cultivation (especially in Indonesia with the introduction of sugar into Java's peasant rice economy), the depression of local wages with the increase in foreign labor supply (especially in colonial Malaya with the massive import of migrant labor from China and India for mines and plantations respectively), the "crowding out" of potential local entrepreneurs by immigrant competitors in the small business sector, and the outflow of profits earned in colonial enterprises to their "mother countries," and remittance of savings to their homelands by diasporic communities.

At the same time, the colonized economies of Southeast Asia did benefit from colonial public and ethnic Chinese private investments in infrastructure (e.g. transportation, utilities) and human capital (e.g. schools, hospitals), and the development of institutions and relationships which increased productivity and facilitated the global market integration that benefited the region's economic growth in the post-colonial period. New migrant inflow and remittance outflow ceased with Japanese occupation during the Second World War, national independence after the war, and the 1949 communist takeover of China which cut that country's links with the outside world, including Southeast Asia, thus eliminating these sources of potential negative impact on host populations.

The post-war emergence of independent nation-states contributed to rooting the Chinese, their investments and enterprise, in their respective countries of domicile, but also subjected them in some places to various forms of ethnic discrimination, including in access to citizenship rights and property ownership, and through restrictions imposed on their previous dominance of trading activities, as happened in Indonesia and the Philippines (Golay *et al.*, 1969). A nationalist backlash against colonialism and those seen as its agents and beneficiaries was complicated by the suspected or actual sympathizing of ethnic Chinese Southeast Asians with the state communism ascendant in China, especially as all countries in the region battled their own internal communist insurgencies. This resulted in further discriminatory restrictions up to and including forced relocation and even repatriation to China.

Anti-Chinese economic policies in the early post-colonial period led to disruptions in internal commerce and external trade which naturally retarded economic growth, particularly in Indonesia, where they were aggravated by the nationalization of Western enterprises as well (Golay *et al.*, 1969). To sustain their livelihoods in the face of ethnic ownership and employment restrictions, Chinese merchants developed so-called "Ali-Baba" relationships with indigenous "sleeping partners" who provided legal "fronts" for their continued trading activities, and "patron-client" relations with government bureaucrats and politicians on whom they were reliant for various licenses and regulatory permissions. This arguably led to the subsequent entrenchment of "crony capitalism," corruption and rent-seeking in the region's economies (e.g. Backman, 1999).

IMPORT SUBSTITUTION AND EXPORT MANUFACTURING

When national development policies turned to import substitution, the import–export business which colonial and Chinese enterprises dominated was undermined. Foreign multinationals which then established local manufacturing for tariff-protected markets often sought or were required to have local joint-venture partners. Chinese-owned businesses were frequently the only candidates with the requisite capital, expertise and connections, including access to ethnic distribution networks by virtue of their previous trading activities, such as acting as agents for the same foreign multinationals. This perpetuation of a *comprador* role with foreign (including Japanese) capital contributed to the rise of what Yoshihara (1988, 1995) has called "ersatz" capitalism in Southeast Asia — or the failure of (mostly ethnic Chinese) Southeast Asian businesses to develop into the globally competitive "national" enterprises which emerged from Japan, Taiwan, South Korea and (to a lesser extent) Hong Kong over the same historical period.

Relying on connections which delivered quasi-monopolistic rents in protected market segments contributed to the evolution in Southeast Asia of conglomerates rather than companies focused on core competences in technology, production or marketing, which did emerge in Northeast Asia (including as the focused business units of larger conglomerates, especially in Korea). This inhibited the development of robust national capitalisms that could drive economic growth, which in Southeast Asia remained heavily dependent on foreign multinationals and indigenous state-owned or government-linked corporations, in part because of nationalist-indigenist fears that domestic private enterprise would end up dominated by ethnic Chinese (who nonetheless, and in response, developed close linkages with foreign and state corporations).

As with import substitution, the development of labor-intensive export manufacturing in the region from the late 1960s was driven mainly by multinationals and other foreign enterprises, including foreign ethnic Chinese from Taiwan and Hong Kong. There were some exceptions, most notably in Thailand (Doner and Ramsay, 1997). Some Southeast Asian Chinese businesses became part of integrated East Asian global manufacturing supply chains, e.g. in garments, textiles, footwear, toys, electronics, computer and telecommunications equipment, while others diversified into rapidly expanding services sectors, finance, construction, properties, infrastructure, tourism and retail, and yet others remained grounded in agribusiness but in higher-value-added operations (such as fruits, vegetables, chicken and seafood), still mostly oriented to global markets. The farnily-owned conglomerate continued to be the typical Southeast Asian Chinese business, with government and external connections becoming more important over time, and regional trade, investment and financial liberalization from the 1980s propelling some cross-border ventures, including into China.

THE ASIAN FINANCIAL CRISIS AND ITS AFTERMATH

The Asian financial crisis of 1997–9 was a setback to Southeast Asia's economic growth. Southeast Asian Chinese business arguably contributed to the build-up of domestic asset bubbles pre-crisis through excessive borrowing and over-investment enabled by the widespread practice of related-party lending between mostly Chinese-owned banks, conglomerates and their many affiliates, as well as the "crony capitalism" resulting from Chinese reliance on government privileges and patronage networks. The crisis then led to the collapse or shrinkage of many Chinese businesses and networks, with the most dramatic example being that of the Salim Group of Indonesia, closely linked with then-President Suharto.

But other than as a consequence of dominating local private sectors, Chinese businesses were not alone or disproportionate in either contributing to or suffering from the crisis. Its causes were largely macroeconomic and regulatory, affecting most regional businesses regardless of ethnicity or nationality, and South Korean financial institutions and conglomerates as well. Except for Indonesia, the other crisis-hit regional economies recovered rapidly, with the assistance of currency depreciation, IMF emergency funds (except for Malaysia, which chose temporary capital controls instead), and a mix of fiscal and monetary policies. Some countries also initially received large amounts of foreign investment, especially in the form of multinational acquisitions of crippled local financial institutions and manufacturers such as automotive and electronics parts suppliers and the capital-intensive cement industry.

REGIONAL ECONOMIC INTEGRATION

Following recovery from the crisis, the integration of the member countries of the Association of Southeast Asian Nations (ASEAN) into global production networks and markets intensified as their export competitiveness improved. The slow-developing ASEAN Free Trade Area (AFTA) finally came into being in 2003. In addition to reductions in intra-regional trade barriers,

ASEAN programs to foster private sector linkages also served to bring Chinese-owned businesses closer together after decades of focusing on national or global markets.

However ethnicity does not appear to have played any role in the still modest number of intra-ASEAN joint ventures. If anything, Southeast Asian Chinese companies have been more likely to be competitors rather than partners, given similar firm-specific advantages and technology levels, with cross-border investments responding more to comparative advantage — as, for example, in the move of Malaysian apparel manufacturers to Cambodia as that country's apparel export industry took off, and of Malaysian oil palm plantations into Indonesia as Malaysian land and labor costs rose.

It is in the growth of trade and investment linkages with "Greater China" — the People's Republic, Taiwan and Hong Kong — that ethnicity may have played some role (e.g. Chong Carino, 1995; Chou, 1998). In the 1980s and 1990s, Taiwan factory owners relocating labor-intensive export manufacturing out of their home base used to say that "language and culture" facilitated their investments in Southeast Asia, which were encouraged by the Taiwan government's "Go South" policy as an alternative to investments in China, then still seen as a political competitor. But in fact there were some tensions between them and local Southeast Asian Chinese businesses, especially in Malaysia, because of the Taiwanese preference for transplanting their entire supply-chains based on home-country networks, rather than partnering with local Chinese, with whom they competed in both product and factor markets. There was also some resentment that Taiwan and Hong Kong manufacturers received foreign investor privileges from host governments. Many if not most Southeast Asian Chinese then also did not speak Mandarin and Hokkien (Taiwan) or Cantonese (Hong Kong), but rather their national languages, and had some concerns about the potential for ethnic tensions arising between the foreign Chinese and their culturally different and unfamiliar indigenous employees. Taiwan and Hong Kong firms also invested heavily in Vietnam which had very few local Chinese left after their post-1975 involuntary exodus. And it was not long before many of them left Southeast Asia for China itself when the latter became more open, in addition to being cheaper and closer, including in terms of "language and culture".

CHINA'S RISE

It is with the rise of China's economy, especially from the 1990s, that ethnicity in the form of linguistic and cultural similarity and networks became a factor in facilitating Southeast Asian Chinese investments in China, particularly from Singapore and Malaysia, and in labor-intensive export industries. This outward investment was intended to improve the competitiveness of Southeast Asian Chinese businesses, and give them eventual access to the anticipated large China market. But many of these companies faltered in China's unfamiliar post-communist environment, where they lacked the firm-specific advantages to compete with foreign investors from more technologically advanced economies like those of the USA, Western Europe, Japan and Korea, and the intimate cultural knowledge, local connections and even languages of native Chinese, Taiwan and Hong Kong investors. Competition and imitation from Chinese state-linked and private enterprises was intense, especially in low-end consumer goods industries such as food processing, and "It is difficult to make money in China" became a common complaint, leading to eventual disinvestment by some Southeast Asian Chinese companies. Those which prospered in the China market usually did so by leveraging firm-specific advantages they had developed at home, e.g. in industries ranging from food, tires and electronic components to hotels, retail and property development.

At the same time, China's rise created competition for Southeast Asian economies both for investment "diverted" there from home-based (mostly ethnic Chinese) companies and third-country multinationals, and in world markets where Chinese goods were often cheaper, especially in the 2000s after its currency became progressively undervalued with the depreciation of the US dollar to which it was fixed. Despite this, Southeast Asia continued to attract significant amounts of foreign direct investment, with occasional dips in particular countries owing more to domestic political developments (e.g. political instability in Thailand since 2006) than to competition from China. Southeast Asian currencies appreciated in large part because of persistent export surpluses, as well as increasing inflows of foreign portfolio capital, both before and after the global financial crisis which most adversely affected developed economies in 2007–9.

Trade liberalization between China and ASEAN — both bilateral preferential trade arrangements like the 2003 China–Thailand Free Trade Agreement in agricultural products, and the 2010 regional China–ASEAN FTA — may have hurt certain economic sectors in Southeast Asia — such as Thai farmers, and Indonesian textile manufacturers. But ethnicity has had nothing to do with this, since trade policy is decided by states at the national level. Indeed, in the case of Indonesia, objection to the China–ASEAN FTA came disproportionately from the local ethnic Chinese business community that would now face intensified competition from cheap Chinese imports. At the same time, China has become a major importer of ASEAN commodities — both natural resources and agricultural products, and the manufactures (electronics, computer parts) which account for over 60% of China–ASEAN trade, reflecting the increasing regional integration of global manufacturing supply-chains in East Asia, with Japan, Korea and Taiwan as well as ASEAN countries exporting parts to China where they are processed and re-exported to world markets. Again, these trade patterns are determined primarily by location-specific comparative and competitive advantage, with little if any role for ethnicity.

Ethnicity may be more important to China's foreign investment in Southeast Asia, which has expanded rapidly since 2000 but is still very small, at less than 5% of total inward foreign direct investment (FDI) into the region, and less than half of the ASEAN FDI flow to China. My current research on this subject shows that availability of local ethnic Chinese managers, employees, partners and agents — if they speak and are literate in Mandarin — facilitates Chinese companies' investment in the region, and in particular explains Malaysia's popularity as a regional headquarters for Chinese companies, given the large (30%) multilingual Chinese population there. For a minority of Chinese companies, the local ethnic Chinese market of consumers for Chinese foodstuffs, medications and other "ethnic" products is an attraction. But most Chinese FDI in ASEAN is non-ethnic in character — about half is invested in globalized Singapore, and there is diverse sectoral distribution, with the largest individual investments by capital invested typically being in natural resource acquisitions and partnerships with local state enterprises. Although it is difficult to evaluate relative impact, one might expect technology transfer to be less in investments by Chinese companies than investments from more technologically advanced countries. There have also been complaints that Chinese infrastructural companies especially prefer importing both low- and high-skilled labor from their China workforce, than employing and training local workers (e.g. Brown, 2009).

Most recently, rising wages and other costs in China, together with the anticipated continuing appreciation of the Chinese yuan, have led to increased interest by global investors in alternative or second-source manufacturing locations outside of China, particularly for labor-intensive export industries like garments, footwear and toys. Chinese companies are also subject to the same pressures, with Southeast Asia — especially its less-developed locations like Cambodia and Vietnam — being the logical targets, given their geographical proximity and lower cost. Relocation by Chinese companies is limited so far, and as with the previous relocation of

Taiwan and Hong Kong companies to the region, ethnicity does not appear to be a factor in location choice.

In the longer term, China's economic rise and continued development of trade and investment linkages with its neighbors will likely both expand the Chinese diaspora in Southeast Asia — as is already happening with both long- and short-term new migrants to the region, especially along the northern borders of mainland Southeast Asia, particularly in Myanmar — and involve more Southeast Asians of all ethnicities, many of whom are now learning the Chinese language as a tool for personal economic advancement. It remains to be seen if the positive growth impact from input enhancement — through new labor migration and capital investment from China — exceeds any negative impact of "crowding-out" local workers and entrepreneurs, similar in many ways to the economic impact of Chinese immigrants in the Western colonial period.

ETHNICITY AND ECONOMIC DEVELOPMENT

In describing the changing economic role of the ethnic Chinese diaspora in Southeast Asia, the foregoing discussion takes a deliberately ambivalent view about the likely developmental impact on their host economies. Definitive evaluation is impossible given the lack of data correlating ethnicity (itself subject to ambiguous definitions especially where intermarriage with non-Chinese is common, as in Buddhist mainland Southeast Asia and the Christian Philippines) with specific economic roles, and with variation by country, location, sector and historical period. As immigrants bringing additional labor, capital and entrepreneurship, the Chinese most likely enhanced output *growth*. But whether they accelerated or retarded economic *development* depends in part on how one evaluates the type of activity they were engaged in, and whether their role was complementary to or competitive with that of the majority indigenous population. For example, the ethnic division of labor which developed during the Western colonial era may have perpetuated the "specialization" of indigenous populations in lower-productivity, lower-income rural and extractive activities, delaying transition to a higher-productivity urban-industrial economy, preempting the emergence of a broader private entrepreneurial class and more sectoral diversity, and inhibiting competition. However this result would have been due not necessarily to the role of the middleman minority per se, nor to its specific ethnicity, but rather to the entire exploitative complex of a colonial plantation or extractive economy.

The political insecurity of an ethnic trading minority, especially if it were "favored" by colonial authorities, might lead in the post-colonial era to "protective" ties with national states involving the creation and distribution of monopoly rents through patronage networks (e.g. Gomez 1999), distorting the allocation of resources. Resentment against the "privileged" minority might also give rise to discriminatory policies and practices that result in inefficiency and slower growth for all. In Southeast Asia, this resulted in the post-colonial preference for state entities that would substitute for and perhaps nurture an underdeveloped indigenous entrepreneurial class, while reducing reliance on the ethnic Chinese minority (e.g. Wibisono 1995). In Indonesia, foreign multinationals were similarly discouraged, while in Malaysia they were encouraged as a means of creating urban-industrial employment and entrepreneurial opportunities for the ethnic Malay population, as part of the New Economic Policy. Even in Singapore, a Chinese-majority city-state, investment by multinationals and state enterprises was promoted as an alternative to local Chinese private business, which was seen as excessively trade-oriented and independent from if not hostile to the predominantly "English-educated" post-colonial state.

These state- and multinational-centered investment strategies, developed as responses to the peculiar economic role of ethnic Chinese minority business, may partly explain the failure of Southeast Asian countries to replicate the vigorous local capitalisms and both large and small- scale, globally competitive private enterprises that emerged in Northeast Asia (Japan, Korea and Taiwan), despite similar macroeconomic and industrial policies which contributed to rapid output and employment growth based on exporting manufactures to world markets. Northeast Asian exporters managed to develop firm-specific manufacturing, technology or marketing advantages that enabled them to maintain and increase their global competitiveness as domestic costs rose and comparative advantage shifted, as examples like Samsung in Korea and Acer in Taiwan demonstrate. But this did not happen in Southeast Asia, for reasons that might derive partly from the minority status of local ethnic Chinese entrepreneurs, including the perpetuation of relationship-based conglomerate structures, continued dependence on multinationals and state support, and actual or perceived ethnic discrimination.

In the case of Malaysia, which for four decades followed a policy of affirmative action for the indigenous Malay population in education, employment and business, economic growth has slowed especially since the Asian financial crisis, making it unlikely that the nation will achieve its goal of becoming a "developed" or "high-income" country by 2020. A major reason is ethnic discrimination, which has caused Chinese Malaysians, especially the highly educated, to emigrate in large numbers, thus depriving the economy of their human capital and financial investment, with neighboring Singapore being the main beneficiary (World Bank, 2011). As a result, the government has embarked on a "New Economic Model" that in addition to moving toward "merit-based affirmative action," envisages a shift from state investment to private-sector-led and market-driven economic growth, while welcoming "talent and skills from anywhere" (Quah, 2010). In a much more dramatic example from the region, communist Vietnam's expulsion of its ethnic Chinese minority in the 1970s contributed to a long period of slow growth which has reversed with market economic reforms, and a welcoming back of emigrant Vietnamese — including Sino-Vietnamese — capital and skills. The outflow of Chinese capital from Indonesia, following anti-Chinese riots in the wake of the Asian financial crisis and subsequent collapse of the Suharto regime, also contributed to the severity of the crisis and the delayed recovery from it.

In short, discrimination against Southeast Asian Chinese communities and business, rather than any actions or inactions of the Chinese themselves, has been partly responsible for some of the more disappointing aspects of economic development in Southeast Asia, including lower output growth, a slower move up the value-chain, and the failure to produce globally competitive national private sector businesses. (Other reasons given for the economic underperformance relative to Northeast Asia include inadequate investment in education, ethnic and religious diversity, and "predatory" rather than "developmental" states.)

PROSPECTS FOR THE FUTURE

Focusing only on internal national developments, the likelihood is that differences — including economic differences — between ethnic Chinese and non-Chinese indigenes in Southeast Asia will diminish over time, as discriminatory policies are eliminated, non-Chinese enter the private sector in larger numbers including in partnerships with Chinese businesses (e.g. Chin, 2007), and Chinese participate more in national politics and government, e.g. in now-democratic Indonesia, thus breaking down the previous ethnic division of labor.

The saga of former Thai Prime Minister Thaksin Shinawatra presents an interesting case-study. The Chinese in Thailand have always been more integrated with the indigenous population than elsewhere in the region, in part because of the ease of intermarriage and social interaction among fellow Buddhists. Thaksin, an ethnic Chinese, operated both in the "Thai" government space (the police) and the "Chinese" business space, leveraging the two to develop the telecommunications company Shin Corp. which made him Thailand's richest man. From this perch Thaksin entered national politics and was elected Prime Minister in 2001 with widespread popular support, including from Bangkok's heavily ethnic Chinese population. Subsequently, however, his monopolistic tendencies both in politics and business, capped by his tax-free sale of Shin Corp., a "national treasure," to Singapore's state-owned Temasek Corp. for $2 billion, caused him to lose the support of Bangkok-based elites as well as other groups. Ousted in a military coup in September 2006, and living as an exile overseas since then, Thaksin nevertheless retained the support of the mostly ethnic Thai rural population in Thailand's North and Northeast, who had benefited from many of his "populist" policies, while earning the ire of many of his fellow ethnic Chinese in Bangkok. The violent clashes between pro-Thaksin "Red Shirts" and anti- Thaksin "Yellow Shirts" in Bangkok in May 2010 did not have any noticeable ethnic cast, with ethnic Chinese business support found on both sides. Thaksin's political influence subsequently declined, but tensions remain mainly along "class" ("elite–mass") and geographical (rural–urban, Central/South–North/Northeast) lines. Interestingly, while some (mostly ethnic Chinese) Thaksin opponents blame him for being "too pro-China" in, for example, his government's negotiation of the Thailand–China FTA in agriculture which supposedly hurt Thai farmers, this does not appear to have dampened his support among ethnic Thai rural voters.

If this example is representative of the possibly declining salience of Chinese ethnicity in Southeast Asian business, politics and economies, the rise of China may be exerting influence in the opposite direction. China's approximately 12% share of ASEAN's trade is already as large as that of Japan and the European Union, and larger than the USA. Its FDI in ASEAN, though small relative to these other regions and to ASEAN's own FDI in China, is growing very rapidly, though thus far mostly concentrated in Singapore and in natural resources. China is already the largest foreign investor in Cambodia, Laos and Myanmar. It is the largest source of foreign tourists to ASEAN countries, sending more than five million visitors a year. Given China's size, the rapid growth of its economy (far surpassing the growth of other regions, especially developed countries), its geographical proximity to, and good relations with, Southeast Asia, these and other economic linkages are bound to expand in both absolute and relative terms. There is also a large migration of students, workers and traders from China to Southeast Asia that is largely undocumented, but possibly reaching as many as half a million in Myanmar alone.

These developments have increased the economic value of Chinese language in the region, resulting in the increased popularity of Chinese language learning among non-Chinese indigenes as well as ethnic Chinese nationals of ASEAN countries. It remains to be seen to what extent cultural assets uniquely possessed by ethnic Chinese add value beyond purely linguistic capabilities that others can also acquire through education. The possible permutations here are many and complex. Already there are cultural as well as linguistic differences within Southeast Asia among ethnic Chinese of different Chinese dialect-groups, geographic and political affiliations, and of different immigrant vintages, nationality, education, occupation and location. Cultural differences are likely to be larger between long-domiciled Southeast Asian Chinese and recent-arriving migrants and visitors from the post-communist "mainland," especially if the latter are economically competitive with the former, and benefit from favored treatment from home or host governments. Southeast Asian Chinese may fear that tensions arising from expanded linkages with China might undermine their own hard-won peaceful relations with indigenous Southeast Asians, or that they might be caught in a new wave of discriminatory treatment aimed at restricting the influence and especially the new immigration of Chinese from China. Although scholars in China tend to view the role and reception of the new Chinese migrants positively (e.g. Zhuang and Wang, 2010), there are reports of resentment over the competition they present for locals in the labor market (e.g. Brown, 2009), and other tensions (e.g. Chan, 2007).

Southeast Asian Chinese may see themselves as benefiting disproportionately from the expanded two-way trade, investment and employment opportunities provided by China's economic rise and closer integration with its ASEAN neighbors. This is most likely to be the case in Malaysia, where the "re-Sinification" of ethnic Chinese as a response to decades of perceived ethnic discrimination under Malaysia's affirmative action policies has resulted in nearly all Chinese under the age of 50 being schooled and literate in Mandarin, as well as Malay and English. This makes Chinese-Malaysians particularly attractive as linguistic interlocutors and cultural intermediaries for businesses from China operating throughout the Southeast Asian region, just as they already are for Western and other Asian multinationals operating in China, Indonesia and other countries.

Overall, China's rise should contribute positively to economic growth and the stabilizing diversification of external economic linkages in Southeast Asia, especially in an era where the region's previously dominant trade and investment partners — the West and Japan — are experiencing slower growth. The Southeast Asian Chinese diaspora may be expected to enhance this interaction and impact, rendering both more positive than they otherwise might be. At the same time, parallels with the Western colonial era are possible, with increases in aggregate output growth coinciding with an uneven distribution of the benefits of that growth to local populations, and with Southeast Asian Chinese unwittingly serving as *compradors*, this time to Chinese companies.

> One wonders if the relationship with China is not reproducing the old colonial division of labor, whereby low value-added natural resources and agricultural products were shipped to the center while Southeast Asian economies absorbed high-value manufactures from Europe and the United States. ... Despite the official propaganda, the China–Asean trade agreement that came into effect on Jan. 1 2010, is likely to disadvantage Asean.
>
> *(Bella 2010)*

If this happens, it could reintroduce the specter of retaliatory or "protective" ethnic discrimination, which I have argued above, is prejudicial to economic development.

CONCLUSION

Southeast Asian Chinese business has played an important role in the economic growth and development of countries in the region since the era of Western colonialism in the nineteenth and twentieth centuries. Often this role has been distinctive, involving specialization in specific economic niches, usually trade and finance. Almost always it has been disproportionate relative to the ethnic group's share of the local population. But it is difficult to argue that it has been definitive, in the sense of driving the growth and shaping the development of national economies, which has been mostly the result of, first, colonial, and later, national government policies, and of global market forces. While ethnic Chinese capital, labor, entrepreneurship and cross-border networks certainly aided the growth of Southeast Asia's economies, in their absence other groups would likely have stepped in, given the region's long, rich and multicultural trading history.

Historical hypothetical assumptions are problematic, but any difference Chinese ethnicity itself made to regional economic development would have had to be due to cultural characteristics or relations with China, both of which could have negative as well as positive impacts on growth. For example, Chinese family structure, culture and ethnic social networks facilitated capital accumulation, risk-taking, labor recruitment, efficient organizations and supply-chains, resulting in higher investment and growth. But the monopolistic family-controlled conglomerates they gave rise to might also have reduced competition, efficiency and equity, preventing both the emergence of indigenous non-Chinese capital, and the transformation of ethnic Chinese capital itself into the globally competitive enterprises which emerged from Japan, Taiwan, Hong Kong and South Korea over much the same historical period. Close relations with China facilitated Southeast Asian Chinese enterprises' access to outside sources of capital, labor, management and technology, as well as a large external market in more recent times. But they also "crowded out" local labor and entrepreneurs, contributing to an outflow of capital through remittances and outward FDI, and creating foreign competition for Southeast Asian export industries.

Regardless of how the positives and negatives of Chinese ethnicity for economic growth might balance out (if they could be calculated), the policy discrimination meted out to the Chinese because of their minority and immigrant status (as distinct from ethnicity per se) has hurt economic development. Discrimination has distorted resource allocation (e.g. diverted it from regulated sectors), reduced long-term investment (e.g. in manufacturing versus shorter-term trade and finance), and led to the outflow of Chinese capital and talent (e.g. emigration of highly educated Chinese). It has also encouraged or necessitated the minority practice of "crony capitalism" and even corruption, based on the need for government "protection" of their investments and for access to state-mediated business opportunities. Fortunately, discriminatory policies are being eliminated, and discriminatory treatment will also taper off in time.

The "wild card" is the rise of China as an economic partner for Southeast Asia. On the one hand, it enhances the region's growth prospects, and also increases the value of Chinese ethnicity (language, culture) in regional business and economic relations, thereby providing more opportunities for ethnic Chinese minorities in Southeast Asia. On the other hand, it may increase competition for Southeast Asia's economies, including for its minority ethnic Chinese business community, and by fostering "re-Sinification" could heighten inter-ethnic tensions leading to the re-introduction of discriminatory policies. Much depends on whether China — which, unlike the region's former colonial powers, is very large, very close by, with a very strong role for the state in its economy and international relations — is viewed by Southeast Asians of all ethnicities as an essentially benevolent power, or not, and on the relations that develop between it and non-Chinese Southeast Asians. China itself is also evolving economically, whether in a more or less ethnically determined direction it is not possible to ascertain. One might expect that continued market liberalization, capitalist development, and both inward and outward globalization would result in reduced ethnic characteristics of China's economy and its state and private businesses. But nearly 30 years ago, I concluded my study of export-oriented, multinational-linked Chinese electronics firms in "capitalist" Malaysia and Singapore with these words:

> as Chinese business enters modern industrial sectors, its traditional distinctiveness declines, as indeed it must for it to compete and survive in international markets. Pre-capitalist modes of operation which may have an ethnic character give way to strictly capitalist forms of business organization and operation in which ethnicity becomes irrelevant. Dependence on ethnically-unrelated multinational corporations and foreign agents for access to factors of production and markets causes Chinese business to become absorbed into the sphere of international capital, where the influence of ethnic and even national identity on firms' operations becomes indiscernible and inconsequential over time.
>
> *(Lim, 1983)*

As it turned out, Overseas Chinese electronics firms, mostly from Taiwan, retained many of their "Chinese" characteristics (family ownership, ethnic networks) as they globalised, obtaining ever-greater shares of manufacturing supply-chains developed with and for their (mostly Western) multinational customers. Ethnic networks and the ability to develop and utilize local government relations, and negotiate boundaries in a culturally distinctive environment, became even more of a global competitive advantage as supply-chains were transplanted to China. Whether this trend will continue as China becomes more central to the world as well as the regional economy depends on the extent to which China's adaptation to universal economic policies, global standards and business practices exceeds or falls short of the rest of the world's adaptation to China's policies and practices. In this context, Southeast Asian Chinese's cultural and business evolution, and their associated contribution to the economic development of Southeast Asia, will lag rather than lead developments in China and the world economy.

REFERENCES

Asia-Pacific Business Review (2005). Special Issue: *Multicultural Organizations in Asia*, 11(4).

Backman, M. (1999). *Asian Eclipse: Exposing the Dark Side of Business in Asia*, Chichester, UK: John Wiley and Sons.

Bello, W (2010). "The China-Asean free trade area: propaganda and reality," *Philippine Daily Inquirer*, 14 January 2010. http://services.inquirer.net/print/print.php?artide?d=20100114-247344.

Brown, PJ (2009). "China labor straining neighborly ties," *AsiaTimes Online*, 11 July 2009. http://www.atimes.com/atimes/Southeast_Asia/KG11AeOl.html.

Chan, KB and BK Ng (2000). "Myths and misperceptions of ethnic Chinese capitalism," in KB Chan (ed.) (2000). *Chinese Business Networks, State, Economy and Culture*, Singapore: Prentice-Hall for the Nordic Institute of Asian Studies.

Chan, YW (2007). "Border encounters: Chinese businesspeople in the Vietnam–China borderlands," in L Suryadinata (ed.) *Chinese Diaspora since Admiral Zheng He with Special Reference to Maritime Asia*, Singapore: Chinese Heritage Centre, Nanyang Technological University.

Chin, YW (2007). "Chinese–Bumiputera partnership in technology-based industries in post-NEP and post-NDP Malaysia," in L Suryadinata (ed.) *Chinese Diaspora since Admiral Zheng He with Special Reference to Maritime Asia*, Singapore: Chinese Heritage Centre, Nanyang Technological University.

Chong Carino, T (1995). "The ethnic Chinese, the Philippine economy and China," in L Suryadinata (ed.) *Southeast Asian Chinese and China, the Politico-Economic Dimension*, Singapore: Times Academic Press.

Chou, Y-M (1998). "The role of overseas Chinese capital in the economic integration of East Asia," in Wang Li-chi and Wang Gungwu (eds.) *The Chinese Diaspora, Selected Essays*, vol. 1, Singapore: Times Academic Press.

Cribb, R (2000). "Political structures and Chinese business connections in the Malay world: a historical perspective," in KB Chan (ed.) *Chinese Business Networks, State, Economy and Culture*, Singapore: Prentice-Hall for the Nordic Institute of Asian Studies.

Doner, RF and Ramsey, RA (1997). "Competitive clientelism and economic governance: the case of Thailand," in S Maxfield and BR Schneider (eds.) *Business and the State in Developing Countries*, Ithaca, NY: Cornell University Press.

Go, BJ (1996). *Myths about the Ethnic Chinese "Economic Miracle,"* translated by Joaquin Sy, Manila: Kaisa Para Sa Kuanlaran.

Golay, FH *et al.* (1969). *Underdevelopment and Economic Nationalism in Southeast Asia,* Ithaca, NY: Cornell University Press.

Gomez, ET (1999). *Chinese Business in Malaysia, Accumulation, Accommodation and Ascendance*, Surrey, UK: Curzon Press.

Hodder, R (1996). *Merchant Princes of the East, Cultural Delusions, Economic Success and the Overseas Chinese in Southeast Asia*, Chichester, UK: John Wiley & Sons.

Journal of Asian Business (2006/7). Special Issue: *The Power of Knowing: Studies of Chinese Business in Asia*, 22(2–3), 23(1).

Khanh, T (1993). *The Ethnic Chinese and Economic Development in Vietnam*, Singapore: Institute of Southeast Asian Studies.

Lee, KH (2002). "The emergence of modern Chinese business in Malaya: the case of the Straits Chinese and Overseas Chinese Banking Corporation," in L Suryadinata (ed.) *Ethnic Chinese in Singapore and Malaysia, A Dialogue between Tradition and Modernity*, Singapore: Times Academic Press.

Lim, LYC (1983). “Chinese business, multinationals and the state: manufacturing for export in Malaysia and Singapore,” in LYC Lim and LAP Gosling (eds.) *The Chinese in Southeast Asia*, vol. 1, *Ethnicity and Economic Activity*, Singapore: Maruzen Asia.

______ (1996). “The evolution of Southeast Asian business systems,” *Journal of Asian Business*, 12(1), 51–74.

______ (2000). “Southeast Asian Chinese business: past success, recent crisis and future evolution,” *Journal of Asian Business*, 16(1), 1–12, Special Issue on Ethnic Chinese Business in Southeast Asia.

Lim, LYC and LAP Gosling (eds.) (1983). *The Chinese in Southeast Asia*, vol. 1, *Ethnicity and Economic Activity*, Singapore: Maruzen Asia.

Lim, LYC and LAP Gosling (1997). “Strengths and weaknesses of minority status for Southeast Asian Chinese at a time of economic growth and liberalization,” in D Chirot and A Reid (eds.) *Essential Outsiders, Chinese and Jews in the Modem Transformation of Southeast Asia and Central Europe*, Seattle: University of Washington Press.

Mackie, J (1995). “Economic systems of the Southeast Asian Chinese,” in L. Suryadinata (ed.) *Southeast Asian Chinese and China, the Politico-Economic Dimension*, Singapore: Times Academic Press.

______ (2000). “The economic roles of the Southeast Asian Chinese: information gaps and research needs,” in KB Chan (ed.) *Chinese Business Networks, State, Economy and Culture*, Singapore: Prentice-Hall for the Nordic Institute of Asian Studies.

Quah, D (2010). “Malaysia’s new economic model: making choices,” *Business Times* (Malaysia), 14 April 2010. http://www.btimes.com.my/Current_News/BTIMES/articles/quah/Article.

Wibisono, C (1995). “The economic role of the Indonesian Chinese,” in L Suryadinata (ed.) *Southeast Asian Chinese and China, the Politico-Economic Dimension*, Singapore: Times Academic Press.

World Bank (2011). “Malaysia Economic Monitor, April 2011 — Brain Drain,” http://siteresources.worldbank.org/INTMALAYSIA/Resources/324392-1303882224029/malaysia_ec_monitor_apr2011_full.pdf.

Yeung, HWC (2007). “The dynamics of Southeast Asian Chinese business,” in Yeung, HWC (ed.) *Handbook of Research on Asian Business*, Cheltenham, UK: Edward Elgar.

Yoshihara, K (1988). *The Rise of Ersatz Capitalism in Southeast Asia*, Singapore: Oxford University Press.

Yoshihara, K (1995). “The ethnic Chinese and ersatz capitalism in Southeast Asia,” in L Suryadinata (ed.) *Southeast Asian Chinese and China, the Politico-Economic Dimension*, Singapore: Times Academic Press.

Zhuang, G and W Wang (2010). “The role of overseas Chinese in economic relations between China and Southeast Asia,” *International Journal of China Studies*, 1(1):174–93. http://cmsad.um.edu.my/images/ics/IJCSVlNl/zhuang wang.pdf.

Chapter 15

STATE POWER AND PRIVATE PROFIT: THE POLITICAL ECONOMY OF CORRUPTION IN SOUTHEAST ASIA

LINDA Y. C. LIM* AND AARON STERN*

This article reviews the extensive political and economic literature since 1990 on corruption in Indonesia, Philippines, Thailand, Malaysia and Singapore. After considering each country's individual recent history of corruption, the article comparatively analyses the relationship of corruption in these countries with, respectively, the roles of the state, the private sector and external actors, democratisation and decentralisation, and the impact of corruption on economic growth and inequality. Our conclusion is that while economic liberalisation, democratisation and centralisation of state power influence the forms of corruption and its impact on national economic performance, they are neither necessary nor sufficient for its decline.

INTRODUCTION, DEFINITIONS AND MEASUREMENTS

Analyses of corruption in developing countries have burgeoned in the 1990s, in part as a result of widespread political and economic liberalisation, democratisation and marketisation, particularly following the emergence of transition economies in Eastern Europe and Central Asia. In the economic literature, theoretical analyses of corruption seek to specify the technical conditions of its likely causes, consequences and possible solutions (for example, Ades and Di Telia, 1999; Bardhan, 1997; Bliss and Di Telia, 1997; Gray and Kaufmann, 1998; Harriss-White and White, 1996; Khan, 1996a; Mauro, 1998; Shleifer and Vishny, 1993), while empirical studies usually run

*This chapter first appeared in *Asia Pacific Economic Literature*, Vol. 16, Issue. 2, November 2002. Reprinted with permission.

Thanks are due to the following colleagues for their very helpful comments: Ramesh Chander, Richard Doner, Allen Hicken, Jomo K. S., Andrew MacIntyre, Pang Eng Fong, Pasuk Phongpaichit, Gavin Shatkin and Elaine Tan.

cross-country regressions to elicit particular cause or result correlations, such as the relationship between corruption and investment, economic growth, or inequality (for example, Ades and Di Telia, 1996; Fisman and Gatti, 2000; Kaufmann and Wei, 1999; Li, Xu and Zou, 2000; Mauro, 1995; Smarzynska and Wei, 2000; Knack and Azfar, 2000; Treisman, 2000; Wedeman, 1997; Wei, 1999, 2000). Multilateral development agencies have been particularly concerned about corruption and have sponsored many of the studies.

This survey does not seek to review the voluminous global literature, though it is referenced where it may be of significance to particular country cases in Southeast Asia. Rather, we concentrate on reviewing the economic and political (not legal, administrative, cultural or ethical) literature on corruption in the market economies (now all also political democracies) of Southeast Asia, focusing in particular on the period of the 1990s when the nature, extent or impact of corruption appeared to change in response to changing domestic political and economic circumstances, most notably democratisation and economic liberalisation. The review is mostly concerned with the causes and, to a lesser extent, the consequences of 1990s corruption in the region, and not with suggested policy solutions (on which see Lederman, Loayza and Soares, 2001; Morgan, 1998; UNDP, 1997; World Bank, 2002).

There is, as yet, no consensus in the global or Southeast Asian literature on a definition of corruption.[1] The broadest and most commonly used definition is 'the misuse of public office for private gain'. Within the political economy literature, this definition has been elaborated in a number of ways, some of which will be presented here to illustrate the diversity of perspectives represented. Analysing corruption in the transition economies of Eastern Europe, Hellman, Jones and Kaufmann (2000) distinguish between 'state capture', the capacity of firms to shape the formation of the basic rules of the game (which regulate the institutional environment of business) through private payments to public officials and politicians; 'influence', the same capacity without recourse to such payments; and 'administrative corruption', referring to 'petty' forms of bribery in connection with the implementation of laws, rules and regulations.

In the Southeast Asian literature, De Dios and Ferrer similarly distinguish between 'bureaucratic corruption' and 'political corruption' (2000, p. 1), using a principal-agent framework to 'examine how and why the

[1]See, for example, the discussion in Lancaster and Montinola (2001).

dominant types of corruption in the Philippines have evolved, from nepotism, to smuggling, to public-works contracts, to debt-finance schemes, asset-privatisations, until the recent descent into underworld-related activities'. For example, they reformulate the principal-agent problem in clientelism as 'one where the politician designs an incentive scheme ... to induce the crucial constituency to perform his bidding, namely election' (De Dios and Ferrer, 2000, p. 12).

Khan and Jomo (2000) and Khan (2000), distinguish between different types of rents (that, for example, can be created through government policy, or are the result of natural resource scarcity), their net social cost or benefit (what Khan calls 'rent inputs' versus 'rent outcomes'), and whether rent-seeking is 'state-led' or 'society-led'. The creation of rents does not necessarily entail waste in the sense of economic welfare if it involves simple transfers, as in the case of state incentives. Ross (2001) distinguishes between 'rent creation, in which firms seek rents created by the state, by bribing politicians and bureaucrats; and rent extraction, in which politicians and bureaucrats seek rents held by firms, by threatening firms with costly regulations ... (and) rent seizing — which occurs when state actors seek rents that are held by state institutions' (Ross, 2001, p. 4) as in the timber industry which he studies.

Hutchcroft (2000) distinguishes between the literature on 'rents' and 'rent-seeking', which focuses on state actions which distort markets (and yield outcomes which enrich both public and private sector 'rent-seekers'), 'clientelism', which studies relationships of power, and 'corruption', which examines how public roles and private influences conflict within state agencies. Kang (2002, p. 15) defines four types of corruption, with two, 'bottom-up' rent-seeking by society and 'top-down' rent-seeking by a 'predatory state', dominating (and alternating) in the Philippines and resulting in large amounts of corruption compared with the 'mutual hostages' situation (collusion by balanced state and business forces) in Korea and *laissez-faire* in (textbook) market economies. Kang's book is entitled *Crony Capitalism*, a term that has been associated with Southeast Asian political economy since the Marcos years, and still resonates in the region today.

Gomez (2002a, 2002b) uses the term 'political business' to define the whole web of reciprocal relationships between business and the state, highlighting 'the extent to which regimes and business in East Asia have been interdependent' (Wedeman, 2002, p. 53); in particular, democratisation in the region has led to '[p]olitical funding by business (which) has contributed to a significant rise in... "money politics", that is, the use of money in the political arena to secure control over the state in order to influence the distribution of state-generated economic rents' (Gomez, 2002a, p. 3).

Since this is a literature survey, we do not employ any particular one of these theoretical perspectives in the review of the country-specific literature. We focus on how political power is used to enrich those in government who wield this power, and their supporters in the private sector. What falls under the rubric of 'corruption' for the purposes of this discussion is guided, first, by the literature itself, and second, by contemporary political discourse in the countries we review. Like the global literature and national and multilateral policy and multinational corporate concerns, both the regional literature and contemporary political discourse in Southeast Asia have moved significantly away from the narrow definition of illegal acts of bureaucratic bribery that dominated the earlier (pre-1990s) literature on corruption in developing countries, and is still largely the context in which the term 'corruption' is understood in developed countries today (for example, Grabosky and Larmour, 2000). In particular, both the regional literature and contemporary political discourse have moved away from focusing only on illegal acts, to include a wider array of business–government interactions, many of which are legal but are considered to violate efficiency, equity and/or ethical or moral considerations. Most notable here is the Indonesian acronym KKN, standing for 'corruption, collusion and nepotism', opposition to which played a role in the downfall of President Soeharto. Similar anti-corruption movements have developed in Malaysia, Thailand and the Philippines in recent years, targeting legal acts of 'cronyism', 'nepotism' and general political favouritism in business.

The five market-economy countries of Southeast Asia are of interest to scholars of corruption for several reasons. The three larger countries, Thailand, Philippines and Indonesia, of different religious, cultural and colonial traditions, have long ranked among the more corrupt of developing countries.[2] The two smaller countries, Malaysia and Singapore, have ranked among the least corrupt, despite extensive state interventions in the economy. Malaysia and Singapore have also had elected governments since independence, while Thailand, Philippines and Indonesia have experienced long periods of military rule followed by more recent democratisation. With the partial exception of the Philippines, all have been among the largest developing country participants in international trade and investment, with

[2]Treisman, for example, notes that Thailand and Indonesia, together with Zaire, were ranked the three 'most corrupt' countries in Business International's corruption data for the early 1980s (Treisman, 2000, p. 400).

some of the fastest growing economies. In the group as a whole, neither rapid economic development nor political democracy appears to have diminished corruption significantly; in some respects and, in some cases, corruption may have even increased with development and democratisation. All five countries are today characterised by systems of state patronage which generate and distribute lucrative rents to those in the favour or employ of the state. They thus collectively form a useful set of countries with which to explore, through their individual histories, many of the theses emanating from the recent global theoretical and empirical literature.

We begin by discussing the trajectory of some conventional measurements of the degree of corruption over time in the five Southeast Asian countries. Tables 1 and 2 present the most commonly used indices. All corruption measurements are necessarily subjective and subject to a plethora of methodological criticisms (see Lancaster and Montinola, 2001). The most serious shortcoming for our purposes is the fact that all three of the measures used[3] reflect components of primary interest to, and the subjective perceptions of, foreign investors, particularly Western multinationals. They

Table 1. Business International and Political Risk Services Corruption Indices, 1980–97

Country	BI 1980–83	PRS 1982	PRS 1987	PRS 1992	PRS 1997
Hong Kong	8.0	6.0	5.0	5.0	4.9
Singapore	10.0	6.0	6.0	4.0	4.0
Malaysia	8.4	6.0	4.0	4.0	4.0
Thailand	1.5	4.0	3.0	3.0	3.0
Philippines	4.5	—	2.0	2.5	3.0
Indonesia	1.5	1.0	—	2.7	2.7
China	—	4.0	3.2	4.5	2.0
India	5.3	3.0	3.0	2.0	3.0

Notes: Together with the Transparency International Corruption Perceptions Index in Table 2, the following are the most common indices used in empirical studies of corruption. BI = Business International, a commercial provider of risk indices subsequently purchased by the Economist Intelligence Unit. The BI Corruption index ranges in value from 0 (high corruption) to 10 (low corruption). PRS = Political Risk Services, a commercial provider of monthly International Country Risk Guide (ICRD) data at www.prsgroup.com. The PRS Corruption in Government variable ranges in value from 0 (high corruption) to 6 (low corruption).

Source: Annual values from which this table draws were constructed by Stephen Knack and the IRIS Center at the University of Maryland.

[3]These are the Business International (BI) index for 1980–83, the Political Risk Services (PRS) index from 1982 to the present and the Transparency International Corruption Perceptions Index (TI-CPI) from 1995 to the present. See Tables 1 and 2.

Table 2. Transparency International Corruption Perceptions Index, 1995–2001

	1995		1998		2001	
	Rank	Score	Rank	Score	Rank	Score
Hong Kong	17	7.12	16	7.8	14	7.9
Singapore	3	9.26	7	9.1	4	9.2
Malaysia	23	5.28	29	5.3	36	5.0
Thailand	34	2.79	61	3.0	61	3.2
Philippines	36	2.77	55	3.3	65	2.9
Indonesia	41	1.94	80	2.0	88	1.9
China	40	2.16	52	3.5	57	3.6
India	35	2.78	66	2.9	71	2.7

Note: Rank is out of 41 countries in 1995, 85 countries in 1998, and 91 countries in 2001. Score is from 0 (lowest/most corrupt) to 10 (highest/least corrupt).
Source: Transparency International (www.transparency.org)

are thus at best only a partial measure of the degree of corruption, and in particular would fail to capture corrupt government or corporate behaviour and practices which do not affect foreign firms, for example, vote-buying, the award of provincial contracts for government services, explicit or implicit loan guarantees for politically favoured private borrowers, bribes and kick-backs that affect only local businesses, and so on. It is thus possible that these indices might denote a decline in the kind of corruption of concern to foreign investors at the same time that corruption affecting domestic constituencies is actually increasing.

There are also inconsistencies among the different indices. For example, the first two columns of Table 1 on the early 1980s have the Business International (BI) index showing Thailand and Indonesia tied for the most corrupt countries in the region (and the world), scoring 1.5/10, with the Philippines at an intermediate level of corruption at 4.5/10; whereas the Political Risk Services (PRS) index shows the Philippines as the most corrupt (0/6), followed by Indonesia (1/6), but with Thailand at an intermediate to good level (4/6). Both indices, however, show Singapore and Malaysia as the least corrupt, with Malaysia ranked at the same level as Singapore in the PRS index (6/6) but not in the BI index (8.42/10 versus Singapore's 10/10).

Between 1982 and 1997, the PRS index shows a decline or worsening of corruption in Singapore, Malaysia and Thailand, but an improvement in the Philippines and Indonesia. The Philippines data suggest a gradual improvement in corruption since the Marcos period (democracy was restored in 1986), whereas the Thailand data suggest a slight worsening of corruption in the democratic period from 1988, but a stabilisation throughout the period. Indonesia saw a worsening of corruption under President Soeharto from 1982 to 1987, but an improvement in the 1990s, despite the fact that this period coincided with a sharp increase in Soeharto's children's business activities, in which foreign investors partnered (see below). It is possible that the Indonesian data (if accurate) reflect a decline in 'bureaucratic corruption' of the petty sort (with the takeover of the customs service by a Swiss private firm during those years), or that foreign investors who partnered with Soeharto's children did not consider this to be corrupt, since it was legal,[4] or were insulated from other forms of corruption by virtue of their privileged relationship with 'the children'. The worsening of corruption in Malaysia seems to follow the 1980s entry of political parties into business, the privatisation of state enterprises, and the subsequent rise of 'crony capitalism' (for example, some of these party ventures and privatised enterprises were spun off into the hands of politically well-connected entrepreneurs). The perceived worsening of corruption in Singapore in the 1990s may similarly parallel the rise of monopolistic government-linked companies with highly remunerated senior management drawn disproportionately from the ranks of the ruling party or civil service.[5]

Table 2 shows changes in Transparency International's (TI) widely cited annual Corruption Perceptions Index in 1995, the year it was first issued, in 1998, the worst year of the Asian financial crisis, and in 2001, the most recent year. In terms of absolute scores, between 1995 and 2001 corruption fell moderately in Thailand and slightly in the Philippines, but increased slightly in Singapore, Indonesia and Malaysia, with Malaysia experiencing the greatest absolute increase. The relative rankings of the five Southeast Asian countries remained stable, with Singapore ranked the least corrupt, followed by Malaysia, Thailand, the Philippines and Indonesia in that order. Rankings are not strictly comparable across years, due to different sample sizes in each year, but some bilateral comparisons may be indicative. Most notably, Thailand and the Philippines moved from being less corrupt than China in 1995 to more corrupt in 1998 and 2001, as China's absolute scores improved substantially, according to the TI-CPI index. But the PRS index in Table 1 shows corruption in China worsening between 1992 and 1997 as

[4]According to my own (non-systematic) interviews of multinationals, the most common form of joint venture partnership with a Soeharto relative was for the relative to be given a minority share in the business without having to put in any equity capital, which probably did not violate any Indonesian or possibly even foreign government laws.

[5]These particular developments in Malaysia and Singapore might be viewed negatively by potential foreign investors for 'crowding out' private (including foreign) competition.

it improved (lessened) in the Philippines. According to the PRS index, in 1997 China was more corrupt than Thailand, the Philippines and Indonesia, but according to the TI-CPI index, in 1998 it was less corrupt than all three. Clearly, these indices are unreliable at best, especially when comparing among countries which are more or less 'equally corrupt'. However, they are all consistent in the ranking of the five Southeast Asian countries to whose recent 'corruption histories' we now turn.

INDONESIA

During the 32-year military-backed autocratic rule of President Soeharto, Indonesia ranked in international comparisons among both the world's most corrupt nations (and the most corrupt in Southeast Asia) and its fastest-growing economies.[6] Explaining this apparent paradox — since most of the literature finds corruption to be negatively correlated with economic growth and development (for example, Mauro, 1995) — has occupied much of the recent work of MacIntyre (1999a, 1999b, 2000, 2002). In his analysis of rent-seeking through off-budget fiscal activity, MacIntyre concludes that centralisation of political and bureaucratic authority under Soeharto's New Order regime meant that the Indonesian President 'achieved something approaching monopolistic rent management and thus had a direct interest in ensuring that government goods were not priced excessively and so did not depress economic activity' (MacIntyre, 2000, p. 267). As he points out, this is in line with Shleifer and Vishny's (1993) theoretical argument that a state exercising strong central political control functions as a single monopoly for bribe-collecting, thus ensuring that 'a healthy share of bribes collected flow upwards, with the remainder being distributed proportionately among relevant officials ... in regulatory agencies (who) are unable to operate independently to maximise their own take' (MacIntyre, 2002, p. 9). In particular, the Soeharto administration was able to ensure that macroeconomic policy never resulted in excessive inflation, which might undermine economic growth and thus its own 'take' from the proceeds of that growth. Bardhan also suggests that 'Indonesian corruption is more centralised ... and thus somewhat more predictable, whereas in India it is a more fragmented, often anarchic, system of bribery' (Bardhan, 1997, p. 1,325) leading to lower economic performance.

[6]Between 1980 and the financial crisis of 1998, only China, Korea, Singapore, Malaysia and Thailand experienced faster annual real GDP growth (World Bank, *World Development Report*, various years).

McLeod carries this argument one step further by postulating that 'the substantial government intervention that existed under Soeharto ... was consciously put in place for the purpose of generating the rents that Soeharto presumably wanted for their own sake, and also needed in order to first attain and then maintain a position of virtually unchallenged authority' (McLeod, 2000, p. 16). It was 'the private corporate sector (which) provided the primary medium through which Soeharto generated his family's enormous wealth and maintained his own power. Early on he realised the effectiveness of private sector monopoly privileges for generating rents' (2000, p. 17) and distributed these privileges and rents disproportionately, not only to members of his own extended family, but also and most notably to otherwise politically vulnerable ethnic Chinese minority entrepreneurs who used these privileges to grow massive family-owned conglomerates.[7] The most important was Liem Sioe Liong of the Salim group which at its height reportedly accounted for 8 per cent of Indonesia's GDP. In return, Salim and other Soeharto 'cronies' who benefited from such monopoly privileges shared some of their rents with the Soeharto clan — for example, by taking family members as sleeping joint venture 'partners' so that some profits could be distributed to them (a practice emulated especially in the 1990s by foreign multinationals as well)[8]; by extending loans or awarding contracts on favourable terms to them or their business cronies; or by making charitable donations to *yayasan*, foundations established and run by Soeharto and his family members. Cronies also helped Soeharto realise some of his national development goals, for example, by making investments in sectors where private enterprise would otherwise not invest — most notable here was Salim's investment in the Krakatua steel-making facility (which subsequently went bankrupt and was bailed out by the government).

Strong central political control may have helped limit rents and direct them in partly productive ways, thus preventing corruption from undermining economic growth, despite the massive personal wealth that Soeharto and his family members accumulated during his rule.[9] But, as MacIntyre

[7]See, for example, Robison (1986), MacIntyre (1990,1994), and Eklof (2002).

[8]The 'who's who' list of multinationals allied with Soeharto's six children alone included Merrill Lynch, Morgan Stanley, GE, Motorola, Lucent, Dupont, General Motors, General Dynamics, Hyatt, BP, Siemens, Deutsch Telekom, Mitsubishi, Mitsui, Marubeni, NEC, Sumitomo, Hyundai, Kia Motor (*Business Week*, 19 August 1996, p. 56).

[9]A *Time Magazine* investigation estimated that Soeharto and his children had assets worth US$15 billion in 1999, a sum already much reduced from its pre-financial crisis levels. See 'Soeharto Inc: All in the Family' and other articles in *Time*, 24 May 1999. Details of Soeharto family businesses are listed in http://www.time.com/asia/asia/magazine/1999/990524/chart.html.

(1999a) and McLeod (2000) further argue, this system was also deeply flawed in being too dependent on the judgment of a single individual, which could change unpredictably, as Soeharto's apparently did at the time of the 1997–98 financial crisis. Erratic policy responses at the time — which may have been due to Soeharto's by-then advanced age (he was in his late seventies), his deteriorating health and mental state following the death of his wife and close companion (an event infused with great mystical significance by many Indonesians, causing them to believe he had lost 'inner power'), or his greater vulnerability to the demands of his 'greedy' children or desire to secure their wealth prior to his own demise or loss of power — both hampered stabilisation of the economy when it was hit by contagion from the Thai crisis, and reduced investor confidence, resulting in massive domestic as well as foreign capital flight. Indonesia subsequently suffered more than any other crisis-hit country, and has recovered the least since. As MacIntyre has put it,

> [w]hereas Thailand suffered policy paralysis as a result of weak multiparty parliamentary government, Indonesia suffered from almost the opposite set of institutional circumstances — massive centralisation of power that left government vulnerable to deep problems of credibility due to unreliable policy commitments (MacIntyre, 1999a, p. 162).

It was not only the Indonesian macroeconomy which suffered with Soeharto's health and loss of power. Fisman (2001) found that the share valuations of publicly traded Indonesian business groups connected with Soeharto also fell significantly more than those of other firms whenever there were rumors of his ill-health during 1995–97, which he takes as an approximation of the value of rents conferred by their relationship with the president.

The financial crisis did lead to President Soeharto stepping down from office in May 1998, following weeks of political unrest and violence. His vice-president and appointed successor, Habibie, whose state-owned IPTN aircraft company had been the beneficiary of government subsidies for decades, was also bedeviled by accusations of corruption, most notably the diversion of US$80 million from Bank Bali to his failed presidential election campaign in 1999. Following the presidential election in 1999, the now factionalised Indonesian parliament — which under a new constitution had severely curtailed the powers of the presidency — chose as president Abdurrahman Wahid (Gus Dur), a Muslim cleric and head of Nadhlatul Ulama, the largest grassroots Islamic organisation in the country (and the world), even though his party commanded only a small share of parliamentary seats. Wahid himself was personally implicated in acts of corruption, particularly the embezzlement of funds by his personal masseuse from Bulog, the government food agency (see Eklof, 2002). He was impeached by parliament and removed from office in 2001, to be succeeded by his vice-president, Megawati Soekarnoputeri (the daughter of Soeharto's predecessor, President Soekarno).

During the Habibie–Wahid period, and continuing into the present Megawati era, Indonesia's economic recovery from the financial crisis has been severely hampered by the politicisation — and associated corrupting — of state economic institutions, most notably the Indonesian Bank Restructuring Agency (IBRA) set up to acquire and manage the assets of the large number of state-owned and private banks and corporations rendered insolvent by the ballooning of their huge debt burdens during the crisis. IBRA has not only been notoriously slow in repackaging these assets for sale; its leadership and senior personnel have changed frequently and been accused of making decisions to sell assets based on political rather than economic criteria, including pressure by former owners eager to repurchase their assets — it is assumed, accompanied by corrupt payments or promises. State macroeconomic institutions have also been compromised, particularly the independence of the central bank.[10]

In contrast to the central political control and rapid economic growth of the Soeharto era prior to the financial crisis, the post-Soeharto governments to date have been as corrupt as, if not more corrupt than, Soeharto's, but have presided over much slower economic growth.[11] MacIntyre's (and Shleifer and Vishny's) analysis suggests that weaker and less centralised political control post-Soeharto has meant that officials of regulatory agencies now act as independent monopolists 'pushing up prices without regard for the effect on overall demand for government goods' (MacIntyre, 2002, p. 9).

At the present time, Megawati's PDI-P party commands a minority of seats in the heavily factionalised elected parliament, resulting in numerous anecdotal reports that 'the going price' for corrupt transactions has increased, while their predictability within a weakened and fragmented bureaucracy has declined, as predicted by MacIntyre (and Shleifer and Vishny). One multinational manager interviewed in 2001, whose views were

[10]'On dangerous ground', *Far Eastern Economic Review*, 3 March 2001, pp. 54–55.

[11]The same was true of the pre-Soeharto era, under President Soekarno, which is not considered here.

echoed by other foreign and local company executives and consultants, complained that

> [i]n the past, under Golkar (S[oe]harto's political party), we always knew whom to pay, and how much, and always got what we paid for. Now, for a single (policy) decision, all kinds of different groups clamor for payment. We don't know who they are, or whether they can really deliver — sometimes they don't deliver, and even if they do, we have to pay much more in total than we did before. And we risk being caught by the anti-corruption authorities.[12]

In a context where 'the best way of influencing policy is to go directly to parliament and buy off the relevant committee',[13] one persistent rumour was that Megawati's husband and political manager, Taufik Kiemas, had set himself up as an extra-parliamentary 'broker' or intermediary for corrupt payments, that is, he would handle payments to the various factions in parliament and to government officials in the bureaucracy, taking a big cut for himself.[14] The fluidity and uncertainty of political power also reportedly makes bribe-takers more demanding and rapacious than before, since they face the risk of quickly losing whatever power they have when the political winds shift.

Political democratisation in Indonesia since 1999 has also introduced a dramatically new institutional change, the 'regional autonomy' policy which is diverting fiscal revenues previously collected and distributed by the central government to the individual districts and provinces from which the revenues are raised. Although intended to redress many decades of imbalance and inequitable distribution of government resources which had benefited the centre at the expense of the provinces, this policy has posed new problems of inequity between rich and poor provinces (based largely on natural resource endowments), as well as of regional authorities' management of the new fiscal process, including revenue collection. Many local and especially foreign companies have complained of increased demands for pay-offs by local authorities, as well as a deterioration in security and

---

[12]Interview conducted by Linda Lim, Jakarta, March 2001.

[13]Michael Vatikiotis, Editor of the *Far Eastern Economic Review*, answering a question following his talk on 'A reflection on the reform era and the future of Indonesian politics', at the United States-Indonesia Organization (USINDO), Washington, DC, 30 January 2002.

[14]'The benefits of prosecution', *Far Eastern Economic Review*, 28 March 2002, pp. 12–16; 'Trading on her father's image', *Economist*, 13 April 2002, pp. 41–42.

property rights, inflexibility in implementing the new regional autonomy rules, and difficulties in resolving legal disputes through the courts, resulting in an outflow of net direct foreign investment.[15] In line with the Shleifer-Vishny/MacIntyre model prediction that political decentralisation would both increase corruption and worsen its economic outcomes, Indonesia's already low position in international corruption rankings has sunk even lower since the advent of democracy in 1999.

Hamilton-Hart (2001) describes the anti-corruption strategies of Indonesia's newly-democratic polity and society, putting forth many reasons why they are unlikely to succeed in the present institutional environment. But recent developments suggest she may be too pessimistic, at least for now. In 2002, Soeharto's son Tommy and other cronies (for example, Hashim Djojohadikusomo) have been arrested and are being tried for various crimes including corruption;[16] central bank governor Syahril Sabirin has been jailed for colluding in the bank corruption scandal related to former President Habibie's election bid;[17] and Akbar Tanjung, the head of Golkar (Soeharto's former party) is also being tried for corruption.[18] At the same time, IBRA under Megawati's appointee appears to be more committed to disposing of seized private assets,[19] including to foreign buyers, as shown by the recent sale of Bank Central Asia, formerly owned by the Salim group, to a US fund, Farallon Capital Management.[20] However, the decision is controversial since it passed over a more qualified bidder, Standard Chartered Bank, and because Farallon is 'a virtually unknown US investment fund with about 40 employees, no banking experience and a local tobacco company

---

[15]See, for example, 'A windfall for Riau' and 'Brave new world', *Far Eastern Economic Review*, 21 February 2002, pp. 42–45; 'Indonesian coal dispute tests moves to decentralize power', *Wall Street Journal*, 10 April 2002, A15, A17.

[16]'Spate of arrests suggests Jakarta is pursuing former untouchables', *Wall Street Journal*, 15 March 2002, A8. Note, however, that as of August 2002, Tommy Soeharto received a relatively light sentence of only 15 years for ordering the assassination of a judge, and central bank governor Sjahrir successfully appealed against his conviction and jail sentence. But three judges have been suspended for allegedly accepting bribes to find a Canadian-owned insurance company, Manulife, bankrupt.

[17]'Jakarta convicts banker in blow to credibility', *Wall Street Journal*, 14 March 2002, A10.

[18]'No rest for the powerful', *Far Eastern Economic Review*, 17 December 2002, pp. 23–25; 'Missed opportunities', *Far Eastern Economic Review*, 31 January 2002, pp. 21–22.

[19]'Steadying the course' and 'You need to fight corruption', *Far Eastern Economic Review*, 30 August 2001, pp. 40–43.

[20]US-led group is picked to buy Indonesian bank', *Wall Street Journal*, 15 March 2002, A6.

for a partner'.[21] It is notable also that all those arrested and convicted for corruption were part of the old Soeharto regime or its crony network, and that the current high-profile cases were all initiated by the previous (Wahid) government. Skeptics either see the latest arrests 'as an internal power struggle within the élite, in which the fight against corruption has become ... a political football as Megawati seeks to balance international opinion against her own domestic interests and those of competing power blocs'[22] or believe that while some 'expendable people' will be punished, the real power brokers allied to her government will escape heavy scrutiny.[23]

Finally, Filmer and Lindauer (2001) find that one explanation commonly given (McLeod, 2000) for Indonesia's historically high level of corruption — low civil servants' salaries — is not valid: while highly educated bureaucrats earn less than equivalently qualified private-sector employees, the gap is modest, and lower-level bureaucrats are actually paid more than they would earn in the private sector.

PHILIPPINES

The Philippines has been a particularly popular country for corruption research — among other reasons (such as a longer tradition of academic and press freedom), because it has long had a reputation for being very corrupt, through periods of dictatorship and of democracy, of the centralisation and decentralisation of state power, of statist economic policy and market liberalisation. In addition, whereas corruption in neighbouring countries coexisted with and arguably did not seem to undermine rapid economic growth (at least until the regional financial crisis of 1997–98), this was not so in the Philippines, which in contrast endured decades of intermittent economic crisis and stagnation even as its neighbours forged ahead in income and industrial development. Both corruption and economic under-performance relative to its neighbours persisted in the Philippines under different political regimes, from post-colonial democratically elected governments (1946–72) and the Marcos martial-law dictatorship (1972–86) through the democratically elected Aquino (1986–92), Ramos (1992–98), Estrada (1998–2001) and current Arroyo governments.

---

[21] 'Bank sale in Jakarta leaves many people surprised, confused' (*Asian Wall Street Journal*, 22 March 2002, Al) also notes, that Farallon 'brought in a high-profile supporter: Hubert Neiss, Deustche Bank AG's top official for Asia and formerly one of the key International Monetary Fund officials who put together Indonesia's emergency finance program in 1998'.

[22] 'The benefits of prosecution', *Far Eastern Economic Review*, 28 March 2002, p. 14.

[23] See note 22, also 'Accountability on trial', *Economist*, 23 March 2002, p. 41.

Most explanations for the Philippines' persistent corruption, and its relatively weak economic performance, begin with the country's social structure — the legacy of pre-colonial indigenous traditions, colonial administrative structures, and colonial and post-colonial concentrated land-holding patterns which shaped economic and political power (Hutchinson, 1997). A rich scholarly and popular literature focuses especially on the domination of the nation's society, politics and economics by large feudal families who either flourish independently of a weak central state, or manipulate that state to their own ends (for example, Gutierrez, Torrente and Narca, 1992; Gutierrez, 1994; McCoy, 1993). This family domination of the political economy means that Philippine corruption is channeled through personalistic patronage networks, as '[t]he political loyalty that was the basis for precolonial Filipino political organisation carried over into the colonial period and into the networks of patron-client relations' (Hawes, 1992, p. 147). But such personalistic — or 'clientelistic' — networks are also characteristic of other Southeast Asian countries, resulting in 'non-market' patterns of corruption which have been contrasted with supposedly more economically efficient (because of competition) 'market-based' processes (for example, Hutchcroft, 2000, pp. 221–2).

What Hutchcroft considers distinctive about the Philippines, compared with its Southeast Asian neighbours, is its history of a relatively weak central bureaucracy, resulting in the emergence during the late nineteenth and early twentieth centuries of commercial land-owners whose economic base lay 'firmly outside the state' (Hutchcroft, 2000, p. 218). Hutchcroft calls this situation of 'a powerful oligarchic business class (which) extracts privilege from a largely incoherent bureaucracy', 'booty capitalism' (Hutchcroft, 1998, p. 50), which he believes continues to this day. He contrasts this with the 'bureaucratic capitalism' of Thailand, where patronage networks lie inside, and are controlled by, a relatively strong centralised state (Hutchcroft, 1998, p. 48). Further, while postwar Thai business and politics were characterised by 'competitive clientelism' (for example, Doner and Ramsay, 1997) which allowed for economic growth propelled by new market entrants, 'monopoly clientelism' in the Philippines served to consolidate the position of oligarchic families and prevent the emergence of new competition (Doner, 1992).

Where Hutchcroft (1998) sees corruption rooted in a powerful oligarchy autonomous from the state extracting spoils from it through different configurations of state power (democracy and dictatorship), Kang (2002, p. 10) sees 'excessive bottom-up rent-seeking by society' 'overwhelming' the state with its demands during the pre-Marcos democratic period, when 'powerful oligarchs were able to overrun the state' (2002, p. 147). Under the subsequent Marcos dictatorship, 'the pendulum swung too far in the opposite direction' (2002, p. 147), with 'excessive top-down predation by Marcos and his cronies' (2002, p. 10). This vacillation between two extremes in the Philippines contributed to incoherent policymaking with resulting poor economic performance. (In contrast, in South Korea a balance between the power of business and the state during both democratic and authoritarian periods limited the degree of predation and the transaction costs associated with corruption, permitting rapid economic growth.)

Sidel, on the other hand, argues that 'control over the agencies of the state has provided the key to capital accumulation' (Sidel, 1995, p. 509) and that

> . . . the Philippine state may appear 'weak' in its failings as a 'developmental state' but is in fact 'strong' as a 'predatory state' (Sidel, 1995, p. 510).

In other words, family or business interests seek control of the state as a means to enrich themselves through its internal patronage networks, in contrast to Hutchcroft's conceptualisation of these private interests operating as actors external to the state who extract 'booty' from it. De Dios and Ferrer argue that '[t]his predatory nature of the state and the failure of formal government to become responsive meant that Filipinos had only non-government institutions to turn to, primarily the family or extended kinship ties, the more basic informal rules of behaviour that. . . are the default mode in traditional societies' (De Dios and Ferrer, 2000, p. 39).

According to Ross, '[w]hen traditional oligarchs and their families moved into politics, they sought out state resources to fund their client networks' resulting in 'rent seizure' through the pillage of state-controlled forestry resources (2001, p. 55). Marcos' declaration of martial law enabled him to gain exclusive control of state 'allocation rights' to forest harvesting, and secured his political control, initially reducing the dissipation of state patronage resources in the form of deforestation licenses and contracts. But as Marcos became more politically insecure in the later years of his rule, he began to expend these resources more rapidly, both to ensure the support of clients and in anticipation of possible loss of monopoly control of forestry allocation rights.

The Marcos era gave rise to the term 'crony capitalism' which is still used to characterise corruption in the Philippines. Cronies were relatives or close associates of Marcos or his wife, Imelda, and included members of groups that had not been represented among the traditional Philippine élite, such as the non-*mestizo* (without mixed native Malay and/or Spanish ancestry) ethnic Chinese minority business community (Hutchcroft, 2000, p. 224).

> Crony capitalism ... entailed the distribution of monopoly rights over key agricultural markets by presidential decree. It also led to the development of private conglomerates in diverse manufacturing and mining sectors through the extension of preferential financing, government contracts, and guaranteed foreign loans approved by the president (Montinola, 1994, p. 200).

Doner (1992) shows how the dominance of one Marcos crony in the auto-assembly industry resulted in high concentration and capital intensity which hampered the industry's development, as compared with the more competitive and labour-intensive ownership and industrial structure found in Thailand. Ross (2001, pp. 79–80) describes the role of several Marcos cronies in the timber sector, while Kang makes a general argument that 'Marcos used the power of the state to expropriate wealth for himself and his associates' (Kang, 2002, p. 10).

Montinola (1994) and De Dios and Ferrer (2000) apply a principal-agent framework of analysis to the Philippine case. Montinola (1994, p. 99) sees politics in the Philippines as 'a hierarchy of principal-agent relationships', with Marcos elected and acting as the agent of citizen principals pre-martial law, and becoming himself the principal (patron) of his cronies (agents/clients) under martial law. While noting that wealth is highly concentrated in a small number of élite extended families, she argues that 'heterogeneous élite preferences' resulted in 'multi-dimensional political competition' (Montinola, 1994, p. 102) for access to the rents from public goods that the president controlled, which has continued in the post-Marcos era. In the same vein, De Dios and Ferrer note the 'long-standing heterogeneity of social interests along various lines' which has caused national affairs to degenerate into 'a contest for the division of spoils among competing particularistic interests' including 'narrower parochial or clan and family interests' (De Dios and Ferrer, 2000, p. 12).

Besides the role of particularistic interests like oligarchs and cronies, most studies of Philippine corruption also focus on the country's weak institutions, particularly its relatively decentralised political system that allows local interests (including oligarchs and cronies) to capture electoral power, and with it control over local state patronage resources and networks as well as some ability through the national legislature to influence central government policy. The Marcos martial-law era was a historical anomaly, in the sense that Marcos sought to centralise political and economic power in the state he controlled, which included 'moving against the entrenched interests of the landed oligarchy and the protected bourgeoisie' (Hawes, 1992, p. 153). Any potentially positive 'developmental' impact this might have had was, however, pre-empted by his grabbing 'a direct proprietary stake in the economy by taking over profitable private firms through a complex series of dummy corporations, setting up monopolies controlled by his political allies, and steering government loans and contracts to enterprises controlled by his cronies' (Wedeman, 1997, p. 470; see also Aquino, 1987; Montinola, 1994; Kang, 2002).

Much of this Marcos-era centralisation and cronyism was dismantled following Marcos' fall, particularly with the policies of liberalisation, privatisation and economic reform embarked on by the Ramos government in the 1990s. However, these market-oriented policies have failed to prevent the accumulation of monopoly power by emergent new élites (for example, ethnic Chinese tycoons, most notably Lucio Tan) or re-emergent old ones (most notably, Marcos' chief crony, Eduardo 'Danding' Cojuangco), who alone possess the capital, connections and business acumen necessary to operate large modern private-sector enterprises, and thus became the main beneficiaries of privatisation. Political democratisation since Marcos has also been dominated by élites with the only difference in respect of corruption being that 'democratic procedures reorient patronage systems toward electoral competition rather than the consolidation of a dictatorial regime' (Hutchcroft, 1998, p. 241), since '[t]he demands of nurturing a political base and winning electoral competition not only encourage corruption, but also promote entirely legal pork-barrel diversions of resources into politicians' hands' (Hutchcroft, 2000, p. 235; see also Coronel, 1998; Ross, 2001; Kang, 2002). Institutionally, the Philippines has an 'unstructured party system' (Hicken, 2001b), with '"catch-all" parties composed of élite families and their client networks rather than class-based parties. Thus, attracting support in each election often required the granting of particularistic benefits for each coalition of families rather than universal benefits for particular classes, making 'access to patronage positions and public works expenditures' necessary for politicians to be elected (Montinola, 1994, p. 103).

There seems to be general consensus that democratisation has led to decentralisation of both political power and corruption in the Philippines. De Dios and Ferrer, for example, consider that 'except for the dictatorship period, corruption in the Philippines may be considered to be generally decentralised' (De Dios and Ferrer, 2000, p. 25). Sidel examines the phenomenon of local 'bossism' — 'the electoral and economic entrenchment of powerbrokers with virtually monopolistic control over entire localities'

(Sidel, 1996, p. 63) — as a consequence of the political democratisation which both Thailand and the Philippines have experienced since the 1980s, and finds more similarities than differences between them. Lacaba (1995) and Coronel (1996) provide more examples of corruption based on the political power of local 'bosses', and Linantud (1998) and Case (1999) document the vote-buying by élites and related irregularities which have typically characterised Philippine elections both before and after Marcos, but which Case believes have been declining through time.

If corruption is now more decentralised, and more related to the outcomes of local rather than national-level elections, does this mean that it has decreased overall? Some authors seem to think so, though for different reasons. Kang believes that post-Marcos, 'the democratic transition brought business and politicians more into a balance ... and many of the worst excesses of rent-seeking and corruption seem to have been eliminated' (Kang, 2002, p. 180). De Dios and Ferrer believe that 'given the obvious checks and balances and risk of exposure entailed by the separation of powers and media freedom ... political corruption ... (is) more modest and selective relative to the years of dictatorship, even as the dilution of central power gives an opportunity for bureaucratic corruption at the local and lower levels to gain more autonomy' (De Dios and Ferrer, 2000, p. 26). While acknowledging that 'the wave of liberalisations and privatisations has provided opportunities for new and large-scale forms of corruption ... these moves ... are in the nature of one-off opportunities for corruption rents and ... do not lead to the recurring economic distortions associated with continuing government economic involvement' (De Dios and Ferrer, 2000, pp. 35–36). Mendoza concurs that 'the transition (to liberalisation) ... affords entrepreneurs of all types new opportunities to capture rents through corruption' but that these might be 'an acceptable one-time cost' (Mendoza, 2001, p. 3).

Investigative reports (for example, Coronel, 2000a, 2000b) continue to detail the breathtaking range and depth of recent acts of corruption linking public officials and private business, including 'pork barrel' projects to benefit particular constituencies and businesses, the diversion of budgetary funds for government health, education and infrastructural services, the perversion of court proceedings and rulings, illegal campaign financing, the suspect creation and allocation of lucrative monopolies, lavish gifts provided to presidents in exchange for favours, police or military complicity in drug-trafficking and kidnapping-for-ransom, and so on. Among scholarly studies, Mendoza (2001) analyses corruption in government procurement, bidding and award of contracts, while Virtucio and Lalunio (2001) discuss corruption arising from government contracts, concessions and privatisation.

Corruption or crony capitalism linked to elected presidents surfaced immediately after Marcos. For example, 'close Aquino supporters appear to have used their proximity to the president to obtain special economic privileges and enrich themselves' (Montinola, 1994, p. 111), while the Ramos administration was associated with 'questionable bids and contracts of large special projects' (Lim and Pascual, 2001, p. 12). Both the Aquino and Ramos administrations 'did not basically try to eradicate the patron-client relations in state institutions and governance structures' with the result that 'this legacy of patronage politics, patron-client relations and informal networks capturing formal structures of authority ... was ... used to the hilt by the Estrada Administration' (Lim and Pascual, 2001, pp. 12–13), and subsequently brought about his downfall.

Estrada, a self-proclaimed 'outsider' (from the oligarchic élite) and 'man of the people' campaigned for the presidency on a populist platform and won a landslide electoral victory. His excesses of corruption ranged from 'crony capitalism'[24] to a stockmarket scam and payoffs from an illegal underground lottery (Lim and Pascual, 2001; see also Coronel, 2000b; Tordesillas and Hutchinson, 2001). Half-way into his term, Estrada was impeached, removed from office and jailed on corruption charges. His successor, Gloria Macapagal-Arroyo, like Marcos' successor Corazon Cojuangco-Aquino, is herself a member of the élite[25] and not exempt from rumours of familial corruption.[26]

THAILAND

Unlike the Philippines, where corruption has a long history and has been much written about, there has been a burgeoning of new research and publications on corruption in Thailand in the past decade. This most likely reflects the impact of democratisation in at least two ways: first, a perceived increase in the incidence and scope of corruption, and a change in its nature from the previous decades of military rule; and second, increased transparency, media and academic freedom, and the flowering of civil society

[24]See, for example, 'Estrada and Co.', *Far Eastern Economic Review*, 12 August 1999, pp. 38–40; 'The crony capitalist: People here never thought I'd survive', *Wall Street Journal*, 30 August 1999, p. 2.

[25]Arroyo is the daughter of a former President of the Philippines, and her husband's family are long-established, large-scale landowners in a sugar-growing area of the country. See, for example, 'More power to the powerful', *Far Eastern Economic Review*, 1 February 2001, 16–18, p. 20.

[26]See, for example, Cecilia Quiambao, 'Bribe linked to husband rebounds on Arroyo', *Bangkok Post*, 31 July 2001, p. 11.

institutions and political participation since the late 1980s, and especially since the restoration of electoral democracy following the last (1991–92) military coup.

Previous analyses of Thai political economy characterised it as a 'bureaucratic polity' (Riggs, 1966) where '[t]he political élite was dominated by civil and military bureaucrats who took a predatory attitude towards business, making business people their clients' (Hewison, 1997, p. 95), especially the minority ethnic Chinese whom Riggs (1966) saw as 'pariah entrepreneurs' reliant on Thai military patrons for protection. Thai business was dominated by large family-owned conglomerates dependent on both national political patronage, and external trade and financial networks (Suehiro, 1992). The dominant Chinese and Sino-Thai businesses cooperated with military leaders, including in the establishment of state enterprises. Both Suehiro (1992) and Hewison (1997) trace the evolution of this partnership between business and bureaucrats through the agribusiness, import-substituting and export-oriented industrial phases of Thai economic development. A centralised, if not particularly 'strong', state co-existed with weak interest groups and non-democratic politics (Rock, 2000, p. 163).

Such clientelist patronage networks did not, however, undermine rapid GDP growth and industrialisation in Thailand. Following Ammar, Vichyanond and Christensen (1993), Doner and Ramsay (2000) and Rock (2000) argue that this was due to the historical insulation from politics of the Thai central bank and finance ministry which conducted fiscal and monetary policy, resulting in a long period of macroeconomic stability and hard budget constraints. In microeconomic sectoral policy, on the other hand, Rock (2000) argues that selective industrial policy favouring large firms and relatively few entrepreneurs advanced Thai industrial development, while Doner and Ramsay's thesis is that 'clientelism helped to facilitate competitive market structures because intra-élite rivalries helped to ensure that aspiring entrepreneurs could find patrons' (Doner and Ramsay, 2000, p. 153). Both agree that a wide range of Thai collective associations played an important role in resolving collective action problems and advancing collective business interests with the state bureaucracy, most notably in the key textile industry. Thus rent-seeking was controlled, and clientelism failed to undermine, and may even have promoted, industrial growth. Khan's (2000) analysis concurs that competition between entrepreneurs seeking to capture the rents created by government policy resulted in good economic growth in Thailand even in the absence of government coercion to reinvest the rents productively (which he argues accounts for South Korea's better economic performance).

All writers agree that things changed with political democratisation. The co-authored works of Pasuk (Pasuk and Baker, 1998, 2000a, 2000b; Pasuk and Sungsidh, 1999; Pasuk, Sungsidh and Nualnoi, 1998) provide the definitive description of the events which followed: the rise of first, Bangkok, and then provincial, business, in challenging military authority; the switch from military-based corruption to electoral corruption, including vote-buying (see also Ockey, 1994; Callahan and McCargo, 1996); the emergence of regional 'godfathers' or *chao pho* (see also Ockey, 2000; Sombat, 2000) who help politicians win seats in the national parliament in exchange for later government favours, and the proliferation of lucrative illegal businesses under the protection of the police, the military and local political kingpins.

While democracy and a free press have also seen the emergence of a Bangkok-based middle-class of professionals, white and blue-collar workers, and small and medium-sized entrepreneurs who are anti-corruption and pro-reform, 80 per cent of the electorate is in provincial rural areas where they are subject to the influence of cultural traditions (Pasuk and Sungsidh, 1999; Jory, 1996; Robertson, 1996) as well as of newer local powerbrokers. The role of electoral competition, factions in fragmented coalition governments, and the short tenure of these governments (an average of 18 months in the 1990s), also increased the importance of political hand-outs (including through cabinet positions) in government formation and survival, and the urgency of using positions for electoral funding, personal aggrandisement, capital accumulation or political pay-offs before one's position collapsed and power and privilege was recycled into rival hands.

Hicken points out that '[w]hen party labels are weak, candidates must rely on building up their personal reputations and personal networks of support in order to be elected. This provides strong incentives for candidates to direct benefits (for example, pork and patronage) towards their narrow constituencies' (Hicken, 2001a, p. 6). He shows that this is what happened in successive Thai elected governments, for whom 'electoral victory (and future electoral success) stemmed from their ability or potential to direct resources to their local constituencies and supports' (Hicken, 2001a, p. 15). In the privatisation of state enterprises, for example, 'concessions were rewarded to those with good political connections on very favourable contractual terms' (Hicken, 2001a, p. 21). The result is that

> [p]olitics have become commercialised. Businessmen dominate parliament and the cabinet to the exclusion of almost anyone else. Many businessmen treat politics as a business. Elections are major economic events. The parliament is a marketplace for contracts, favours and deals ... Economic policy-making is all too obviously distorted by private interests (Pasuk and Baker, 1998, p. 321).

Wingfield details some of these policies, concluding that "'democratisation" has been subverted by the dominance of capital over the political process (2002, p. 282). Political democratisation thus contributed to economic decentralisation as politicians (many of whom were businessmen) directed state resources to their electoral constituencies. Not all of this was 'corrupt' (see Montesano, 2000; Arghiros, 2000; Ueda, 2000; LoGerfo, 2000), but it did involve an increase in the power of provincial interests and a corresponding decline in the authority of the central state. Just as politicians had to turn to business for financial support, and business entered politics to further its own interests, the vast and widening gap in remuneration and power between business and the bureaucracy led to an exodus of educated talent from the latter to the former (Pasuk and Baker, 1998, p. 321), compromising the efficiency and autonomy of government institutions which had previously been able to ensure that the economy prospered. Among other things, this deterioration in government policy-making under democracy contributed to the financial crisis of 1997–98 (Doner, and Ramsay, 2000; Hicken, 2001a).

The crisis accelerated various institutional changes that had been afoot since the early 1990s, including a new constitution, a National Counter Corruption Commission (NCCC), and a new bankruptcy law and other financial sector reforms, including the opening of this previously closed sector to competition from foreign investment. The new constitution was expected to reduce the number of political parties, the degree of factionalism and vote-buying, and the power of local interests (for example, Hicken, 2001a), leading to a decline in corruption (Pasuk, 2001). At the same time, 'in the wake of the crisis, domestic capital has become much more focused on capturing or influencing the state, and restoring the state's historic role as the protector of domestic capital' (Pasuk and Baker, 2002, p. 5); Thaksin was seen as 'the leader with the best credentials for managing globalisation' (Pasuk and Baker, 2001, p. 6).

Perhaps because of the tension between these two contradictory (with respect to corruption) trends, the results of political reform so far have been disappointing, as 'political business' interests have managed to subvert both constitutional reform and financial restructuring (Wingfield, 2002). Reverses have escalated since the election of Thaksin Shinawatra, the country's wealthiest individual, as prime minister in 2001. Thaksin's wealth came from monopoly telecommunications licenses he obtained while in the police, and he stood accused by the NCCC of concealing assets while serving as deputy prime minister in 1997. The Constitutional Court subsequently acquitted him of this offense by a controversial and suspect 8:7 vote. Thaksin campaigned on a nationalist and populist platform, and has begun re-centralising power under his government, a coalition with a large majority in parliament. Within his first year in office he replaced the independent central bank governor in a policy dispute over interest rates, imposed protectionist barriers on foreign investment (later relaxed as investment plunged), initiated a telecommunications policy that would benefit his own family's companies, was suspected of wanting to use government funds to bail out heavily indebted local firms (especially those belonging to political cronies) via the Thai Asset Management Corporation, called for the powers of the Constitutional Court and the NCCC to be curtailed, promoted conservative military officers sympathetic to him, tolerated the violation by big business of a 1999 competition law to remove monopolies, and threatened the continued freedom of the press.[27]

But these reverses have been accompanied by some advances, such as the first-ever convictions for corruption of senior politicians from the previous government, and the current investigation of Constitutional Court judges who ruled in Thaksin's favour in his corruption trial. Pasuk and Baker (2001, 2002) interpret Thaksin's actions as a move 'to institutionalise the ways in which businessmen gain access to state power' (Pasuk and Baker, 2002, p. 8), through direct participation in political parties (in this case Thaksin's party Thai Rak Thai), parliament and the cabinet, as happens in more mature democracies like the United States. In doing so, the big Bangkok business groups allied with Thaksin (including his former chief competitor in the telecoms industry, the Charoen Pokphand or CP Group) have undermined the power of local 'godfathers' or *chao poh*, a development which could lead to a diminution of the type of corruption which burgeoned in the 1990s (as Shleifer and Vishny's 1993 analysis would also suggest).

But the resulting appearance of more private-sector monopolies, in contrast to the 'competitive clientelism' of Thailand's recent past, together with the need to dissipate rents to other political clients 'to buy their acquiescence'[28] may result in slower economic growth (Pasuk and Baker, 2002, pp. 8–9).

[27]See the following articles in the *Far Eastern Economic Review:* 'Thailand Incorporated', 18 January 2001, pp. 16–18; 'Reform on the rocks', 15 March 2001, pp. 50–52; 'Thaksin turns back the clock', 19 April 2001, pp. 46–49; 'A clash of wills', 7 June 2001, p. 53; 'All the power in his hands', 16 August 2001, pp. 16–19; 'Thai defence chiefs march out of step', 13 September 2001, pp. 16–19; 'Thaksin at a crossroads', 7 February 2002, pp. 18–20, 22; 'Prickly Premier', 11 April 2002, 15–16, p. 18.

[28]For example, buying the electoral support of Thailand's rural areas through Thaksin's promised 'populist' programs of agrarian debt relief, village capital funds and cheap health care.

MALAYSIA

Despite the existence of patron–client cultural traditions within the politically dominant Malay community, corruption did not become a major issue of public or political discourse in Malaysia until the late 1980s. Although its place in international rankings of corruption has fallen (to lower rankings, meaning more corruption) and is now behind Taiwan, Singapore, Hong Kong and Japan, Malaysia remains well ahead of (less corrupt than) Korea, the other Southeast Asian nations, China, India and most other developing countries. It has had an elected government since independence in 1957, with the same coalition of race-based political parties, dominated by the Malay party UMNO.

The many works of Gomez (1990, 1991, 1994, 1999, 2000), Jomo (1995) and Gomez and Jomo (1999a, 1999b, 2000) amply document the country's descent into 'money polities', which had its origins in the electoral politics of race. In 1970, following post-election race riots in 1969, the Malay-dominated government instituted a New Economic Policy (NEP) which sought to bring the largely rural-based Malays into the urban labour and capital markets then dominated by the much wealthier urban-based Chinese minority. Affirmative action quotas for Malays in higher education, government and large private-sector company employment, and credit and contract allocation, together with the 'market nationalisation' through international stock purchases of previously foreign-owned plantation and mining corporations and their conversion into state-owned enterprises run by Malays, accelerated the emergence of a Malay professional and managerial class. Related restrictions on largely non-Malay private sector enterprises (for example, under the 1975 Industrial Coordination Act) caused Chinese business to seek patrons among local and national Malay politicians, bureaucrats and businessmen, as their own race-based party, MCA, weakened (Heng, 1992). At the same time, UMNO established its own party-owned and controlled businesses, many of them later collected together under the umbrella of the Renong Group. Revenues, or 'rents', earned by these privileged 'private' businesses, as well as government funds, were distributed to ensure the party's return to power in elections, and the rise of particular factions and individuals within its own internal hierarchy.

> ... control over the state appears to have become a necessary prerequisite in the race for political power ... UMNO's vast patronage machinery has been pivotal in enabling the party to win and maintain the electoral support of rural Malays, its primary power base (Gomez, 1994, p. 280).

At the same time, race-based affirmative action privileges led to the emergence of

> ... a growing circle of Malay businessmen whose corporate holdings have been considerably bolstered by opportunities made available through such government concessions. This has led to the burgeoning of a capitalist class with close links to UMNO (Gomez, 1994, p. 291).

The rise of a group of élite Malay capitalists fulfilled a long-time political goal of Prime Minister Mahathir Mohamad, and was achieved with the assistance of his political lieutenant, sometime finance minister and controller of the UMNO purse-strings, Daim Zainuddin, who himself had earlier become a successful businessman. The Malay 'entrepreneurs' that Daim favoured rapidly accumulated large conglomerate empires through intricate mergers, share-swaps and takeovers, rather than through the organic growth of self-built businesses which directly participated in production to create value (Sieh Lee, 1992; Gomez, 1994). This process of creating 'Malay millionaires' as business leaders of their community was justified on the grounds of 'redressing the imbalance' of economic power between Malays and non-Malays. But a few key non-Malay tycoons (for example, Vincent Tan, Ting Pek Khing, Ananda Krishnan) closely connected with the UMNO leadership also benefited enormously from their business associations with politically prominent Malays. The 'privatisation' of previously Malay-run, state-owned corporations, beginning in 1985 and accelerating with the Privatisation Master-plan issued in 1991, contributed greatly to this development. In a non-transparent and often non-competitive manner, public assets were transferred to hand-picked, politically well-connected private monopolists, and/or only partially privatised through the sale (for example, through management buy-outs) of some shares of companies whose control continued to rest with government entities.[29] Privatisation thus enabled a few individuals to become extremely wealthy without significantly reducing government control of the resources transferred to them.

But while definitely 'clientelist' and 'rent-seeking' (in Hutchcroft's typology, above), and referred to by Jomo as 'rentier cronyism' (Jomo 2001b, p. 161), the above developments were not necessarily 'corrupt' in the sense of being technically illegal. Jomo also distinguishes between rents which promoted industrialisation and capital accumulation, that is, were productively invested, and those which were used for inter-ethnic redistribution as part of Malaysia's race-based affirmative action policies.

[29] For details on Malaysia's extensive privatisations, see Jomo (1995).

He further distinguishes between 'redistributive measures that also enhance productivity and those that merely involve wealth transfers' (Jomo, 2001b, p. 159). In any event, widespread cronyism did not curtail Malaysia's rapid GDP growth from the late 1980s to the late 1990s, which was largely predicated on the success of foreign-owned, export-oriented electronics manufacturing, and for the most part did not undermine the historically stable macroeconomic policy management.

There was, however, struggle over control of state resources and party patronage networks within UMNO itself. Competition between business groups linked to Anwar Ibrahim — who led a major faction in UMNO and had been elected Deputy Prime Minister and thus Mahathir's apparent successor — and others within the party, apparently culminated in Anwar's eventual ouster, arrest and long-term incarceration on charges of corruption and sodomy during the turmoil of the financial crisis in 1998. In 1997, Malaysia succumbed to financial contagion from the collapse of the Thai baht, as (both foreign and domestic) investor confidence plunged. This loss of confidence was exacerbated by Prime Minister Mahathir's vociferous claims that the crisis was the result of an international conspiracy, and by actions subsequently taken by his government to prop up the stockmarket and use government funds to bail out the heavily debt-burdened Renong and other crony-controlled companies hard-hit by the fall in the ringgit and rising interest rates (Jomo, 1998a). Anwar Ibrahim as Finance Minister cut back on government mega-projects, but his authority was progressively undermined by Mahathir and Daim, concerned that conventional fiscal and monetary austerity would worsen economic contraction and severely weaken heavily-indebted Malay tycoons.[30] Finally in September 1998, the ringgit was pegged, capital controls imposed, and Anwar himself sacked and then arrested. Mahathir centralised power in himself, including retaining the post of Finance Minister, and later dispensed with the services of Daim Zainuddin, several of whose protegees have since lost control of their business empires.

Following the crisis, the government set up two state agencies, Danaharta to take over the non-performing loans of banks and financial institutions, and Danamodal to recapitalise the banks. Their activities served to stabilise the banking system and restore financial confidence, but also helped politically-favoured interests to consolidate and extend their businesses (Jomo, 2001a, Gomez, 2002b). There has also been a stream of bail-outs of crony companies

[30]Resort to IMF emergency funding was never considered, reportedly because of the belief that IMF policy conditionality would include a cut-back in affirmative action and crony-support policies.

by Petronas, the national oil company, and various government-controlled funds (for example, the Employees' Provident Fund), including of Mahathir's son Mirzan's shipping company — part of a wave of 'de-privatisation' or 're-nationalisation' of financially strapped utilities and infrastructure enterprises. In the 'restructuring' of the corporate sector, financially distressed businesses which retained Mahathir's patronage were rescued, while those closely aligned with Anwar Ibrahim, and more recently with Daim Zainuddin, were allowed to go under or had their assets transferred to more 'loyal' crony businesses (Gomez, 2002a).[31] Johnson and Mitton (2001) found that Malaysian capital controls provided a screen behind which favoured firms could be supported; approximately 32 per cent of the estimated US$5 billion gain in market valuation of Mahathir-connected firms during September 1998 was due to the increase in the value of their connections.

In the political arena, the financial crisis precipitated popular outcries against corruption and cronyism, initiated by Anwar Ibrahim and gathering momentum especially after the downfall of Soeharto in May 1998 and Anwar's arrest in September 1998. Corruption has become an issue, especially among the Malay community with whom UMNO and Mahathir have lost a great deal of support — though not enough to lose the general election in November 1999. UMNO was given strong Chinese support, motivated in part by fear of the Islamic opposition which has emphasised the need to do away with corruption and cronyism from which it has never benefited. There has been some *bona fide* financial and corporate restructuring, though not devoid of suspicions that companies owned by Anwar corporate allies (for example, Phileo, Rashid Hussain) have been disproportionately or unfairly targeted for 'restructuring'. The crisis has highlighted the erosion of ethnic divisions in the Malaysian business community, with Chinese–Malay partnerships prominent in both the Mahathir and Anwar camps, and with Mahathir himself announcing that 'some Chinese would be allowed to take over companies owned by Malays to prevent the latter from going bankrupt' (Gomez, 1999, p. 196). Searle's analysis concludes that the rise of Malay capitalism has involved the 'blurring of such categories as the state, the party and the private sector' (Searle, 1999, p. 243) and that 'the most striking features of the new Chinese (business) groups was the extent to which their capital was integrated with Bumiputra capital and the interdependence of that relationship' (1999, p. 248). According to Searle, both are based on state patronage, and the associated need to be approved by the man who

[31] 'Doom and gloom for Daim's boys', *Economist*, 30 March 2002.

now controls the reins of the state more tightly than ever, the world's longest-serving prime minister, Mahathir Mohamad.

SINGAPORE

Singapore has a long-established reputation as one of the least corrupt countries in the world, and the least corrupt in Asia by a wide margin. At the same time, the state owns and controls much of the economy and intervenes heavily in the private sector (for example, Rodan, 1997), and is 'formally democratic but illiberal' (Khong, 1999, p. 302) — conditions that in other countries have been positively correlated with corruption. Lim (1998) gives an official explanation of Singapore's anti-corruption strategies that relies heavily on conducive values, meritocracy, stiff penalties and institutional efficiency. Quah (1999) and Wei (2000) remind us that the generous financial rewards available to public servants vitiate any need for enrichment through corruption. For example, 'Singapore's cabinet ministers' salaries are pegged to those of the CEOs in the largest multinational firms in the world. The Singapore Prime Minister's pay is several times that of the United States President' (Wei, 1999, p. 18).[32] To quote then-Prime Minister Lee Kuan Yew, 'it's a simple choice. Pay political leaders the top salaries that they deserve and get honest, clean government or underpay them and risk the Third World disease of corruption'.[33] High pay for senior civil servants, even in times of recession, has recently become a source of political controversy in the context of widening income disparities within the country (Lim, 2001a). Yet for a privileged few 'star performers' it represents but a fraction of the full packet of financial remuneration (augmented by large bonuses, board member fees and other perks) they can expect to receive legally during a working life spent in the civil service, military, or employment in statutory boards and government-linked companies (GLCs).

Haggard and Low (2002) explain the lack of corruption in Singapore in terms of the relative economic weakness of the local private sector in the post-colonial era, due in part to the PAP government's political crackdown on the local business-financed, Chinese-educated left in the 1960s and 1970s, and its own social democratic ideology of the time which did not allocate a

[32]Note that Wei's comparison is overstated with respect to Singapore cabinet ministers' salaries, which are linked to those of the top few Singapore tax-paying CEOs in a few selected professions and industries, not to the much higher salaries of CEOs in 'the largest multinational firms in the world.'

[33]*The Straits Times*, 23 March 1985, cited in Quah (1999, p. 117).

major role to domestic capital in national economic development. The result was that 'the PAP did not rely heavily on political support from business, did not develop an ideology that gave pride of place to indigenous firms, and therefore did not look to the local private sector as a central object of either policy or patronage' (Haggard and Low, 2002, p. 310). They acknowledge that 'the GLCs ... provide opportunities for members of the political élite to advance their careers and create bases of power' (2002, p. 317), and are famously non-transparent in terms of financial and business disclosure (2002, p. 305). But they note that 'grumbling about political insiders and nepotism has not extended to charges that the Lee family or other officials have abused office for personal gain', focusing instead on the observation that 'the GLCs provide a field for the political élite to exercise economic power through their control of a variety of assets' (2002, p. 319). Haggard and Low conclude with an interpretation that sees GLC operations 'less in terms of the political and career incentives of politicians and civil servants and more in terms of a gradual interpenetration if not fusion of public and private interests' (2002, p. 319). Yet for several years now, and especially following the general election and economic recession of 2001, the government has sought to reduce its own role in the economy and to promote the emergence of domestic entrepreneurs, in line with the now-official belief that '[w]hat really matters for East Asia is a shift towards open, competitive markets, and away from the state-driven industrial policies and the collusive domestic networks that have led to low returns on investment.'[34]

Tan (2002) documents the vested interests associated with the government and ruling party whom he suggests are likely to resist the government's oft-announced intention to withdraw from business. He identifies five categories of individuals whose often multiple or sequential sources of employment, income and ownership are in or closely connected with the government's business activities: relatives of senior government leaders, former senior government officials, former senior military commanders, current senior government officials, and current and former ruling party politicians (Tan, 2002, p. 1). In addition to their past and current well-paid, high-level occupations in the public and (government-linked or state-dependent) private sectors, some of these individuals hold multiple and lucrative board positions in GLCs and their numerous subsidiaries, which can multiply their income and wealth (for example, through stock offerings and options).

---

[34]Tharman Shanmugaratnam, the (then) recently appointed Senior Minister of State for Trade and Industry, quoted in Tan (2002).

Thus, for example, 'DPM (Deputy Prime Minister) Lee (Hsien Loong) and his father Senior Minister Lee Kuan Yew are at the helm of GIC (Government of Singapore Investment Corporation), possibly Singapore's largest GLC in terms of assets. DPM Lee's wife, brother, and a few other relatives are also holding key positions in GLCs' (Tan, 2002, p. 2). Deputy Prime Minister Lee's wife, Madam Ho Ching — like himself and his brother, also a former military officer — served concurrently as chairman, deputy chairman or director on the boards of several large GLCs, most notably the Singapore Technologies conglomerate; in June 2002, she assumed the post of executive director of Temasek Holdings, the holding company which controls some 40 GLCs.[35] Ho Ching's brother, Ho Sing, is vice-president and director of two Singapore Technologies units. Deputy Prime Minister Lee's brother Lee Hsien Yang is chief executive of the SingTel Group and director of other GLC units, while his wife Lee Suet Fern is director of SembCorp Logistics and her sister is senior vice-president of SembCorp Utilities, both subsidiaries of the large GLC conglomerate SembCorp. The Deputy Prime Minister's maternal uncle and maternal and paternal cousins also serve in top positions of various GLC units. This listing is perhaps less an indicator of nepotism, since the individuals are all highly qualified in terms of education and past employment — Tan himself refers to this as 'presumably a coincidental outcome of a free market meritocracy' (Tan 2002:2) — and more an indicator of the extreme pervasiveness of GLCs and their collective monopolistic position as employers of senior local talent, whose scarcity in a small population has been given by the government as the reason for their overlapping tasks and multiple income sources. Of the other four groups of GLC managers and board members identified by Tan, it is notable that current senior government officials also hold paid appointments in GLCs while still in government.

A comprehensive report on the status of GLCs highlights the frequent local criticism that their government backing and favour gives them unfair competitive advantages in the local market, where they have 'crowded out private investment and usurped entrepreneurial activity' (US Embassy, Singapore, 2001, p. 1).[36] Other criticisms are that the GLCs' diversified

[35] 'The Insider', *Business Week*, June 24, 2002, pp. 52–3.

[36] According to the US embassy report, official estimates of GLCs' share of GDP range from 21.8 per cent to 60 per cent, but another report from the Singapore Department of Statistics estimates GLCs' contribution to GDP in 1998 at 12.9 per cent, or more than a quarter of local-controlled companies' 46 per cent contribution to GDP (Singapore, Department of Statistics, 2001).

conglomerate structure and their management by former civil servants or military officials, who would tend to be risk-averse, results in economic under-performance, even though most GLCs are 'both competently administered by professional managers and profitable' (US Embassy, Singapore, 2001, p. 5).

> A study done by KPMG Consulting in 1999 on listed manufacturing firms in Singapore included three GLC subsidiaries among the top five 'destroyers of shareholder value', but no GLCs among the top five 'creators of shareholder value' ... in several cases in recent years where the Government wanted to turn around an underperforming GLC (examples include Neptune Orient Lines Ltd in shipping and DBS Bank in banking and finance), it appointed foreigners to push through radical restructuring (US Embassy, Singapore, 2001, p. 10).

At the same time, the overseas ventures of GLCs have to date been notably unsuccessful outside of the oligopoly or monopoly market position that they enjoy at home in Singapore, and their state ownership has, on occasion, made it difficult for them to acquire companies in countries like Hong Kong, Malaysia and Australia. Still, led by GLCs, Singapore is the largest foreign investor in corrupt neighbouring countries like Burma and Vietnam.

GLCs are the most prominent current example of state intervention in the Singapore economy, and have yielded lucrative above-board returns to their government-associated managers and directors. Ideologically, at least in its public pronouncements, the government seems to have turned against this model, but dismantling it — given the vested interests already established and the absence of private sector capacity to take over GLC functions and enterprises — is likely to be slow and partial at best. Many GLCs were created by 'corporatisation' of previous statutory boards and this process continues. At the same time, '[t]he extensive economic and political reach of the Singapore state necessarily conditions the activities of the locally based private sector. Dependence on the state for contracts and awareness of the political nexus between the civil service and the PAP has promoted co-option rather than forceful interest representation to the government' (Rodan, 1997, p. 160). In the political arena, state control of the economy, housing and social services, and its successful record of delivering economic progress, has contributed to the PAP's continuous electoral victories. Despite this, the government has explicitly linked 'government public-spending programs to the extent of voter support of the government, not just in individual constituencies, but also in individual wards within constituencies. Rather than the government being accountable to the people, the people were now explicitly made accountable to the government' (Khong, 1999, p. 294).

None of these actions are considered 'corrupt' by the international community, as evidenced by Singapore's continued high standing in international corruption rankings (above the United States and United Kingdom, for example). But they could be considered the (perfectly legal) dispensation of state patronage (GLC senior management positions and board appointments, physical 'upgrading' of public housing units) to favoured individuals (state employees, party members) and electoral constituencies (which vote in the ruling party), in clientelistic party-based networks resembling those in Malaysia, if not in the other Southeast Asian countries. In terms of rent-seeking, it is arguable that rents generated by government monopolies like GLCs are 'internalised' by being distributed to individuals within those monopolies, without involving the private sector which provides those rents through its payments for corporatised public services, for example. The end result, as in the other countries, is to maintain the government in power (Haggard and Low, 2002).

CORRUPTION IN THE FIVE COUNTRIES COMPARED

The following discussion considers the implications of a comparative analysis of the five Southeast Asian countries for various subjects of importance in the regional and global corruption literature. 'The state' figures prominently in this literature where, depending on the study, it may refer to the national or local bureaucracy or political authority, or to state-owned or government-linked enterprises. For the sake of brevity, these distinctions will not be drawn here, but the reader should be aware that they exist and may have differential impacts on corruption outcomes.

THE ECONOMIC ROLE OF THE STATE: RENTS, LIBERALISATION AND PRIVATISATION

The early economic literature on corruption attributed it to state interventions in the market which created monopoly rents[37] that both distorted the allocation of resources and were misused by those who appropriated such

[37]Rents are factor (land, labour, capital) incomes greater than could be earned in the factor's best alternative employment. Monopoly creates rents for the monopolist by artificially restricting supply and competition, and thus raising prices. Monopolies are usually created by governments which hold or allocate the rights to them.

rents, resulting in economic inefficiencies and loss of output (Krueger, 1974). Khan (2000) challenges this literature by showing that there are different types of rents (for example, those due to monopoly, industrial policy or scarce natural resources), that they are not all created by the state (for example, as in natural resource scarcity), and that they do not necessarily result in economically inefficient outcomes—much depends on the type of rent, how it is allocated and used, and by whom. For example, a well-designed industrial policy (protection, subsidies) that creates temporary rents which are competitively allocated among private sector actors according to performance can accelerate domestic capital accumulation, industrialisation and economic growth. This is arguably what happened in East Asian economies like Japan, South Korea and Taiwan, all of which were characterised by relatively high levels of both state intervention and corruption during their respective periods of rapid industrial growth.

Khan's analysis can also explain why Singapore, despite decades of industrial policy and state intervention, grew rapidly, apparently without corruption — presumably because state-created rents were efficiently allocated, without illegal payments, mostly to foreign multinationals which enjoyed tax breaks, infrastructure and other subsidies on the input side, but had any output-side rent-seeking checked by the simultaneous need to compete on international markets. State-created rents also accrued to state agencies and government-linked corporations which enjoyed domestic market monopolies but were held to the high performance standards necessary to attract foreign private investment in other sectors of the economy (from which their rents were ultimately derived). Rents earned in monopolistic GLCs and a persistently huge government budget surplus were reinvested to increase efficiency and economic growth, and distributed, legally and transparently, to senior management, civil servants and political leaders in extremely generous emoluments. In terms of Ross' (2001) analysis (which he does not apply to Singapore), '[r]ent-seizing politicians need not storm the fortress. They are already inside the walls' (Ross, 2001, p. 4) and can thus create or dismantle state institutions to facilitate or block their access to state-based rents.

The significance of the Khan analysis and the Singapore and other East Asian examples is that state economic interventions may be rent-creating and even (but not necessarily) corrupt, but the allocation and use of such rents need not be either corrupt or inefficient, thus permitting the coincidence of a high degree of rent-seeking and high economic growth. For example, Campos argues that in the absence of modern legal and market institutions, 'rents and corruption have been essential to the credible enforcement of contracts and thus to the large inflows of investment' which led to high economic growth in East Asia (Campos, 2001, p. 3).

In line with the traditional economic analysis that tends to equate state intervention with monopoly, rent-seeking and corruption, it follows that liberalisation (for example, dismantling of import controls and other protective barriers) and privatisation of state-owned economic entities should reduce both rents and corruption by increasing market competition. Thus, for example, Haggard and Low argue that in Singapore, '[t]he country's small size and the corresponding pressures to maintain liberal trade and investment rules partly foreclosed the opportunities for rent-seeking available elsewhere in the region' (Haggard and Low, 2002, p. 301). This is in line with predictions in the global literature that there is a negative relationship between economic 'openness' and the incidence of corruption, that is, more open economies tend to be less corrupt. Ades and Di Telia find that 'corruption is higher in countries where domestic firms are sheltered from foreign competition by natural or policy induced barriers to trade, with economies dominated by a few number of firms, or where antitrust regulations are not effective in preventing anticompetitive practices' (Ades and Di Telia, 1999, p. 992), and also that corruption is higher in countries with more active industrial policy (Ades and Di Telia, 1997). But Treisman finds that the effect of trade openness is 'depressingly small' (Treisman, 2000, p. 439), and Knack and Azfar (2000) find that the relationship between corruption and trade intensity disappears when sample selection bias in favour of large countries in previous studies is removed.

Among our five Southeast Asian countries, it is true that corruption is greater in the Philippines, Thailand and Indonesia, which have higher trade barriers than the less-corrupt Malaysia and Singapore. But corruption did not diminish as trade barriers fell during the 1990s (Table 3). Ownership of the corporate sector is also much more concentrated in Indonesia, the Philippines and Thailand than in Malaysia and Singapore, even though the latter ratios are also high by international standards (Claessens, Djankov and Lang, 1999).

Malaysia and Singapore have definitely received more foreign direct investment, in both absolute and relative terms, than their three more-corrupt neighbours (see UNCTAD, 2001). But both Malaysia and Singapore have practised statist industrial policy much more than their three more corrupt neighbours, and have large state-owned sectors and very state-interventionist economic policies; that these have not meant higher levels of corruption may be due to the fact that they were export and

Table 3. Weighted Mean Tariffs, Selected Southeast Asian Countries (per cent)

Indonesia	13.2 (1989)	6.2 (1999)
Philippines	22.5 (1988)	6.7 (1999)
Thailand	33.0 (1989)	15.0 (1995)
Malaysia	13.8 (1988)	4.9 (1997)
Singapore	0.5 (1989)	— (1995)

Source: World Bank, 2001. *World Development Indicators 2001*, World Bank, Washington, DC.

Table 4. Economic Growth and Freedom, Selected Countries

	Economic growth (real GDP, per cent per annum)		Economic freedom		Political freedom	
	1980–90	1990–2000	1995	2002	1990/1	1999/00
Singapore	6.7	7.8	2 (1.50)	2 (1.35)	4, 4, PF	5, 5, PF
Malaysia	5.3	7.0	18 (2.40)	79 (3.10)	5, 4, PF	5, 5, PF
Thailand	7.6	4.2	17 (2.35)	32 (2.40)	2, 3, F	2, 3, F
Philippines	1.0	3.2	54 (3.20)	70 (2.95)	3, 3, PF	2, 3, F
Indonesia	6.1	4.2	69 (3.40)	105 (3.35)	6, 5, PF	4, 4, PF
China	10.2	10.3	77 (3.60)	121 (3.55)	7, 7, NF	7, 6, NF
India	5.8	6.0	89 (3.80)	121 (3.44)	2, 3, F	2, 3, F

Notes: Economic freedom: first figure is rank out of 101 countries in 1995, 155 in 2002; Second figure in parentheses is (Score) from 1 (high) to 5 (low).
Political freedom: first figure is political rights, second is civil liberties, with 1 (high) to 7 (low). F = free, PF = partly free, NF = not free.
Sources: Growth: World Bank, 1992 and 2002. *World Development Report*, World Bank, Washington, DC; economic freedom Heritage Foundation (www.heritage.org); political freedom Freedom House (www.freedomhouse.org)

foreign-investment-oriented, both of which imposed external competitive disciplines on local firms and governments (Lim, forthcoming).

Table 4 shows the Heritage Foundation's Economic Freedom Index for all five countries in 1995 and 2002, which should be read together with Table 2's listing of Transparency International's Corruption Perceptions Index for 1995 and 2001. With one exception, the two tables show that the more 'economically free' country is also 'less corrupt', with Singapore ranked first and Indonesia last among the five countries. The exception is Malaysia which in 1995 ranked as less free than Thailand and in 2002 ranked as less free than both Thailand and the Philippines, but remained less corrupt than either. Malaysia's sharp drop in 'economic freedom' between 1995 and 2002 most likely reflects the imposition of capital controls in 1998, though by 2002 they had been substantially liberalised. In terms of absolute scores on both indices, Malaysia became substantially 'less free' (and 'more corrupt', the largest increase of the five), while Thailand became slightly 'less free' (but also 'less corrupt'), Indonesia slightly 'more free' (and 'more corrupt'), the Philippines significantly 'more free' (and 'less corrupt') and Singapore significantly 'more free' (but also slightly 'more corrupt'). So, based on this small sample and short period of time, the relationship between 'economic freedom' (as a proxy for 'openness') and corruption is ambiguous.

Privatisation of state-owned enterprises in Malaysia and their 'corporatisation' in Singapore contributed to the enrichment of politically-connected 'private' entrepreneurs (in Malaysia), and of GLC managers and directors (Singapore), without diminishing the control of the state, and especially the ruling party, over national resources. There have been similar results in the Philippines, with privatisation disproportionately transferring such resources into the hands of cronies of current or past presidents, and the otherwise politically well-connected. Thailand and Indonesia have successfully resisted major privatisation, which is likely to continue in Thailand under Thaksin, but shows signs of reversing in Indonesia under Megawati, despite considerable local opposition.[38]

Thus, the literature and evidence from Southeast Asia to date is largely inconclusive with respect to the relationship between state intervention, liberalisation and privatisation on the one hand, and rent-seeking and corruption on the other.

THE ROLE OF THE PRIVATE SECTOR: PATRONAGE AND CLIENTELISM

Most of the empirical literature on Southeast Asia analyses corruption as the result of a struggle over the control of rents, whether state-created or naturally occurring, as in the timber industry (Ross, 2001). Politicians seek access to state power — whether by means of military coup or martial law (for example, Soeharto, Marcos and successive military regimes in

[38]'Jakarta turns deaf ear to privatisation nay-sayers', *Asia Times Online*, 29 March 2002, *www.atimes.com*.

Thailand), or by popular election (in the democratic era), in order to gain 'allocation rights' (Ross, 2001) to rents, which are then distributed to political supporters or the public at large in exchange for political support, or to friends, relatives and themselves, for personal or familial enrichment.

Families figure prominently in analyses of corruption in Southeast Asia. The Philippine literature, in particular, emphasises the power of landed families in instigating and appropriating state-generated rents under different political regimes (democracy and dictatorship), including by their members gaining access to local or national political office and influencing policy that affects rent creation and distribution. The Indonesian literature, especially of the 1990s, focuses heavily on the rent-seeking business activities of President Soeharto's children and other family members. From the 1980s, in both Thailand and Malaysia, attention has been paid to the politically favoured business ventures of family members of ruling political leaders — who in Thailand have changed frequently through elections, but not in Malaysia. Much of the prospering of families of political leaders is not strictly illegal (for example, the easy access to loans or loan guarantees from state or private banks, the privileged purchase of privatised state-owned enterprises, the award of state contracts or licences, or the receipt of equity stakes in private sector ventures) but may still be widely perceived both at home and abroad as being uncompetitive, unethical or corrupt (and thus reflected in the international corruption rankings discussed previously). The prospering of relatives of political leaders does not arouse the same approbation as, for example, in the United States. Thus, although immediate and extended family members of Senior Minister Lee Kuan Yew in Singapore are particularly prominent in highly paid management and board positions of state agencies and GLCs, this is not widely seen to constitute corruption.[39]

Families aside, the appropriation of rents by close personal or political associates of local or national political leaders has given rise to the term 'crony capitalism' now widely used throughout Southeast Asia. This term is generally interpreted as reflecting 'patron-client' (often, 'clientelist') or 'principal-agent' relationships of various origins and degrees of complexity. Where these relationships have a personal rather than social, political or institutional foundation, they are referred to as 'personalistic'.

[39]Haggard and Low (2002, p. 306) cite a 1999 Gallup international survey which showed that only 10 per cent of Singapore respondents worried about graft compared with 41 per cent of respondents in the other 50-plus countries surveyed.

One type of 'clientelist' and usually 'personalistic' relationship distinctive to Southeast Asia is that between indigenous political leaders and ethnic Chinese business. Their political vulnerability as immigrants and members of a small minority everywhere but Singapore, dominating the private sector but often discriminated against, made the Chinese business community reach for political protection and patronage from indigenous political leaders, in both authoritarian and democratic regimes (Gomez, 1999, 2000; Lim, 2000; Doner and Ramsay, 1997, 2000). The changes that democratisation brought to Thailand included the entry of Chinese businessmen into politics on their own account, rather than through native patrons or clients, and the increasing direct or indirect participation of provincial Chinese business leaders in the national polity (McVey, 2000). In Indonesia, a few Chinese have now been elected to parliament, and some occupy ministerial positions in the cabinet of President Megawati; here they represent national interests and seek to give a voice to the vast majority of Chinese-Indonesians who were never cronies of Soeharto, but are often targets of a corrupt officialdom. In Malaysia, the Chinese community is politically divided between government and opposition parties, and its business members include both tycoons allied with UMNO politicians and business interests and small-town small and medium enterprises, some of whose owners reportedly appreciate the absence of corruption in the states ruled by PAS, the Islamic opposition party.

Singapore again stands out, not so much because ethnic Chinese are the majority, but rather because of the absence of close political connections between the government and the local private sector, which has tended to be crowded out from domestic factor and output markets by multinationals and the state (Lim, 2002). Whereas the government has been dominated by English-educated professionals since independence, Chinese-educated entrepreneurs have populated the local private sector, and at times in the past have even funded left-wing opposition to the ruling party (Haggard and Low, 2002). As noted above, the PAP did not rely on political support from business so the private sector was not an object of patronage. Since the rents the party controls are largely within the public sector, access to them (which may be for national development or party-political rather than personal purposes) does not involve the local private sector.

Khan (1996b) argues that whether corruption will have positive or negative efficiency effects depends on 'the distribution of power between the state and the organisations competing over the creation or allocation of rights' (Khan, 1996b, p. 695). Khan does not consider them directly, but in this analysis the Southeast Asian countries (except the Philippines) are characterised by 'patrimonial patron–client networks' under which: 'If the state officials acting as patrons can appropriate part of the rents, they are likely to allocate the right in response to bids being made by competing agents who wish to acquire the rent. This allocative procedure can be efficiency-enhancing because it favours the allocation of scarce resources to users who are most likely to maximise returns' (Khan, 1996b, p. 694). The Philippines, in contrast, is characterised by a 'clientelist patron-client network' in which 'clients or clientelist groups with superior organisational power are likely to get payoffs for their support in the form of allocation of rights ... (which) will not always ... go to individuals or groups who are the highest value adding users' (Khan, 1996b, p. 694), thus contributing to inefficiency and lower growth.

Despite the considerable variation in both the nature of the private sector and of its relationship with the state in Southeast Asia, the former needs to 'capture' or 'influence' the latter (Hellman, Jones and Kaufmann, 2000) in order to preserve or gain access to rents controlled by the latter. How this is done depends a great deal on the nature of national political institutions.

THE ROLE OF POLITICAL INSTITUTIONS: DEMOCRATISATION AND DECENTRALISATION

In the literature analysing the influence of political institutions on corruption, Lederman, Loayza and Soares (2001) find that democracies, parliamentary systems, political stability, and freedom of the press are all associated with lower corruption. They conclude that political accountability reduces corruption. But Treisman (2000) finds that democracy is associated with less corruption only in countries which have been democratic for decades, which has not been the case in Southeast Asia.[40] Lederman, Loayza and Soares (2001) argue that his finding that countries with a British legal tradition (in our sample, Malaysia and Singapore) tend to be less corrupt disappears once political variables are included in the regression.

In the 1990s, democratisation occurred in Thailand and Indonesia, and continued in the Philippines. Although not necessarily worsening corruption (see the discussion of Table 2 above), democracy increased the need of

[40]Although Malaysia and Singapore have been governed by elected governments since political independence from 1957 and 1963 respectively, both are dominant-party states which have not experienced any change of government for four decades, and are usually considered to be 'authoritarian democracies' without full press freedom or independent judiciaries.

politicians for financial backing in order to win elections, and also dispersed parliamentary seats, political power and fiscal revenues to the provinces where vote-buying is more common (for example, in Thailand) and local business interests can wield more influence over local bureaucrats and politicians. This led Gomez to conclude that 'following democratisation ... the influence of capital over politics has increased appreciably' (Gomez, 2002b, p. 3) and to argue that 'if a more genuine form of democracy is to emerge ... the influence that capital can acquire over the state has to be curbed by preventing politicians or parties from seeking funding from business' (Gomez, 2002b, p. 20). But business funding of politicians and parties is the prevailing system in the democratic United States.

Malaysia, like Singapore, has not abandoned electoral politics since becoming a nation-state, but with the expansion of state patronage, 'money politics' has become more important and is now entrenched in the electoral process. It includes, among other things, 'favouritism, conflicts of interest and nepotism in the award of state-created rents, securing votes during federal and party elections by disbursing current and future material benefits, and the direct and indirect interference of political parties or influential politicians in the corporate sector' (Gomez, 2002a, p. 83). These developments are a major reason why anti-corruption has become a major policy platform of opposition political parties and the *reformasi* movement in Malaysia. Singapore has not become noticeably more democratic or politically open despite reaching economic affluence by the 1990s; instead, government spending is increasingly used as both carrot and stick before, during and after elections, to encourage people to vote for the PAP and not its enfeebled opposition.

Democratisation is often or usually accompanied by a decentralisation of political and economic power away from a centralised authoritarian state or dictatorship, which accounts for the concern in the literature with the relationship between decentralisation and corruption. Fisman and Gatti (2000) find a strong negative relationship between decentralisation in government expenditure and corruption, that is, more decentralised polities tend to be less corrupt. Treisman on the other hand finds that 'Federal states were robustly perceived to be more corrupt than unitary ones, controlling for the level of economic development ... this ... suggests a reason for caution in decentralising political power in countries at low levels of development' (Treisman 2000, pp. 440–1). Knack and Azfar (2000) argue that this is because large countries tend to be federal, and are over-represented in sample surveys which show them to be more corrupt than smaller countries — a result which disappears when selection bias is corrected for.

Some of the literature suggests that centralisation can impose limits on rent-seeking and corruption, and perhaps channel rents into productive directions that facilitate, or at least do not hamper, economic growth. But the literature also recognises that this prediction is uncertain and fragile, that is, central power is neither necessary nor sufficient to restrain corruption, nor to ensure that it does not forestall growth. In Indonesia, the centralisation of power under Soeharto hampered recovery from economic crisis, eventually bringing about his downfall; while in the Philippines, centralisation under Marcos' military regime was accompanied by increased, and increasingly concentrated, corruption. In the post-Marcos democratic era, however, term limits imposed on the presidency to restrain its strong central authority are 'likely to extract more corruption rents and generate greater political instability among investors' than in a 'well-run authoritarian government' (De Dios and Esfahani, 2001, p. 127).

In Thailand, as in post-Soeharto Indonesia, democratisation was accompanied by decentralisation, which changed the forms of corruption, but the available empirical evidence on whether corruption increased or decreased is ambiguous (see discussion on Table 2). The re-centralisation of power that Thaksin is now attempting appears to be associated with more corruption in terms of benefiting his own business and family. But as argued by Pasuk and Baker (2002), and in line with Shleifer and Vishny's (1993) thesis, it may in the longer term reduce corruption by curtailing the power of provincial 'godfathers' to extract rents.

In Malaysia, however, the progressive concentration of power under Mahathir in the 1990s was accompanied by more 'money polities', rent-seeking and clientelism (Searle, 1999; Gomez, 2002b). In Singapore, the PAP's strong hold on power has virtually eliminated the usual forms of corruption, but at the same time it has built up a huge state patronage machine that has financially (if legally) benefited the élite of the civil service and GLCs.

It is in the political arena that the Southeast Asian experience may most contradict the conventional wisdom emanating from theory and from cross-country empirical studies. Singapore and Malaysia, the least corrupt countries, each with a British colonial heritage and legal tradition, four decades of continuous elected government, and a much higher level of economic development than their neighbours, rank lower than the Philippines, Thailand, and post-Soeharto Indonesia in many of the indices of political freedom and accountability, such as freedom of the press and participatory democracy (see 1999/00 Freedom House ranking and source in Table 4). Unlike Taiwan and South Korea, with which it is often compared, Singapore has not become significantly more democratic with the attainment of affluence and high education standards. Malaysia has actually slid backwards, curtailing many political and economic freedoms in recent years. Yet both are economically prosperous, relatively politically stable and less corrupt than their more conventionally democratic neighbours. It is likely that two factors previously discussed account for this: heavy dependence on trade and foreign investment (which requires a certain amount of competitiveness and transparency to limit rent-seeking and corruption), and the limitation and efficient channeling of rents due to the centralisation of power.

Ross (2001), for example, argues that the more secure in power a government or political leader is (for example, the stronger and more centralised the grip on power), the slower it/they will be to dissipate the rents under its/their control, since there is no need to do so to attract political support, but there is an incentive to phase rent extraction out over the relatively long period of anticipated rule. Ross uses this argument to explain periods of relatively restrained extraction of natural resource rents in the Marcos and Soeharto regimes when their rule was relatively secure. It could also explain the relatively low level of corruption in Malaysia and Singapore with their dominant-party governments, and a possible decline in corruption in Thailand as power is centralised, and rent-seeking institutionalised, under the Thaksin government. Ross also argues that parliamentary systems like Malaysia's, where the executive and legislative branches are 'fused', may be better able to preserve or resist the dissipation of rents than presidential systems like the Philippines where there is a greater struggle over rents by the different branches of government. In contrast, Hicken (2001b) argues that 'presidentialism has advantages over parliamentarism when it comes to policymaking in unstructured party systems' (Hicken, 2001b, p. 22). He compares privatisation in the Philippines (privatisation under a relatively powerful president) and Thailand (no privatisation under a relatively weak prime minister). However, other interpretations are possible in these cases, such as stronger (or politically better-connected or protected) private-sector interests eager to access formerly state-controlled rents through the privatisation process in the Philippines, as compared with Thailand.

THE ROLE OF EXTERNAL ACTORS

The literature has speculated, although only lightly, on the role of external actors in corruption in Southeast Asia, and in the fight against corruption. These countries are among the most open in the world in terms of international trade and investment. While conventional wisdom has it that foreign investment is likely to reduce corruption because of the preferences of foreign investors for transparency and no added 'hidden costs', and their greater efficiency than local competitors burdened with such costs, we have seen (above) that many multinationals, from the west as well as Asia, were willing to bear these costs to invest in Indonesia under Soeharto. Transparency International's most recent Bribe Payers Index[41] also shows very high levels of bribery in 15 leading emerging market countries by foreign corporations from 21 home countries. On its 0 (high bribery) to 10 (low bribery) scale, US and Japanese companies both scored 5.3, or tied for thirteenth place, with France at 5.5 (twelfth), Germany at 6.3 (ninth) and the United Kingdom at 6.9 (eighth). Outward-investing Singapore companies tied for ninth place with a score of 6.3, Malaysian and Hong Kong companies for fifteenth place with 4.3. Domestic companies scored 1.9, below the most bribe-prone of the twenty-one investing countries.

Multilateral institutions like the World Bank and the International Monetary Fund have unwittingly provided funds that have been siphoned off, for example, by Marcos in the Philippines and Soeharto in Indonesia. The World Bank admits that there have been large 'leakages' from past disbursements of its aid to the Indonesian government. In the 1990s, however, multilateral aid agencies like the World Bank and Asian Development Bank launched research and assistance programs focused on corruption and governance and, following the financial crisis, foreign donors including the IMF have begun to demand bureaucratic reforms and transparency that should reduce corruption.[42] President Bush has also expanded US foreign aid for 'countries with good governance'.[43]

THE IMPACT OF CORRUPTION ON ECONOMIC GROWTH AND INEQUALITY

The dominant concern in the global literature on corruption appears to be with the relationship between corruption, investment and economic growth, finding it to be generally negative. Wei (1999, 2000) reports on studies that find that corruption discourages foreign investment, including in China and the rest of East Asia, resulting in a capital inflow structure more likely to lead to currency crises. It also discourages wholly-owned subsidiaries relative to joint-ventures (Smarzynska and Wei, 2000). Mauro (1995) finds a negative

[41] www.transparency.org/pressreleasesarchive/2002/2002.05.14bpi.en/html
[42] 'Donor fatigue', *Far Eastern Economic Review*, 29 November 2001, p. 28.
[43] 'A feast of giving', *Economist*, 23 March 2002, p. 71.

relationship between corruption, and investment and GDP growth. Li, Xu and Zou (2000) find a weaker negative relationship between corruption and growth. They also find that 'inequality is low when levels of corruption are high or low, but inequality is high when corruption is intemediate. Corruption alone also explains a large proportion of the Gini differential[44] across continents.' (Li *et al.*, 2000, p. 157). At a firm level, Kaufmann and Wei (1999) find that firms that pay more bribes also spend more management time negotiating with bureaucrats, and face a higher cost of capital.

In Southeast Asia, however, with the exception of the Philippines (which had low growth) and Singapore (which had low corruption), relatively high levels of corruption have been associated with decades of very rapid GDP growth. This subject has preoccupied scholars of corruption in the region. Most studies conclude that the positive relationship is explained by institutional variables — the particular nature of the state, its economic policies and involvements, and its rent creation, control and allocation process, as discussed above. Where these have resulted in rent-seeking activity that did not hinder and in some instances may even have promoted efficient domestic or foreign investment, economic growth did not suffer. Campos, Lien and Pradhan argue that 'Corruption regimes that are more predictable ... have less negative impact on investment than those that are less predictable. In many of East Asia's miracle economies, corruption is said to be well organised and systematic so that the degree of predictability is relatively high' (Campos *et al.*, 2001, p. 20–21). Investment, especially foreign direct investment, and economic growth have recently fallen in Southeast Asia, but this is much more as a result of the US and Japanese economic downturns, some increased competition from a rapidly reforming China,[45] and perceptions of heightened political risk due to shaky democracies and post-September 11 fears of radical Islamic terrorism, than of investors' aversion to corruption. In Southeast Asia, external economics has generally dominated domestic corruption in the impact on economic performance.

[44]The most widely-used measure of income inequality.

[45]But note that in 2000, ASEAN countries still received nearly five times more US direct investment than the much larger economy of China *(Survey of Current Business September 2001*, US Bureau of Economic Analysis), which is significant since US investors are usually considered to be the most corruption-averse. According to Transparency International, in 2001 Thailand, the Philippines and Indonesia were perceived to be more corrupt than China (see Table 1). The US data also shows Indonesia to be the second-largest recipient of US direct investment, after Singapore.

THE IMPACT OF CORRUPTION ON FINANCIAL CRISIS AND RECOVERY

Still, nearly all the post-1997 literature cited in this survey concurs that corruption in its many forms, especially crony capitalism, had a role to play in the region's 1997/98 financial crisis, which has been analysed in a voluminous body of literature that we will not address here (see for example, Jackson, 1999; Pemple, 1999; Hill, 1999; Pasuk and Baker, 2000a, 2000b; Haggard, 2000; Jomo, 2001a, 2000b). Various forms of rent-seeking, including by foreign capital providers, and the 'moral hazard' resulting from state ownership of, or perceived support for, large or well-connected borrowers, contributed to excess domestic lending and large over-investment bubbles that eventually collapsed.

Long-existent rent-seeking, corruption and cronyism were not, however, the main causes of the bubbles and their collapse, which also resulted from unsustainable (overvalued) quasi-fixed exchange rates, premature capital market liberalisation, weak domestic financial institutions, flawed crisis management policies, and regional financial contagion. Jomo argues that the problem lay in financial liberalisation which 'directly challenged the institutional arrangements that underpinned (Malaysia's) economic governance system, that is, arrangements that had rent-seeking and corruption at the very core of the country's "shared growth" phenomenon' (as stated in Campos, 2001, p. 7). But he concurs that rent-seeking and cronyism, fueling the need or desire to protect or appease political constituents and vested business interests, were responsible for some of the flawed crisis management policies which were undertaken in Indonesia, Thailand and Malaysia (Jomo, 2001b). Hicken notes that in Thailand, '[c]riticisms of the government's response often point to the lack of decisiveness on the part of policy makers and their ties to narrow, special interests', citing Thai economist Ammar's 1997 comment that IMF intervention was initially welcomed because it 'filled a gap in authority' (Hicken, 2001a, p. 181–2).

Crisis recovery policies, including those imposed by the IMF as conditions for its emergency foreign-currency loans in Thailand and Indonesia, did, however, include institutional reforms, especially in financial and corporate restructuring. These gave increased emphasis to competition, transparency, accountability and 'good governance' — in addition to the 'old standbys' of accelerated market liberalisation and privatisation. If fully implemented, these reforms — together with major government and constitutional changes in the political arena in Thailand and Indonesia, resulting in part from the crisis — are likely to presage a decline in corruption. But the region's rapid, export-led recovery from the financial crisis was not the result of these reforms, just as its current economic slowdown will not be reversed by them alone.

CONCLUSION

In-depth political economy studies of Southeast Asian countries do not provide any clear or easy answers to the central theoretical and policy questions which preoccupy the flourishing and contentious global literature on corruption and development. Instead, they indicate the inherent difficulty of generalising from the results of cross-country surveys to generate analytical predictions and policy recommendations for individual countries which are very different in their socio-historical, political and institutional circumstances. Longitudinal studies of individual countries do help to explain their experiences with corruption and its consequences, but are not able to be uniformly generalised, nor are they predictive, even for the country studied itself. A very corrupt country like Indonesia experienced rapid economic growth for three decades under a centralised authoritarian regime, whose nature eventually brought about its own collapse; the subsequent democratisation and decentralisation has been accompanied by lower growth and no apparent reduction in corruption. Democratisation and decentralisation in Thailand have also not significantly reduced corruption as yet, and have been accompanied, since the financial crisis, by slower growth. Democratisation in the Philippines may have reduced corruption but it remains high and economic growth low, regardless of the degree of centralisation of power. Malaysia and Singapore have been good economic performers with 'democratic-authoritarian' governments which have been elected to power for over 40 years without liberalising their political systems; if anything, judicial independence and freedom of the press have declined in Malaysia in recent years, and not changed much in an open direction in Singapore. Perhaps because of the high degree of centralised state power in both countries, control of the state continues to provide channels for legal capital accumulation, without necessitating the illegal acts so common in their neighbours, and apparently without jeopardising economic growth so long as open trade and investment regimes are maintained. Our (weak) conclusion is that while economic liberalisation, democratisation and centralisation of state power influence the forms of corruption and its impact on national economic performance, and may reduce its extent, they are neither necessary nor sufficient for its decline and disappearance.

REFERENCES

Ades, A and R Di Telia (1996). The causes and consequences of corruption: a review of recent empirical contributions. *IDS Bulletin*, 27(2), 6–ll.

______ (1997). National champions and corruption: some unpleasant interventionist arithmetic. *The Economic Journal*, 107(443), 1,023–42.

______ (1999). Rents, competition and corruption. *American Economic Review*, 89(4), 982–93.

Ammar, S, P Vichyanond and S Christensen (1993). *Thailand: The Institutional and Political Underpinnings of Growth*, World Bank, Washington, DC.

Aquino, B (1987). *Politics of Plunder: The Philippines Under Marcos*, University of the Philippines College of Public Administration, Manila.

Arghiros, D (2000). The local dynamics of the "new political economy": a district business association and its role in electoral polities. In *Money and Power in Provincial Thailand*, McVey, R (ed.), pp. 123–53. Honolulu: University of Hawaii Press.

Bardhan, P (1997). Corruption and development: a review of issues. *Journal of Economic Literature*, 35(3), 1,320–46.

Bliss, C and R Di Telia (1997). Does competition kill corruption?. *Journal of Political Economy*, 105(5), 1,001–23.

Callahan, WA and D McCargo (1996). Vote-buying in Thailand's Northeast. *Asian Survey*, 36(4), 376–91.

Campos, JE (2001). *Corruption: The Boom and Bust of East Asia*. Quezon City: Ateneo de Manila University Press.

Campos, JE, D Lien and S Pradhan (2001). Corruption and its implications for investment. In *Corruption: The Boom and Bust of East Asia*, Campos, JE (ed.), pp. 11–24. Quezon City: Ateneo de Manila University Press.

Case, W (1999). The Philippine election in 1998: a question of quality. *Asian Survey*, 39(3), 468–85.

Claessens, S, S Djankov and LHP Lang (1999). *Who Controls East Asian Corporations?*, Working Paper No. 2054, World Bank, Washington, DC.

Coronel, SS (1996). *Patrimony: 6 Case Studies on Local Politics and the Environment in the Philippines*, Philippine Center for Investigative Journalism, Manila.

______ (1998). *Pork and Other Perks: Corruption and Governance in the Philippines*, Philippine Center for Investigative Journalism, Manila.

______ (2000a). *Betrayals of the Public Trust: Investigative Reports on Corruption*, Philippine Center for Investigative Journalism, Manila.

______ (2000b). *Investigating Estrada: Millions, Mansions and Mistresses*, Philippine Center for Investigative Journalism, Manila.

De Dios, ES and RD Ferrer (2000). *Corruption in the Philippines: Framework and Context*, The Political Economy of Corruption Studies in Transparency and Accountable Governance No. 1, Transparent and Accountable Governance (TAG) Project, Manila.

De Dios, ES and HS Esfahani (2001). Centralization, political turnover, and investment in the Philippines. In *Corruption: The Boom and Bust of East Asia*, Campos, JE (ed.). Quezon City: Ateneo de Manila University Press.

Doner, R (1992). Politics and the growth of local capital in Southeast Asia: Auto industries in the Philippines and Thailand. In *Southeast Asian Capitalists*, McVey, R (ed.), pp. 191–218. Ithaca: Cornell University Press.

Doner, RF and A Ramsay (1997). Competitive clientelism and economic governance: the case of Thailand. In *Business and the State in Developing Countries*, Maxfield, S and BR Schneider (eds.), pp. 237–76. Ithaca: Cornell University Press.

——— (2000). Rent-seeking and economic development in Thailand. In *Rents, Rent-Seeking and Economic Development: Theory and Evidence in Asia*, Khan, M and KS Jomo (eds.), pp. 145–81. Cambridge: Cambridge University Press.

Eklof, S (2002). Politics, business, and democratization in Indonesia. In *Political Business in East Asia*, Gomez, ET (ed.), pp. 216–249. London: Routledge.

Filmer, D and DL Lindauer (2001). *Does Indonesia Have a 'Low-Pay' Civil Service?*, Working Paper No. 2621, World Bank, Washington, DC.

Fisman, R (2001). Estimating the value of political connections. *American Economic Review*, 91(4), 1,095–102.

——— and Gatti, R (2000). *Decentralization and Corruption: Evidence Across Countries*, Working Paper No. 2290, World Bank, Washington, DC.

Gomez, ET (1990). *Politics in Business: UMNO's Corporate Investments*, Kuala Lumpur: Forum.

——— (1991). *Money Politics in the Barisan Nasional*. Kuala Lumpur: Forum.

——— (1994). *Political Business: Corporate Involvement of Malaysian Political Parties*, James Cook University, Townsville.

——— (1999). *Chinese Business in Malaysia: Accumulation, Accommodation and Ascendance*. Richmond: Curzon Press.

——— (2000). In search of patrons: Chinese business networking and Malay political patronage in Malaysia. In *Chinese Business Networks: State, Economy and Culture*, Chan, KB (ed.), pp. 207–23. Singapore: Prentice-Hall.

——— (2002a). Political business in Malaysia: party factionalism, corporate development, and economic crisis. In *Political Business in East Asia*, Gomez, ET (ed.), pp. 82–114. London: Routledge.

——— (2002b). Introduction: political business in East Asia. In *Political Business in East Asia*, Gomez, ET (ed.), pp. 1–33. London: Routledge.

——— (2002c). Paradoxes of governance: ownership and control of corporate Malaysia, Paper presented at Ninth Southeast Asia Business Research Conference, University of Michigan Business School, Ann Arbor, 18–19 May (unpublished).

Gomez, ET and KS Jomo (1999a). *Malaysia's Political Economy: Politics, Patronage and Profits*. Cambridge: Cambridge University Press.

——— (1999b). Malaysia. In *Democracy, Governance, and Economic Performance: East and Southeast Asia*, Marsh, I, J Blondel and T Inoguchi (eds.), pp. 230–60. New York: United Nations University.

——— (2000). The Malaysian development dilemma. In *Rents, Rent-Seeking and Economic Development: Theory and Evidence in Asia*, Khan, M and KS Jomo (eds.), pp. 274–303. Cambridge: Cambridge University Press.

Grabosky, P and P Larmour (2000). *Public Sector Corruption and its Control,* Trends and Issues in Crime and Criminal Justice No. 143, Australian Institute of Criminology, Canberra.

Gray, CW and D Kaufmann (1998). Corruption and development. *Finance and Development*, March: 7–10.

Gutierrez, E (1994). *The Ties That Bind: A Guide to Family, Business and Other Interests in the Ninth House of Representatives*, Philippine Center for Investigative Journalism and Institute for Popular Democracy, Manila.

______, IC Torrente and NG Narca (1992). *All in the Family: A Study of Elites and Power Relations in the Philippines*, Institute for Popular Democracy, Quezon City.

Haggard, S (2000). *The Political Economy of the Asian Financial Crisis*, Institute of International Economics, Washington, DC.

______ and Low, L (2002). State, politics, and business in Singapore. In *Political Business in East Asia*, Gomez, ET (ed.), pp. 301–23. London: Routledge.

Hamilton-Hart, N (2001). Anti-corruption strategies in Indonesia. *Bulletin of Indonesian Economic Studies*, 37(1), 65–82.

Harriss-White, B and G White (1996). Corruption, liberalization and democracy. *IDS Bulletin*, 27(2), 1–5.

Hawes, G (1992). Marcos, his cronies, and the Philippines failure to develop. In *Southeast Asian Capitalists*, McVey, R (ed.), pp. 145–160. Ithaca: Cornell University Press.

Hellman, JS, G Jones and D Kaufmann (2000). *Seize the State, Seize the Day: State Capture, Corruption and Influence in Transition*, Policy Research Working Paper No. 2444, World Bank, Washington, DC.

Heng, PK (1992). The Chinese business elite of Malaysia. In *Southeast Asian Capitalists*, McVey, R (ed.), pp. 127–44. Ithaca: Cornell University Press.

Hewison, K (1997). Thailand: capitalist development and the state. In *The Political Economy of Southeast Asia*, Rodan, G, K Hewison and R Robison (eds.), pp. 93–120. Melbourne: Oxford University Press.

Hicken, A (2001a). Governance and growth in Thailand. In *Corruption: The Boom and Bust of East Asia*, Campos, JE (ed.), pp. 163–182. Quezon City: Ateneo de Manila University Press.

______ (2001b). Party systems, political institutions and policy: policymaking in Thailand and the Philippines, Paper presented at the 2001 Annual Meeting of the American Political Science Association, San Francisco (unpublished).

Hill, H (1999). *The Indonesian Economy in Crisis: Causes, Consequences and Lessons.* Singapore: Institute for Southeast Asian Studies.

Hutchcroft, PD (1998). *Booty Capitalsm: The Politics of Banking in the Philippines.* Ithaca: Cornell University Press.

______ (2000). Obstructive corruption: the politics of privilege in the Philippines. In *Rents, Rent-Seeking and Economic Development: Theory and Evidence in Asia,* Khan, M and KS Jomo (eds.), pp. 207–47. Cambridge: Cambridge University Press.

Hutchinson, J (1997). Pressure on policy in the Philippines. In *The Political Economy of Southeast Asia*, Rodan, G, K Hewison and R Robison (eds.), pp. 64–92. Melbourne: Oxford University Press.

Jackson, K (1999). *Asian Contagion: The Causes and Consequences of a Financial Crisis.* Boulder: Westview Press.

Johnson, S and T Mitton (2001). *Cronyism and Capital Controls: Evidence from Malaysia*, NBER Working Paper No. 8521, National Bureau of Economic Research, Cambridge, Massachusetts.

Jomo, KS (1995). *Privatizing Malaysia: Rents, Rhetoric, Realities.* Boulder: Westview Press.

——— (1998a). Malaysia: from miracle to debacle. In *Tigers in Trouble: Financial Governance, Liberalisation and Crises in East Asia*, Jomo, KS (ed.), pp. 181–198. London: Zed Books.

——— (ed.) (1998b). *Tigers in Trouble: Financial Governance, Liberalisation and Crises in East Asia.* London: Zed Books.

——— (2001a). *Malaysian Eclipse: Economic Crisis and Recovery.* London: Zed Books.

——— (2001b). Governance, rent-seeking and private investment in Malaysia. In *Corruption: The Boom and Bust of East Asia*, Campos, JE (ed.), pp. 131–62. Quezon City: Ateneo de Manila University Press.

Jory, P (1996). Corruption, the virtue of giving, and Thai political culture, Proceedings of the 6th International Conference on Thai Studies, Chiang Mai, 14–17 October: 111–26.

Kang, DC (2002). *Crony Capitalism: Corruption and Development in South Korea and the Philippines.* Cambridge: Cambridge University Press.

Kaufmann, D and S-J Wei (1999). *Does 'Grease Money' Speed up the Wheels of Commerce?*, Working Paper No. 2254, World Bank, Washington, DC.

Khan, M (1996a). A typology of corruption transactions in developing countries. *IDS Bulletin*, 27(2), 12–21.

——— (1996b). The efficiency implications of corruption. *Journal of International Development*, 8(5), 683–96.

——— (2000). Rent-seeking as process. In *Rents, Rent-Seeking and Economic Development: Theory and Evidence in Asia*, Khan, M and KS Jomo (eds.), pp. 70–144. Cambridge: Cambridge University Press.

Khan, M and KS Jomo (2000). *Rents, Rent-Seeking and Economic Development: Theory and Evidence in Asia.* Cambridge: Cambridge University Press.

Khong, C-O (1999). Singapore. In *Democracy, Governance, and Economic Performance: East and Southeast Asia*, Marsh, I, J Blonde and T Inoguchi (eds.), pp. 287–304. New York: United Nations University.

Knack, S and O Azfar (2000). *Are Larger Countries Really More Corrupt?*, Working Paper No. 2470, World Bank, Washington, DC.

Krueger, AO (1974). The political economy of the rent-seeking society. *American Economic Review*, 64(3), 291–303.

Lacaba, JF (1995). Boss: *5 Case Studies of Local Politics in the Philippines*, Philippine Center for Investigative Journalism and Institute for Popular Democracy, Manila.

Lancaster, TD and GR Montinola (2001). Comparative political corruption: issues of operational-ization and measurement. *Studies in Comparative International Development*, 36(2), 3–28.

Lederman, D, N Loayza and RR Soares (2001). *Accountability and Corruption: Political Institutions Matter*, Working Paper No. 2708, World Bank, Washington, DC.

Li, H, LC Xu and HF Zou (2000). Corruption, income distribution and growth. *Economics and Politics*, 12(2), 155–82.

Lim, JY and CG Pascual (2001). *The Detrimental Role of Biased Policies: Framework and Case Studies*, The Political Economy of Corruption: Studies in Transparency and Accountable Governance No. 3, Transparent and Accountable Governance (TAG) Project, Manila.

Lim, LYC (2000). Southeast Asian Chinese business: past success, recent crisis and future evolution. *Journal of Asian Business*, 16(1), 1–12.

______ (2001). Income inequality in Singapore, Speech to Singapore students at Stanford University, 8 April (unpublished).

______ (2002). Shrimps among whales: local business, multinationals and the state in Singapore, Speech at the MIT-Singapore Forum, Massachusetts Institute of Technology, Cambridge, Massachusetts, 28 February (unpublished).

______ forthcoming. Southeast Asia. In *The Future of Asian Business Systems*, Westney, E (ed.). New York: Oxford University Press.

Lim, SG (1998). Integrity with empowerment: challenges facing Singapore in combating corruption in the 21st century. *Asian Journal of Political Science*, 6(2), 132–9.

Linantud, JL (1998). Whither guns, goons and gold? The decline of factional election violence in the Philippines. *Contemporary Southeast Asia*, 20(3), 298–318.

LoGerfo, JP (2000). Beyond Bangkok: the provincial middle class in the 1992 protests. In *Money and Power in Provincial Thailand*, McVey, R (ed.), pp. 221–700. Honolulu: University of Hawaii Press.

MacIntyre, A (1990). *Business and Politics in Indonesia*. Sydney: Allen and Unwin.

______ (1994). Power, prosperity and patrimonialism: business and government in Indonesia. In *Business and Government in Industrialising Asia*, MacIntyre, A (ed.), pp. 244–67. Sydney: Allen and Unwin.

______ (1999a). Political institutions and the economic crisis in Thailand and Indonesia. In *The Politics of the Asian Economic Crisis*, Pempel, TJ (ed.), pp. 143–62. Ithaca: Cornell University Press.

______ (1999b). Indonesia. In *Democracy, Governance and Economic Performance: East and Southeast Asia*, Marsh, I, J Blondel and T Inoguchi (eds.), pp. 261–86. Tokyo: United Nations University Press.

______ (2000). Funny money: fiscal policy, rent-seeking and economic performance in Indonesia. In *Rents, Rent-Seeking and Economic Development: Theory and Evidence in Asia*, Khan, M and KS Jomo (eds.), pp. 248–73. Cambridge: Cambridge University Press.

______ (2002). Investment, property rights, and corruption in Indonesia. In *Corruption: The Boom and Bust of East Asia*, Campos, JE (ed.), Manila: Ateneo University Press.

Marsh, I, Blondel J and Inoguchi T (1999). *Democracy, Governance, and Economic Performance East and Southeast Asia*, United Nations University, Tokyo.

Mauro, P (1995). Corruption and growth. *Quarterly Journal of Economics*, 110(3), 681–712.

——— (1998). Corruption: causes, consequences, and agenda for further research. *Finance and Development*, March: 11–4.

McCoy, AW (1993). *An Anarchy of Families: State and Family in the Philippines*, Center for Southeast Asian Studies University of Wisconsin, Madison, Wisconsin.

McLeod, RH (2000). Soeharto Indonesia: a better class of corruption. *The Indonesian Quarterly*, 228(1), 16–27.

McVey, R (1992). *Southeast Asian Capitalists*, Cornell University Press, Ithaca.

——— (2000). *Money and Power in Provincial Thailand*, University of Hawaii Press, Honolulu.

Mendoza, Jr., AM (2001). The industrial anatomy of corruption: government procurement, bidding and award of contracts. *The Political Economy of Corruption: Studies in Transparency and Accountable Governance*, Case Study No. 2a, Transparent and Accountable Governance (TAG) Project, Manila.

Montesano, MJ (2000). Market society and the origins of the new Thai polities. In *Money and Power in Provincial Thailand*, McVey, R (ed.), pp. 97–122. Honolulu: University of Hawaii Press.

Montinola, GR (1994). The foundations of political corruption: insights from the Philippine case. *Asian Journal of Political Science*, 2(1), 86–113.

Morgan, A (1998). *Corruption: Causes, Consequences, and Policy Implications, a Literature Review*, Working Paper No. 9, The Asia Foundation, San Francisco.

Ockey, J (1994). Political parties, factions, and corruption in Thailand. *Modern Asian Studies*, 28(2), 251–77.

——— (2000). The rise of local power in Thailand: pro-vincial crime, elections and the bureaucracy. In *Money and Power in Provincial Thai-land*, McVey, R (ed.), pp. 74–96. Honolulu: University of Hawaii Press.

Pasuk, P (2001). Good governance: Thailand's experience, Paper for the Asia-Pacific Finance Association Annual Conference, Bangkok, July (unpublished).

Pasuk, P and C Baker (1998). *Thailand's Boom and Bust*. Chiang Mai: Silkworm Books.

——— (2000a). '*Chao Sua, Chao Pho, Chao Thi:* lords of Thailand's transition'. In *Money and Power in Provincial Thailand*, McVey, R (ed.), pp. 30–52. Honolulu: University of Hawaii Press.

——— (2000b). *Thailand's Crisis*. Bangkok: Silkworm Books.

——— (2001). Thailand's Thaksin: New populism or old croynism, Johns Hopkins University School of Advanced International Studies, Washington, DC (unpublished).

——— (2002). Good governance, money politics, and honest mistakes, Monash Asia Institute, Monash University, Melbourne (unpublished).

Pasuk, P and P Sungsidh (1999). *Corruption and Democracy in Thailand*. Chiang Mai: Silkworm Books.

Pasuk, P, P Sungsidh and T Nualnoi (1998). *Guns, Girls, Gambling, Ganja: Thailand's Illegal Economy and Public Policy*. Chiang Mai: Silkworm Books.

Pempel, TJ (1999). *The Politics of the Asian Economic Crisis*. Ithaca: Cornell University Press.

Quah, JST (1999). Accountability and anticor-ruption agencies in the Asia-Pacific region, in *Combating Corruption in Asian and Pacific Economies*, Asian Development Bank and OECD, Manila, pp. 101–24.

Riggs, FW (1966). *Thailand: The Modernization of a Bureaucratic Polity.* East-West Center Press, Honolulu.

Robertson, Jr., PS (1996). The rise of the rural network politician: Will Thailand's new elite endure?. *Asian Survey,* 36(9), 924–41.

Robison, R (1986). *Indonesia: The Rise of Capital.* Sydney: Allen and Unwin.

Rock, MT (2000). Thailand's old bureaucratic policy and its new semi-democracy. In *Rents, Rent-Seeking and Economic Development: Theory and Evidence in Asia,* Khan, M and KS Jomo (eds.), pp. 182–206. Cambridge: Cambridge University Press.

Rodan, G (1997). Singapore: economic diversification and social divisions. In *The Political Economy of Southeast Asia,* Rodan, G, K Hewison and R Robison (eds.), pp. 148–78. Melbourne: Oxford University Press.

Rodan, G, K Hewison and R Robison (1997). *The Political Economy of Southeast Asia.* Melbourne: Oxford University Press.

Ross, ML (2001). *Timber Booms and Institutional Breakdown in Southeast Asia.* Cambridge: Cambridge University Press.

Searle, P (1999). *The Riddle of Malaysian Capitalism: Rent-seekers or Real Capitalists?.* Sydney: Allen and Unwin.

Shleifer, A and RW Vishny (1993). Corruption. *Quarterly Journal of Economics,* 108(3), 599–617.

Sidel, JT (1995). Coercion, Capital and the Post-Colonial State: Bossism in the postwar Philippines, PhD dissertation, Cornell University, Ithaca.

______ (1996). Siam and its Twin? Democratization and bossism in contemporary Thailand and the Philippines. *IDS Bulletin,* 27(2), 56–63.

Sieh Lee, ML (1992). The transformation of Malaysian business groups. In *Money and Power in Provincial Thailand,* McVey, R (ed.), pp. 103–26. Honolulu: University of Hawaii Press.

Singapore, Department of Statistics (2001). Contribution of Government-Linked Companies to Gross Domestic Product. Occasional Paper, March, Department of Staitstics, Singapore.

Smarzynska, BK and SJ Wei (2000). *Corruption and Composition of Poreign Direct Investment: Firm-level Evidence,* Working Paper No. 2360, World Bank, Washington, DC.

Sombat, C (2000). Local godfathers in Thai polities. In *Money and Power in Provincial Thailand,* McVey, R (ed.), pp. 53–73. Honolulu: University of Hawaii Press.

Suehiro, A (1992). Capitalist development in postwar Thailand: Commercial bankers, industrial elite and agribusiness groups. In *Southeast Asian Capitalists,* McVey, R (ed.), pp. 35–64. Ithaca: Cornell University Press.

Tan, BS (2002). Why it might be difficult for the government to withdraw from business, Singapore Window (www.singapore-window.org/sw02/020210gl.htm).

Tordesillas, E and G Hutchinson (2001). *Hot Money, Warm Bodies: The Downfall of Philippines President Joseph Estrada.* Anvil Press, Manila.

Treisman, D (2000). The causes of corruption: A cross-national study. *Journal of Public Economics,* 76(3), 399–457.

Ueda, Y (2000). The entrepreneurs of Korat. In *Money and Power in Provincial Thailand,* McVey, R (ed.), pp. 154—94. Honolulu: University of Hawaii Press.

United Nations Conference on Trade and Development (UNCTAD), (2001). *World Investment Report 2001*, UNCTAD, Geneva.

United Nations Development Program (UNDP) (1997). *Corruption and Good Governance*, Discussion Paper No. 3, Management Development and Governance Division, Bureau for Policy and Programme Support, UNDP, New York.

US Embassy, Singapore, (2001). Singapore government-linked corporations face the future, US Embassy, Singapore (unpublished).

Virtucio, MAG and MP Lalunio (2001). *Tender Mercies: Contracts, Concessions and Privatization*, The Political Economy of Corruption: Studies in Transparency and Accountable Governance No. 2b, Transparent and Accountable Governance (TAG) Project, Manila.

Wedeman, A (1997). Looters, rent-scrapers, and dividend-collectors: corruption and growth in Zaire, South Korea, and the Philippines. *The Journal of Developing Areas*, 31(4), 457–78.

——— (2002). Development and corruption: the East Asian paradox. In *Political Business in East Asia*, Gomez, ET (ed.), pp. 34–61. London: Routledge.

Wei, SJ (1999). *Corruption in Economic Development: Beneficial Grease, Minor Annoyance, or Major Obstacle?*, Working Paper No. 2048, World Bank, Washington, DC.

——— (2000). *Corruption, Composition of Capital Flows, and Currency Crises*, Working Paper No. 2429, World Bank, Washington, DC.

Wingfield, T (2002). Democratization and economic crisis in Thailand political business and the changing dynamic of the Thai state. In *Political Business in East Asia*, Gomez, ET (ed.), pp. 250–300. London: Routledge.

World Bank, (2001). *World Development Indicators 2001*, World Bank, Washington, DC.

——— (2002). *World Development Report 2002: Building Institutions for Markets*, World Bank, Washington, DC.

CPSIA information can be obtained
at www.ICGtesting.com
Printed in the USA
LVHW101503011019
632853LV00014B/738/P

9 789813 225251